TEMPORARILY YOURS

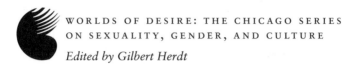

WORLDS OF DESIRE: THE CHICAGO SERIES
ON SEXUALITY, GENDER, AND CULTURE
Edited by Gilbert Herdt

TEMPORARILY *Yours*

Intimacy, Authenticity, and the Commerce of Sex

Elizabeth Bernstein

THE UNIVERSITY
OF CHICAGO PRESS
Chicago and London

Elizabeth Bernstein is assistant professor of sociology at
Barnard College, Columbia University, and coeditor of
Regulating Sex: The Politics of Intimacy and Identity.

The University of Chicago Press, Chicago 60637
The University of Chicago Press, Ltd., London
© 2007 by The University of Chicago
All rights reserved. Published 2007
Printed in the United States of America

Chapter 5, "Desire, Demand, and the Commerce of Sex," was
originally published as "The Meaning of Purchase: Desire,
Demand, and the Commerce of Sex" in *Ethnography*. It
is reprinted here by permission of Sage Publications Ltd.
Copyright © Sage Publications, 2001.

16 15 14 13 12 11 10   4 5

ISBN-13: 978-0-226-04457-6 (cloth)
ISBN-13: 978-0-226-04458-3 (paper)
ISBN-10: 0-226-04457-2 (cloth)
ISBN-10: 0-226-04458-0 (paper)

Library of Congress Cataloging-in-Publication Data

Bernstein, Elizabeth, 1968–
  Temporarily yours : intimacy, authenticity, and the
commerce of sex / Elizabeth Bernstein.
      p.   cm.
  Includes bibliographical references and index.
  ISBN-13: 978-0-226-04457-6 (cloth : alk. paper)
  ISBN-13: 978-0-226-04458-3 (pbk. : alk. paper)
  ISBN-10: 0-226-04457-2 (cloth : alk. paper)
  ISBN-10: 0-226-04458-0 (pbk. : alk. paper)
  1. Prostitution. 2. Sex-oriented businesses. I. Title.
HQ118.B47 2007
306.740973—dc22

                                        2006034203

CONTENTS

To Kerwin Kaye, always

ACKNOWLEDGMENTS

So many people have helped to guide and inspire me through the myriad loops and twists that this project has taken. From fieldwork to theorizing to the multiple writings and rewritings that would eventually give shape to the final text of this book, the fiction of individual authorship has been belied by the wide array of friends, kin, and colleagues who have been my partners in dialogue at every stage. Though the creation of this book would have been impossible without the critical interpersonal and institutional support that I have been so fortunate to receive, any errors, omissions, or misinterpretations that appear in the following pages should of course be considered solely my own.

I am first and foremost indebted to the hundreds of women and men who shared their experiences and stories with me. Taken together, they comprise a vast and varied group, one with wide-ranging reserves of expertise. In San Francisco, the nightly companionship of Carol Leigh in the cold, damp streets of the Tenderloin was particularly important during the early stages of my research. I am enormously grateful to her for "adopting" me at the project's outset and for introducing me to many of the sex workers and activists who would make crucial contributions to my subsequent investigations. I have benefited tremendously from the insights that Norma Hotaling offered at the inception of this project and from the warmth and wisdom that Victoria Schneider has shared with me over many years. Ulla-Carin Hedin, Arne Randers-Pehrson, Petra Östergren, Marieke van Doorninck, Ida Koch, Sven Axel Månsson, Jan Visser, Gert Hekma, Kersten van Dalen, Jackie, Ulrika Dahl, Anna Gavanas, Licia Brussa, Pye Jacobssen, Bo Hansson, Anders Gripelov, Annicka Ericcson, and Marjan Wijers were wonderfully informative and generous hosts to me while I pursued my research in Scandinavia and the Netherlands. I am also extremely thankful to the members of the diverse sex-worker organizations—including COYOTE, SAGE, PROMISE, US-PROs, CAL-PEP, de Rode Draad, Pro-Sentret, the Prostitution Project, Street Survival Project, and Iris—and to the members of the Oakland, San Jose, San Francisco, Copenhagen, Göteborg, and Stockholm police departments who allowed me to tag along with them while they went about their work, patiently indulging my questions and scribbling. I owe a special debt of gratitude to my coparticipants on the San Francisco Task Force on Prostitution, who provided the original context in which my thinking on this issue developed.

In this book's prior incarnation as a doctoral dissertation in the sociology department at the University of California at Berkeley, my faculty advisors served as a significant source of intellectual and emotional support. Over the nearly two decades that I have known her, Kristin Luker has been an especially significant mentor and role model. Her deep commitment to the sociological study of gender and sexuality, one which is premised on both worldly relevance and theoretical rigor, has been a motivating example for my own research. I am grateful to Loïc Wacquant for his creative and dynamic input into this project as it unfolded, to Jerome Skolnick for his facilitation of vital components of my field research, and to Lawrence Cohen for his astute engagement with the incubating thoughts that comprised my early chapter drafts. To Ruth Rosen, I owe the inspiration that her own groundbreaking study of modern-industrial prostitution provided. I owe extra special thanks to the members of my dissertation group—Laurie Schaffner, Lucinda Ramberg, Will Rountree, and Jackie Orr—who accompanied me on research outings whenever necessary, read everything from chapter drafts to anxiously scrawled memos, and helped me to realize my dream of vibrant intellectual community. Thanks also to Stacy Lawrence, Michael Burawoy, Nancy Chodorow, and Ronald Weitzer for their assistance with this project during its earliest, conceptual stages—long before I had any idea that it might someday become a primary intellectual focus, let alone a dissertation or book.

In New York City and beyond, I am so grateful to the many friends and colleagues who read chapter drafts and provided all variety of encouragement and commentary along the way. I would especially like to thank Kelly Moore, Penelope Saunders, Clare Corcoran, Sealing Cheng, Mark Padilla, Lynn Chancer, and Katherine Newman. At Barnard and Columbia, Janet Jakobsen, Rob Smith, Elizabeth Castelli, Carole Vance, Ali Miller, Paige West, Katalin Makkai, Lisa Gordis,

Gary Dowsett, and Deb Minkhoff have been wonderfully supportive colleagues and mentors. Emily Dobbins, Liam MacLeod, Antonia Levy, Kate Broad, and Magdalena Ruiz provided vital research, artistic, and transcription assistance. I am indebted to Siobhan Brooks, Hima B., Darby Hickey, Winddance Twine, Don Kulick, Salvador Vidal Ortiz, Ben Shepard, Denise Brennan, Casey Green, Melissa Ditmore, Rhys Williams, and Christina Crosby for their support of this project, and to Gail Kligman, Adrian Favell, Viviana Zelizer, David Greenberg, Steven Seidman, Ann Pellegrini, Miryam Sas, Kay Levine, Ruth Milkman, Mitch Duneier, Laura Agustín, and Elizabeth Wood for providing valuable and generous feedback at different stages. I wish also to thank my deeply supportive cohort of friends in Barcelona—Marçal Solé, Magda Solé, Monsterrat Guntín, Manolo García, Paco Abril, and Ana García—who have contributed so much to my life and work over many years.

I am extremely grateful to the following institutions and fellowships for providing funding for this work: the National Science Foundation, the Woodrow Wilson Foundation, the Mellon Post-Doctoral Fellowship in the Humanities, the University of California Chancellor's Dissertation Fellowship, and the Phi Beta Kappa Alpha Chapter. This funding was absolutely crucial to the successful execution of this project: it afforded me the all-too-rare gifts of time and material resources that are a prerequisite for sustained research and thinking. At the University of Chicago Press, I am greatly indebted to Gil Herdt, Doug Mitchell, Timothy McGovern, Susan Olin, and the reviewers of this manuscript who offered thoughtful and astute readings of the text. Their contributions strengthened my analysis, sharpened my argument, and enhanced the readability of the final book.

Finally, I would like to thank my parents, Ruth and Bernard Bernstein, my sister and brother-in-law, Jan and Tom Chargin, and my grandparents, Sylvia and Arthur Rubenstein—who in subtle ways set much of the political and intellectual backdrop for this project. Kay Brook, Alan and Judy Bernstein, Linda Ringel, S., and H. offered much appreciated emotional support and encouragement to me during difficult times. In addition to sharing with me the fruits of his ample reading and thinking about commodity exchange, my father read an early draft of the manuscript and provided detailed feedback on core dimensions of the argument. My mother, who for years provided me with a steady stream of clippings about any- and everything relevant to sexual commerce, tragically did not live to see this book reach completion.

On her deathbed, she listened attentively to me read the concluding chapter to her aloud. Then, as always, she was among my most provocative critics.

More than any other single individual, I am indebted to Kerwin Kaye, who has made innumerable contributions to every aspect of this project. His tremendous gifts to me—intellectual, emotional, and otherwise—are what enabled me to sustain this work during periods both joyous and trying. With all my heart, I dedicate this book to him and thank him for his presence.

1 | Sexual Commerce in Post-industrial Culture

In the back room of a discreetly furnished apartment in a quiet San Francisco neighborhood, I am sitting on a brown leather sofa talking with Amanda, who has just said goodbye to the day's first customer. We drink tea as the early afternoon sunshine streams into the room, illuminating many overstuffed bookcases, an exercise bicycle, and Amanda herself—a slender woman in her late thirties with dark hair and serious eyes. Amanda is a former copy editor and a graduate of a prestigious East Coast university who has been working in the sex industry for six years. Smiling slightly, she shrugs when I ask her how the session with her client went:

> Actually, I spent most of the time giving him a backrub, and we also spent a lot of time talking before we had sex. In the end, we went over [time] by about seven minutes. . . . You know it's really funny to me when people say that I'm selling my body. Of all the work I've done, this isn't abusive to my body. Most of my clients are computer industry workers—about half. Sometimes I ask myself: what about *their* bodies? These men spend forty hours a week hunched over a desk. They live alone, eat alone, drive to work alone. Other than seeing me, they don't seem to even have time for a social life.

Amanda goes on to explain that today's client was a marketing executive for a prominent Silicon Valley software company. This client is a "regular," someone she has seen before, who has often complained to her that he is overworked and too busy to meet women. I wonder aloud how it is that he nonetheless has the time to drive two and a half

hours on his lunch break to come and see her. Amanda observes with
bemusement that for the majority of her client pool—educated, professional men who have contacted her via an online ad—such paradoxes
represent the norm.[1]

This book is about the ways in which recent transformations in
economic and cultural life have played themselves out at the most intimate of levels: the individual experience of bodily attributes and integ-
rity, and the meanings afforded to sexual expression. The lens through
which I examine these transitions is sexual commerce, the exchange of
sex for money in the late capitalist marketplace. Although the analysis
of sexual commerce is my jumping-off point, it is not my sole destination. It is my contention that experiences such as those of Amanda and
her clients reflect and thus offer insight into broader trends at work
within urban life in the contemporary West. Explicating the changes
that are occurring within the field of paid sex and their relationship to
broader social dynamics constitutes the work of this study.

This inquiry is organized around three main questions: What is the
relationship between contemporary markets in sexual labor, the proliferation of other forms of service work, and changes in labor processes
more generally? How have campaigns against prostitution in postindustrial cities served to remap the boundary between licit and illicit
forms of sexual expression? What is the significance of the widespread
availability of sexual commerce to the white middle-class men who
constitute the overwhelming majority of its consumer base?

For generations of social thinkers, there has been an assumption
that women's increasing participation in legitimate paid employment
and a decline in the gendered "double standard" would eliminate the
social reasons behind the existence of prostitution, as well as other
commercial sexual activities.[2] Departing from this premise, diverse
groups of reformers have at various historical moments sought to curtail sexual commerce by providing occupational alternatives to the
women who sell sex and legal deterrents to the men who buy it. Since
the 1990s, states and municipalities have implemented a variety of
innovative measures to stem the rising tide of the sex trade—zoning
restrictions and stepped up enforcement against the perpetrators of
"quality of life" crimes, the criminalization and "reeducation" of male
sexual clients, and even (somewhat paradoxically) the legalization of
brothel keeping. Despite these measures, in both the developing world
and in the postindustrial cities of the West (cities with local economies
weighted heavily toward tourism, business and personal services, and
high technology) the sex industry has not "withered away" as predicted

but has instead continued to flourish. Furthermore, it has diversified along technological, spatial, and social lines. Feminist and sociological analyses of prostitution have yet to adequately account for the persistence and diversification of the sex trade or for the transformations that have occurred in intimate relationships, labor, and consumption in postindustrial cities more generally.

Increasingly, public attention has been directed toward the "traffic in women" as a dangerous manifestation of global gendered inequalities. Media accounts have rehearsed similar stories of the abduction, transport, and forced sexual labor of women and girls from developing nations, whose desperation and poverty render them amenable to easy victimization in first- as well as third-world cities.[3] While I do not dispute the existence of the devastating social realities that inspire such narratives, this book tells a very different story about the role of globalization in facilitating contemporary patterns of commercial sex. I focus not on victimized women and their exploitation by "bad men," but on the structural factors and social locations that incline women and men toward specific labor and consumptive practices and produce particular embodied subjectivities. Though I am well aware that violence, brutality, and exploitation characterize many corners of the sex trade, my own research and that of other social scientists indicates that these experiences stretch unevenly across social space and occupy a variety of different forms. I believe, furthermore, that the causes of oppression within sex work have been consistently misidentified by those commentators who endeavor to explain all commercial sex within the singular rubric of the "traffic in women." While it is clearly impossible to understand the accelerated entry of women, men, and transgendered individuals into the contemporary sexual economy without situating this participation within a broader context of structural violence (i.e., conditions such as poverty, racism, homophobia, and gendered inequalities), one question that this book raises is whether engagement in commercial sexual activity always and inevitably constitutes a further injury to those concerned, or whether it might sometimes (or simultaneously) constitute an attempted means of escape from even more profoundly violating social conditions.[4]

Recounting sex workers' diverse experiential realities, including those of social suffering, forms an important piece of my narrative, yet such experiences do not adequately convey the entire story. Indeed, part of the message I wish to convey revolves around the way that relatively privileged people—women as well as men—have entered into commercial sexual encounters in response to new subjective and social meanings that append to market-mediated sex. Although the global sexual economy continues to draw participants from the most disadvantaged strata of the working poor, it increasingly incorporates members of other social classes as well—in particular, individuals pertaining to what has been variously termed the "new" middle class, the "creative class," or the "new petite bourgeoisie." [5] Yet it is precisely one of the enabling conditions of this development—namely, the expanded presence of the white middle classes in gentrifying urban centers as both residents and tourists—that has made street prostitution and other "older" styles of sexual commerce (which share an association with urban blight) less socially acceptable.

In the chapters that follow, my aim is to illuminate the diverse and shifting social geographies of contemporary sexual commerce, the disparate state interventions that have facilitated the remapping of "public" and "private" zones within postindustrial cities, and the emergent subjective meanings that are drawing new groups of people into commercial sexual transactions and transforming them from within. By detailing the relationship between money and sex on the "micro" level of bodies and subjectivities, I aim to reveal the relationship between economy and desire more broadly. I shall argue that the global restructuring of capitalist production and investment that has taken place since the 1970s has had consequences that are more profound and more intimate than most economic sociologists ever choose to consider. [6] The desires that drive the rapidly expanding and diversifying international sex trade have emanated from corporate-fueled consumption, an increase in tourism and business travel, and from the symbiotic relationship between information technologies and the privatization of commercial consumption. [7] At the same time, a rise in service occupations and temporary work, an increase in labor migrations from developing to developed countries, and the emergence of new paradigms of family and community have fueled the growth and diversification of sexual labor. For many sectors of the population, these shifts have resulted in new configurations of intimate life as well as in new erotic dispositions—ones which the market is well poised to satisfy.

TRANSFORMATIONS IN ECONOMY, KINSHIP, AND SEXUALITY

GIRLFRIEND FOR HIRE! So you've been thinking you're working too hard, and enjoying it less. You'd have a girlfriend, if only you had time. You want someone presentable, fun loving, toned, and oh so naughty. I'm like that exquisite condo in Hawaii. Beautiful and serene. Just the person to

make you feel like a KING. I provide great memories well after the retreat.
Outcalls available. Serving peninsula and Silicon Valley. Incalls by appt.
Reduced rates for extended assignments.

Advertisement on San Francisco Bay Area erotic Web site, 2001

There is an abundant literature on the transformations that have taken place within the global economy over the last thirty years. These works have traced the nature and significance of postindustrialism and the emergence and impact of the service economy and the new information technologies, as well as ensuing sociodemographic changes.[8] Sociologists of the family have extended this project, exploring the connections between recent economic transformations and the structure and meaning of American kinship, detailing the postmodernization of family forms and the "queering" of domestic life.[9] In her well-known book, the *Time Bind,* for example, the feminist sociologist Arlie Hochshild has analyzed the cultural transposition of emotional meaning from the sphere of domesticity to the sphere of public commerce, arguing that such symbolic inversions are a consequence of the changing material realities of both public and private spheres.

Sociologists of culture have furthermore pointed to a general trend of "disenchantment" or "cultural cooling," whereby intimate exchanges have increasingly come to resemble other forms of utilitarian transaction, even within private-sphere, nonmarket emotional exchanges.[10] Whether in the guise of Taylorized, efficiently managed "quality time" with one's own children, or via an emerging ideology of romantic love that "endorses flexibility and eschews permanence," public-sphere market logics have become intricately intertwined with private-sphere emotional needs. In the process of this comingling, the nature and purpose of both domains have been radically transformed.

Yet the abundant and continually expanding literature on postindustrial cultural formations has had relatively little to say about the changing nature of sexuality and how it might reflect and facilitate transformations in other social domains. Though sociologists and historians of sexuality have aptly described the "modernization" of sex, they have barely begun to theorize its "postmodernization" in the contemporary period. Social historians such as Kristin Luker and John D'Emilio have linked the "relational" model of sexuality (sometimes referred to as "amative" or "companionate") to the rise of modern romance and the nuclear family under capitalism, contrasting it with the prototypically procreative orientation of preindustrial society. Thus, Kristin Luker has deciphered contemporary abortion debates in the United States in terms of a contest between procreative and relational worldviews, linking women's ideological positions on the question of abortion to disparate sets of material interests. In similar fashion, John D'Emilio has explained the ways in which the peculiarly modern notion of gay identity could only emerge within a sexual ethic premised on intimate relationship, since both were products of the individualizing freedom from domestic production and extended kin networks that was provided by a system of wage labor.[11]

The works of several recent social thinkers do begin to theorize shifts in the sexual sphere that have occurred in concert with contemporary economic transitions. Manuel Castells has, for example, spoken of the new economy's "normalization" of sex; Steven Seidman has described the emergence of "unbound eros," Anthony Giddens has evoked "plastic sexuality," and Zygmunt Bauman has referred to a "postmodern erotic revolution."[12] In a sweeping journey through global sexual politics, emergent sexual subcultures, and different varieties of globalized sex commerce, Dennis Altman has perhaps gone furthest, declaring it his aim to "connect two of the dominant preoccupations of current social science and popular debate": globalization and the preoccupation with sex.[13] Altman excepted, most of the existing efforts to link sexuality and globalization are implicitly premised on a naturalism which, post-Foucault, should give us significant pause.[14] In these analyses, "sex" is something which exists beneath the social layers of human existence, by which it can either be constrained or freed. Although I diverge from Foucault in granting primacy to material conditions, with him I suggest that there is no "true" form of sex that lurks beneath its socially paradigmatic expressions.

Elaborating on these theoretical efforts, and following Luker's and D'Emilio's analyses of the emergence of a relational sexual ethic during the rise of industrial capitalism, it is my claim that the proliferation of forms of service work, the new global information economy, and "postmodern" families peopled by isolable individuals have produced another profound transformation in the erotic sphere. Both the traditional "procreative" and the modern "companionate" models of sexuality are increasingly being supplemented by what sociologist Edward Laumann and his colleagues have referred to as a "recreational" sexual ethic.[15] Instead of being premised on marital or even durable relationships, the recreational sexual ethic derives its primary meaning from the depth of physical sensation and from emotionally bounded erotic exchange—what I here term *bounded authenticity*. As Zygmunt Bauman writes, within the postmodern social field "sex free of reproductive consequences and stubborn, lingering love attachments can be securely enclosed in the frame of an episode, as it will engrave no deep grooves on the constantly re-groomed face being thus insured against limiting the freedom of further experimentation." [16] Whereas domestic-sphere, relational sexuality derived its meaning precisely from its ideological opposition to the marketplace, recreational sexuality bears no antagonism to the sphere of public commerce. It is available for sale and purchase as readily as any other form of commercially packaged leisure activity.

When sex workers advertise themselves as "girlfriends for hire" and describe the ways in which they offer not merely eroticism but authentic intimate connection for sale in the marketplace, when overworked high-tech professionals discuss their pursuit of emotional authenticity within the context of paid sexual transactions, and when municipal politicians strategize about the best means to eliminate the eyesore of street prostitution while encouraging the development of corporate "gentleman's clubs," we are witnessing the unfolding of precisely this transformation. In postindustrial cities throughout North America and Western Europe, the defining features of modern street prostitution (the prostitute as public, and therefore disreputable woman; the exchange of cash for expedient sexual release as ideological antithesis to private-sphere sex and love) have become increasingly muted. In their place has emerged a brave new world of commercially available intimate encounters that are subjectively normalized for sex workers and clients alike.

SEXUAL COMMERCE AND SOCIOLOGICAL INQUIRY

The nature of money resembles the nature of prostitution. The indifference with which it lends itself to any use, the infidelity with which it leaves everyone, its lack of ties to anyone, its complete objectification that excludes any attachment and makes it suitable as a pure means—all this suggests a portentous analogy between it and prostitution.

GEORG SIMMEL, "Prostitution," 1907 [17]

The exchange of sex for money has been a symbolically laden transaction for successive generations of social thinkers. Starting with Marx and Engels, continuing on through the iconoclastic interpretive sociology of Georg Simmel and through the functionalist tradition of Kingsley Davis and Talcott Parsons, and extending forward to the sociology of deviance in the 1960s and 1970s, prostitution has (explicitly or implicitly) been the paradigmatic example of the moral difficulties that ensue when bodily attributes are commodified for a wage. For Marx and Engels, prostitution served as the supreme metaphor for the exploitation inherent in wage labor, representing the commodification of the most "market inalienable" of human capacities.[18] Writing in 1844, Marx noted the association between forms of modern wage labor and prostitution in observing that they were undergirded by a shared (and morally troubling) principle: "You must make everything that is yours *saleable,* i.e. useful."[19] Engels declared that only with the advent of communism would the twin institutions of women's oppression—capitalist monogamy and prostitution—be curtailed.[20] For Simmel, who argued in his landmark treatise, *The Philosophy of Money,* that "the nadir of human dignity is reached when what is most intimate and personal for a woman . . . is offered for such thoroughly impersonal, externally objective remuneration," what was disturbing about prostitution was the contradiction it posed to the assumption that the proper domain of women's sexual expression was the intimate, romantic relationship in the private sphere.[21] At historical junctures when the scope and reign of the market is experienced as particularly problematic, social critics from Marx, Engels, and Simmel onward have returned to ponder the meaning of this and other limiting cases.[22]

In the United States, the first burst of sustained political attention and writing about prostitution occurred in the late nineteenth and early twentieth centuries, in tandem with social reformist attempts to address anxieties about urbanization, industrialization, and changing gender norms. Attention to prostitution as a social problem built steadily through the middle decades of the nineteenth century, eventually finding expression in Dr. William Sanger's mammoth *History of Prostitution,* written in cooperation with the New York City police. Sanger soberly declared it "a fact beyond question that . . . vice . . . was attaining a position and extent . . . which cannot be viewed without alarm."[23] As the social historian Ruth Rosen has explained, the Victorian policy of "quiet toleration" and the view of prostitution as a "necessary evil" were ultimately replaced during this period by a new focus on prostitution as a *social* evil.[24]

The "social evil" framing found expression not only in moral reform movements with broad-based constituencies, but in a spate of texts which sought to capture the problem of prostitution using new social-scientific frameworks. The idea that prostitution constituted an evil which could no longer be tolerated often focused on the specter of "white slavery" (i.e., the forced prostitution of white rural women who migrated to cities only to be imprisoned by male—often Jewish—pimps).[25] In the United States, public anxiety around this issue peaked between the years of 1910 and 1914 and was captured in numerous exposés by muckraking journalists as well as in highly influential investigations of prostitution such as George Kneeland's *Commercialized Prostitution in New York* (1913) and Abraham Flexner's *Prostitution in Europe* (1914), two data-rich tomes published with the sponsorship of John D. Rockefeller and the Bureau of Social Hygiene.[26] As David Langum has observed, in the *Reader's Guide to Periodical Literature,* between 1890 and 1909 thirty-six entries appear under the heading "prostitution," and forty-one entries appear between 1915 and 1924. Between the crucial years of 1910 and 1914, however, there were 156 separate entries.[27]

Very few of these commentators were sociologists, however. By the end of the nineteenth century, two grand scientific enterprises were emerging side by side—sociology and sexology—destined to professionalize as two autonomous disciplines. Together, these two modernist projects would serve to institutionalize a common understanding regarding the distinction between life's social and biological realms, creating a framework which placed sexuality outside of the social sphere. Thus, in contrast to Marx, Engels, and Simmel, Weber and Durkheim had relatively little to say about either prostitution specifically or sexuality in general.[28] In the early twentieth century, the task of explaining the social meaning of prostitution would be increasingly assumed by several new sets of commentators—sexologists, psychoanalysts, and a handful of psychoanalytically inclined structural-functionalist sociologists—who imputed meanings to the commercial sexual encounter which stood in stark contrast to the formulations of Progressive Era social critics.

Early twentieth-century sexological, psychoanalytic, and structural-functionalist interventions around prostitution recast the Victorian "necessary evil" framework in a scientific guise, naturalizing the male desires that were seen to underpin the institution of sexual commerce. Such accounts rendered prostitution not only unproblematic but structurally integral to the institution of marriage. Writing in this vein, for example, Sigmund Freud famously maintained that

> In only very few people of culture are the two strains of tenderness and sensuality duly fused into one; the man almost always feels his sexual activity hampered by his respect for the woman and only develops full sexual potency when he finds himself in the presence of a lower type of sexual object. . . . Full sexual satisfaction only comes when he can give himself up wholeheartedly to enjoyment, which with his well-brought up wife, for instance, he does not venture to do.[29]

And as the sexologist Havelock Ellis argued in a chapter of his monumental *Studies in the Psychology of Sex,* "The history of the rise and development of prostitution enables us to see that prostitution is not an accident of our marriage system, but an essential constituent."[30] Within the newly emergent fields of sexual science, sexology, and psychoanalysis, men's patronage of prostitutes was normalized, while women's path into prostitution was deemed to be largely a question of individual psychopathology. And within the tradition of psychoanalytically influenced structural-functionalist sociology, later commentators such as Kingsley Davis surmised that without prostitution, "Marriage, with its concomitants of engagement, jealousy, divorce, and legitimacy, could not exist."[31]

Though yielding few publications, some Chicago school ethnographers ventured into the terrain of sexuality during the interwar years to produce accounts which would complicate this trend.[32] In 1923, William I. Thomas published *The Unadjusted Girl,* which situated the female prostitute's experiences within a framework of rising expectations in a burgeoning consumer economy, and William C. Reckless located transformations in post–Progressive Era Chicago vice in terms of broader urban trends. Paul Cressey, in his well-known monograph on the taxi dance hall (a public dance hall in which women exchanged dances with their customers for payment), recast the conventional narrative of women's "moral decline" into one of downward social mobility.[33] Melding the "academic principles of sexology and the compassion of social reform," various of the Chicago school ethnographers also sought practical applications of their research, collaborating with local organizations who were committed to eliminating prostitution (as well as homosexuality) in the city.[34]

It was not until the late 1960s and 1970s that a new spate of empirically based sexuality studies were conducted under the purview of the sociology of deviance—a field of American social science research which reached its fruition at about the same time. Responding to the predominant social currents of the day, researchers pertaining to the sociological subfield called "labeling theory" sought to explain the power of institutions of social control to shape people's identities and behaviors (i.e., "to restrict people's ability to 'do their own thing'").[35] As with earlier sociological interventions, the focus of such works largely remained fixed on the female prostitute, who now served as the emblematic figure of the breakdown of normative consensus.[36] Rejecting a psychodiagnostic perspective, Wayland Young was among the first to reframe prostitutes and homosexuals as the paradigmatic social

Others.[37] And in her 1965 study of women institutionalized for prostitution offenses, Nanette Davis drew on labeling theory and symbolic interactionism to argue that prostitutes provided the exemplary case study of the "internalization of a deviant self-conception." [38]

In the late 1980s and the 1990s, commercialized sex became a central focus of the sharply polarized feminist "sexuality debates." Emerging out of earlier discussions regarding the significance of pornography, sadomasochism, and "butch-femme" coupling in lesbian relationships, feminist activists and academics engaged in heated theoretical disputes over the implications of prostitution (or "sex work") for women's subordination and empowerment.[39] Rejecting the word "prostitute," with its connotations of shame, unworthiness, or wrongdoing, some feminists introduced the term "sex worker" to suggest that the sale of sex was not necessarily any better or worse than other forms of service work or embodied labor.[40] Echoing the reformist critiques of the early twentieth century, other feminists maintained that prostitution and pornography were among the clearest indicators of female sexuality as "that which is most one's own, yet most taken away." [41] For scholar-activists such as Kathleen Barry, Sheila Jeffreys, and Catharine MacKinnon, sexuality was seen to be at the root of women's subordination to men, with sexual objectification constituting the egregious substratum of all forms of gendered exploitation.[42]

Meanwhile, burgeoning sex workers' rights organizations, along with their "prosex" feminist allies, had begun to articulate positions which stood in sharp contrast to the analyses of prostitution as sexual oppression advanced by MacKinnon, Jeffreys, Overall, and others.[43] "Prosex" feminist writings sought to reconstrue sex work as a form of labor that was primarily distinguishable from other varieties of low-status employment by virtue of its better pay. As Anne McClintock argues,

> The female prostitute puts a price on her labors. The sex-worker cocks a snook at Johnson's famous edict that "on the chastity of women all property in the world depends"—demanding, and generally getting, better money for her services than the average, male, white-collar worker. Society demonizes sex workers because they demand more money than women should, for services men expect for free.[44]

In these texts, the female sex worker might also be figured not just as someone making do under the inevitable constraints of patriarchy but as the subversive strategist par excellence: "I've always thought that whores were the only emancipated women," wrote Margo St. James, founder of the sex workers' rights organization, COYOTE (Call Off Your Old Tired Ethics). "We are the only ones who have the absolute right to fuck as many men as men fuck women."[45] Overwhelmingly, the initial phases of the feminist sexuality debates surrounding prostitution were carried out at an abstract, theoretical level: they were matters of ideological rather than empirical dispute.

Since the mid-1990s, there has been a veritable explosion of writing on contemporary forms of sexual commerce, rivaling the obsessive attention that was devoted to the matter by the social reformers of a century ago. Feminist sociologists, anthropologists, and other scholars working in the interdisciplinary field of gender and sexuality studies have produced a growing body of theoretically informed, empirical work on different varieties of contemporary commercial sexual exchange.[46] Recent studies have even broadened their focus to include the heretofore invisible male participants in the commercial sexual encounter—male sex workers, profiteers, and clients—and they have begun to dissect transnational patterns of commerce such as sex tourism and migratory sexual labor.[47] These academic studies have been supplemented by a rapid succession of first- and third-person accounts of erotic labor by journalists, social activists, self-proclaimed allies, and popularly appointed "sex-perts."[48]

Finally, filmmakers, broadcast- and cyberjournalists, talk-show hosts, and fiction writers have also jumped on the commercial-sex bandwagon, churning out all variety of fictional, semifictional, and "real-life" accounts of commercial sex work at a dizzying pace. The HBO network has produced its weekly television exposé of strip clubs, *G-String Divas*, as well as *Cathouse*, an "insider's" view of Nevada's legal brothels, in addition to *Hookers*, a documentary series on street prostitution in diverse U.S. cities. Although the figure of the prostitute has been a staple figure of popular cinema for over seventy years—from *Shanghai Express* (1932) to *Belle du Jour* (1967) to *Pretty Woman* (1991)—the last decade has produced an unprecedented spate of filmic images and narratives about sexual commerce. Recent cinematic blockbusters have included *The Full Monty* (1997), *The People vs. Larry Flynt* (1997), *Moulin Rouge* (2001), *Monster* (2003), *Sin City* (2005), *Hustle and Flow* (2005), and *Memoirs of a Geisha* (2005)—to name but a few. Independent filmmakers have been no less interested in the sex industry and have often focused on aspects of the business that extend beyond the usual heteronormative bounds—e.g., depictions of male hustlers in *My Own Private Idaho* (1992), *Hustler White* (1996), *Star Maps* (1997), and *Johns* (1997). Finally, enterprising documentarians have also issued exposés of various facets of the industry, such as *Fetishes* (1996), *Live Nude Girls Unite* (2000), *Big Girls: Big Beautiful Women in the Adult Entertainment Industry* (2000), and *Inside Deep Throat* (2005). By 1999, the cities of San Francisco, Portland (Oregon), and Berlin were hosting annual sex-worker film and video festivals at major theaters.

Although the political winds have shifted in the postmillennial, post–September 11 world, bringing the moral values of the Religious Right into greater ascendance, the intense cultural focus on sexual commerce has not been stemmed. While many treatments of the issue have employed a condemnatory, moralizing tone (in both feminist and antifeminist guises), the production of explicit texts that rely on the visual and rhetorical tropes of sexual commerce as a basis both for their sales and for their political claims (what political theorist Wendy Brown might term "the mirror of pornography") has continued at a steady pace.[49] Recent films in this genre include the academy award-winning documentary *Born into Brothels* (2004), by Zana Briski, and the highly influential Swedish film, *Lilya 4 Ever* (2002), by Lucas Moodyson.[50] In 2005, the Lifetime cable network screened a well-promoted two-part miniseries focused on sex trafficking, while television shows as diverse as "Frontline," "Law and Order," and "Battlestar Galactica" have also devoted various special episodes to the issue. Whether presenting "pro" or "con" positions, the abundant and diverse representations of the sexual economy can best be seen as subsidiaries of the sex industry itself and are likely attributable to the same cultural and structural features which drive demand for other kinds of sexual commodities.

The discursive explosion that has taken place around sexual commerce cannot be isolated from the significant material transformations that the industry itself has undergone in recent years—transformations which, I shall argue, are emblematic of a broadly shared moment in economic and cultural life. By all accounts, the sex industry has far exceeded its prior bounds to become a multifaceted, multibillion dollar industry, produced by and itself producing developments in other sectors of the global economy, such as hotel chains, tourism, long-distance telephone carriers, cable companies, and information technology, and creating burgeoning profits for right- and left-wing entrepreneurs alike.[51] Inevitably, comparisons will be drawn to the sheer numbers of women employed as prostitutes in, for example, turn-of-the-century London or New York.[52] What is new in the current economy is the scale of the profits being generated, the diversification of the modes in which sexuality is transacted, and the increasingly businesslike and even corporatized structure of many profiteers.[53]

The cultural critic Linda Williams has described a shift from "ob/scenity" to "on/scenity," whereby "discussions and representations of sex that were once deemed obscene, in the literal sense of being off (ob) the public scene, have today instantly appeared in the new public/private realms of Internet and home video." She coins the term "on/scenity" to refer to "the gesture by which a culture brings on to its public arena the very organs, acts, bodies, and pleasure that have heretofore been designated ob/scene and kept literally off scene."[54] In his recent study of the contemporary California pornography industry, the journalist Eric Schlosser has observed a similar "mainstreaming" of the ob/scene, noting that "most of the profits being generated by porn today are being earned by businesses not traditionally associated with the sex industry—by mom and pop video stores; by long-distance carriers like AT&T; by cable companies like Time Warner and Tele-Communications Inc., and by hotel chains like Marriott, Hyatt, and Holiday Inn that now reportedly earn millions of dollars each year supplying adult films to their guests."[55] Just as the availability of hard-core pornographic films on videocassettes fueled the popularization of the home VCR, pornography on CD-ROM and over the Internet has been responsible for the acceptance and popularization of these new technologies. More recently, executives from some of the world's largest telecommunications companies convened to discuss the profits to be generated by providing "explicit sexual content" via handheld communication devices, such as iPods and cell phones.[56]

Despite burgeoning cultural attention, most contemporary social theorists who are concerned with the phenomenon of globalization have neglected to consider the meaning and impact of sexual commerce—perhaps because, like some of their predecessors, they have relegated matters of the body and eroticism to the spheres of nature and physiology. In contemporary sociology, some sociologists have continued to regard sexuality as a presocial aspect of human experience, not amenable to sustained sociological reflection. States, markets, organizations, labor practices, families, even attitudes and beliefs are regarded as falling within the proper purview of social inquiry, but not bodies or desires. This book is intended as a corrective to that trend. By focusing on the political economy of bodily practices and desires, my intention is to push the sociological envelope to its logical conclusion, linking together economic, cultural, and libidinal realms of human experience.

THE SETTING AND THE APPROACH

The analysis which follows situates the lives and motives of the diverse participants who populate the contemporary sexual economy within the broader framework of postindustrial transformations of sexuality and culture. Drawing from nearly a decade of research involving ethnographic fieldwork with female and male sex workers, clients, police officers, government officials, local activists, and representatives of social service agencies, as well as a review of relevant policy documents and print and electronic media, I detail the ways in which new economic currents have altered the forms and meanings of commercial sexual encounters for sex workers, clients, and other inhabitants of postindustrial cities.[57] In order to most vividly convey the transformed realities that I seek to describe, I have interspersed my theoretical discussions with closely edited extracts from my field notes, moving back and forth between my analysis and prostitution strolls in urban tenderloins, between luxury brothels in suburban outskirts and police holding tanks for arrested streetwalkers, between meetings with municipal policy makers and sexually oriented Internet start-up companies. The juxtaposition of distinct analytic and ethnographic voices within the text is also intended as a device for denaturalizing both representational strategies—a goal which is consistent with the "reflexive turn" in recent ethnographic writing.[58] To best avoid the exoticizing and "othering" stance which has characterized much of the existing sociological literature on prostitution, I have sought to keep my own situatedness and embodiment as a fieldworker discernible in my field notes.[59] At the same time, I have taken care to avoiding constructing myself as the substitute-object of a voyeuristic gaze. Though any discursive treatment of commercial sex will invariably be trapped within a pornographic hall of mirrors (i.e., the very same libidinal economy that the author endeavors to describe), in this text I have deliberately sought to minimize such refractions to the extent possible.[60]

A more complete discussion of the range of considerations which guided my ethnographic approach as well as my strategies for conducting research in different cultural settings is available in the methodological appendix, but I offer a brief summary here. I situate my work within sociological and feminist ethnographic lineages that seek to understand local behaviors and identities in terms of their enabling political-economic and historical conditions.[61] I place my own research on transformations in contemporary sexual markets in explicit dialogue with a broad array of empirical and theoretical work on recent economic and cultural transformations, building my argument both from my own ethnographic data and from the large body of secondary research that has been done by urban sociologists, economic geographers, social historians, and cultural critics of contemporary sexuality. In contrast to social researchers who aspire to apprehend their data in the absence of any contaminating theoretical apparatus, my own fieldwork developed with an aim to address specific—albeit evolving—sets of paradoxes and questions. Because I sought to capture historical change and to connect "micro" with "macro" levels of social transformation, my ethnographic approach has been both multisited and polyperspectival. Rather than locating my study within the enclosed space of a singular streetwalking stroll or commercial sex venue, I have pursued social meaning and analytic insight through the strategic juxtaposition of multiple field sites, allowing social spaces and actors to mutually illuminate one another's diverse principles of functioning.

My primary field site is the San Francisco Bay Area, which, by the late 1990s, was one of the hearts of the "new economy" and thus emblematic of its attendant economy of desire. Although the Bay Area is neither a typical nor a "representative" U.S. location, I maintain with other commentators that the fact that postindustrial cultural transformations occurred in a manner that was "more condensed, rapid, and exaggerated" here than elsewhere likely rendered them easier to perceive.[62] Because my ambition has been to be able to make claims about more than merely "one world" of advanced welfare capitalism, I conducted parallel research in Amsterdam, the Netherlands, and Stockholm, Sweden, as well as other cities.[63] Including these sites enabled me to simultaneously track the thriving commercial sex trade in cities comparable in size and economic structure to San Francisco but which still reaped the benefits of relatively strong welfare states, with more tightly constrained market sectors and fewer social inequalities than are prevalent in the United States. As nodal points of transnational economic and cultural processes, all three cities were key sites of sexual transformation as well, giving rise to the rapid proliferation of sexual commerce.

The bulk of my fieldwork was conducted during six distinct intervals between 1994 and 2002. During these periods, my research involved an average of ten hours per week of "participatory observation" on streetwalking strolls, with sex-worker activists and their clients at

meetings, in their homes, and in their professional venues. For methodological rather than substantive reasons, my ethnographic research on
the streets did not include a sustained focus on the experiences of male
hustlers or transgender prostitutes. These latter groups concentrated
on different strolls and did not typically mix with the women. Among
indoor sex workers, however, gender divisions were less enforced, both
at the level of ideology and at the level of community, and my research
was able to encompass the experiences of both women and men. Many
of the indoor female and male sex workers that I met attended the same
organizational meetings, advertised in the same venues, and at times
even shared clients. In two neighboring municipalities, I accompanied
the vice squad on its twice-weekly prostitution patrols during a three-
month period, climbing into the paddy wagon with apprehended sex
workers and watching as prospective clients were arrested. I also attended San Francisco's pretrial diversion program for customers seeking to purge their arrest records. From 1994 to 1997, I served as a
participant-observer on the San Francisco Task Force on Prostitution.
Comprised of sex-workers' rights activists, government and police officials, and neighborhood representatives, the task force was created to
review and amend prostitution policy in San Francisco.

Of the forty-five in-depth interviews with sex workers and fifteen
in-depth interviews with clients that I conducted, the majority were
with individuals that I had already come to know over the course of my
fieldwork. Other sex workers and clients were recruited through the
"snowball sample" method, and some clients were recruited through
ads placed in local heterosexual and gay male sex newspapers. In-depth
interviews were conducted face-to-face, tape-recorded, and lasted from
one to four hours each. For both sex workers and clients, I sought to
capture a diversity of experiences pertaining to a range of different sex
markets, including massage parlors, brothels, the streets, escort agencies, and strip clubs.

TERMINOLOGY

Readers with some exposure to the feminist sexuality debates described earlier will surely wonder about my slippage between the terms
"sex work" and "prostitution." Empirically inclined sociologists may
similarly perceive a slippage in this text between different objects of
analysis: prostitution, on the one hand, and more disparate forms of
sexual commerce, such as exotic dancing and pornography, on the
other. Motivated by political considerations, many recent academic
writers have elected to use the term "sex work" as a nonstigmatizing

and broadly encompassing designation for all forms of sexual labor. Such writers may deliberately attempt to blur the boundaries between prostitution and other forms of sexual labor, suggesting that the sale of heterosexual intercourse needn't be regarded as categorically distinct from the explicit or implicit eroticism that characterizes much of women's labor (from prostitution at one extreme to cocktail waitressing at the other). While I abide by the same convention throughout much of this book, I will also use the terms "prostitution" and "sex work" in ways that are more precisely delimited. Where possible, I will employ the preferred terminology of the female and male participants in particular settings as a tool for discerning subjective variations in the experience of selling and buying sex.[64] In addition, when the criminal and stigmatized nature of the commercial sexual encounter is paramount to my analysis, I will opt for the term "prostitution."[65] When the legal, social, and phenomenological specificity of the practice is not germane, I will rely on the broader and more neutral designation of "sexual commerce" or "sex work" instead. Although my primary focus is on the set of commercial sexual practices falling under the legal rubric of prostitution, I have sought to make clear when and where my analysis pertains to trends within the sex industry more generally.

My use of the term "postindustrialism" is also potentially fraught. The period of the last thirty years has been variously described as "globalized," "postmodern," "postindustrial," "post-Fordist," "late capitalist," "millennial capitalist," "neoimperial," and "neoliberal."[66] Each of these terms highlights a different dimension—cultural or economic, spatial or temporal, organizational or political—of the multifaceted social changes that have transpired during the last thirty or so years. Although I shall alternate between these various designations to some extent, tailoring my usage in accordance with the aspects of contemporary cultural and economic life that I seek to highlight in a given instance, in general I have opted for the rubric of postindustrialism, a term which in my view captures with the most precision and simplicity the extent to which these new social formations have been premised on the demise of an industrially based economy.

STRUCTURE OF THE ARGUMENT

My argument in this book is organized as follows. In chapter 2, "Remapping the Boundaries of 'Vice,'" I examine the shifting literal and metaphoric boundaries of "vice" in modern-industrial and postindustrial cities. Drawing on the works of key social historians and economic geographers, I describe the origins of modern prostitution in nineteenth-century North American and European cities, sketching this development in terms of transformations in legal frameworks, patterns of urban development, and paradigms of sex, gender, and intimacy. Focusing on the case of San Francisco, I examine the spatial dimensions of successive waves of legal and economic transformations that have occurred over the last two centuries, serving to reshape not only inner-city neighborhoods and patterns of classed, raced, and gendered exclusion but also prevailing paradigms of commercial sex.

The next two chapters, "Modern Prostitution and Its Remnants" and "The Privatization of Public Women," focus on changing forms and meanings of commercial sexual transactions from the perspectives of diverse strata of contemporary sex workers. I do not endeavor to describe and interpret the full range of commercial sexual services that currently exist in well-touristed postindustrial cities: in the city of San Francisco alone, a comprehensive study would, at a minimum, have to encompass the diverse experiences of the thousands of female, male, and transgender sex workers who advertise each week in local newspapers and online sex guides,[67] the additional two thousand or so women and men who work at San Francisco's seventeen legal sex clubs, the employees of the nearly one hundred escort agencies and sixty-five massage parlors that advertise in the San Francisco Yellow Pages, the fifty to one hundred young women, men, and transgender individuals who walk the streets each night, the hundreds of men and women involved in the local heterosexual and homosexual pornography industries (print, video, and online) and employed as phone-sex operators, and the inestimable numbers of individuals who sell sex via informal networks or in exclusive brothels and houses which do not advertise. For purposes of the argument that I wish to make here, I have chosen to focus on the experiences of two broad (and themselves, multiply constituted) subdivisions within the myriad realities that comprise the contemporary sex industry: streetwalking and indoor, self-employed sex work. The disparate realities presented by these distinct markets in sexual labor are exemplary both in revealing the ways in which the practice and subjective experience of selling sex vary in accordance with the structural location of the participants, and in suggesting declining and emergent sectors within the sexual economies of postindustrial cities.

Although feminists and other scholars have debated theoretically what exactly is being purchased in the commercial sexual transaction, and whether sex can be "a service like any other," they have scarcely begun to unravel such questions empirically. Chapter 5, "Desire, Demand, and the Commerce of Sex" draws on field observations of and interviews with male clients of commercial sex work in order to probe the meanings that they give to different types of commercial sexual exchange. Building on my analysis in chapter 4, I elaborate on the emergence of "bounded authenticity" as a particularly desirable and sought after sexual commodity. I frame this discussion in terms of the paradoxical coemergence of recent state efforts to problematize heterosexual male desire and an increasingly normalized ethic of male sexual consumption.

Despite the diversity of legal approaches to prostitution that have prevailed in recent years, the common focus of most state interventions has been on eliminating the visible manifestations of deviance and poverty in urban spaces, rather than the exchange of sex for money per se. In chapter 6, "The State, Sexuality, and the Market," I situate the changes that I observed in San Francisco alongside two other recent and noteworthy attempts to amend prostitution policy in the West: the 1998 passage of the Violence against Women Act in Sweden, which unilaterally criminalized the purchase of sex for customers, and the legalization of the commercial sex trade in 2000 in the Netherlands. The Swedish and Dutch cases are particularly interesting to consider, both because they constitute the two poles of contemporary European approaches to the state regulation of commercial sex, and because they have served as exemplars for diverse factions of feminists, sex-worker advocates, and policy makers around the globe. I argue that the failure to situate sexual commerce within a broader political-economic framework can lead advocates to argue for opposing tactics which, once implemented, may have surprisingly similar effects on the ground. Whether sex work is decriminalized, legalized, or criminalized, the interests of real estate developers, municipal politicians, and business owners may overshadow the concerns of feminists and sex workers.

How are we to ethically and politically assess the broad transformations in sexuality, commerce, and culture that the following pages describe? By way of conclusion, chapter 7 engages contemporary normative debates around sexual commerce and evaluates the proposed political interventions that have emerged from the course of such discussions. This chapter also argues for an ethical assessment of sexual commerce that melds feminist concerns around gendered power with a broader consideration of the commodity form. Rather than taking commodification to be a self-evident totality, I stress the necessity of distinguishing *between* markets in intimate labor, based on the social location and defining features of any given type of exchange. At a more general level, I seek to complicate the view that the commodification of sexuality is transparently equatable with diminished intimacy and erotic experience. Such an argument does not do justice to the ways in which the spheres of public and private, intimacy and commerce, have interpenetrated one another and thereby been mutually transformed, making the postindustrial consumer marketplace one potential arena for securing authentic, yet bounded, forms of interpersonal connection.

2 | Remapping the Boundaries of "Vice"

I am standing on my usual corner in the San Francisco Tenderloin when a white car drives up to me and a loud, commanding voice bellows, "Start walking!" I quickly scurry away before I even have time to make sense of what happened. My first thought was that the men in the car were pimps and that I'd invaded their territory. Then I vaguely recall that the one who leaned his head out the window was white, mustached, and wearing a badge. I realize they were cops.

When I return to my post, there are a half dozen or so sharp-tongued, tough-as-nails young women there, much to my relief. I am intrigued by the fact that they handle themselves so well on the streets, can defend themselves so adeptly among even the most infuriating of street harassers (and there are so many!), yet seem so timid and fearful when it comes to the police. Every once in a while, a girl will shout out "six" to signal to the others that the cops have been sighted. As Lydia, one of the women on the stroll, explained to me my first night, "It's 'six' for cops, 'heads' for pimps; if you hear either one, scram!"

Business is unbearably slow this evening, and the seven of us remain on the corner for what seems to be an eternity. A few heterosexually coupled tourists walk past us, arm in arm. Although we have all done our best to look "classy" (silky blouses, pencil-thin miniskirts, heavily lacquered hair, and French-manicured nails), the theater- and restaurant-goers do not mistake us for their own kind. The fact that we stand immobile, watchful, and unescorted by male partners is the dead give away. We are on this street precisely because of its proximity to the tourist district, yet the tourist-women walk by us scowling in disapproval and cling firmly to their husbands, who are careful not to meet our eyes. "I hate theater nights," complains the woman next to me. "We stick out like sore thumbs."

After standing on our feet for hours, Kelly, a red-wigged, spunky mother of two, begins to moan to the wind, "Don't nobody wanna fuck me?" The petite black woman at my side muses that perhaps she never really can tell when she looks ugly and when she looks good—as if that were the source of the problem, rather than the desolate streets. "I really want to make some money . . . ," she wails. The night seems so long and hopeless that when a cabbie drives by offering to take the women over to Hyde Street to watch two police decoys working, they pile into the cab and go. I remain on the street corner, with two homeless men that I know only by face for company. I'm lost in thought when an old, 1970s model gray sedan pulls over close to me, and a non-uniformed Asian man of about forty leans his head out the window. He screams: "If you're still here when I go around the block, you're going to jail." I nod and begin to cross over to the other corner. A random male passerby, who I don't bother to study too closely, asks me if I want "life insurance" to walk across the street. Without looking up, I politely decline. Now Lydia and Beverly have appeared, making their way up from the corner of Mason and O'Farrell, where the other women they were working with have just been arrested. I ponder the fact that these scantily clad female bodies have been forcibly removed from public streets for "lewd behavior," while the equally revealed, yet lifeless feminine forms on the billboards that surround me have been allowed to remain.[1]

After another twenty or so minutes, I decide to call it quits. It's too cold, and my nose is beginning to run. My attire, chosen for the sake of aesthetic conformity, affords me little protection from the frigid night air. I say good-bye for now, and tell them I'll be back tomorrow night.

FIELD NOTES, SAN FRANCISCO TENDERLOIN, DECEMBER 1994

Despite the frequent equation of prostitution with "the oldest profession," what many of us typically think of as "prostitution" has not existed for very long at all. The rise of large-scale, commercialized prostitution in the West is a recent phenomenon, emerging out of the dislocations of modern industrial capitalism in the mid-nineteenth century. It is also a distinctly urban phenomenon, premised on the existence of an organized and relatively autonomous sphere of public commerce, as well as on individuals who are sufficiently disembedded from traditional kin networks so as to serve as a consistent source of both "demand" and "supply."[2]

As numerous social historians have described, the attendant features of modern-industrial capitalism—phenomena such as urbanization, the expansion of wage labor, and the decline of the extended kin-based "traditional family"—brought with them new cultural ideologies of gender and sexuality, and new symbolic boundaries between public and private life.[3] The development of "work" as an autonomous, rationalized, and prototypically masculine sphere of economic activity outside the home produced a sexual "double standard" and an unprecedented gender division of life activities, dichotomizing women along class lines.[4] While white, bourgeois, married women served as caretakers and practiced an ideology of sexual restraint in the private sphere, many working-class women and women of color joined men in the public sphere as wage laborers or as sexually available prostitutes.[5] By the early twentieth century, numerous "vice commissions" had been created to study—and definitionally constitute—the social problem of modern prostitution.[6]

By contrast, the forms of sexual commerce that prevailed prior to this period were self-organized, occasional exchanges in which women traded sexual favors during limited periods of hardship. Early modern prostitution was small in scale, frequently premised on barter, and generally took place within the participants' own homes and communities. Only with the onset of modern industrial capitalism and an increasingly gendered social divide between public and private spheres did a new class of specially demarcated "public women" come under increasing scrutiny and control. In contrast to the casual and informal exchanges that had previously transpired in coffeehouses, taverns, and pubs, large numbers of women now found themselves sequestered in a space which was physically and socially separate, and affixed with the permanently stigmatizing identity of "prostitute."[7] In the United States, it was not until the Progressive Era in the early twentieth century that a statutory definition of prostitution even existed. As the historian Timothy Gilfoyle has observed, prior to this time the crime of prostitution was primarily "a condition of vagrancy and being female."[8]

During the first decades of the twentieth century, gathering public outcry around the expansion of sexual commerce led to the shutdown of the red-light districts and to the criminalization of the organized sex trade. A succession of municipal and state-level "Red Light Abatement Acts" and the passage of the federal Mann-Elkins "White Slavery" Act officially brought the first era of wide-scale, commercialized prostitution to a close.[9] Yet the decline of the red-light district and the brothel as a prevailing commercial-sexual form did not fundamentally alter the gendered meanings of prostitution, which still marked the female prostitute (but not her male customer) as a deviant outsider. Instead, associations with the image of a dangerous and gritty underworld were dramatically exacerbated, sexual commerce was increasingly confined to the streets of poor, immigrant, and other "socially disorganized" neighborhoods, and prostitutes now had to cope with the added risk and stigma of criminality.[10] Control of the prostitution transaction continued to shift from madams and prostitutes to male middlemen, as well as to organized crime.[11] Nor did criminalization serve to significantly curb the sex trade's supply, demand, or gross profits. As the historian Barbara Hobson has noted, "The laws and general strategy of repression seem to have had remarkably little effect on the prostitution economy. . . . Turning out the red lights and dismantling the districts merely dispersed the trade and produced a new set of institutions in the prostitution economy."[12] In a study conducted shortly after the closure of the red-light district in Chicago, the sociologist William C. Reckless thus reported only a modest decline from 1,020 "vice resorts" in 1910 to 731 venues in 1931. He further observed the rise of new erotic commercial venues in the city, including taxi-dance halls, roadhouses, and cabarets. Commenting on the case of San Francisco, Neil Shumsky and Larry Springer similarly note that legal changes dramatically revamped spatial patterns between 1880 and 1934 but ultimately did little to deter the existence of prostitution.[13]

In Europe, although the prostitution transaction itself was not criminalized, a similar pattern prevailed. Antiprostitution campaigns in the United States had counterparts in France, Germany, Holland, Sweden, Finland, Denmark, and the United Kingdom. The goal, in all cases, was the dismantling of the organized sex trade and the regulated system.[14] In Sweden, a French-style regulatory system, premised on the rationalized enclosure of the *maison de tolerance,* was established in 1859 but abolished by 1918.[15] In the Netherlands, a regulatory system was introduced during the French occupation (1810–13), but by the second half of the nineteenth century an alliance of Christians, feminists, and some socialists were fighting to eliminate it. Their efforts culminated in the passage of the Public Morality Act of 1911, which sought to wipe out prostitution through the prohibition of brothel keeping.[16] Yet, as in the United States, the abolitionist agenda did not ultimately prove to be effective in dismantling the European sex trade.[17]

SEXUAL COMMERCE AND URBAN SPACE

In addition to shifts in law and policy, the evolution of sexual commerce was also intimately tied to transformations in the spatial contours of life in industrializing cities. In a 1981 essay, Neil Shumsky and Larry Springer point out that while scholars have frequently analyzed prostitution as a social, cultural, economic, political, or psychological issue, they have rarely considered it in terms of shifting patterns of urban geography.[18] To the extent that contemporary scholars have considered questions of space and mobility in relation to urban sex work, they have tended to emphasize individual sex workers' mobility as a response to an ever-present flight from law enforcement.[19] Yet such analyses often beg the question of *why* particular laws and law enforcement patterns emerge when they do, and what the underlying determinants of such patterns might be. In the early decades of the twentieth century, it was not only the rise of various moral reform movements by feminists, purity crusaders, and social hygienists but also phenomena such as urban expansion, the rise of the automobile, growth in the entertainment and leisure industries, and burgeoning immigration that led to the increasing regulation of sexual commerce in modernizing cities.[20]

In the predominantly male social world of mid-nineteenth-century San Francisco, women arrived from many different cities and nations to work as prostitutes, but Chinese prostitutes were the first to be singled out for special treatment by the state.[21] Although the city's de facto prostitution zone between the years 1849 and 1917 was the broad sweep of terrain bounded by Powell, Montgomery, Broadway, and Market streets (including the well-known "Barbary Coast" and the area immediately south), early efforts were made to control the spatial trajectories of an expanding population of Chinese prostitutes. In 1854, a committee was assembled to discuss the removal of Chinese prostitutes "from the more inhabited line of streets," and, in 1866, the San Francisco Board of Supervisors issued an "Order to Remove Chinese Women of Ill-Fame from Certain Limits in the City."[22] Although the attorney for the Board of Supervisors eventually persuaded the board to delete "Chinese" from the statute's final wording, its intent remained clear: Chinese women were to be the target of the crackdown. During the same year, the California legislature passed the "Act for the Suppression of Chinese Houses of Ill Fame," and San Francisco police began to ready themselves to close down all Chinese brothels in the city until the prostitutes and brothel owners consented to occupy "only certain buildings and localities under restrictions imposed by the Board of Health and Police Commissioners."[23]

The Barbary Coast had initially been located in a "transitional zone" between areas of work and areas of residence; it was an area that San Francisco's largely male population could "reach equally well from either work or home."[24] However, in response both to external pressures to curb prostitution and to the rapid expansion of the city's central business district, by the final decades of the nineteenth century the San Francisco Board of Supervisors began to pass a series of laws that would both confine the red-light district and enable the westward expansion of the city's burgeoning downtown. As the city's central business district expanded, it came to encompass several blocks which had been major parts of the zone of prostitution. As Shumsky and Springer note, "[when] the shopping district moved in, the prostitutes moved out." By 1915, Maiden Lane, which had been one of the most notorious streets in the entire city, "had clearly become the core of the women's apparel-shopping district. Out of 188 women's apparel shopping establishments in the central district, 47 (25%) had taken up locations in it, and another 16% had located in the two blocks to the east and south." [25]

A new series of municipal ordinances pertaining to prostitution were passed in order to accommodate this expansion. The first new law was General Order 2191, issued in 1890, which "prohibited persons from keeping, maintaining, or becoming an inmate of or visiting any house of ill fame . . . within a district bounded by California, Powell, Kearny, and Broadway streets." Although the law was not uniformly enforced, the Board of Supervisors supplemented it with further orders to confine the district over the course of the next several years. In 1909, the Police Commission decided to create an even more restricted zone, one which was contained within the contours of the Barbary Coast (where the highest concentration of brothels existed): prostitutes were "not allowed to solicit outside of this territory nor on the streets, nor . . . to reside anywhere except within this prescribed district." [26] In 1911, the city delimited the district still further, confining it to the area bounded by "Commercial Street from the westerly line of Kearny Street to the easterly line of Grant Avenue; Jackson Street between Kearny and Grant Avenue north to Pacific Street; Pacific Street from the easterly line of Montgomery Street to the westerly line of Front Street . . . Washington Place . . . from the north side of Washington Street between Kearny and Grant Avenue North to Jackson Street." [27] That same year, the San Francisco Board of Supervisors stipulated that to avoid arrest, prostitutes would be required to undergo biweekly examinations for venereal disease, and to live within the confines of the narrow strip between Washington and Pacific streets (see figure 1). [28]

More dramatic spatial changes were wrought with the passage of the California Red Light Abatement Act in 1913. After the law was upheld by the California State Supreme Court in 1917, eighty-three brothels were immediately closed and 1,073 women were put out on the street. [29] According to journalistic accounts from the period, very few prostitutes chose to abandon the sex trade despite offers from groups like the YWCA and the Civic League to help them find other vocations.[30] Thus, with the Barbary Coast abolished, a new "red-light non-district" gradually emerged to take its place.[31] Although some prostitutes chose to remain in the old area, the majority moved to the region southwest of Union Square, the up-and-coming hotel and entertainment district. As streetwalking became a more prominent feature of city life, the area that came to be known as the San Francisco Tenderloin was transformed into the city's primary prostitution zone and would remain so for the next seventy-five years (see figure 2).

In European cities, where prostitution was not criminalized, the pattern varied to some extent. The historian Alain Corbin has dated the decline of the brothel and the rise of street prostitution in Paris to 1925 (before the official dismantling of the regulated system), but he has also documented the emergence of the *maison d'abattage* in

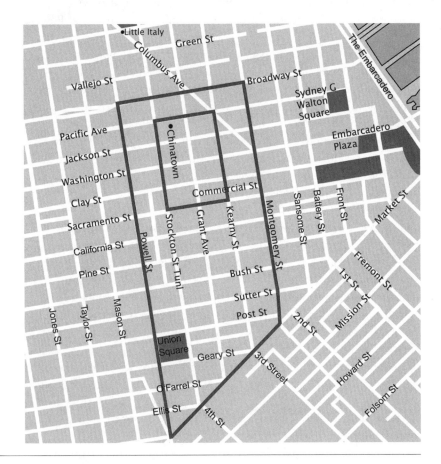

1 Primary zone of San Francisco prostitution, inner and outer limits, 1849–1917.

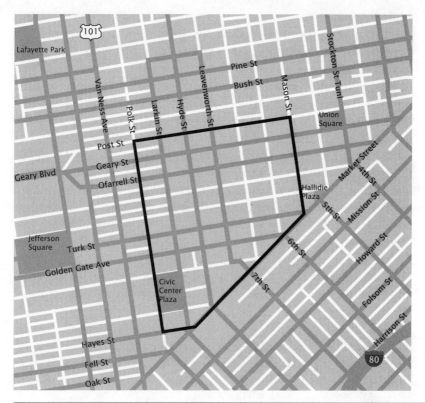

2 Primary zone of street prostitution in the San Francisco Tenderloin, 1917–1994.

the interwar years, characterized by "concentration, rationalization, and standardization"—what he has termed "Taylorized coitus" and "conveyor-belt sex."[32] In Swedish cities, prostitution was relatively small-scale and confined to informal exchanges on the streets until the emergence of "sex clubs" and escort agencies in the early 1960s.[33] In Amsterdam and other Dutch cities, many prostitutes chose to work in the streets or clandestine brothels of the new semiofficial red-light districts after the passage of the 1911 Public Morality Act, including in the Oudeskerksplein (today's well-known prostitution district for tourists).[34]

THE POLICING OF URBAN MARGINALITY
IN POSTINDUSTRIAL CITIES

Commenting in the early 1980s on the situation in the United States, the historian Ruth Rosen noted that streetwalking—along with its at-

tendant social realities of crime and violence—had become the dominant means of prostitutes' solicitation since the 1920s.[35] Despite the
growth of massage parlors and escort agencies during the 1960s and
1970s as commercial sexual forms, the streetwalker has remained
largely synonymous with "the prostitute" in both the popular and the
policy maker's imagination.[36] The miniskirted, stiletto-heeled figure of
the street prostitute has continued to grace the covers of recent sociological texts on the contemporary sex industry (even if the contents of
these volumes describe a far more varied reality).[37] Yet by the end of
the 1980s, prominent sex-workers' rights activists were estimating that
streetwalkers comprised a mere 20 percent of the prostitute population
in urban areas like San Francisco.[38] In 2001, the time by which I had
completed the bulk of my research, my own calculations suggested that
2 percent might be an even more accurate figure.[39] Over the course of
the seven years that I conducted my fieldwork, I watched as the number
of female prostitutes on the streets of San Francisco dwindled from several hundred to as few as ten or twenty a night, while the overall size of
the sex industry expanded and diversified. Meanwhile, the 1995 introduction of San Francisco's First Offender Program (colloquially known
as "John School") was transformed into an effective tool for systematically removing male clients from city streets. In Western European
cities with diverse legal regimes I witnessed a similar reorganization of
the commercial sex trade during the same period (see chap. 6).

In 1994, when I first began studying prostitution in San Francisco,
there were three principal streetwalking strolls in the Tenderloin, each
just blocks away from the posh shops, corporate hotels, and expensive real estate of Union Square—which had by then become the main
tourist and shopping district of the city. At the time, most streetwalkers could be easily distinguished not only because of their distinctive
dress but because they were practically the only women inhabiting
the sparsely populated, poorly lit streets. I was befriended by women
like Olivia, a twenty-seven-year-old African American mother of two
who took the BART to work each night from Oakland.[40] When she
arrived at the local $20 per hour SRO (single-room occupancy hotel),
she would change into the short skirt and towering heels that she called
her "uniform," then hit the streets. Most of her nights were spent dodg-
ing pimps and police officers and waiting for customers to approach,
either by car or on foot. As my research progressed, Olivia and the
other women on her stroll spent an increasing number of their working
nights—sometimes, as many as four nights a week—in jail.

The predominantly Thai and Vietnamese immigrants who staffed the cluster of small-scale, "mom and pop" erotic massage parlors which were concentrated in the Tenderloin also came under siege. By 1998, there had been an unprecedented series of worker arrests, nearly a third of the twenty-six massage parlors in the area had been shut down or targeted for closure, and the Board of Supervisors had approved a permanent ban on the building of any new massage parlors in the area.[41]

The late 1990s were of course the peak years of dot-com and high-tech investment in the city, when San Francisco became the global headquarters of the Internet economy and the repository of over a third of the nation's venture capital. As a consequence, the nine-square-block area that had housed the city's primary street prostitution strolls and commercial sex venues for over seventy-five years was on its way to being incorporated into the Union Square shopping and tourism district. At the same time, advertisements for prostitution in the newspapers and through the new online services exploded, as did prostitution in eleven of the city's seventeen legal (and increasingly corporate-run) strip clubs.[42] In similar fashion, the number of licensed massage parlors in the city overall was actually *increasing,* despite the police crackdown on Asian-run massage parlors in the Tenderloin.[43]

Many of the same women who had been working on the streets or in Tenderloin massage parlors now began to get cell phones and to take out ads, or to look for work in different indoor venues. These venues were not concentrated in the center of town but dispersed throughout the city, housed in Victorians in quiet residential neighborhoods or relocated to the city's suburban periphery. This explosion of large-scale, commercialized sexual services and individually run, off-street operations in the city's residential periphery drew relatively little attention from the police—despite their intense focus on commercial sexual transactions in the gentrifying core. The timing of my research thus coincided with the demise of inner-city street and massage parlor prostitution in San Francisco and the flourishing of new, high-tech, and decentered forms of sexual commerce.

From the fall of 1994, when I first began my study, to the early part of 1997, street prostitutes were steadily "pushed" by police sweeps deeper and deeper into the Tenderloin. Periodically, when a politician or an important convention was in town, the police would conduct even more systematic sweeps of the area. By the time of the prominent 1997 Mayor's Convention (to be held just blocks away from the city's principal street prostitution zone), local politicians and police

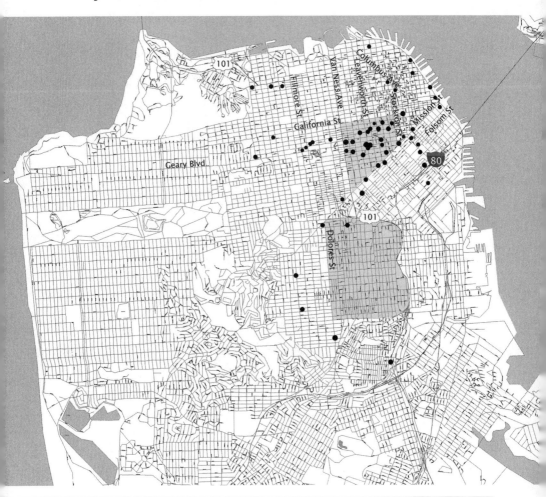

3 Distribution of licensed massage parlors in San Francisco, 1997 (source: San Francisco Police Department).

had made a more definitive decision regarding street prostitution in San Francisco: they decided to eliminate it. As a sergeant from the San Francisco Street Crimes unit informed me, the city's "no tolerance policy on hookers" was to involve nightly sweeps, incessant patrolling, and a stepped up "decoy program" for arresting johns. "We have always had the capability to do this," he explained. "It's just been a question of incentive." The "incentive," in this case, was provided not simply by a single, if important, celebrity event in the city, but by deeper transformations that had been transpiring quietly for years,

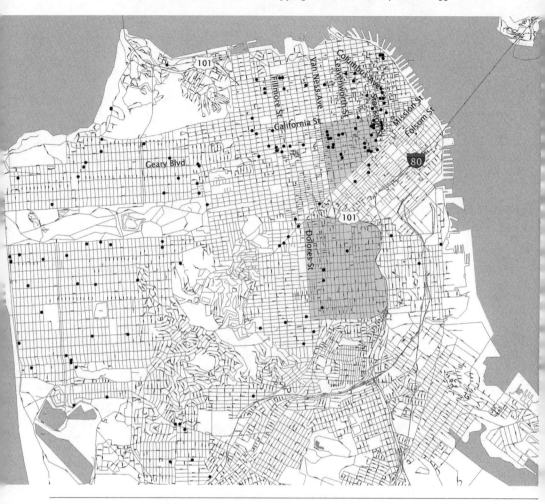

4 Distribution of licensed massage parlors in San Francisco, 2005 (source: San Francisco Department of Public Health and Alix Lutnick, St. James Infirmary).

such as the increasing gentrification of the city's Tenderloin district.[44] As in other U.S. and Western European cities, rigorous, combative policing became a "frontline strategy" for purging sex workers and other perceived members of the "deprived underclass" from newly desirable downtown real estate.[45]

The crackdown on prostitution followed a spate of aggressive policy measures designed to remove the homeless and other undesirable populations from city streets. Most notable among these was the MATRIX program begun under Mayor Frank Jordan in 1992, which

5 San Francisco prostitution arrests by neighborhood, January–December 1994: Tenderloin, including Polk Gulch, 2,280, or 65 percent; Mission, 950, or 27 percent; other street arrests, 226, or 7 percent; other indoor arrests, 39, or 1 percent (source: San Francisco Task Force on Prostitution 1996, app. D).

resurrected a panoply of city and state ordinances against public drunkenness, trespassing, littering, and obstructing the sidewalk, and which targeted its initial enforcement efforts in San Francisco's downtown neighborhoods (including Union Square and the Tenderloin).[46] Initially, some of the sex workers in these neighborhoods relocated to the Mission district, the predominantly Latino neighborhood just east of downtown, which since the 1980s had housed the city's central drug corridor. This strategy worked until the late 1990s, when the inner Mission district began to undergo its own gentrification process, and neighborhood antiprostitution activism mounted steadily.[47] Eventually, the sex and drug trades would be curtailed on these streets as well, leaving only a small strip of commerce on Sixteenth and Capp streets by the time I completed my research.

The changing topography of San Francisco's Tenderloin and Mission districts in the 1990s was portended by broad structural transformations that swept through diverse postindustrial cities throughout the same period. As the urban geographer Neil Smith has explained, the 1990s marked the decline of inner-city tenderloins as a dominant urban form which, since the era of post–World War II suburban expansion, had served as the city's primary haven for the poor and socially dispossessed:

> [T]he terrain of the inner city is suddenly valuable again, perversely profitable. This new urbanism embodies a widespread and drastic repolarization of the city along political, economic, cultural, and geographical lines since the 1970s, and is integral with larger global shifts . . . global economic expansion in the 1980s;

the restructuring of national and urban economies in advanced capitalist countries towards services, recreation, and consumption; and the emergence of a global hierarchy of world, national, and regional cities. These shifts have propelled gentrification from a comparatively marginal preoccupation in a certain niche of the real estate industry to the cutting edge of urban change.[48]

As urban economies have reoriented themselves away from productive labor and toward services and consumption, a "new geography of centrality and marginality" has emerged: the white middle classes increasingly seek out the city center for their residences and leisure activities, while the urban industrial proletariat is reduced in numbers and relocated to the city's periphery.[49]

In the 1970s, the San Francisco Tenderloin was the poorest neighborhood in the city: low-income seniors, the disabled, and "drifters" in SROs were its principal residents, sustaining themselves through casual

```
      CHILDREN ARE EXPOSED TO PROSTITUTES EVERY DAY ON
CAPP STREET IN THE MISSION. CAPP STREET AT 19TH STREET
IS AN OPEN MARKET FOR PROSTITUTES.
      STREET PROSTITUTION IS CONSIDERED LOW PRIORITY BY
MAYOR JORDAN AND THE POLICE.
      PROSTITUTION IS NOT A VICTIMLESS CRIME. CHILDREN
FORCED TO HEAR OBSCENITIES AND WITNESS DEGRADING ACTS
ARE BEING PSYCHOLOGICALLY VICTIMIZED DAY AND NIGHT.
      MAYOR JORDAN HAS NO EFFECTIVE POLICY FOR REMOVING
THE PROSTITUTES AND PIMPS FROM RESIDENTIAL STREETS
WHILE HE TELLS HIS CONSTITUENTS THAT STREETS ARE CLEAN
AND CRIME IS DOWN, THE STREETS IN THE MISSION ARE FILTHY
AND CRIME IS RAMPANT. MATRIX HAS TURNED THE MISSION
INTO MAYOR JORDAN'S WASTELAND.
      PROSTITUTES SHOULD NOT BE ON RESIDENTIAL STREETS
PROSTITUTION WILL NEVER BE ERADICATED WITH SELF-SERVING
MORAL FERVOR. WE HAVE TO LEGALIZE IT, REGULATE IT, ZONE
AND TAX IT, AND GET IT OFF THE STREET.

      HOW CAN ANY CITIZEN OR CANDIDATE CLAIM TO CARE ABOUT
THIS CITY AND OUR CHILDREN WITHOUT MAKING THIS ISSUE A
PRIORITY?
```

6 Flier posted in the San Francisco Mission district, fall 1995.

labor or through meager stipends from General Assistance. Local store-fronts were frequently boarded up and grafittied, their interiors left unoccupied. Many San Francisco residents regarded the neighborhood as little more than "a containment zone for drug dealing, prostitution, and public drinking," where illicit activities could occur with relatively little police interference, and liquor stores and massage parlors were licensed in greater numbers than anywhere else in the city.[50]

By the 1980s, the city's economy was becoming increasingly dependent on tourism, and the Tenderloin's central location, proximity to the Union Square shopping and theater district, and abundance of residential hotels made it especially appealing to the San Francisco tourist industry.[51] The first major step toward neighborhood transformation occurred in the late 1970s, when large numbers of SROs were emptied of their tenants so that their buildings could be converted into budget tourist accommodations (a more profitable enterprise for owners than charging reduced-rate monthly rents). The next step came in 1980, when three national hotel chains announced plans to build luxury hotels in area: Ramada, Hilton, and Holiday Inn. Despite fierce protests by local residents and social service agencies, the developers emerged from the struggle triumphant, and the hotels were erected.

Over the course of the next decade, the tension between the "old" and "new" Tenderloins would become even more heated. Although the peak years of high-tech expansion in the 1990s created great economic benefits for the city's affluent classes, they also created a more entrenched social divide. On the streets, crack cocaine joined heroin as drugs of choice and brought more violence to the neighborhood, while the area's low-income residents confronted a dwindling supply of housing, federal aid, and social services. Among local activists and nonprofits, who were also stretched thin for adequate resources, there was a new tendency to think in terms of the "deserving" versus the "undeserving" poor.[52]

JOHN SCHOOL, GENTRIFICATION, AND
THE SAN FRANCISCO TASK FORCE ON PROSTITUTION

It was within this context of neighborhood transformations that a Task Force on Prostitution was convened in 1994 by then-Supervisor Terence Hallinan in response to complaints from local residents and merchants about the "increasingly problematic" nature of the sex trade—in particular, problems such as noise, litter, and empty condom wrappers on their streets.[53] The task force comprised leaders of resident and merchant associations from the city's Tenderloin and Mission districts, representatives from the police and health departments, nearly a dozen sex-worker activists, and a handful of other interested parties.[54] Unprecedented in the history of policy reform, the strong presence of sex-worker activists on the task force meant that they were to play a vital role in revising prostitution policy in the city. [55] And, in notable contrast to antiprostitution movements of eras past, complaints by the residents' groups were explicitly aimed at the "quality of life" problems caused by visible street prostitution in the Tenderloin, Mission, and other neighborhoods, rather than at the moral difficulties entailed by the existence of sexual commerce per se. As Michael, a small business owner from the group "Save Our Streets" insisted at an early task force meeting, "We're upset not because it's illegal or immoral, but because it disturbs our lives." [56]

After two years of biweekly meetings, in which the task force members considered various solutions, a *Final Report* was at last issued. In it, the task force noted that "despite their concerns about noise, traffic, etc., most residents supported decriminalization or legalization of prostitution." These concerns could effectively be dealt with by focusing "on the perceived fallout or side effects of street prostitution" rather than by policing the sex industry in its entirety.[57] The task force's *Final Report* thus advocated both further crackdowns on street prostitution through the use of public nuisance laws and other municipal codes, *and* the decriminalization of the indoor sex trade.

After the report was issued, the recommendations of the task force report were never officially adopted, but they nonetheless became de facto policy in the city. According to statistics provided by the California Bureau of Justice, the number of arrests for the crime of prostitution in San Francisco decreased steadily between the years of 1994 and 2003, declining from 2,749 to 1,276 cases annually. Arrests for the misdemeanor offense of "disorderly conduct," on the other hand, came to replace charges for prostitution and thus surged during this same period, from 166 to 929.[58] To further appease some of the disaffected neighborhood residents, Hallinan (who was by now the city's District Attorney) also put in place another policy, his ground-breaking "First Offender" program for arrested clients, which would eventually serve as a template for prostitution regulation in numerous North American and Western European cities.[59] The program involved stepped up arrests of male clients and an all-day reeducation program (akin to traffic school) for johns. In practice, since the only men arrested were those who patronized street prostitutes, both the de facto decriminalization of indoor sex work and the emergence of "John School" would serve to

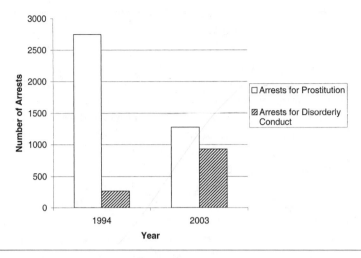

7 Prostitution and disorderly conduct arrests in San Francisco, 1994 and 2003 (source: California Bureau of Justice Statistics).

further curtail outdoor sex markets, redirecting both sex workers and their customers to the burgeoning indoor and online sectors.

The transformation that was underway in San Francisco thus did not solely concern the fate of a few hundred street prostitutes and their customers but was about a wide-sweeping reallocation of urban space, in which the inner city found itself being reclaimed by the white middle classes, while those at the social margins were pushed to the city's literal periphery. In tandem with the excision of the homeless, the unemployed, the poor, and most racialized Others from the new "bourgeois playgrounds" of the inner city, San Francisco's de facto red-light districts came under increasing scrutiny and censure. Witnessing a similar reconfiguration of the sex industry in Portland, Oregon, during these years, the sociolegal scholar Lisa Sanchez has described this shift under the rubric of "spatial governmentality," in which spaces rather than offenders are targeted for reform.[60] In notable contrast to Progressive Era social reformers, the groups who opposed flagrant and visible prostitution on their streets did not issue a critique about the intermingling of sexuality and the market. To the contrary, the young, white professionals who flooded the city during the 1990s to work in high-tech, multimedia, and other industries—necessitating the "renewal" of formerly impoverished areas—were at the forefront of a new economy in sexual services, both by creating a demand for them and by facilitating new conditions of production. The sex trade was not eliminated but instead changed its predominant form. As the following chapters shall reveal, the world of modern-industrial street prostitution, along with its classic paraphernalia—the pimp, the police officer, the prostitute as "public" and therefore disreputable woman—had begun to recede into the distance, while an array of spatially dispersed sexual services rapidly emerged to take its place. Transformations in the forms and functions of urban space were accompanied by important changes in the prevailing practices and meanings of commercial sex.

3 | Modern Prostitution and Its Remnants

I parked on Sixteenth Street tonight, within eyeshot of the all-night diner, and hid my bags beneath the seat. Tonight Evelyn and I will be handing out condoms and fliers advising the women to take care, since four women who work this area have been shot during the past month—two fatally. Most of the street-walkers, it turns out, have not only heard about the killer, but knew one or more of the women who were victimized. Some have been talking to cops and reporters all day. "Dana was a smart girl," says one woman who we stop to talk with. "She had a lot of street sense." Other women strive to calculate their own level of personal risk: "They were all blonde with blue eyes, so I think I'm okay."

A slender, twentyish, dark-haired woman recounts the week's horror stories to us: "Lisa was found beaten and naked in a box." She describes the two most recent rapes that she managed to survive, and says she'll try to remember to call us tomorrow with the johns' license plate numbers. The rapes were brutal and traumatic, but she went along with them so she didn't get too hurt. One of her assailants was a small, scrawny guy, but she was high on heroin so she couldn't defend herself. She carries a pair of large rusty scissors with her most of the time, but when she's half–passed out they don't do much good.

We move on to cover more of the stroll, and Evelyn stops to introduce me to several of the men she used to shoot drugs with, the women she used to solicit with, and the shabby but surprisingly well-scrubbed Florida Hotel (where many of the women take their tricks) owned by a bespectacled, middle-aged Indian man. As we walk through the area, I observe that prospective customers outnumber the street women by a ratio that exceeds ten to one: behind us, there is a row of headlights that extends for several streets. At the hotel, Evelyn explains that women can rent rooms for $20 (plus an additional $10 when they come with a trick). I note with some puzzlement the sign taped to the hallway door, which reads "No Illegal Activities or Prostitution Permitted on Premises." When I inquire about this directly with the owner, he says that he's powerless to stop what happens in the dark behind closed doors—that's the residents' private business.

As we continue walking, we encounter women every block or so, alone or in pairs, before we soon come across a heavy-set streetwalker named Drew who appears to be in her late thirties. Drew has the spunk and charm of a one-woman comedy show, with a bilevel haircut, a magenta pantsuit that is ornamented with bangles and baubles, and the distinctive extra-sweet perfume that I have come to recognize from other prostitution strolls. She tells us that she has been out of jail for three days after doing six months' time, and is now trying to get her life together so that she can leave the streets. Drew recounts some of her experiences while incarcerated, describing how the women were supposed to break chicken necks as part of their work duty, but she alone refused: "I'll sell my pussy but I won't sell my soul. At least you can wash your pussy off." She pauses contemplatively to consider the "outdated morality" that landed her in the state penitentiary in the first place: "For selling sex, I get thrown in jail and my children get taken away, while we've got seven-year-old schoolgirls walking around in pint-sized 'Madonna' corsets. What's going on?"

FIELD NOTES, SAN FRANCISCO MISSION DISTRICT, NOVEMBER 1995

In the mid-1990s there was still an abundant and diverse street prostitution scene in San Francisco. Beginning each evening and lasting until the early morning hours, hundreds of female, transgender, and male prostitutes would take to one of several prostitution strolls in the city's de facto red-light districts. On "good" nights, streetwalkers would greet lineups of paired headlights that ran twenty cars deep, and fortunate sex workers could have ten or more fifteen-minute dates in an evening. On "bad" nights, proportionately more waiting and watching were required, as was the exercise of extreme vigilance for pimps, assorted social predators, and the police. Unbeknownst to the most of the women who walked the streets, a conjoining of political and economic interests were all the while conspiring to eliminate their predominant means of earning a living. As the women watched and waited, the social landscape of prostitution was quietly being transformed.

This chapter highlights the world of street prostitution that I came to know during a period when stepped up arrests of street-based sex workers and the city's implementation of an unofficial "no tolerance" policy on public soliciting were radically reducing its scope and visibility. While many women moved off the streets during this time, those who remained found themselves confronting heightened stigma, sequestration, and physical risks from both clients and police. In this chapter, I draw on my fieldwork as a volunteer outreach worker handing out condoms, needles, and safety tips to street-based sex workers; as a "street decoy" dressed to blend in with the other women in order to better experience street dynamics from their perspective; and as a companion to the police (in the patrol car and in the paddy wagon with arrestees) during their biweekly prostitution patrols for streetwalkers and their customers.[1] Focusing on the defining features of modern prostitution that streetwalking has represented—the nature of the commodity that is sold and bought; the social construction of female streetwalkers as an isolable class of "public women"; the locus, organization, and modes of state intervention which have shaped the exchange—the analysis presented here serves as a contrast case to my discussion in subsequent chapters of the new, "postindustrial" forms of sexual commerce that have emerged in the wake of modern prostitution's decline.

SAN FRANCISCO STREETWALKING STROLLS: A TOPOGRAPHY

As the peak years of street prostitution in San Francisco were drawing to a close, the women who walked the streets of the San Francisco Tenderloin and Mission districts were likely to describe themselves as pertaining to one of three distinct "classes": the "upper-class" women of the stroll located at the intersection of Geary and Mason streets, the "middle-class" women at the corner of Leavenworth and Geary, and the "lower-class" women who concentrated on O'Farrell Street between the cross streets of Taylor and Jones. For streetwalkers, these classes were widely recognizable and could be distinguished not merely by geographic location and by hourly rates but also by sex workers' physical attributes, or what sociologists might term their "bodily capital"—a symbolic currency often acquired by members of the dominated fractions of society who, deprived of other forms of social power, cultivate their bodies as value-producing investments.[2]

"Class" in the sense of economic origin was relatively uniform in all three terrains. Nearly all of the women that I encountered had tenth- or eleventh-grade educations and came from working-class or poor families. The younger women were often runaways; many of the older women were mothers themselves. Ages typically ranged between fifteen and thirty, with most women in their late teens and early twenties.[3] A cursory glance at the available socioeconomic data suggests that the most immediate and tangible "cause" of their participation in paid sexual labor—as numerous social scientists have noted for prostitutes since the early part of the century—had much to do with poor labor market prospects and family disruption.[4]

On the crowded and brightly lit Geary-Mason stroll, the predominantly white, Asian, and light-skinned black "circuit girls" commanded the highest prices. These women of the "West Coast circuit" (consisting of Portland, San Francisco, Las Vegas, Los Angeles, San Diego, and Honolulu) generally traveled together from city to city to work the streets. In the vernacular of the commercial sex trade, the term "circuit girls" has served to distinguish high-end, pimp-managed streetwalkers from women who trade sex for drugs or who work the streets sporadically and informally. Young, slim, and expensively dressed, the circuit girls' tightly fitted suits, sweater sets, and fur or leather jackets coded them for a relatively upscale market. Physically, only their somewhat shorter-than-average skirts, artfully teased and layered hair, and diligently applied makeup set them apart from many of the dressed-up female tourists or theater- and restaurant-goers who walked past them, and the differences were often quite subtle. For women working this "upper-class" stroll (which included a few "independents," as well as the circuit girls), prices would start at $100, and it was not uncommon to make as much as $400 for what was typically a fifteen-minute "date."[5] Many of the women who worked this stroll boasted that they could easily make $800 to $900 a night, depending on how "brave" they were. "Bravery" might be defined as getting into cars with dates—for many, an unquestionably dangerous activity—rather than insisting that dates accompany them back to one of the numerous high-priced hotels in the area, or to the Diamond Palace, a less expensive hotel on a neighboring street where they had an arrangement with the manager.

Just a few blocks over, deeper into the Tenderloin and further away from the posh shops and upscale hotels of Union Square, were the "middle-class" women who worked on the two prostitution strolls formed by the intersections of Leavenworth with Geary and O'Farrell streets. This area formed something of a continuum with the "lower-class" stroll, the nucleus of which was situated a few blocks to the west. Unlike the already gentrified area directly adjacent to Union Square, these sections of the inner Tenderloin were still characterized by neglected apartment buildings and a smattering of liquor stores, dimly lit bars, and SROs. While drug dealers, their customers, and pimps formed the main foot traffic, potential clients drove by in automobiles, craning their necks out of rolled down windows and honking their horns to express interest. On these streets, more streetwalkers of color were apparent; women's outfits were scantier and less formal; and there was a greater range of ages and body styles. Dates generally ranged from $20 to $100, with prices corresponding both to services offered and to precise geographical location (those standing closer to Union Square, on the "middle-class" stroll, charged more than women deeper in the Tenderloin). Typically, the self-employed "hos," "hookers," or "working girls" who worked here would rent their hotel rooms either for the evening or by the hour, though sometimes after a hotel bust those without good connections might be denied access to a room and forced to go into dates' cars.

Commercial sexual exchanges also regularly took place at the corner of Hyde and O'Farrell streets and on Capp Street in the Mission, though on these streets prostitution was not a night-time occupation but a daily survival strategy.[6] Amid the weathered and peeling SROs and congregations of drug dealers and panhandlers, sexual commerce was an all-day, everyday activity, since most of the prostitutes were homeless women with no place to go until enough money could be scraped together for a hotel room. More often, women would "sell pussy" for the $20 that could be directly applied to the purchase of a vial of heroin, crack, or "speedballs" (a combination of heroin and cocaine). In the standardized economy of these streets, a $20 bill was the ubiquitous note of exchange, good for a blow job or a hand job, a hotel room, or drugs.[7] Sometimes the women would skip the middle step altogether, bypassing any exchange of currency, and simply "turn tricks for rocks."

Streetwalkers in the Hyde and Capp street drug markets might initially be difficult to identify as such, lacking some of the traditional visual markers of sexual availability. In contrast to the self-identified "career prostitutes" concentrated on the other strolls, they did not change into a "uniform," did not travel to a special place to work, and did not cultivate their sexual capital as an abstracted feature of the self. They were also likely to be older than other prostitutes (streetwalkers from other strolls might "retire" to these strips) or they might be adolescent runaways, dressed in down jackets, tennis shoes, and jeans. Peer-based outreach projects that frequented the neighborhood employed the term "survival sex" (rather than "sex work" or even "prostitution") to designate the pattern of exchanging sex for small

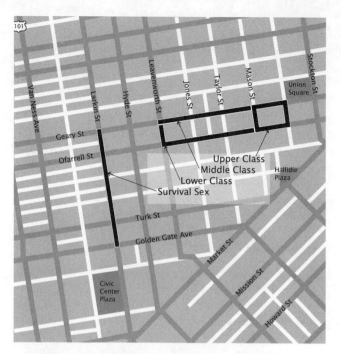

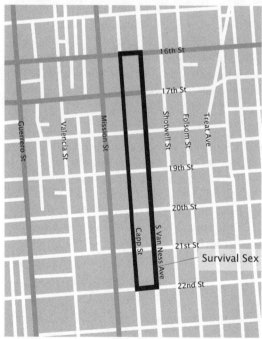

8 Streetwalking strolls in the Tenderloin (above) and Mission districts (below), 1994–1997.

amounts of money, for drugs, or for a place to stay that usually took place on these streets.

VARIETIES OF "CAREER PROSTITUTION": PRACTICES AND MEANINGS

How most women explain prostitution when they first start out is "I felt an incredible sense of power." When I started turning tricks, the world finally made sense to me. I thought, I can do this, this is something that I know how to do. It wasn't just to buy heroin. . . . It had all kinds of other meanings for me. It's an incredible sense of power to turn a date, an incredible sense. Suddenly, I could do something that was very natural for me and feel good.
    EVELYN, Capp Street, San Francisco

I have actually had clients who have wanted to marry me. But then I explain to them: I cannot have a romance with you because you have no idea who I really am. What you see is completely an act! The only reason that you think everything works so well between us is because I am pretending. And the only reason that I am willing to pretend is because you pay me.
    RITA, Stockholm, Sweden

Tricks can get loud, especially on weekends. They'll yell from their cars if they see a sexy girl. But most of the tricks are middle-aged blue-collar and white-collar men who are quiet and nervous—they want to be discreet. A lot of them are married businessmen. Usually, they're not even interested in talking to you. What they want is quick sex. They'll say "hi" and "bye," but in terms of conversation, that's about it.
    EVE, Geary and Leavenworth streets, San Francisco

Once when I was home with my husband, I forgot who I was with. And I started to moan and act—I thought I was working! Then suddenly I realized what was happening. He didn't notice, but I did. I was sweating. And I knew it was time for me to get out [of the business] because it was becoming more and more difficult to keep the different parts of myself apart, to keep the different roles separate. I didn't want to be a hooker 24 hours a day. It's enough work to do it for two or three.
    CRISTINA, Göteborg, Sweden

Contemporary analyses of prostitution, whether authored by academics, activists, or policy makers, often fail to distinguish *between* markets in sexual labor and the different meanings, practices, and regulatory strategies that each market entails.[8] This is especially true when it comes to analyses of street prostitution, where commentators are apt to generalize from the experiences of drug-dependent and/or pimp-controlled women to street prostitution in general or even to sex work as a whole.[9] The analysis of prostitution provided in *Backstreets,* for example, an early feminist ethnographic treatment of street prostitution, is emblematic of this trend. As is revealed in the volume's table of contents, the authors Cecilie Høigård and Liv Finstad organize the various chapters of their book under thematic subheadings intended to capture not only the lived realities of prostitution for the particular drug-dependent streetwalkers in their study, but as intrinsic and generalizable qualities of sexual labor in all its diverse forms (e.g., "A Life under the Influence," "The Customer—Faceless and Nameless," "In It for the Money: The Economics of Prostitution from the Women's Point of View," "Fast Fuck: The Women's View of What the Customer Buys," and "'I've Left My Body on the Street': Delayed Damage to the Women").[10] Antiprostitution activists such as Donna Hughes and Melissa Farley, as well as feminist academics such as Catharine Mac-Kinnon and Carole Pateman, have similarly sought to emphasize the common underpinnings of diverse forms of sexual labor—specifically, the experiences of sexual trauma, alienation, objectification, and exploitation which they claim are shared by women working in all facets and tiers of the sex industry.[11] Only recently have some feminist scholars begun to tease out the distinctive empirical realities of particular sexual markets and to demonstrate the divergent meanings, motivations, and embodied practices that can adhere to the sale of sex, across and within social spaces.[12]

My own fieldwork on the streets of the San Francisco Tenderloin and in various Scandinavian and Dutch cities also revealed the extent to which the exchange of sex for money could encompass a diverse range of experiences, even within the twenty-block radius of a single municipality. In contrast to the survival sex and strategic barter prevalent among the women of Hyde and Capp streets, for example, a majority of the street prostitutes on the "upper-," "middle-," and "lower-class" strolls of the Tenderloin tended to frame their commercial sexual activity as *labor,* and they explained to me that there was no other job at which they could make anywhere near a comparable wage.[13]

Female prostitutes' framing of prostitution as "work" is a theme which appears frequently in the historical and contemporary sex-work literatures, and it was also prominent in my own street-based fieldwork and interviews.[14] What has been less frequently remarked on by most commentators is that contemporary streetwalkers' decisions to frame their commercial sexual activity as rationally chosen and (comparatively) well-paid labor reveal a paradigmatically *modern* understanding of prostitution, one that is by no means shared by all sex workers. Such an understanding is premised on the structuring dualisms of home and work, private and public, interior and exterior, and formal vs. casual employment. The idea of heterosexual desire as "natural" and dually gendered also structures many women's narratives, and plays itself out in both routine and innovative ways.

During a late-night interview at a local diner, for example, Eve, a twenty-six-year-old streetwalker from Canada, recounted to me her experience of running away from home as a teenager and scrambling to find a job working long, hard hours as a fast food cashier. Over mouthfuls of french fries and cola, she described her initial decision to become a prostitute this way:

> Unless you have a college degree, and maybe even then, only mini- mum wage jobs are open to you, and it just ain't enough to get by. It's been an answer to a lot of things over the years. . . . I have more independence than the women who have to do it for their husbands and make their dinner . . . women do it all the time.

Throughout our conversation, Eve conceptualized her work as a form of highly paid wage labor, "a regular job." In the same spirit, Olivia, who shared a corner with Eve, was fond of quipping to police officers who chided her about still being on the streets at the age of twenty- seven that she'd "call in sick" the next day if they ever agreed to "re- tire her" on their pensions. These framings reveal a conceptual tem- plate which explicitly situates prostitution in terms of the likely array of other available working-class jobs. They also provide context for the findings of Martin Weinberg and his colleagues, who noted that 70 percent of Tenderloin street prostitutes that they surveyed reported the importance of having "a regular work schedule" (working on aver- age 5.2 days per week) when they engaged in sexual labor.[15]

Several of the women on Eve and Olivia's "middle-class" stroll also stressed the difference between "career prostitutes" and "crack pros- titutes," emphasizing not only the cash-for-sex instead of drugs-for- sex transaction, but also the clear division between private and pub- lic selves that the former mode of exchanging sex entailed. For these women, the bounded and routinized world of "career prostitution" was constituted explicitly in opposition to the disordered informality of "crack prostitution."[16] Eve, for example, explained to me early on that, unlike career prostitutes,

> crack prostitutes . . . live full time in the hotel we work at, going back and forth to the guys who sell drugs. [In crack prostitution]

you don't choose to make your living this way. I can go work in a massage parlor, or for an escort service, but they can only do what they're doing. For them, drugs is their career, and not prostitution.

In paradigmatically modern fashion, the self-identified "career prostitutes" maintained clear public/private boundaries by keeping separate spaces for "living" and "working." These boundaries were also maintained via a careful remapping of erotic bodily geography, in which certain sexual practices, aspects of the self, and segments of the body were kept strictly off limits. As the sociologist Susan Edwards has observed,

> The belief that, for women who supply the service, "anything goes," is widespread, as women who sell sex forfeit the right to say "No." . . . On the contrary, while sections of the public world may hold this view, the selling of sex by prostitute women is carefully circumscribed. . . . Prostitute women care less about the genitals and breasts, and much more about the mouth, the lips, the kiss, and tenderness, for them the truest meaning and expression of intimacy.[17]

In addition to extreme vigilance about the use of condoms (as both a physical and a psychological barrier)[18] and working "straight" (rather than drunk or high), most of the street-based "career prostitutes" that I interviewed insisted that they would not engage their clients in a mouth-to-mouth kiss. As with prostitutes' economic justifications for engaging in sex work, the reluctance to kiss clients is a commonplace in the contemporary prostitution literature, one which has been taken by some critics to represent an evident distaste for the labor that one is required to perform.[19] While this is no doubt true in some instances, female prostitutes' refusal to kiss clients must also be situated alongside other occupational practices such as the adoption of "working names" or the donning of "uniforms" (as Olivia and others often described their work attire), practices which, taken together, emerge as general occupational strategies for enforcing the separation between public and private selves.[20] During my fieldwork with street prostitutes in Oslo, Norway, it was in this spirit that one woman asserted that her work had "nothing to do" with her sexuality, because "the most intimate thing that I have is not what I, as a prostitute, am selling. I am simply selling the man his orgasm." As with many other working-class jobs, the displeasure of doing the work can intermingle with a more general division between "work" and "nonwork" selves. Karolyn, a Swedish street prostitute, explained:

> If you work like this, you need to have unseen borders you don't let people trespass. If you do [let them trespass], then you start to drink or use drugs, because you can't bear to see yourself in the mirror afterwards. There are things that you allow, and there are things that you don't allow, things that you won't do for money. There has to be a private place inside of you. You can't be the same person when you go out to work.

Still another woman described the emotional labor involved in "leaving my private me at home so that I can go to work."[21] She added that she knew it was time to think about getting out of the business when the labor involved in her psychic transformation began to take up more and more time, as a twenty-minute process eventually came to occupy all afternoon and most of the evening.

In the context of street prostitution, a "career" often describes an occupation that is held for an average of four years, and for which its practitioners rarely speak in terms of acquiring skills, providing "services," or honing a sales pitch; rather, it is the body as product, as saleable object, that is key.[22] After a number of months of doing condom distribution and outreach on the Geary-Mason stroll of the San Francisco Tenderloin and witnessing the streetwalkers' frequent arrests, I decided to attempt a sociological experiment to see how I would be treated by the police, and by others, if I dressed to look as much as possible like the other women and stood with them on the street. When I first discussed my plans with several women to go on the street as a "decoy," they pointed out that if I actually decided to work, I could make many hundreds of dollars. It did not occur to them to ask me if I knew how to "do" anything. Either I apparently knew all I needed to know, or any such knowledge was irrelevant. Youth, body capital, and the enhancements of sexualized clothing and makeup were regarded as the primary determinants of moneymaking ability. For these women, much of the "work" resided in the preparation, packaging, and grueling nightly display of the body that sells itself (rather than in specifically sexual labor, per se).

On the "upper-" and "middle-class" strolls, if prostitution was typically conceptualized as highly paid (yet unskilled) labor, it was also conceived of in functionalist terms as the result of dually gendered heterosexual desire. In her essay, "Love for Sale," Eva Pendleton has described the ways that the "overt economy" of commercial sexual exchange often "brings to light the greater economy of heterosexuality in general . . . 'queering' heteronormativity and forcing a closer examination of various modes of exchange between men and women."[23] While the "career prostitutes" of the Tenderloin indeed denaturalized the commonsense view of prostitution as the bestowal of a fundamentally private, interior self for economic benefit, they nonetheless *renaturalized* understandings of heterosexual relations which posit the inevitability of particular configurations of masculine desire. During our late-night diner interview, Eve mused that she had enjoyed sex exactly two times in her life. Yet she went on to argue that prostitution was potentially empowering to women because—unlike conventional heterosexual relationships—it at least compensated women for their (presumably joyless) submission ("I have more independence than the women who have to do it for their husbands and make their dinner . . . women do it all the time"). She remarked,

> I've had boyfriends over the years that I had sex with because that's what you were supposed to do. I didn't enjoy it, it was like a chore . . . so it's like the same thing but you're getting paid for it, you're gaining something. . . . On the streets, the common view is that the average man is stupid and insensitive. We're not being victimized, we're being smart and getting what we can for it.

Drew, a twenty-two-year veteran of the streets, was similarly passionate in conveying her experience of gendered empowerment through "getting paid." During a focus group that I helped facilitate with Drew and several other street-based workers,[24] she explained,

> I was married to a battering fuck for some twenty years and had never turned a trick. Then one day someone wanted to bone me for money! The whole thing is an ego rush. I didn't have an ego until I became a whore. I felt disgusting before. I was delighted when someone finally offered me money after years of being raped by my husband.

Trisha, an incest survivor and a streetwalker for thirty years, put it in equally blunt terms for me during the first day that I accompanied her to visit the Hyde Street stroll: "All fucks are tricks anyway, and you're always doing it for the money. If you sleep with your husband and later he gives you $50, it amounts to the same thing." From the perspective of women like Drew, Trisha, and Eve, the real crime, abuse, and humiliation in heterosexual relations would be to "put out" and not get paid. Despite the risk, prevalence, and brutality of sexual assault on the streets, many street-based "career prostitutes" that I met insisted that engaging in prostitution was the first time that they had ever experienced the notion of "consent" as at all meaningful.[25] For them, degrees of consent and compensation were the most significant variables in heterosexual relations; the content of "sex" itself was a given.

NAVIGATING THE STREETS:
PIMPS, PREDATORS, AND POLICE

On the corner, I notice that Lydia is standing unusually close to the curb to-night and waving down cars—something I haven't before seen her do. Later she explains to me: "See that guy in the blue and white jacket. That's my man. I hate it when he watches me. He's already mad because I only made $200 last night, and tonight I'm wearing jeans, so he doesn't think I'm go-ing to make any money. But it's so fucking cold out. And besides, I think I look good. . . ." Lydia pauses to give me time to express my agreement with the last point (which I enthusiastically do). "Besides, it's so hard to make money when the weather's bad. No one wants to come out. I was up on Post Street before, but no money. And the cops are everywhere! My man wants me to move to another street, but shit, the police are gonna grab me!" Bev-erly, who is standing behind us, overhears this last comment and scowls. "Fuck him. She can't move. We have to watch each other's backs." Caught between a rock and a hard place, her pimp and the police, Lydia's predica-ment this evening is clear.

"Heads up!!!" Everyone runs into the liquor store to the booming musi-cal accompaniment of a passing pimp car. I look up and am surprised to discover that, true to stereotype, it is dark, shiny, and has tinted windows. "Those guys messed with me real bad. . . . You know Nancy, who works here sometimes? He's her guy," Beverly begins to explain on our way out. "He got some other guy to slap me around, but he better watch out cause he's gonna get his. My man's a *real* pimp," she says proudly.

FIELD NOTES, DECEMBER 18, 1994

In addition to framing sexual labor as "work" and to the enforcement of a gendered public/private divide, another important hallmark of modern prostitution that historians have identified is the prostitute's reliance on third-party managers.[26] Prior to the criminalization of brothels during the Progressive Era, these were typically brothel own-ers or madams; in the period following the elimination of official red-light districts, for many women such control shifted to the pimps who work the streets.[27] Although in the popular imagination, the pimp is typically conjured as a smartly dressed, smooth talking, and relatively youthful African American male, legally speaking, a variety of different arrangements could conceivably come under the penal code's broad definition of pimping; California's legal code, for example, defines a pimp as "Any person who, knowing another person is a prostitute, lives or derives support or maintenance in whole or in part from the earnings or proceeds of the person's prostitution." [28] While such a legal definition could, for example, potentially include a prostitute's children or siblings (or even any of the local store owners), in practice most of those charged with pimping are working-class men of color who act as "manager-boyfriends" to various women. [29]

The shift to street work has simultaneously given some women greater autonomy than the brothel-based workers who were their historical predecessors, while also creating dependencies which leave others open to greater levels of exploitation. In the iconography of contemporary Hollywood cinema and music videos, the figure of the pimp has been critical in lending a deviant aura to the subculture of street prostitution—with the pimp exemplifying not only the women's exploitation but also raising the specters of interracial sex and polygamy. Yet as my own and others' ethnographic research demonstrates, the reality of pimp/prostitute relations is far more complex. The circulations of power which characterize such relations are reflected in multiple levels of exchange of sex and money, making these relationships significantly less straightforward than those which typically existed between the sex workers and brothel owners of eras prior. [30]

At an initial level, the tentative control that pimps hold over women is highlighted by the fact that many women on the street chose to work without pimps—perhaps a third of the women working the "middle-" and "upper-class" strolls. Several of these "independent" women were adamant in our discussions about the ability of women to work alone. Eve, who was "turned out" by a pimp at the age of thirteen but later took to working for herself, explained it this way:

> A lot of girls come into town and they're square, they lead regular lives, and they meet this sexy guy who charms them. They think they have to have a pimp. They call it "choosing." If they're treated really bad—there is a huge domestic violence problem with these girls—they sometimes give their money to another guy. He calls her pimp, and says she's now his. . . . All of the pimps talk to me, but I'm not stupid. If they try to take my money, one of us is going to die trying.

The majority of the women who worked independently were comparatively older (mid- to late twenties) and had a fair amount of experience navigating their way around the streets. Those who were younger
and less experienced were more likely to rely on pimps to handle the
mundane organizational details involved in street prostitution: figuring
out how to contact, select, and satisfy clients; learning how to dress;
and determining on what streets to stand to generate the most income.
Olivia, like Eve, described being "turned out" by a pimp at a young
age, only to later realize that she could work independently:

> I was turned out when I was 16, after listening to a person tell
> me I was so beautiful . . . I grew up in Richmond [across the Bay
> from San Francisco], the only girl, the only virgin on the block,
> all the boys were chasing me. One day, the guy I was seeing asked
> me to go out to dinner with him, and said "wear a mini-dress."
> We came here to San Francisco. I didn't know what I was doing.
> I believed that he was taking me to dinner. I ended up turning my
> first date in an alley. Watching everyone else, I was like, "Okay,
> let me try. What the hell." After that, he went one way and I went
> another, and it was just extra income.

As occurred in Olivia's case, many pimps obtained access to women
only in the course of turning them out, rescinding control as the women
gradually moved on to higher-status men or to working for themselves.
    Nevertheless, approximately two-thirds of the women in the "mid-
dle" and "upper" tiers did have pimps, a fact which may speak less
to the streetwalkers' need for outside management than to the ability
of the pimps to sell themselves to the women. In this sense, the pimp
does not simply offer management expertise but also commodifies his
own sexuality in exchange for a prostitute's wages. It is primarily for
this reason that pimps may go to great lengths to dress well and "talk
smooth," to display their material success prominently, and in some
cases to promote their services to the women on the street via business
cards with original motifs ("Invest in Smooth and You Can't Loose";
"Smooth Cross Country: Serious About You Now or Later"). While
pimps are often referred to by the women as their "men" or "boyfriends," they typically will have not have sex with "their" women for
pleasure, but only in exchange for payment.[31]
    In a sociological study of Canadian pimps and their relationships
with street prostitutes conducted in the early 1990s, James Hodgson
observed two distinct methods of procurement among the pimps

9 Pimps' business cards may serve as a vehicle for self-promotion to streetwalkers (source: Victor Vigna, Las Vegas Police Department).

that he observed and interviewed: what he termed the "seduction" and the "stratagem" methods of procurement. While in the former, pimps typically seduce the most young and inexperienced women into prostitution through the strategic deployment of affection; in the latter, the pimp emphasizes his role in facilitating a lifestyle of grandeur and ease.[32] In accordance with Hodgson's findings, on the streets of the Tenderloin pimping could also be both a labor and an erotic contract, but it was not (as the men sometimes claimed) primarily about the women's protection. Although the streetwalkers were indeed at exceptionally high risk of physical violence, by their own accounts the chief danger existed when they were alone with a client—in a car or hotel room—not when they were standing on the street. Pimps were of little or no use in this regard, as one early excerpt from my field notes illustrates with startling clarity:

Olivia told us that a new girl was found cut up last night. She'd gotten into a car with a twenty-one-year-old guy in an old blue Toyota, but after the trick paid, he slashed her face. A bloody, gory mess. May lose an eye. They threw her somewhere. Some pimps found her, but they didn't know who her man was, so they brought her to the women on Geary and Leavenworth who brought her to the hospital. Why did she get in the car? Because the cops are

all over the place lately! They just raided the hotel, and now you can't get in
unless the doorman knows you.

[FIELD NOTES, OCTOBER 1994]

Streetwalkers were well aware that the stigma and criminality of
their work placed them at exceptionally high risk of physical violence.
While their identification as publicly sexual women ("whores") undoubtedly played a role in inspiring the aggressions of sexual predators,
women who worked under conditions of urgency for the next fix or
who turned car dates—sometimes to avoid police interception—were
undoubtedly the most vulnerable. In the midst of one particularly grue-
some series of attacks on prostitutes in the Mission district, the police asked Drew to help them look for the serial murderer. Drew was
asked if anyone had ever taken her to China Basin (an industrial zone
within the city) and raped her. The brash and outspoken mother of
seven found this to be a laughable question. "Who hasn't been taken
down to China Basin and raped," she responded, "like every week?"
Although women working the "lower-class" strolls faced the most difficulties in these regards, encounters with violence from clients and
harassment and arrest from the police formed a common experiential
core among all streetwalkers.

If a pimp protected a woman at all, it was most likely to be from
other pimps, from their harassment or encroachment on "his" (i.e.,
her) territory. The nights I stood with the women as a decoy, I discovered this firsthand. The women were indeed afraid of talking to other
pimps, and they warned me of the many potentially terrible consequences of not fleeing when they approached—robbery, beatings, kid-
napping, and so on. Two avowed "independents" assured me that the
real fear was inspired by what might happen to a girl later at home if it
was found out that she had spoken to another man. Yet I also discovered that the women's own collaborative signaling system (issuing the
warning cry of "six" for cops and "heads" for pimps; taking down license plate numbers; keeping eyes and ears open when colleagues took
their dates to hotel rooms) seemed a more effective means of providing
protection for one another than that offered by pimps, especially since
their men were often elsewhere anyway, returning only sporadically to
"empty the traps." [33]

Despite the constraints and dangers of working for a pimp, having
a "real" one was often seen as an accomplishment. Beverly was not
alone in boasting that her man was a "real" pimp; other women proudly
displayed the watches and jewelry that they had hoisted from clients

in order to adorn the bodies of their men ("Don't you think this ring will look *great* on my guy?"). It is also of significance that most of the women in the sex-for-drugs economy were generally unable to or uninterested in obtaining pimps, as their drug use rendered them incapable of generating the surplus cash required to invest in a male manager-companion. In her interview-based study of drug-injecting prostitutes in the San Francisco Mission district, María Epele reported that only a small number of the twenty-five women she spoke with had ever worked with pimps ("Controlling all profits and threatening women with physical violence, pimps tend to give them only a small amount of drugs").[34] Epele's and my own findings also resonate with the words of a Norwegian street prostitute interviewed for a study conducted by Cecilie Høigård and Liv Finstad, who noted simply that, "Junkies can't afford to have pimps. What they earn goes straight into their veins."[35] By contrast, nearly all of the women on the "upper-class" stroll did have pimps, as did about half of the women working the "middle-class" stroll.

Notably, pimps were unable to provide any protection from one of the most frequent threats to female streetwalkers—the police—from whom they themselves seemed to have a surprising degree of immunity.[36] Even if (by many of the women's accounts) San Francisco's police officers were less dehumanizing than those of other cities, one of the more striking things on the street was the women's relative fearlessness with potential johns compared to their timidity and submissiveness in the face of—sometimes explicit, often implicit—sexualized domination by the police. Depending on the stroll, a woman's "seniority," her street wisdom, and her own relationship with particular police officers, a woman might go to jail as often as four times a week. For example, women on the "upper-class" stroll—which directly bordered the Union Square shopping and tourist district—went to jail much more frequently than women on the other strolls, and less experienced streetwalkers also tended to be arrested more often. A woman might be arrested for soliciting or, more likely, for a "public nuisance" or "disorderly conduct" violation; or she might be issued a citation for jaywalking.[37] The vast majority of cases were never prosecuted;[38] after spending several hours in jail women were typically dismissed and would immediately catch a cab back to "the strip" to try and make up their lost earnings.

I was quite shocked the first time I witnessed a police sweep, which seemed to amount to the systematic removal of all women present from public space. The women involved were standing quietly while waiting for clients to approach them and had not perceptibly broken any law; the yelling, honking men on the sidewalk and in the streets certainly created far more of a "nuisance." On another evening a few months into my fieldwork, I was handing out condoms on the "middle-class" stroll and had just said goodbye to a streetwalker named Sherry, who was hoping for an early night so that she could get back home to care for her young son. Within about a minute, I was startled by a booming voice behind me: "I'm the first customer of the evening—get in the car!!!" I turned on my heels to see Sherry being pushed into a police car and pleading, "Aren't you going to give me a warning first? I'll go home. Please, please, I have to get my kid tonight . . . " Later that night Eve mused to me and to her other companions that, although Sherry would probably be at the station until five o'clock in the morning, "it could be worse . . . like when they call your name out through a megaphone and force you to stand in the middle of the road!"

During my nights as a decoy on Geary and Mason streets, the police demanded to see my identification, searched me, and threatened to bring me to jail various times, although I was meticulously law-abiding and indicated that I was there for research purposes. As in the two graphic accounts below (the first from the "lower-class" and the second from the "middle-class" stroll), other women shared stories with me of police officers who asked to exchange blow jobs for dropped citations or who "thrilled from the chase" when they were hiding behind trees, who revealed their identity as officers and arrested them *after* sexual services had been rendered, or who "popped them" with a date, stole their money, then gave half of the cash back to the customer when he claimed not to have finished.[39] Women who were considered by the police to be "known prostitutes" also shared stories of getting stopped and apprehended while on their way home with groceries or even of being arrested on their nights off while making a midnight run for cigarettes.

> The day I got busted I didn't have any money. I had medicine, no food. Can't do the medicine without the food. I was like, well I gotta make some money, so that's why I came here. Son of a bitch, he saw me standing on a corner sucking on a lollipop and he made eye contact—that's the game, you know. He pulls over right away, he rolls down his window, and he goes, "Well, I got a lollipop you can suck on for twenty-five dollars." So I get in the car and he goes, "You got a condom?" and I go "Oh yeah." Bingo.[40] We went right around the block, right around the corner to jail. And

10 The author, being apprehended by the police while conducting fieldwork in the Tenderloin (video by Carol Leigh; still by P. J. Starr).

he grabbed the lollipop, pulled it out of my mouth, and he started getting rough with me. . .

When I finally got out of jail, I walked straight across the street and this cop followed me, followed me down, just past Sixth Street, pulled me into an alleyway and asked me if he could come over and have sex with me, if I was dating. I knew if I said no I'd go back to jail, 'cause he could have picked me up for jaywalking. So he knew that, and he pulled over, and I'm thinking, don't try it with me, don't, I just want to go home. I want breakfast. I want to go home and tweak.

VICTORIA, Hyde Street

On the street, the police is our main problem. . . . They'll come up to our hotel room and bust us, but they won't say nothing to the manager. Johnny, this one police officer, he knocked on the door when I was finishing once. He asked the guy, "How much money did you just give her?" and I said, "I'm not giving you my money." They don't prosecute our cases, but they don't give us our money back, either. If they catch you with a date and the guy says, "I gave her sixty bucks," the cop takes the money and gives both of you a ticket. Then you get a thing in the mail saying there are no charges, the case was dismissed. But where's our money? The last time I was in the room arguing for an hour 'cause I didn't want to give him my money. So he took the guy outside saying, "Your job, your wife's gonna find out," and finally the guy said he gave me $80. The cop said he'd call a lady police officer to search me.

Sherry's been popped by Johnny like twelve times already. He popped her and asked the guy if they were finished and said, "Give me the eighty bucks, I'm gonna give you half and I'm taking half." That's why I'll eat my money before they take it. I'm not giving kickbacks to the city. Do they have some kinda special fund with the money they take? It ought to go back to the person when the case is dismissed. . . . They always go by what the guy says. They give them tickets, but they're dismissed just like ours. If the guys tell them they didn't finish, they get half their money back. I'd like to go to the police department and get my money back for like, the last eleven years.

OLIVIA, Geary and Leavenworth streets

WHOSE QUALITY OF LIFE?
THE STIGMA OF THE STREETS

The prostitute is the prototype of the stigmatized woman. She is both named and dishonored by the word "whore." The word "whore" does not, however, refer only to prostitutes. It is also a label which can be applied to any woman. . . . The word "whore" is specifically a female gender stigma.
GAIL PHETERSON, "The Whore Stigma"[41]

Prostitutes are among the disorderly—they are among the "disreputable or obstreperous or unpredictable people: panhandlers, drunks, addicts, rowdy teenagers . . . loiterers, the mentally disturbed."
JAMES Q. WILSON AND GEORGE L. KELLING, "Broken Windows"[42]

In a well-known essay entitled "The Whore Stigma: Female Dishonor and Male Unworthiness," the feminist critic Gail Pheterson has described the diffuse and generalized sense of dishonor that can adhere to women who are perceived to be engaging in "indiscriminate" and, most especially, commercially profitable sex. She traces the historical equation of female prostitutes with disease as well as with "(adulterous) sex, (dark) race, (dirty) money, (deserved) abuse, and (taboo) knowledge."[43] Pheterson argues that the "whore stigma" ultimately serves as a patriarchal tool of control over all women, who, by virtue of the prostitute's example, are threatened with a similar loss of honor should they traverse accepted norms of sexual propriety. Pheterson's analysis of the cultural circulations of stigma draws its inspiration from Erving Goffman's classic study, in which he noted that "the dynamics of shameful differentness" have the tendency "to spread from a stigmatized individual to his [*sic*] close connections," a phenomenon that he terms "courtesy stigma." [44]

On the streets of the Tenderloin, both the "whore stigma" and "courtesy stigma" appended not merely to those who violated conventions of female sexual propriety but were functions of the associations of prostitution with poverty and disorder that have been the hallmark of "broken windows" policing since the 1980s. [45] Although some version of the whore stigma was a constant for streetwalkers, it worsened in scope and intensity precisely during the period when "quality of life" campaigns in the neighborhood were gathering steam. In addition to the staple difficulties of having to fend off police, pimps, and "bad tricks," streetwalkers would increasingly describe being followed and harassed by organized groups of neighborhood residents and business owners such as SOS (Save Our Streets), the Polk Street Merchants' Association, and the Guardian Angels. They also described being honked at, yelled at, pelted with eggs, or "tailed" by residents who hoped to shame them away. One woman recounted to me a story of being shoved so hard by a scoffing passerby that she was propelled through a plate glass window.

The well-lit liquor store on the Geary-Mason stroll that was the streetwalkers' most valued source of cigarettes and gum was also one of the few places that the women could dash to for cover and find welcome shelter from pimps, harassing customers, and the police. By contrast, most of the other restaurants and businesses in the area overtly refused entry to even the most immaculately dressed of the female streetwalkers—and to me, when I was with them. The potential ferocity of these reactions first became apparent to me one stormy December evening, when I cajoled Beverly—a blonde, statuesque, and meticulously put-together streetwalker—to join me for something to eat at the all-night diner just diagonal from our stroll. After reluctantly trying to explain to me that she was "not supposed to be there," she eventually agreed. We had just settled down in our booth when the waitress came over and demanded that Beverly leave. "No prostitutes here!" the waitress snapped, in a voice that was sufficiently audible to cause all surrounding heads to turn. When I began to protest, she immediately volleyed back: "And if *you're* one you shouldn't be in here either." Feeling sheepish and embarrassed about having "provoked" the uncomfortable situation in the first place by not heeding Beverly's warning, I followed her out of the booth and back into the rain.

Two high-profile legal cases further illustrate the ways in which the stigma of being seen as a "public woman" in the Tenderloin exacerbated streetwalkers' physical risks and social marginalization during this period of stepped up police interventions and heightened antiprostitution activism. They also illustrate the structural obstacles that most street prostitutes faced in advocating for justice on their own behalf. Notably, the two cases discussed below became newsworthy precisely because they featured protagonists who had resources generally unavailable to the intended targets of the majority of "quality of life" campaigns.[46]

The first case involved Yvonne Dotson, a forty-eight-year-old African American registered nurse with a master's degree in public health from the University of California at Berkeley. One February evening in 1993, Dotson had just left a birthday party at a Union Square restaurant and was walking toward her car when two police officers drove up beside her and arrested her on suspicion of prostitution. After the officers ran a computer check on her driver's license and turned up an old infraction warrant, they handcuffed her and took her to jail. Although Dotson protested that an error had occurred, she was not allowed to post bail and was eventually booked, fingerprinted, and photographed before being released.[47] Dotson's police report indicates that she was assumed to be guilty because she was standing "next to a known prostitute" within "an area known to be frequented by prostitutes."[48] After her release, Dotson was able to demonstrate that the eight-year-old infraction warrant had actually been for a dog leash violation in neighboring Marin County, and she decided to sue. Although she received an $85,000 settlement from the case, the city never admitted liability.[49] Dotson's recounting of her experiences constituted an important piece of testimony during the San Francisco Task Force hearings, and in Margo St. James's (unsuccessful) bid for the city's Board of Supervisors one year later.[50]

Dotson's status as an African American woman (however light-skinned) was one possible factor which contributed to her initial apprehension by the police—as well as their unshakable perception of her as a prostitute despite her protests and the contravening evidence of idiosyncratic age and attire. The literature on policing is rife with accounts of the disparate burden of arrest borne by African Americans, but these patterns may intersect with an additional and less straightforward policing dynamic leading to disparately racialized outcomes on the streets. Lisa Maher has described racial "acontexuality" as the single most significant factor in determining which women will be arrested on a given stroll (meaning that white or black streetwalkers

LIKE MANY WOMEN ARRESTED FOR PROSTITUTION, YVONNE DOTSON WAS HANDCUFFED, FINGERPRINTED AND INNOCENT.

11 Image of Yvonne Dotson, as featured in a COYOTE publicity poster during Margo St. James's bid for Supervisor (reprinted with permission).

are more likely to be arrested when working in a Latino neighborhood, for example, or vice versa).[51] Since Dotson was arrested on Post Street, the outer limit of the "upper-class" stroll, it is likely that the police regarded prostitution as the only conceivable explanation for her presence amid the largely white theater- and restaurant-goers who regularly populated the neighborhood.

Where Dotson's case illustrates the extra burden of stigma borne by African American women on the streets, a second case demonstrates the particular susceptibilities that could be faced by transgendered sex workers. Victoria Schneider was a sex worker from the Hyde and Capp street corridors who had legally changed her sex from male to female. One evening, after she was picked up for soliciting and placed in a men's holding cell as a form of harassment and intimidation, then forcibly strip-searched while officers looked on and snickered (allegedly to determine her "true sex"), she decided to sue. Due to her established record of activism, Victoria was able to enlist the help of a lawyer at a prominent city firm who agreed to take her case pro bono. Not only did she emerge from her lawsuit victorious, but the jury awarded her an unprecedented $750,000 in damages for violations to her civil rights. This was an uncommon victory which stood in sharp contrast to the numerous stories of abuse I was told about that never got a public hearing.[52]

STRUCTURAL TRANSFORMATIONS

It is dark now, and at some point I realize that the paddy wagon has started moving. I assume that they cannot be taking us to jail yet, since there are only three of us, but I begin to get a little bit nervous when we get on the freeway. . . . Arrest Team One pulls up again, this time with a small, sickly, heavily made-up white woman, with bleached blond hair, a white tank top, and a visibly swollen belly. She remains passive and says nothing while the two burly officers remove the handcuffs from her thin, pale arms, and place their hands on her narrow shoulders to guide her in the direction of the wagon. The two African American women who are seated beside me joke about the arrest of the "snow-bunny" as she climbs in. The officers seem to know this new woman (although they act surprised to find her still working the streets) and they refer to her by name. After giving them her vital statistics (which include the obvious fact that she is pregnant), she moves over to the far end of the bench seat and slumps quietly.

Minutes later, another African American woman is brought in. She is the most disheveled and jittery of the group, and arrives barefoot and with one breast exposed. Apparently, she lost her shoes after she decided to run for it when she realized that she was dealing with the police. In slurred speech, she tells us over and over again how shocked she was that the guy was a cop, since he felt her up, all over, inside. How could he be a cop? The cars should have tapes or video cameras, she declares. And the cops who arrested her had no right to hit her, she says, rubbing her head.

Later that night when we return to the station, I will ask Sergeant Brenner what happened to the woman who arrived with no shoes. "These women are used to a lot of violence," he says, "then they complain when the police are a little rough with them." "They are used to talking themselves in and out of trouble. . . . Maybe the cops get numbed and a little callous to them, but they're not like you and me. These women are very unstable."

FIELD NOTES, POLICE RIDE-ALONG, JUNE 1995

Despite the fact that many streetwalkers recounted stories of demeaning police treatment with great frequency and passion (and on occasion, I myself served as an uncomfortable witness to such occurrences), women's reported experiences of harassment and humiliation at the hands of the police were not ubiquitous. Eve, for example, described an overwhelmingly positive relationship with San Francisco police officers—she explained that as a "tenured" prostitute, officers would often warn her before a sweep, advise her what nights not to work, and even suggest that she change streets on particular evenings. She also noted proudly that she got arrested only about five times a year, far less frequently than any of the other women she knew.[53]

During my ride-alongs with the vice and street crimes units in two different Bay Area municipalities, I encountered a number of police officers who displayed a caring and sympathetic attitude toward the streetwalkers on their beats. Laura, for example, a thirty-year-old street crimes officer, expressed what appeared to be genuine concern for the streetwalkers' well-being, and characterized her relationship to the twenty-five or so women on the stroll she patrolled as "very friendly, very good." She also told me that she was on a first-name basis with the majority. Yet even Laura's kindly disposition toward the women might become irrelevant in the face of orders that were handed down to her from her superiors. As Laura herself observed, there had been significantly more street prostitution in the city prior to the implementation of "Project Hollywood" in 1992, when the police decided to make a concerted effort to get rid of the street industry, "tailing every girl they could find until they drove her out of town." In most cases, the chief problem was not simply "bad" police officers with a penchant for abuse; rather, it was the growing *structural* imperative to intervene in the women's lives, an imperative derived from the more general restructuring of the welfare state away from social services and toward heightened police control and surveillance.[54]

Of the various prostitution strolls that existed in San Francisco in the mid-1990s, pared down versions of the sex-for-drugs corridors of

Hyde and Capp streets are all that currently remain. The career prostitution strolls have largely been eliminated by the insistent, rigorous
police sweeps that are often the means by which "urban renewal"
is physically accomplished. Most of the SROs around the Geary-
Leavenworth intersection have been closed down, and the neighborhood is now peppered with growing numbers of stylish restaurants,
bars, and nightclubs. The few women who still walk the streets have
been consolidated into two more isolated and delimited areas: in the
Tenderloin, the triangular three-block terrain bounded by O'Farrell,
Market, and Van Ness streets, and in the Mission, the stretch of Sixteenth Street that runs between Valencia and Capp streets.

As the gentrification of the city spreads, it is likely that even these
two remaining street prostitution strolls will be subject to greater police
intervention, creating added pressure on the women who work them
to make potentially dangerous decisions. Criminologists Lisa Maher
and Richard Curtis note that when prostitution strolls are compressed,
"conditions of extreme competition and increased hostility between
sex-workers . . . exacerbat[e] the atomization and social isolation of
[the] women." Increased competition then leads to price deflation,
which in turn spawns "a self-selection process of cheaper 'rougher'
dates, which has made the strolls themselves 'rougher' and more violent places to work." [55] For those women who have chosen to remain
on the streets—whether in order to have proximity to drug dealers,
because of their underage status or lack of confidence in their ability to
secure other kinds of work, or for a complicated mix of personal and
structural reasons—it is unlikely that police intervention alone will
inspire them to leave the sex trade, no matter how frequent or how
fierce.

> I desperately want to get my shit together. I'm too old for this. I've
> been out on parole for nine months. Being homeless, you're shoved
> out on the street all day long if you stay in shelters. . . . I've been on
> methadone for a week. If you don't have medical—which you can
> only get through SSI [Supplemental Security Income]—you have
> to pay $12 a day to detox. Being on GA [General Assistance], and
> not having a place to live, you're forced out on the streets. . . . I'm
> trying to find low-income housing. I can't get SSI because I was in
> prison and am a drug addict. I can't get a job because my record is
> so bad, and my age, and because I have no education or training,
> since I had six children. I've spent thirteen years on parole, at least
> ten incarcerated for petty thefts. Another arrest could mean life

in prison for me.[56] I've got petty thefts trailing me. I don't want to go back to jail. I'm having a very difficult time getting my life together. I don't know where to go. . . . I'm not capable of holding a job. Who's going to hire a woman who's fifty-eight years old who's never worked? I just want a little place to live. I don't think I could hold a full-time job. But I don't want a criminal life no more. We get $172 every two weeks on GA. That don't even pay for a room![57] But it does keep us out here.

    JANEY, Capp Street Focus Group, May 1996

LEAVING THE STREETS

Although the streetwalkers on all of the strolls that I studied sought to navigate a safe path between police officers, johns, and others who sought to harass them, it is important to recognize the extent to which the practices and meanings of sexual labor varied in the different prostitution strolls. Within the street-level drug economy, the predominant form of sexual labor that was practiced shared structural features with the sexual barter that social historians have described as the most prevalent type of sexual commerce prior to the late nineteenth century: self-organized, occasional exchanges that generally took place within women's own homes and communities. (In a recent study of the sex-for-crack scene in San Francisco, for example, Harvey Feldman and his coauthors note that "the exchange of sex for crack . . . did not always have overtones of degradation . . . but more closely resembled a bartering situation." Women might negotiate sex for crack "not as a way of begging or losing control but as a way of eliminating an unnecessary and intrusive financial proceeding.")[58] The sexual labor of "career" streetwalkers, on the other hand, fit squarely into the paradigm of modern-industrial prostitution that social historians have articulated: commercial sexual exchange was conceptualized as "work" that resided in the public display of the body, an enforced division between "public" and "private" selves, and the expedient fulfillment of men's "drives" through quick, impersonal, sexual release.[59] This latter is the form of prostitution that was most dramatically redefined by the broader structural transformations of the postindustrial city.

As stepped up police harassment made it increasingly difficult to work the streets, the "career prostitutes" of the Tenderloin who were my closest confidantes—Olivia, Eve, Sherry, Beverly, and Victoria—made a variety of different choices. Beverly and Sherry eventually got cell phones and decided to place ads for private clients in a local newspaper, while other women from their stroll got jobs in local strip clubs (where recently installed "private booths" made it possible to engage in prostitution without risk of arrest).[60] Olivia got a paid position doing street outreach at a local social service agency and abandoned sex work entirely, while Eve and Victoria left town to seek opportunities in other cities.

These decisions were not made without some remorse. Although the world of street-based "career prostitution" that they had known could be labor-intensive and risky, they were also adamant about the advantages that this form of labor entailed—above and beyond the high pay. For Eve, the best aspect of working the streets was that "you're your own boss, you talk to who you want . . . you're out in the open, in public, familiar with the territory. There are people around if anything goes wrong." Olivia similarly emphasized the sense of autonomy and control she derived from streetwork, in contrast to her experience during a brief stint at an escort agency ("I'd be tired, have done three or four calls, have driven to Oakland and San Jose to Pleasanton and back, made six or seven hundred dollars, and be ready to go to sleep. They call you at 3 or 4 a.m., saying 'I can't find anybody to take this call, please take it.' If you don't take it, they don't give you any calls the next day"). Olivia further emphasized that the streets provided her with a sense of discretion regarding clients that the brothels did not, the power to refuse men that she found unappealing ("In the brothels, they'll tell you to date McGuilla Gorilla. You can say 'no,' but if the guy really wants to go with you, they will give you a really hard time"). All of the women I knew on the "middle-" and "upper-class" strolls expressed a sense of choice and volition regarding their decision to work the streets, *despite* the evident dangers and *even if* they might also have preferred the luxury of a better set of vocational possibilities.

In his book, *The Trouble with Normal,* the queer theorist Michael Warner describes the ways that diverse "sex publics" became endangered by the Giuliani administration in late 1990s New York City. Focusing primarily on the demonization of gay sex venues, Warner reminds us that it was not the moralizing agenda of the Christian Right but a broad-sweeping and multifaceted "politics of privatization" that cast the initial pall over class- and race-integrated cultures of public sex.[61] Yet the neoliberal policies which systematically eliminated "public sex" in postindustrial cities did not eliminate commercial sexuality altogether—far from it. Ultimately, these policies were even less successful (and arguably, less interested) than their Progressive Era counterparts in eliminating sexual commerce in its entirety. Whereas Progressive Era social activists drew on the language of moral critique to shut down the organized brothel system and to drive prostitutes outdoors, neoliberal "broken windows" policing in the 1990s drove the sex industry back inside. Commercial sexual encounters were thus relocated to spatially dispersed interior venues where they could be marketed to class- and race-segregated customers, while the marginalized populations left behind bore the burden of the heightened police presence associated with gentrification.[62]

Following Warner's analysis of the sexual transformations that transpired in Giuliani-era New York, one can similarly note the ways in which postindustrial economic transformations led to a privatization of sexual commerce in San Francisco, impacting the world of public streetwalking (and thus, the social institution of modern prostitution) in at least three key ways: *spatially,* privatization occurred through prostitutes' retreat back indoors after the prohibition of brothels nearly a century earlier; *socially,* privatization represented a shift away from a street-based social milieu to one-on-one, technologically mediated encounters with clients through cell phones and the Internet; and, as I shall discuss in the next chapter, privatization also had a significant impact at an *emotional* level for sex workers by altering the nature of sexual labor itself, propelling women to provide their clients with ever more profound and more intimate forms of erotic connection—what I term "bounded authenticity."

The spatial, social, and emotional privatization of sexual labor that has occurred in recent years has endowed sexual commerce with historically unprecedented forms and meanings. Alongside the early modern prototype of sexual barter and the modern prototype of organized commercial prostitution, modes of commercial sexual exchange have emerged, diversified, and proliferated to create new forms of domination for many sex workers, but also (at least for some) new possibilities for creative entrepreneurship, intimacy, and community. In the pages that follow, it is to this new "postindustrial" paradigm of sexual labor that I turn.

4 | The Privatization of Public Women

Citylove.com, San Francisco's first on-line "Adult Entertainment Guide," is housed on the bottom floor of an inconspicuous Victorian in a quiet, residential neighborhood. The company, a full-service advertising agency for "independently employed erotic entertainers," is one of the myriad legal and legitimate online sex businesses that have helped to usher in the cyber age. The site makes its money by creating and posting the advertisements of some five hundred local escorts, fetish specialists, and erotic masseuses and masseurs for a fee which ranges from $25 to $120 a month, depending on size of photos, video capabilities, and other "extras." One ad features Stephanie, a "sensuality expert," who combines "clinical massage training with years of Tantra study." Another is for Andrew, "a very clean, very well-developed personal trainer" who offers "sensual pleasures for sensual women." Because novelty confers sex workers a strong market advantage, every two weeks the ads are rotated to appear in the section entitled "New Additions."

When I first arrive for my interview with the company's founder, I am struck by the bustling "newsroom" atmosphere of the premises as the energetic young staff attempts to deal with the latest crisis: the DSL lines have gone out all over town. But for a few telltale details (one or two seductive posters, some provocative lacy garments on the coat rack) the atmosphere here is surely no different than that of any other new and profitable Internet start-up company. Today, there are a dozen or so college-aged women and men present, dressed in sweatshirts and jeans. While some talk rapidly to one another or respond to the incessantly ringing telephones, others sit with their faces glued to the computer monitors as their fingers race across the keyboards.

Sara, one of the company's two founding partners, pulls away from the confusion to come over and greet me. Statuesque and striking, with long, auburn ringlets and layers of dark clothing, Sara has worked as a stripper and also has advanced degrees in graphic design and photography. She has been living in San Francisco for eleven of her thirty-three years. Sara created the company with her lover Greg in 1997 and is currently responsible for the creative side of the business—Web design, staff supervision, helping sex workers to manage their publicity, and placing ads for the company in local media. Since they started the company four years ago, two important competitors have emerged, but by this she is pleased: competition has been good for business. Company growth has averaged 45 percent a year.

"In the beginning, no one even really knew what the Internet was," she explains. "We had to call the newspaper ads to get advertisers interested; now people hear about us through word of mouth, or online. Before, the only thing that sex workers knew about the Internet was the sensationalism around child pornography and corrupt politicians. And of course, they didn't want to be associated with these kinds of people! There seemed to be a dire need for the service that I wanted to provide. Four years ago in San Francisco, newspapers were "above" their advertisers. They would take your money, but they would have a negative reaction as soon as you told them what section you wanted to place the ad in. And there was no advertising company that catered to professionals in the adult entertainment industry. Only *Playboy* and *Penthouse* had access to the services of high-quality, professional advertising agencies. It was impossible for an escort to go into an agency and say, 'Help me work on my image, help me with copyrighting and photography, make sure that my banners and my image go together, that it fits me and my phone message.' But we came along and gave advertisers a choice. Being able to advertise on the Internet has been a huge boon to self-employed sex workers.

"Part of our image is that we will not have full frontal nudity or pornographic banner exchange with other Web sites. I personally don't have an issue with it, but here the perception is that showing too much is vulgar. Doing it this way also gives people more access to our site from offices. We have 20,000 visitors a day, and our peak hours for hits are from 12:30 to 1:00 in the afternoon and from 5:30 to 6:00 in the evening. So people are obviously coming to us from businesses, and we don't want them to get sued for sexual harassment if they have our Web site on their computer screen. The biggest compliment I ever received was from a man who said to me, 'I just want to thank you for your Web site. When I go there I feel comfortable with myself. I don't feel like I'm doing something dirty. I feel like I'm doing something normal.'

"The most important thing about the Internet is that it has hastened the acceptance of adult entertainers as competent people. A lot of us are intelligent and very shrewd businesspeople, people to be reckoned with. And many entertainers are writing and publishing on the Internet, so you can't ignore them, or pretend that everyone is just a gum-chewing, fishnet-wearing, miniskirted prostitute with big hair and sunglasses. More and more individuals are forced to accept the reality: those of us who work in the sex industry are normal people."

FIELD NOTES, SAN FRANCISCO, MARCH 2001

Yvonne Dotson and Victoria Schneider's accounts of being illegally apprehended and arrested on the streets of the Tenderloin were not the only sex-work related stories to attract the attention of the local and national media during the late 1990s. At the same time that street-based workers were encountering unprecedented levels of stigmatization and harassment, a different contingent of San Francisco sex workers was making legal, political, and cultural strides. In 1996, Margo St. James—a self-described "ex-hooker," former and current sex-worker organizer, and the founder of the world's first prostitutes' rights group, COYOTE (Call Off Your Old Tired Ethics)—mounted a campaign for election to the San Francisco Board of Supervisors, securing the endorsements of some of the most prominent political figures in the city.[1] St. James had recently returned from an eight-year sojourn in the south of France to serve on the newly assembled San Francisco Task Force on Prostitution and to resume her leadership of the organization she had founded two decades earlier.[2] By the winter of 1996, the task force was ready to recommend that San Francisco become the first U.S. city outside of Nevada to decriminalize indoor sex work, and St. James hoped to carry the political momentum that was being generated on to an electoral victory. Though St. James did not win one of the six seats on the board, she finished seventh in the general election, a mere 12,000 votes behind the victorious sixth-place candidate.[3]

Other sex-worker activists were also making headlines. In 1993, several members of COYOTE splintered off to found the Exotic Dancer's Alliance (EDA), targeting their protests at unfair labor practices in the city's erotic theaters. Partnering with the Service Employees International Union (SEIU) Local 790, the women sought to combat troubling health and safety issues in the clubs as well as the implementation of mandatory "stage fees" for club employees. According to EDA activists, the stage fees effectively transformed the theaters into clandestine, pimp-managed brothels, compromising their freedom and their safety. Indeed, some of the newest crop of performers or "independent contractors" in these refurbished commercial venues were the same women who had previously engaged in prostitution on Tenderloin streets. Though tacit, the reorganization of the clubs was ensured by the construction of "private rooms" as well as through the implementation of a system of steep stage fees. The creation of private rooms in the strip clubs—cubicles featuring a bench, sofa, or bed cordoned off from the rest of the club by opaque curtains or even a door—occurred simultaneously with the sudden imposition of the stage fees, whereby dancers were reclassified as "independent contractors" (rather than employees) and were required to pay fees of up to $200 per shift in order to be able to work. Since the stage fees were often more than women would earn from an entire evening's worth of striptease performances and lap dances, club management explicitly encouraged dancers to take their clients into the private rooms where they could engage in more "lucrative" activities.[4]

Rather than regarding these exploitative conditions as intrinsic to sexualized labor and fighting for its elimination (as their abolitionist feminist peers might have done), the members of the EDA instead sought to reform the industry from within by arguing for exotic dancers' rights as workers. Numerous EDA members filed wage and hour claims with the California Labor Commission, culminating in a successful class action lawsuit against one of the largest erotic theaters in the city, the Market Street Cinema. As described by former dancer-activist Heidi M. Kooy, "The courts ruled that . . . employers were required to pay at least minimum wage for hours worked; and that requiring dancers to pay stage fees was illegal. The California Labor Commission later reiterated the San Francisco court's ruling, outlawing clubs throughout the state from charging dancers for the right to make a living."[5] The trend toward the normalization and legitimation of sexual labor *as labor* appeared to advance still further in 1996, when the city's only "women-owned, women-managed" erotic theater, the Lusty Lady, became the first fully unionized exotic dancing venue in the nation.[6]

By the end of the decade, the burgeoning Internet economy was in full swing, and many Bay Area sex workers hoped to profit from the new billion-plus-dollar-a-year online pornography industry.[7] As a national debate unfolded around the meaning of presidential sexual peccadillos, media stories abounded which suggested that the Internet was pushing contemporary culture toward new frontiers of sexual tolerance by eliminating the biggest obstacles to selling pornography and other sexual services: shame and ignorance.[8] Commentators highlighted the ease and efficiency of the new technologies and the ways in which online sexual commerce had shifted the boundaries of social space, blurring the differences between underworld figures and "respectable" citizens:

> The boom is reflected by strippers diversifying their assets and morphing into business-savvy Internet artists, porn actors transforming into full-time producers/distributors, women . . . directing major market trends, and "respectable" companies and professionals (doctors, lawyers, bankers, etc.) who, with the help of insider high-tech specialists, are discreetly establishing their own websites, both for profit and pleasure.[9]

"Online sexual entrepreneurs" such as Danni Ashe were on their way to becoming new Horatio Alger figures, with many sex workers hoping to make the transition from dancing for tips to managing multimillion dollar Web sites.[10]

Less frequently commented on in the spate of news stories surrounding this trend were the broader cultural implications of the new forms of technologized sexual exchange.[11] Nor was there much discussion of the socioeconomic transformations that linked seemingly disparate cultural phenomena together (i.e., the new vibrancy of sex-worker organizing efforts and the rise of Internet pornography). How did the emergence of new communications technologies transform the meaning and experience of sexual commerce for sex workers and their customers? In what ways did the new technologies serve to exacerbate shifts that were already occurring in the sexual geography of postindustrial cities? What were the underlying connections between the new "respectability" of sexual commerce and the new classes of individuals who were participating in commercial sexual transactions?

Drawing on ethnographic fieldwork conducted during the seven-year period in which these changes transpired, in the rest of this chapter I seek to situate this series of transformations within a broader cultural and economic context. My discussion derives from on-site observations in a variety of work spaces and erotic performance venues, attendance at sex workers' political meetings and support groups, fifteen in-depth interviews with local sex-worker activists, and an immersion in sex workers' own (published and unpublished) writings and documentary films.[12] Focusing on the varieties of sexual labor practiced by Bay Area sex-worker activists, I here consider the distinctively *postindustrial* forms and meanings of sexual commerce that flourished in late-1990s San Francisco, noting the paradigmatic contrasts with their modern-industrial counterparts. Before proceeding, a word of caution is in order: although "trafficked women and children" have recently become some of the most iconic figures of the new global economic order, they are not the main protagonists of these pages.[13] Instead, my discussion in this chapter highlights the experiences of sex workers who are overwhelmingly white, native-born, and relatively class privileged, women and men who have *also* recently found their way into sex work in increasing numbers as a result of global economic restructuring. My primary aim is to explain the participation of a new and unlikely set of social actors in the contemporary commercial sexual economy, and how it has been facilitated by—and itself facilitates—new modes of sexual exchange. A second goal of this chapter is to explore some of the key transformations that are occurring within privatized commercial sexual transactions, including the emergence of "bounded authenticity" as a particularly desirable and sought after sexual commodity.

A NEW FACE OF SEXUAL LABOR?

Tonight we have decided to gather at Sybil's house—a modern, beautifully decorated, in-law unit in a lush, view-filled section of San Francisco's Cole Valley. After the last COYOTE meeting, Sybil was concerned that Anna, who's relatively new to the business, might need some advice from "an older, more experienced sister." So she invited a group of young women over to her apartment (including myself) for an intimate evening of informal information-sharing, food, and drink.

Sybil chats casually about the challenges of domestic life (she's thinking of exchanging sexual services for cooking lessons from a friend of hers who's a chef) while preparing pasta and a salad, then opening a bottle of wine. Nearly forty years old, she's a former dancer and performance artist who is still in terrific shape and moves fluidly in her black, clingy outfit. "Make yourself at home, honey . . ." she says to me, in a mock southern drawl. Her repertoire of accents and performance styles are so impressive that even though I usually think of myself as an outgoing person, I begin to feel self-conscious and shy in her presence.

Nearly half an hour passes before the others start to arrive. Allison—who I haven't met before—is first. She looks like a typical college student, carrying a backpack and wearing baggy, neutral-toned clothing. She seems pensive at first, but only for a few moments. Somewhat abruptly, she turns toward me and asks cheerily if I'm a sex worker too. "No, I'm a sociologist," I say. She explains that she wanted to study human sexuality at San Francisco State [University], but they don't have a bachelor's program. Now, she works in a massage parlor and at a strip club and is also an actor. "Not an actress?" I ask. "No, an *actor*." Like Sybil, she has a charming, flirtatious manner, and an engaging laugh.

Anna arrives next. A novice sex worker from Colorado, Anna is the one who asked for beginner's tips after the last meeting. Blonde and girlish, today she is wearing jeans, a studded leather dog collar, and other miscellaneous bondage gear. She hardly seems the innocent that she did two weeks ago. Sybil, too, remarks on the difference. The last to arrive is Ruby, a quiet woman with freckles and red hair who works in Berkeley giving "outcalls" and carrying a massage table with her everywhere she goes. She explains that in Berkeley, you don't need a massage license to work out of your home, and you're less likely to have legal hassles. Unfortunately, although there's more tolerance, there's also less money.

Ruby gets excited when I tell her that I want to write a book about the local sex industry. "Forget wages for housework! How about wages for sex work?! That's what we're really valued for!" All agree that the truly feminist dimensions of sexual labor are too infrequently acknowledged. What about streetwalking? I ask. Is that feminist too? "What's more feminist than running away from an abusive father and declaring your own boundaries?" asks Anna. "As a prostitute, you learn to say no." Eventually, everyone sits down at the small table in the kitchen to eat and drink wine and continue the conversation.

As the evening wears on, I ask the others about the ways that they conduct their work. Sybil is "in business for herself" which she much prefers to the competitive house where she worked in the past. She says that she finally got smart and placed an unbeatable ad of the "Mrs. Robinson" sort in the local sex newspaper. She won't tell us what's in it exactly—it's a trade secret. But working this way, she explains, *she* gets to be in control: there's no boss, no competition with the other women in the house, and she makes $200 per hour and keeps all of it. She has more time and more respect. Allison and Anna tell me about the massage parlor where they work together in Marin. "Most houses charge $120 but ours charges $140 'cause we're the best." It's $80 for them and $60 for the house. They are *proud* of where they work. In contrast to Sybil's narrative, they celebrate the pleasure and solidarity of women working together, making referrals for one another, and sharing clients ("Today Allison and I peed on this guy together—it was wonderful!").

Anna explains that she got started in the business when she answered an ad in the newspaper after running out of money. "I didn't want to go back home to my parents' house in Aurora [an upper middle-class Colorado suburb], and I didn't want to work for $5 an hour. I wish I'd thought of this sooner." At some point, she'd like to go back to graduate school, maybe even at Berkeley, but it would be difficult to give up all the money she is making. She was recently offered an internship in her field that would have wowed her at one point in her life, but at $7 an hour, now she thinks she'd be a fool to take it. Allison got started at the house through a friend she'd made while stripping at the Lusty Lady erotic theater. Her parents know that she's a stripper but they don't know about the massage parlor work. She enjoys stripping because it gives her an opportunity to express herself sexually. As an attractive woman, she explains, she's never been able to flirt with men, because they'll take her too seriously. At the Lusty Lady she can, because she's behind plates of glass and it's a safe environment. Like Anna, she emphasizes that she's pretty, thin, and good at what she does. Isn't that worth something? "You bet!" the others chime in. "Not just money, but self-esteem."

FIELD NOTES, SAN FRANCISCO, SEPTEMBER 1994

COYOTE, the national sex-workers' rights organization, was founded in San Francisco in 1973 by Margo St. James—at the time a young, bohemian feminist and prostitute living in Marin County. Although there are several other sex-workers' rights organizations in the country, and a growing number globally, COYOTE is arguably the best known, most visible, and most historically significant.[14]

The members of COYOTE have sometimes reacted defensively to their critics from alternative advocacy groups such as CATW (Coalition Against Trafficking in Women), SAGE (Standing Against Global Exploitation), PROMISE (Prevention, Referral, Outreach, Mentoring and Intervention to End Sexual Exploitation), and WHISPER (Women Hurt in Systems of Prostitution Engaged in Revolt), who maintain that COYOTE's celebrations of "happy hookerdom" are the result of white, middle-class privilege, and that they are atypical and unfit spokeswomen for the majority of women that perform sexual labor—whose "choice of profession" is made under far greater constraints.[15] On one level, these criticisms appear to be difficult to dispute: COYOTE's members are, practically to a person, white, middle-class, and well educated, just as their political opponents claim. They are overwhelmingly self-employed escorts, exotic dancers, fetish or tantra specialists, and erotic masseurs and masseuses. Many work out of expensively furnished homes or rented work spaces by placing ads online or in newspapers, earning enough money not only to cover expenses but to help finance alternative artistic and intellectual careers.[16] Others work in lavishly decorated, view-filled houses run by madams in San Francisco, Berkeley, or Sausalito. At the time of this writing, the average hourly fee (depending on the precise nature of the service) was between $140 and $350.

Although COYOTE's members may not be speaking for all sex workers when they seek to reframe sexual labor in terms of a respectable and esteem-worthy profession, some of the most interesting questions go unasked and unanswered if we limit ourselves to this critique: Why are these women doing sex work? Can sex work be a middle-class profession? Can engaging in sexual labor entail pleasure for the worker? Most crucially, if sexual labor is regarded as, at best, an unfortunate but understandable choice for women with few real alternatives, how are we to explain its increasing appeal to individuals with combined racial, class, and educational advantages? In order to begin to answer these questions, it is important to delineate the social origins, definitional parameters, and embodied sets of practices that are implied by the term "sex work."

SEX WORK FOR THE MIDDLE CLASSES

The term "sex work" was invented by COYOTE member Carol Leigh, who "began working and writing as a prostitute in 1978." [17] Unlike the word "prostitute," with its connotations of shame, unworthiness, or wrongdoing, the term "sex worker" tries to suggest an alternative framing that is ironically both a radical sexual identity (in the fashion of queer activist politics) and a normalization of prostitutes as "service workers" and "care-giving professionals." [18] For COYOTE's sex workers, the meaning and appeal of their work reside in this seeming contradiction.

As articulate writers and spokespeople, COYOTE members have historically produced more "theory" than they have "data" for the social researcher studying prostitution. At conferences, in members' own publications and films, and on Web sites, they have sought to emphasize prostitution as a liberatory and transgressive leap over the rigidly enforced good girl/bad girl, Madonna/Whore divide. [19] Meanwhile, feminists on the other side of the political fence have objected violently to the efficacy of these images as general characterizations of women in the sex industry. But perhaps these images should not be dismissed so readily simply because they cannot serve as general characterizations. While not applicable to everybody, these theories are socially illuminating in that they may be at least partially true for the group that produces them.

12 Advertisement in the *San Francisco Bay Guardian,* a free weekly, December 13, 1995.

The "good girl/bad girl" divide that they call attention to may itself help to explain wherein resides the ideological appeal of their theoretical formulations. While there is little transgressive about one who is socially expected (due to classism and racism) to be a "bad girl" becoming one, COYOTE's members were born and raised to be "good girls," and as prostitutes, they have arguably crossed a certain line.[20]

The bimonthly COYOTE meetings that I attended over a period of several years were a prime site for the refashioning of sex work as a category of radical sexual identity: members (many of whom also belonged to queer activist groups such as ACT UP or the Harvey Milk Democratic Club) organized sex-work conferences for artists and academics; discussed media strategy and talk show appearances; planned

Web pages and e-mail discussion groups; and took contributions for the monthly publication, "Whorezine." [21] New members often introduced themselves by telling their "coming out" stories ("I graduated from Smith College with a BA in philosophy, then I moved here to become a sex worker"), receiving words of encouragement and hearty applause from the other forty or fifty sex workers in the room. At COYOTE meetings, being a sex worker was about taking pleasure in sex, unleashing repressed energies, and exploring the dangerous border zones of eroticism.

This is not, however, to suggest that economic considerations were irrelevant to members' erotic and professional decision making. Even during the peak years of the Internet economy, well-paid, part-time work—especially for women pertaining to what Richard Florida has termed the "creative classes"—was, more often than not, difficult to come by.[22] Despite the huge expansion of jobs in San Francisco's booming postindustrial economy, patterns of gendered inequality within the city's high technology sector meant that even white, college-educated women were likely to be excluded from the highest paying positions.

Compared to men with similar forms of educational capital and class provenance, middle-class women in postindustrial economies are much more likely to find themselves working in the lowest paid quarters of the temporary help industry, in the service and hospitality sectors, or in other poorly remunerated part-time jobs.[23] Journalists Jenny Scholten and Nicki Blaze have written about their experience living in San Francisco during the dot-com boom years and supporting their nascent writing careers by working as strippers, coining the term "digital cleavage" to refer to a gender-specific version of the more frequently remarked "digital divide." Observing the disparity between their "noncorporate type" female friends who worked in the sex industry and many of their male counterparts who easily drifted into well-paid work in the high-tech sector, they note that "College hadn't prepared these men for systems administration anymore than it had prepared us for pole tricks. We'd all learned our trades on the job."[24] With women constituting a mere 28 percent of the employees in the IT industry (and occupying the lowest rungs within it), the decision to provide lap dances was regarded by Scholten, Blaze, and many others as a more reliable source of revenue. Notably, by the late 1990s, the UC Berkeley student newspaper, the *Daily Californian,* was as likely to feature "Help Wanted" ads for exotic dancers ("Earn up to $300 to $500 a day. Friendly work environment. Safe & clean"), escorts ("Earn $2500 per week part time"), and pornographic models ("Adult website $100/hour. Private studio, Comfortable settings") as it was for "computer geeks" ("Help local retailer with 486/Windows 95 applications. Part time, your schedule").[25]

Given the gendered disparities of postindustrial economic life, the relatively high pay of the sex industry (compared to other service sector jobs) provides a compelling reason for some women from middle-class backgrounds to engage in sexual labor. "Girl-X' "s narrative of her decision to become a phone-sex worker, which appeared in a special "Sex Industry" issue of the alternative parenting zine, *Hip Mama* (based in Oakland), exemplifies one common route of passage into the Bay Area sex industry in the mid-1990s:

> I had gotten bored with my day job, which was—and still is—unworthy of mention. I decided I'd had enough of the outside world, and wanted to work from home somehow. The idea [of doing phone sex] excited me. . . . I would no longer be subject to the indignities that came along with my previous jobs in the service industry, slinging espresso, records, books, or trendy clothes. I could barricade myself in my cave-like studio apartment all day and all night if I wanted, leaving only for special occasions, like the appearance of a Japanese noise band at one of those divey punk clubs.[26]

Where "Girl-X" exemplifies the transition from low-end service work into sexual labor, Zoey's account of trying to support a middle-class lifestyle on $17.75 an hour (despite holding bachelor's and master's degrees) exemplifies another. The close friend of several prominent sex-worker activists when I met her, Zoey was a thirty-year-old former social worker who was currently working as an erotic masseuse. During a conversation over tea in her apartment in the Oakland Hills, she described her transition into sexual labor this way:

> A year out of school I was very burnt out on the low pay, and really wanted to make more money. I was working in a really rough environment, I was constantly depressed, and I was feeling really frustrated that I had these prestigious degrees and was making so little money. My boyfriend at the time had a good friend who had been doing sensual massage for many years and had found it tremendously lucrative. And she looked like she had a hell of a lot more freedom than I did! And so, I thought, oh, this would be a great ground for me to, you know, skip over years of torturous

low pay [laughter] and actually then, to practice things that were truly dear to my heart.

During an interview with Elise, who was pursuing a doctoral degree in comparative literature when she began what would eventually evolve into a ten-year stint as an escort, she pointed to a related set of motivations that had underpinned her own decision to engage in sexual labor:

> I had reached a point in my life where I just wasn't sure what I wanted to do. I had recently met these women who were sex workers—like one in particular, my friend who was working as a fetish model. And I saw that this looked easy, like an easy way to make lots of money. . . . I was working on my dissertation and I had to teach and to take out huge student loans. That was like a huge factor in deciding to do sex work because I felt like I couldn't afford to go into any more debt. So yeah, I started doing sex work at this agency where my friend worked. And then eventually I started working from home.

Economic factors also served to shape COYOTE sex workers' choices in other ways, ways which were not directly related to the pursuit of material sustenance in a high-tech economy but which pertained more generally to members' class-specific cultural dispositions. In *Distinction,* Pierre Bourdieu's careful analysis of the material and social underpinnings of taste, he describes "the new petite bourgeoisie" as comprised of individuals with two primary class trajectories: on the one hand, "those who have not obtained from the educational system the qualifications that would have enabled them to claim the established positions their original social position promised them" (e.g., women like Anna, the novice sex worker from Colorado, who had yet to pursue an advanced degree); and, on the other hand, "those who have not obtained from their qualifications all they felt entitled to" (e.g., women like Zoey or Elise, who were dismayed that their educational credentials had not lifted them to greater heights).[27] Given either trajectory, individuals who pertain to the new petite-bourgeois class fractions are likely to settle into subordinated spaces within the institutions of cultural production and exchange. According to Bourdieu, what is most distinctive about these new class fractions, however, is the distinctive ethos which infuses the cultural goods that they produce and consume. Unlike the "old" petite bourgeoisie—which sought to distinguish itself from the working classes via an ethic of self-sacrifice and "virtue"—the new petite bourgeoisie seeks its occupational and personal salvation (and thus its sense of distinction) via an ethic of "fun":

> [W]hereas the old morality of duty, based on the opposition be-tween pleasure and good, induces a . . . fear of pleasure and a rela-tion to the body made up of "reserve," "modesty" and "restraint," and associates every satisfaction of the forbidden impulses with guilt, the new ethical avant-garde urges a morality of pleasure as a duty. This doctrine makes it a failure, a threat to self-esteem, not to "have fun." [28]

COYOTE members' identification with the "bad girl," their em-brace of an ethic of sexual experimentation and freedom, must thus be seen not only in terms of feminist politics or sexual ideology but as a particular strategy of *class differentiation* as well. In contrast to the old petite-bourgeois values of upwardly mobile asceticism and restraint (which themselves serve to distinguish this class from the working class beneath them, a class whose ethos rejects "pretense" and striving), the new petite bourgeoisie regards fun, sexiness, pleasure, and freedom as ethical ideals worthy of strenuous pursuit. The embrace of these ideals serves as a means for members of the new petite bourgeoisie to distin-guish themselves from the old petite bourgeoisie, an invisible boundary separating classes of individuals who might seem, at first glance, to exist in close proximity.

The relationship between class-based ethical ideals and the mean-ing of sex work was inadvertently well illustrated by two different se-ries of "before" and "after" photographs featuring San Francisco sex workers, both published in 1998, with each series telling a very differ-ent morality tale. The first series, published in *Life* magazine, featured streetwalkers who had left prostitution and committed their lives to helping other women leave the trade. The *Life* series of photos was in-tended to illustrate the women's successful completion of a longed-for transition from "disreputable" street life into the respectable middle classes (the "old" petite-bourgeois ethic). The second series of photo-graphs derives from sex-worker activist and performance artist Annie Sprinkle's "Transformation Salon," the stated aim of which is to "bring out the inner slut/whore/porn star/pinup in any woman and capture it on film for her and her loved ones to marvel at for years to come." [29] In contrast to the *Life* magazine pictures, Sprinkle's photos illustrate a new petite-bourgeois rejection of the pursuit of respectability in favor of a celebration of the "fun ethic." One of the frequent hallmarks of the middle-class entry into sex work is the explicit challenge that is

NICHOLE SYLVIA-ZENO, 31 In her 1993 mug shots she's a victim; today, a victor.

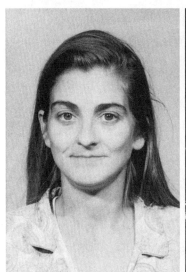 

AUTUMN BURRIS, 33 "Nothing made me sicker than seeing a wedding ring on a trick, or a baby seat in back," says Burris (in 1995 mug shots and, right, today).

13 Old and new petite-bourgeois cultural strategies. Two series of sex worker "before" and "after" photos, both published in 1998, including original captions. The series on the left appeared in *Life Magazine;* the series on the right derives from sex-worker activist and performance artist Annie Sprinkle's "Transformation Salon."

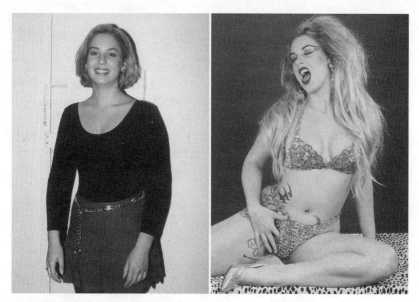

Jill, a university student from San Francisco . . . is CHASTITY CHURCH.

Cora Emans, a mother and singer from Amsterdam . . . is HARD CORA.

posed to precisely these standards of respectability, standards which are experienced as hindrances to freedom rather than embodied strategies of class advancement.

Although the dividing line between good girls and bad girls is challenged for COYOTE's sex workers, another inviolable boundary is sometimes erected to take its place. There is a crucial—and only occasionally denied—distinction that is enforced between "professional sex workers" and those who walk the streets. It is not just the distinction between trained professional and unskilled labor that is at stake here, but a fierce reluctance to hover anywhere near (let alone to cross!) the class divide. When I asked sex workers if they had ever or would ever consider working the streets, one male prostitute responded that he couldn't, because "his clothes were too good and he had all his teeth." Others said that it was "too risky and dangerous," and very fortunately, unnecessary, for sex workers like themselves with a college education. While statements such as these may convey an accurate assessment of street-level risks, they also convey a more general sensibility which placed certain kinds of sex work (most especially streetwalking, but also some brothel-based work) socially beneath them.

It's 1:00 a.m., and Celia (a new friend I have met through my research) and I have decided to go out for a drink. Celia finally asks me the question I've been waiting for all along during the course of this project: "Have you ever considered doing prostitution yourself?" My response to her is both diplomatic and true: "Of course I think about what it would be like. It's part of working on this topic." She tells me that she knows a madam in Noe Valley who's looking for women in their twenties and thirties. A nice, Jewish lady who deals with successful business men. Totally safe; she checks the men out thoroughly, would tell me exactly how to do it, what they like. She goes on to tell me that she knows it would be a big deal for me to "cross the line," to transgress the Madonna/Whore barrier. But it's abundantly clear to me that this conversation is also about something else. Celia knows that I have been doing fieldwork on the streets of the Tenderloin, and she is concerned. I sense that she is telling me not to cross another line, the streetwalking line. Streetwalking is simply not appropriate for a middle-class girl like me, not even the upper-tier "career prostitution" of the Union Square strip where I have been spending most of my time.

Even though it's late and we're both tired, a fascinating conversation ensues about the differences between streetwalking and middle-class sex work. Celia can't understand why anyone would streetwalk rather than work out of their home. I suggest that it may actually feel more exploitative to sell an hour of feigned intimacy rather than twenty minutes of body mechanics and a smile. She concedes my point, but again, emphasizes the differences in personal risk. For her, safety is key.

Before leaving, Celia asks me about the madam again. This turns out to be an extremely useful thought experiment for me, really forcing me to think seriously about "what, if anything, is wrong with prostitution" (the persistent question in feminist discussions of the issue). I explain to Celia that it's not so much the commodification of sex, the taboo of sex for money that keeps me from doing sex work, but having to subordinate myself to a man for an extra hour when I already feel that this is something I too frequently have to do in the course of my academic career. "What's your economic situation?" she asks me, with a knowing tilt of her head. When I tell her about my fellowship, she is quick to respond: "I bet you might change your mind if you really needed the money."

FIELD NOTES, DECEMBER 1, 1994

ORGANIZING THE EXCHANGE FOR AUTHENTICITY

Middle-class sex workers' sense of distinction vis-à-vis their work was found not only in an unwillingness to consider streetwalking (an unwillingness that extended beyond questions of safety) but also in the types of work situations that they favored. As researchers Melissa Ditmore and Juhu Thukral have observed, the goal for most indoor sex workers (of whatever class background) who remain in the business is usually to be able to work independently. A common trajectory is to enter the industry working for someone else (e.g., in a brothel, massage parlor, or dungeon) and to gradually build up one's own clientele.[30] While professional autonomy was indeed desirable for COYOTE's sex workers, there were other organizational criteria that were important to them as well. During whatever period of time that they might spend engaged in brothel-based work with third-party management, they were inclined to remove themselves from locales that seemed to foster a purely instrumentalist relationship to the labor. As Bourdieu writes, new petite-bourgeois "need merchants" "sell themselves as models and as guarantors of the value of their products . . . [they] sell so well because they believe in what they sell."[31] Although the sex workers I interviewed described an array of experiences with third-party management which ranged from positive to negative, some of the most troubling situations for women did not involve violent coercion or physical danger but circumstances which seemed to exemplify crude economic self-interest and a lack of authenticity (the very qualities which would have endowed their work with the sense of value and distinction that made it desirable to engage in in the first place). Although "bad" managers were also those who were negligent when it came to safeguarding their workers' well-being (leaving them vulnerable to clients or the police), even these narratives stood in contrast to the stories of violent control over one's person that were a common negative pimping narrative among women who worked the streets.

> The first time I did massage, I was green, green, green. I don't think that there was a hell of a lot of camaraderie or direction shared among the women. I know that there was male ownership or at least male management and I don't think that the commissions were fair. I think the structure of the situation itself was set up for entrapment, verbal entrapment, because if the guy would pay forty or fifty bucks for a massage, it was up to the worker to negotiate a sex act for money, which is in and of itself entrapment verbally.[32] So there were not a lot of clues given to me about how to determine when it was okay. The only rule I think I remember is that he had to be grabbing on me first. So that's not an empowerment situation, that's him trying to grab your booty or touch your breast. I do remember one phrase, "greasing down pigs." I remember always thinking about the oil, and touching, and thinking of the men as pigs. So we're not talking real true blue pleasure here. And after an incident where I walked a guy to his car, thinking he was such a sweetheart, and he flashed a cop I.D. at me, I just decided to quit. Real or fake, it scared the shit out of me.
>
> DIANA, 38, independent escort

> I used to work for this couple who often left me alone in the house when I was seeing clients. I was really upset with them one time because a man, an attorney that I saw on an outcall basis through them, he was very mentally distressed. He lived in a beautiful home that was completely disheveled and slovenly, and was on an alcoholic roll that was life-threatening. I was dropped off there and I had to take a taxi home. And the management said to me, "Go ahead, take the check from him," because he was lonely, because he needed company, and because they weren't giving him any break on my time. He had to come up with "X" amount per hour, whether we were fucking or talking. Mostly we talked. And um, by even the second time, I said to Laura, one of the women in the couple, "This place is gross. I don't even want to lie in his bed," and she said, "Well honey, here, take a sheet." After he

died, they told me that his wife has frozen the funds on the account, and they weren't going to cover the last check that he gave me. They didn't seem to feel any remorse that he died, and they wouldn't cut me any slack, even though I had spent six fucking hours with him.

SYBIL, 40, independent escort

I worked at a place once in a sort of gourmet neighborhood in Berkeley—alternative but ritzy. It had hardwood floors and potted plants, candles and cut flowers, things like that. But even though they acted like we were a co-op—they expected us to do all of the cleaning and answering the phones, and required us to do the laundry during our shifts, stuff that a madam would normally do—all they did was come in and collect the money. They acted as if we were equals when we weren't. The rule there was that you could do "massage with a happy ending" but you couldn't do full sex, even though hand jobs are less money [than intercourse] and also the same crime. They also made us come to staff meetings in addition to our regular schedule. These meetings were unpaid, a waste of our time. Then at meetings, they would say things like "We're not making enough money, so we should light a candle together and say a prayer." And I was like, "If we're not making enough money, maybe we should buy some more advertising." I finally left when I got a chance to open my own place in the city. Anyway, to me, selling erotic massage was too much of a legal risk for too little money.

AMANDA, 38, independent escort

By contrast, "good" places to work were not only those with managers who took the women's physical and emotional well-being into account and paid them fairly, but places which seemed to foster an ethic of authenticity and genuine care, both between client and worker and between worker and manager. Pye, a sex-worker activist and a newspaper columnist who I met during my research in Stockholm, was proud of the fact that the strip club she danced at and managed was run as a (genuine) cooperative. She emphasized that at her club, the workers not only maintained close relations with one another as well as with the management, but equally divided up all wages and tips ("We're like friends and family to each other—one girl plays the violin; another is in a folk band; another is studying English lit"). And in Zoey's account below, the attention paid to organic foods is important precisely because it serves as a symbol of the wholesome and genuine interactions that prevailed among the individuals she describes:

> The owners of the brothel where I worked were often on site; they played a really sweet role, which is actually part of why I stayed for so long: I felt a real sense of community. They were both very nurturing. I mean they had food in the house: organic yogurt and whole wheat bread and organic orange juice, and fruits and vegetables and salads. The message that I got from them was that they felt that it was a special group of women and they really were dedicated to keeping this group of women together and invested in us being happy. Once, I hung out with them and we went to this really, really nice restaurant and they just bought me a wonderful meal. And I didn't feel like it was buying my love. I felt like there was *already* a loving bond, you know? Another time, I had a terrible stomachache and Danielle gave me a stomach massage. It's just how she is in her life, very generous. She was generous with everybody she came in contact with, and nurturing and loving. With them, it wasn't just like, "Oh this is what I do for business."

Perhaps the closest thing to what at first glance might seem to resemble a more conventional pimping arrangement was the present manner of working described by Amanda, who had current and former male lovers serving as her "drivers" (taking her to the homes of "outcall" clients, and waiting for her until she was finished) or providing security for her with "incall" clients (staying in an adjoining room of her rented workspace and being ready to intervene in case of any mishaps). Amanda's drivers typically received $35 per date; those who did security for her received a $100 flat fee for a five-hour shift. But in speaking with her and in observing firsthand the way that she worked, the differences between her system and a conventional pimping arrangement became immediately clear. Amanda liked to refer to the three men who worked for her as her "sofa boys," whose main job it was to sit on the couch, to chat with her during slow periods, and to help her clean up at the end of a shift. Far from controlling Amanda, these men were essentially friends she had recruited to act as her paid employees. Zoey's experience highlights the importance that middle-class sex workers placed on establishing an emotionally safe working environment, one which enabled an authentic relation to sex work to develop. Amanda similarly spoke of taking care to make sure her rented work space felt like it was "hers," proudly displaying to me her candlelit bedroom with its lush velvet curtains and extra-soft featherbed (as Amanda noted,

"It's really more for me than for them. The decor doesn't really make much of a difference to them at all—I've discovered that they'll only leave if the place is filthy").

Like their counterparts on the street, middle-class sex workers must still concern themselves with questions of legality and the police. Not surprisingly, however, this relationship varies significantly from the "revolving door" between jail and the streets that most women in the Tenderloin experienced.[33] Only a handful of the self-employed sex workers that I spoke with reported having been arrested (a more common scenario was to have a too-close-for-comfort run-in with someone suspected of being a police officer), and even those who were arrested were generally able to get their records cleared. In the interview extract below, Elise—a thirty-seven-year-old escort and nonfiction writer who has worked in the sex trade for ten years—describes the one occasion during which she was apprehended by the police. What is especially noteworthy about this account is precisely its atypicality, both within the context of Elise's own experience as well as within the broader community of San Francisco sex-worker activists that I came to know. In fact, the brief spate of arrests and the illegal fining of indoor workers that occurred during the period that Elise describes (which continued to be a regular and ubiquitous experience for women on the streets) was so unprecedented and unusual that it made local newspaper headlines for several weeks.[34]

> I was working with Jenny, who was high profile but also had a lot of political connections and was very savvy in terms of the screening process. She didn't actually require the guy to show an I.D. this time because he said he left it in the car. But anyway, they were after her, which is the real reason I think I got arrested.
>
> What happened is that I went to her place and the client came in and talked for a long time, about real estate and things. I retreated to the other room, he came in and took off his clothes and he like tried to get me to look at the money and tried to get me to say something. I didn't count it or anything because that's not something I do, but I didn't take the money either. And he was naked and I actually had my hand on his cock, I think I was like putting on a condom or something. And then these people just busted in. They came in the room and they were like, "You're under arrest!"
>
> There were three undercover officers, all men. And so I ended up getting dressed, and they ended up taking me to the police

station and separating me from Jenny. And then for like five hours they tried to get me to talk. And since I had gone to a legal training workshop, I knew not to say anything except: "I want to speak to my attorney." And the cop who arrested me got madder and madder. He threw phone books on the table, he would just leave me in this witness room and come in and say things like, "Well, you know, we realize that she was exploiting you." It was very condescending.

Eventually, they released me, and I got a ticket with a court date on it and then I got a letter in the mail that referred me to a criminal diversion program. And it was not like a real criminal diversion program—it was just like "pay us money in cash or a money order." Fortunately, I was pretty much connected with the other sex workers in town, who knew that some other people had gotten arrested lately too. They told me not to pay it. And when I went to the court house on my court date, I discovered that I wasn't even on the docket. My charges had been completely dropped. I went up to a bunch of people in the room to try to find out what was going on, just to try and track down what was on file, but they couldn't bring up anything. They had a record of Jenny being arrested, but there was nothing whatsoever with my name on it.

Like Elise, most women learned how to navigate their way around the criminal justice system through careful and meticulous business practices and through regular information sharing—for example, by circulating the telephone numbers of police officers who were suspected of posing as clients—and by doing legal training with a local activist attorney. Amanda conducted her incall business in typically prudent fashion, taking $250 in cash from each client as soon as he walked through the door, before any services were rendered. She would not discuss the particulars of her practice on the telephone, and took care to dispose of used condoms (the potential "evidence") after every date. She only gave cash to her "sofa boys" after the workday was finished. But perhaps the most important factor in making her arrest unlikely was the relative lack of concern that police departments demonstrated toward the white, middle-class sectors of the sex trade. Police officers in three distinct Bay Area municipalities that I spoke with all confirmed that their priority in prostitution arrests was street-level transactions. Although a high-profile madam like Jenny could briefly attract notice, or a particular indoor business might come to their attention if a caller complained, the officers bluntly informed me that it was the street trade that generated the most concern from residents and which was the biggest "visual distracter" from neighborhoods. As one sergeant from a local vice squad said simply, "Our main goal is to contain prostitution in such a way that my parents do not have to see it."

THE ROLE OF NEW TECHNOLOGIES

Recent journalistic accounts have noted that indoor sex workers were among the first and most consistent beneficiaries of the technological innovations that defined the "new economy." [35] Despite the broader structural trend situating many middle-class women on the wrong side of the "digital cleavage," the Internet has indeed reshaped predominant patterns of sexual commerce in ways that some sex workers have been able to benefit from. For many indoor sex workers, it has become easier to work without third-party management, to conduct one's business with minimal interference from the criminal justice system, and to reap greater profits by honing one's sales pitch to a more elite and more specialized audience.

During an interview over dinner in my San Francisco apartment, Amanda was quite explicit about the ways that the new technologies had revolutionized her practice. She recounted how, after her brief stint working in a Berkeley brothel in which she was consistently "passed up" by the predominantly working-class clientele "in favor of younger, bustier, blonde women," she decided to give sex work another try when a friend suggested to her that she could advertise on the Internet and work out of her own space:

> I started realizing that there was a lonely pool of frustrated men out there, earning good money in Silicon Valley. So I placed an ad with some pictures of myself in a garter belt, stockings, and lingerie. It said "East Coast transplant. Kind, playful, smart, slender brunette with a sensitive touch." I wouldn't have been able to continue doing sex work if it had not been for this. Now, I only advertise on the Internet. It insures me a reliable pool of well-educated, professional men with predictable manners and predictable ways of talking. When they make appointments, they keep them. My ad attracts a lot of first timers. I seem "safe," like someone they would already know, since it's clear that I have the same kind of background as they do and I seem easy to talk to. White educated women like me have a lot of appeal to professional white men.

Sybil, an aspiring dancer, described a similar transition from brothel work to self-employment:

> At the brothel, I would always get sold short. Jennifer, the woman who ran it, would always say things to customers like "Well I have Christy, who's a busty blonde, very tan, very lovely, she's literally a Swedish girl, and then I have Roxette, who's the cutest, most petite, diminutive little redhead. And then I have Sybil, a lanky brunette dancer. I was always presented in the number three or number four position, brunette being a big negative. Jennifer would say to me: "Sybil, the men who come here know what they want before they even call. They want a busty blonde." But the great thing about Jennifer is that she told me, and it went over my head like a low flying jet, "Sybil, you're old enough, you're good enough, and gosh darnit you know how to sell yourself. Just take out a fucking ad and work out of your own crib." I am so grateful. For less than the commission price of one client at Jennifer's, I have created a monster by virtue of six words, a knowledge of language, and marketing skill.

By advertising through specialty Web sites, members can pitch their ads toward clients who harbor an interest in their specific physical characteristics (e.g., fat women, older women, Asian women), or in the precise sexual services for which they can offer expertise (e.g., tantra, sadomasochism, erotic massage). Many such sites are even linked to client Web sites which feature restaurant-style "reviews" of their services.[36] Other Web sites contain links to escorts' "blogs," in which the day-to-day musings of the sex worker are intended to serve as a window into her personality. There are also a number of Web sites where sex workers can advertise if they are interested in working sporadically or informally ("Rainy Day Massage Special!"; "Prostate Pleasure—Deep, Slow, and Caring"). Perhaps the best known of these is "Craig's List," a community Web site with classified listings, where ads for sex workers simply appear in the "services" section, sandwiched unobtrusively between the headings for computer help, event planning, skilled trades, and real estate.

PROFESSIONALIZING SEXUAL LABOR

As Bourdieu observes, one way that members of the new petite bourgeoisie have found to embrace a sense of social distinction is via the adoption of "reconversion strategies," in which cultural capital is employed to "professionalize" marginal spaces within the labor market

#2-from Diamond Heights, Indoors
This person has been calling around again lately. His name is Andy. He is a large, Mexican American & Irish , lives on Moreland (near Diamond Heights) uses numbers 239-011_, 239-707_, fax 834-918_, smooth sweet way of talking, other names as well, Robert, Paul, Rick. If you make a date, and you're supposed to call back, if you hang up, and if you don't call back within two minutes, then he calls and says why didn't you call me back. 5'10-6ft, light skin, dark hair, thirties, 240-260 lbs., stocky, been to prison, lots of tattoos on arms, neck, chest, said he's been in gang, asks for garter belts & lingerie on phone. In person he wanted her to dance and keep asking for more money as she danced. One woman reported that he did not use a weapon. Another stated that he lives with his mother. Another woman said he threatened her on the phone, saying that he would find her and rape her if she did not come to his house.

━━ ━━ ━━ ━━ ━━ ━━ ━━

#3-from Marin, Indoors
He calls for Friday afternoon 3-5. He may make the appointment earlier in the week. He uses a couple of phones numbers, 753-552_, or 499-061_. He is between 5'10" and 6' muscular, stocky, strong upper body, thirties, dark hair, buzz cut, shows up in jeans shorts, sweat pants, dark shirt or sweatshirt, sometimes barefoot, targets sensual masseuses, roundish cheeks. Once asked "What if I don't want a full body massage?" He has piercing blue eyes that everyone notices. Once he had green eyes (maybe contact lenses). Comes in, very nice, sometimes nervous. When the woman is turned around he pulls a knife or gun and says, "If you do everything I say, I won't hurt you. If you scream I will hurt you." He may see person a couple of times without rape. Names are Kevin or Mike, One person mentioned that he seems like he is in the military. He's very strong in that he got maced last weekend in Marin- The woman's husband was home. He came in when he heard what was happening. The husband maced him, but he was able to run out, even with husband chasing him. Also the woman had a panic button to police station. She pressed the button. The cops came right away.

14 Example of a "dirty trick list," distributed at a COYOTE meeting (1995).

and to invest them with a sense of personal meaning and ethical value.[37] At COYOTE meetings, members made efforts to professionalize their trade through activities such as the demonstration of "penetration alternatives," discussions of novel and tested safe sex techniques, and presentations of statistical studies documenting the incidence of HIV in body fluids. Meetings were also a common place for members to make referrals to one another and to circulate written materials such as "dirty trick" lists (featuring the names and phone numbers of clients who were suspected of being dangerous); legal, investment, and tax advice; and safer sex guidelines.

Over the course of the last decade, there have been a number of print and Web-based "how-to" guides which serve a similar purpose, distributing accumulated know-how worldwide.[38] The volume *Turning Pro*, for example, features chapters on "Marketing Your Services" (offering detailed guidelines on how to set up a Web page, create signature files, and secure search engine placement), "Continuing Education within the Field" (a listing of books and classes which can aid in the development of particular sexual skills), and "Planning for the Future" (a discussion of how to invest money wisely and, when the time comes, navigate a career transition). In similar fashion, the *Escorting Tip Guide*, published by the Web site www.escortsupport.com, contains a list of frequently asked questions ("Q: What is the best way to screen clients? A: Get their full name, phone number . . . and make them aware that you will be asking for photo identification when you first meet them") as well as a set of probing "self-knowledge" questions for prospective sex workers to consider ("Was it money alone that attracted you? Were you trying to prove something to yourself or others? Do you have any internal stigma about working? . . . There are far too many women in the business who thinks all it takes to succeed is tits and ass").

In contrast to the naturalization of heterosexual relations that prevailed among the streetwalkers, for COYOTE members sex work implied a distinctive skill set that could be elaborated through education and training. Amanda, Elise, Aaron, and Zoey all spoke explicitly about their deliberate pursuit of special skills as a means of enhancing both their experience of doing sex work and their earning power. The forms of training that they pursued ranged from massage certification to yogic breathwork (useful, Amanda explained, with clients who were interested in tantric sex) to sexual surrogacy courses to the self-conscious embellishment of skills left over from prior careers. Zoey, for example, who had completed graduate school and an internship in social work, considered her earlier training as a therapist to be vital to her current work as an erotic masseuse:

> The model that I have always chosen in doing this work has actually been a psychotherapy model. In order to do psychotherapy well, in a way that most deeply serves the client, you must be doing lots of behind-the-scene work. If you go to the psychotherapy empty—without having done the behind-the-scenes work—and then you provide just what the client wants from you, you're not really serving the client. And your burn-out rate will be quite

high. So, what this work called for when I first got started . . . was to first heal myself in certain ways. As a therapist, in order to continue working with repetitively traumatized children, I had to be doing a ton of behind-the-scenes work so I could hold my ground and have something to give them of value. And so it's the same exact thing. Because of my training as a therapist I knew, intimately, how to do that; so, I brought that to sex work too.

For Amanda, her best training for sex work came from sex-educator classes, from yoga, and from years of experience teaching preschool ("Even though there's no nap time, both jobs are really about connecting nonverbally. And in both cases, you often have to repeatedly set boundaries and clean up the mess."):

> I had been doing sex work for about two years when I decided to take a class at SFSI [San Francisco Sex Information, a nonprofit hotline]. I was getting psyched about sex education, about the sexual healing work that I was doing as a prostitute. So I was kind of inspired, thinking maybe I would go on to be a sexual surrogate. I wanted to know more, to get more training, and to be in a sex-positive environment with other sex workers where I could talk about my work. And when I got there, I saw that there were a lot of students there like me, a hundred or so in the class.
>
> One day, they brought in a sex therapist who used sex surrogates to speak with us. He was a male sex therapist, a very nice guy. During the small group discussion with the sex surrogate, I learned that even after you go through all this training, it's still technically illegal to be a surrogate, and you get paid less and have to work harder. Plus, you still can't tell most people you meet what you do for a living.
>
> They gave us a guide to the most reliable condoms—that was really useful—and also a guide to nonlatex condoms. At some point in the training though, I realized I wasn't really cut out to be a sexual healer. I can be kind of grouchy. I'm not really enough of an earth mother.

In addition to the acquisition of skills and training, the strategic deployment of educational and cultural capital came into play for COYOTE's middle-class sex workers in other ways. Lisa got her job at a Sausalito massage parlor when she "faked a French accent and answered an ad for a European blonde." Sybil, like other women, screened her clients closely, and could restrict her practice to powerful businessmen

15 Banner for "www.escortsupport.com," a Web site for sex workers which extends tips and networking to a broad online community.

once she knew "how to ask the right questions." Whereas on the streets, women described their previous private-sphere heterosexual relations as constituting sufficient preparation to engage in sex work, for middle-class women, cultural capital, work experience, and special training constituted vital components of the labor.

THE BODY FOR SEX WORK

COYOTE's middle-class sex workers often imbue their labor with an ethic that demands that they are themselves "sold" on what they are selling, as we have seen. In this manner, sex work is more than an occupation that offers concrete material rewards—it also comes to offer opportunities for "personal growth" and deep meaning.[39] Sex workers' embrace of both an ethic of physical pleasure and a therapeutic language of personal growth in turn give rise to what might be termed "body-positive" approaches to sexual labor. Ascribing to the ideal of the pleasure-seeking, pleasure-deserving, sensuous female body, middle-class sex workers often stand in ambivalent tension with the conventional standards of beauty that the job would seem to demand.

While many sex workers did indeed display their own shrewd understanding of the importance of bodily capital, it was talked about in a way that was quite different from that of the streetwalkers. For

WHORE COLLEGE
P.O. Box 210256, San Francisco, CA 94121
Dean of Academic Studies: Carol Leigh
Author,
Unrepentant Whore: Collected Works of Scarlot Harlot

Whore College is a day of classes for sex workers and our communities* on May 4th,Wednesday during the San Francisco Sex Worker Festival. Each class is $20, but $40 will buy an all day pass, good from 11-5. Evening class, DIY webcam, is $30.00 (scholarships). There are partial scholarships available for sex workers, so please don't hesitate and let us know by phone or email if you need a scholarship. Earn your diploma by attending all classes! Please register early to be sure you have a seat at: http://www.bayswan.org/swfest2005/college registration.html or write info@bayswan.org

11 AM Sex Worker Well-Being
This workshop focuses on a broad range of occupational health and safety issues for sex workers

* Sex Worker Stretch
Instructor: Frog (see Frog's bio at art exhibit page)

* Safer Oral Sex Techniques
Instructor: Headmistress, Kimberly Cline

* "Six Herbs That Can Cure Anything" with a focus on genital health.
Instructor: Kymberly Cutter is a working prostitute, political activist, poet, mother, herbalist, and parenting educator.

* Spiritual Tools
Instructor: Aphrodesia

* San Francisco Resources for Sex Workers
The Bay Area has many sex worker groups and resources for men; women and transgender people, including support groups, sex worker rights organizations, the St. James Infirmary, health and other resource agencies and clinics, therapists, attorneys, etc.
Instructor: Scarlot Harlot has been collecting information about Bay Area services for sex workers since the early 80s. She is webmistress of bayswan.org and director of the SF Sex Worker Film and Arts Festival.

1 PM Self-Defense
Fun, interactive self-defense workshop. Learn practical ways to keep yourself safe at work and in daily life. Share safety skills in a supportive environment. We will discuss safety and prevention, learn physical self-defense techniques, and do boundary roleplays.
Instructor: Yalith Fonfa

2 PM Discussion and Panel: Beauty Standards and Sex Work
Are you beautiful? As sex workers many of us overcome, seek to expand and ultimately capitalize on 'beauty'. What can we teach each other and society about these standards as we work towards a healthier society and prosperous business?
Moderator: Sadie Lune

3:30 PM "The Business"
This workshop examines various facets of erotic service businesses in the Bay Area, focusing on issues for sole proprietors.

---

16 Web description (extract) of "Whore College," a professional development seminar held at the Fourth San Francisco Sex-Worker Film and Arts Festival, 2005.

some women, particularly those operating in the uppermost tiers of the industry, body and appearance were described as "company assets," and their diligent care was calculated directly into the monthly budget (not just makeup and clothes, but gym membership, lingerie, and visits to the tanning salon and hair stylist).[40] Yet women's strategies for managing their bodily capital were in the main complex, since there was a fairly wide range of ages and body types, with many individuals appealing to specialized rather than mainstream sexual markets. Indeed, for several of the sex workers I spoke with, doing sex work became an occasion for developing an acceptance of their own bodily deviations from the mass-mediated ideal of the sleek, big-breasted silhouette. It was common for me to hear women describe feeling "sexy," "beautiful," and "powerful" only *after* they had begun to engage in sexual labor and were receiving consistent praise from their clients.[41] Taking this notion one step further, Heather MacAllister, a Bay Area "fat activist" and the founder of an erotic lap-dancing troupe featuring "women of size," has argued that erotic performance can provide a means for larger women to affirm a sexuality "which has been underaffirmed and made negative in the popular culture." McAllister's express purpose for integrating lap dances into her erotic performances is "to give the dancers' self-esteem a boost. . . . It is important for women to shake their big butts in somebody's face and get paid for it."[42] Sex work was also described by various women as a job which enabled them to revel in the delights of their own physicality, in a way that more "intellectually oriented" professions did not often permit:

> [U]nlike some people who dissociate with sex work, I find that I feel very much there in my body when I am doing it. Probably part of it is just the adrenaline. But I think it is more that it is a departure from my other life, which is all about, you know, putting different structures together in my mind. Like actually doing sex work has allowed me to be less of a disembodied brain than I sometimes have been, which is a really good antidote. . . . It kind of takes me out of my head.
>
> ELISE, 37, independent sex worker and freelance writer

> After I've had a busy day, you know, like four or five clients, I totally have a major buzz—I feel great! I also think it's good for me because I grew up in a very intellectual family and I have a very intellectual bent and this makes me get into my body. So my self-care practices around my body are so much better than they ever were. Before I did this work, I used to stuff my feelings away by

17 Developing bodily pride through sex work: Heather MacAllister (center) and her Fat-Bottom Erotic Revue (photo by Kina Williams).

> eating. . . . You know, I don't have perfect tits and I'm not a skinny person and for a long time I had issues with my breasts, which I still do to some extent, but I actually feel like it's helped me a tremendous amount knowing that my clients are so appreciative.
>
> ZOEY, 30, erotic masseuse and former social worker

Whereas street-based workers tended to develop instrumental relations to their bodies (dividing them into "public" and "private" regions; studiously transforming their appearances for public display), middle-class sex workers self-consciously attempted to integrate an ethos of bodily pleasure, appreciation, and authenticity into their occupational practices and their aesthetic ambitions.

BOUNDED AUTHENTICITY AND THE SINGLE SELF

Ironically, it is precisely among the sex workers who are the most strident purveyors of the term "sex work" that sexual labor is most likely to implicate one's "private" erotic and emotional life. Those who have fought hardest for the social and political recognition of prostitution as "work" (as opposed to a uniquely degrading violation of self) are also those for whom the paid sexual encounter is likely to include emotionally engaged conversation as well as a diversity of sexual activities (bodily caresses, genital touching, cunnilingus, and even occasional mouth-to-mouth kisses, rather than simply intercourse or fellatio), requires a larger investment of time with each client (typically at least an hour, as opposed to fifteen minutes for streetwalkers), and is more likely to take place within the confines of one's own home.[43] Since sex workers generally charge by the hour rather than for specified acts, their sexual labor is diffuse and expansive rather than delimited and expedient.

With the relocation of sexual labor from the street to indoor venues such as private homes, rented apartments, and "gentlemen's clubs," both the setting and the quality of sexual labor are transformed. The practices and meanings that accompany sexual labor have shifted in accordance with the new geographic boundaries of vice. In modern prostitution, what was typically sold and bought was an expedient and emotionally contained exchange of cash for sexual release. To survive in the trade, prostitutes learned to develop strategies to distance themselves from their labor, to treat their commercial sexual activity as "work." Many streetwalkers whom I spoke with gave evidence of this strategy when they stressed the importance of maintaining a division between public and private selves and of keeping certain sexual practices, aspects of the self, and segments of the body off limits. By contrast, within the emergent postindustrial paradigm of sexual commerce that I have been describing, what is bought and sold frequently incorporates a great deal more emotional as well as physical labor within the commercial context. Just at the historical moment when some women are fighting to reclassify "prostitution" under the banner of "sex work" (a morally neutral, rational market activity), the sexual labor that is performed within the transaction is more likely to involve emotions and eroticism that had formerly been relegated to the private sphere.

Yet the attachment of a monetary fee to the transaction constitutes a crucial element in the erotic exchange, not merely for the sake of material provision but at emotional levels as well. As I shall describe in more detail in the next chapter, sex workers who recounted occasionally offering "bargain rates" or unpaid sexual arrangements to preferred clients soon discovered that they wound up repelling the very clients they wished to keep. As with other forms of service work (therapy, massage, etc.), successful commercial transactions are ones in which the market basis of the exchange provides an important emotional boundary for

both worker and client, but one which can also be temporarily subordinated to the client's desire for authentic interpersonal connection.[44]

In contrast to the quick, impersonal "sexual release" associated
with the street-level sex trade, much of the new variety of sexual labor
resides in the provision of what I call "bounded authenticity"—the sale
and purchase of authentic emotional and physical connection. Beginning with Dean MacCannell's classic study, *The Tourist*, students of
tourism have connected the rise of the tourist industry to the pursuit of
the "authentic" in a world in which capitalism is perceived to have rendered more and more quarters of social life "artificial." Contemporary
theorists of middle-class tourism to the third world have extended this
insight, noting that for the new middle classes in particular, the pursuit
of "the authentic" in consumption and travel often provides consumers
with a sense of distinction, the sense that one is capable of appreciating
that which is "untouched" and accessible to only a few.[45] In her recent
study of strip club patrons, the anthropologist Katharine Frank has
noted that men's visits to strip clubs resemble a form of "postmodern
touristic practice" in that men often place a premium on "realness"
(authenticity) in their interactions with strippers. Frank argues that
clients' desire for authenticity is palpable even amid the postmodern
simulations of makeup, costumes, breast implants, and stage names
(not to mention cash exchange). This desire finds expression in their
frequently stated preference for exotic dancers who exhibit the "natural look," who personify "the girl next door," and who can engage
in conversation with frequency and ease.[46] Drawing on ethnographic
observations and in-depth interviews, Frank documents the numerous
ways that clients seek to signal authenticity in their commercial sexual
transactions with strippers, including payments through gifts or cock-
tails (more personal than cash transactions) and their persistent interest in dancers' real lives and identities.[47]

In my own research, evidence of middle-class sex workers' efforts
to manufacture authenticity resided in their descriptions of trying to
simulate—or even produce—genuine desire, pleasure, and erotic interest for their clients. Whereas in some cases this involved mere "surface
acting" (as with Amanda, below) it could also involve the emotional
and physical labor of manufacturing authentic (if fleeting) libidinal and
emotional ties with clients, endowing them with a sense of desirability,
esteem, or even love. In contrast to the "counterfeit intimacy" that
some sociological researchers have presumed to occur in the commercial sexual encounter, many sex workers' depictions of their work ex-
emplified the calling forth of genuine feeling that Arlie Hochschild has

termed "deep acting" and that Wendy Chapkis has described as the "emotional labor" of sex:[48]

> When I first started out, I enjoyed the sex. I'd go to work and "have sex." Now, I don't have that association as much. But my clients seem to think that being a nice guy means being a good lover. They do things to me that they should do with a girlfriend. Like they ask me what I'm into, and apologize for coming too soon! So I need to play along. They apparently have no idea that the best client is the one that comes immediately.
>
> AMANDA, 38, escort

> What I've noticed is that a lot of people really want to be witnessed when they come. They really want to feel that. You know, I totally get their desire and I want to be able to offer that. And so what I've learned how to do is to look at them deeply and very, very lovingly. . . . For them, it feels great, like it's so personal, like girlfriend stuff. But I feel that I'm just offering them . . . love from the earth, coming up my feet and coming out to them. So they get love. I'm just channeling love.
>
> ZOEY, 32, erotic masseuse

This experience was also common among the middle-class male escorts with whom I spoke:

> In a way, I'm surprised that there isn't *more* of a market among men for prostitution. . . . You'll hear people talk about "cold, mechanical, detached." But to me it's one of the most beautiful things you can do. It's like a sacred, wonderful, beautiful thing to do for other people and to get money for doing that. I think if more people knew that with a good whore you're getting a lot more than sex, you know? The down side of that for me, and maybe for the clients—is that I get seized sometimes by a horrible loneliness after it. That's why it's so hard to do more than one [client] a day. Because it's like I gave someone all that love and all that affection and everything, and then suddenly it's all over, boom.
>
> MICHAEL, 37, escort

In addition to satisfying clients' desires for bounded authenticity, many sex workers placed a premium on ensuring that the labor felt meaningful to themselves. Through the recent development of "blogging," a growing number of middle-class women have taken to

About Me: i work as a sexuality educator and research & write for a sexual health organization. through my academic studies, i explore larger sexual themes of identity and experience. sex work allows me to synthesize these fields. i love being a sex worker and more specifically i love being a whore. i am not ashamed of the work i do as i believe i am improving my clients' quality of life (as well as my own) through our encounters. yes, i worry about legal issues and being outed to certain conservative friends and family members, but these sentiments are similar to those surrounding my queer identity. however, i also feel sex worker community and visibility are important to constructing the support system necessary for positive sex work experiences.

18 Excerpt from a sex-worker blog, www.educatedslut.com. (The site is no longer active).

writing about their experiences doing sex work and the satisfactions and disappointments that they have encountered. Part advertisement for their services and part vehicle for self-expression, Web sites for escort-bloggers boast hundreds of members nationwide. On one popular escort blogspot, Magdalene Meretrix describes the philosophy that she brings to her experience of sex work as "a combination of mysticism, meditation, and the magical arts." Meretrix makes clear that she regards her work as more than an occupation, noting that it has been a "vital component of her spiritual path." In a similar vein, Zoey spoke to me during our interview about creating meaning and authenticity for herself in sex work by offering her clients only the kinds of erotic experiences that she herself enjoyed giving ("I start out each session with a meditation, getting them into their breath and guiding them through a body awareness exercise. I don't go into those sessions teaching my client how to pleasure me like a lover, but I *do* teach them how to pleasure me by receiving the service that I offer"). As Frank's research and my own both make clear, what is bought and sold in many contemporary commercial sexual transactions is something that is at once distinct from both premodern and modern-industrial paradigms of sexual exchange. The transactions that I have been describing resemble neither the informal barter of premodern exchanges nor the (prototypically modern) emotion-free, Taylorized provision of sexual release. In postindustrial sexual commerce, emotional authenticity is incorporated explicitly into the economic contract.

As opposed to the "double self" that many streetwalkers drew on as an emotional resource for facilitating their engagement in sex work,

COYOTE's sex workers aspired to a "single self" with no steadfast divisions between "front stage" and "back stage" or between public and private erotic domains.[49] Not incidentally, many of the members of COYOTE that I met were unpartnered and without children, and the majority described themselves as nonmonogamous, bisexual, and experimental. Many members espoused an ideology of sexual fluidity that (along with the necessary economic capital) enabled them to serve as both sellers and occasional buyers of sexual services.[50] In fact, the ethical and social world they inhabited was a fair approximation of "the universal market in bodies and services" that Carole Pateman predicted would arise if the logic of contract were allowed completely free reign.[51]

SEX-WORKER CHIC

In a dimly lit, cavernous nightclub, located in the fashionable South of Market district in San Francisco, Fairy Butch (the ambiguously gendered and flamboyant hostess) presents an erotic cabaret on alternate Friday nights of each month. The show features performers—and audience members—of diverse sexual orientations and gender presentations. The show's unstated ambition is to subvert the conventional status-based hierarchies that have characterized most commercial sexual transactions (in which young, attractive women with excessively marked feminine attributes provide sexual services to typically older, typically richer, typically less attractive men). Here, by contrast, there is no sharp line drawn between women and men, between objects and subjects, or between bodies and desires.

Tonight, the crowd is predominantly white, female, and young—from twenty to thirty years of age. There are butch women in jeans with shaved heads and tattooed biceps; women in three-piece suits with skinny neckties; apple-cheeked young women in college sweatshirts; and women in high-femme regalia with deep red lips. The few men present are markedly queer: one sports a lime-green mane of hair and a tight t-shirt; another wears a tiny halter top that exposes his well-muscled chest, pierced nipples, and smooth skin.

To the right of me is a bar packed six-deep with patrons. Many clamor to catch the attention of the one harried bartender; others are there to take advantage of the sturdy wooden railing to support their weight, since seating is so scarce. For those who lack the stamina to weave their way through the hundred-some sweaty bodies that block the path to the stage, there are small television monitors suspended from the ceiling at regular intervals to broadcast the floor show. Far at the other end of the club resides the small, spotlighted, platformed stage. It is surrounded by a ring of delicate metal tables—built for two, but in this case, accommodating as many as six or seven, piled high and precariously on one another's laps. The area is jam-packed, the atmosphere, flirty and boisterous, and the erotic tension palpable, even before the event begins.

Around 10 p.m., Fairy Butch makes her much-anticipated entrance onto the stage to inaugurate the show. Fairy Butch is a large, solid woman who appears to be in her early thirties, with a dark crew cut, a square jaw, and a broad smile. Tonight, she is dressed in classic cabaret-host style, with a tuxedo, tails, and a neat bowtie. She hams it up during her opening monologue, much to the delight of the very appreciative and engaged audience members, who revel in shouting back snappy and sexually explicit retorts. Before exiting, she plugs some of the other products and services that are available for purchase on her Web site: a new sexual advice book that instructs women on the fine points of "strap-on sex," and multilevel instructional seminars (as well as private lessons) on a variety of sexual techniques. Among the classes listed are "Dyke Sex Tips for Straight Couples" and a "Sex and Identity Intensive Workshop." Her final gesture is to solicit interested audience members to audition for an upcoming erotic review that features performers who are at least forty years of age.

The lights dim even further, a dramatic chord sounds from the speakers, and the first exotic dancer of the evening appears. Dressed seductively in black leather with a slim, muscular physique, short black hair, and a masked face, the performer's gender is a mystery—at least, for the moment, to me. The arms move with bold, sleek gestures over chest and leather-clad pelvis, which gyrates to the accelerating beat. Then the dancer leaps from the stage and out into the audience, straddling the thighs of those audience members who have beckoned for individual attention, and planting deep tongue kisses on the mouths of the most eager. In response, the audience members place rolled up five-dollar bills in the dancer's tight leather pants pockets. Finally, after the music changes to mark the end of this suspenseful opening sequence, the mask, shirt, and trousers are whisked away to reveal the compact form of a young, wiry Asian man. The crowd, shocked and delighted, roars.

FIELD NOTES, SAN FRANCISCO, MARCH 1998

The contingent of San Francisco sex workers that I have been describing calls into question a number of common feminist presuppositions about what is actually for sale in the commercial sexual encounter, and the likely impact of such transactions on the body and psyche of the sex worker (recall Høigård and Finstad's *Backstreets*, which summarized these as quick and anonymous sexual encounters predicated on mind/body dissonance and economic desperation). As my discussion here has revealed, COYOTE sex workers engage in forms of sexual labor that pose a potent challenge to commonsense perceptions about what erotic labor consists of and the configurations of gender, sexuality, and labor that underpin it. To be clear: I am not arguing that the newly emergent forms of sexual labor that COYOTE sex workers represent are unconnected to individuals' material conditions or to their structural locations within a social world that is characterized by increasingly profound inequalities. I *am* suggesting, however, that contemporary sex workers are often situated in highly complex ways vis-à-vis axes of domination and subordination (both economically and sexually) and that the forms of oppression they experience within sex work may be less severe than those they experience elsewhere.

I am also suggesting that the forms and meanings with which they have endowed their labor are connected to a historically specific set of conditions of possibility. These conditions include a postindustrial economy that has rapidly driven up the cost of living in desirable urban centers, while at the same time creating a highly stratified occupational sector (one with a limited number of time-intensive, highly paid, and hard-to-acquire professional positions, but with ample quantities of poorly paid, temporary, and part-time "junk" jobs).[52] These economic developments are intricately connected to some of the ways that increasing numbers of young, urban middle-class people are restructuring their intimate lives—either by delaying marriage and childbearing until these are more economically viable options, or by defying the expectations of heterosexual monogamy entirely.[53]

Middle-class participation in sexual labor must also be situated in terms of a broader cultural "mainstreaming" of sexual commerce, the supply and demand for which have arguably been facilitated by some of the same economic and social conditions. A significant transformation of public culture has occurred in recent decades, one which is in need of more serious theorizing than the moralizing commentary of the Religious Right (and certain feminists) has offered. The most tangible markers of the new public culture of sex commerce have included the mainstreaming and ubiquity of pornography, the normalization of commercial sexual products for women consumers (e.g., lingerie, sex toys, and instructional videos), and the surging popularity of the "sex-worker memoir" as a literary genre.[54] Despite the recent challenges posed by an increasingly conservative federal government, the sex-workers' rights movement has continued to flourish and to receive greater visibility. One sign of this visibility has been the emergence of *$pread Magazine,* the first-ever monthly magazine about the sex industry that is available at newsstands and geared toward industry workers as well as the general public. Another important sign has been the continued expansion and diversification of the field of sex-workers' rights organizations. In February of 2005, the UCLA branch of the Sex Workers' Outreach Project (SWOP-USA) became the first officially registered student sex-worker organization at a major university.[55]

Notably, all of these developments occurred during the very same period when public streetwalking was being eliminated from major urban centers and a new global panic around third world and child prostitutes was beginning to gather steam. In New York City, for example, at the very same moment that Manhattan's sex clubs, street-walkers, and porn stores were being banished by Rudolph Giuliani's famous "adult entertainment" zoning ordinances, new members-only erotic events were being mainstreamed for a white, middle-class, and largely female clientele, who crowded into upscale "sex parties" by the hundreds.[56] At the same time that Times Square's Harmony Burlesque Theatre was shut down, Victoria's Secret was replacing the district's "live nude girls" with mannequins posed as strippers and donning frankly pornographic lingerie. Meanwhile, the ethos of the strip club continued its spread into privatized spaces, as "cardio-striptease" and "sensual dance" classes became staple features of the home video market and city gyms.[57]

The magnitude of this shift was well-illustrated for me again recently when a former sex-worker activist and current PhD student in sociology, Siobhan Brooks, gave a guest lecture in my Sociology of Gender class at Barnard College. Brooks began her lecture with a reference to the changing racial profile of women in the local sex industry, referring not to the influx of third world women into sexual servitude but to the *whitening* of the sex trade, which she attributed to the rise of "sex-worker chic" among the urban middle classes. "The new face of sexual labor," she explained, "looks a lot like the women in this room." To illustrate her point, she asked the sixty-some students present (the vast majority of whom were white, class-privileged young women) how many of them had friends who had ever worked in the sex industry. Approximately a third of the students in the room raised their hands. As this pedagogical exercise and the comparative research that I conducted in Stockholm and Amsterdam make clear (see chap. 6), the transformations that I observed during the course of my research in San Francisco were not unique to a particular set of individuals or even to a particular city but portended a much broader cultural trend.[58]

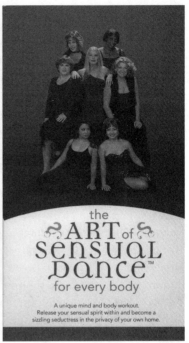

19 Domesticating sex work: a Victoria's Secret display window in New York City's Times Square, and an instructional video, "The Art of Sensual Dance for Every Body" (photo by author).

CONCLUSION

In this chapter, I have argued that the emergence of "sex work" as both an ideological term and a set of lived possibilities is a development that must be situated socially and historically. The normalization and professionalization of commercial sexual exchange as "sex work," as much as the receding landscape of the deviant underworld of "prostitution" that I described in chapters 2 and 3, are phenomena reflective of interrelated features of postindustrial life: transformations in economic practices and intimate relations, the reconfiguration of urban space, and changing social norms around gender and sexuality.

In contrast to modern forms of sexual labor such as streetwalking, COYOTE sex workers bring a constellation of subjective meanings and embodied practices to commercial sexual exchange that would not have been possible at earlier historical junctures. These new meanings and practices emanate from an explicit challenge to the symbolic dualisms that have characterized paradigmatically modern forms of sexual labor: between private and public, home and work, "good girls" and "bad girls," and between sexuality and the market. Deeply implicated in these cultural inversions, their sexual labor cannot be reduced to matters of socioeconomic deprivation, in the conventional sense of the term. And, crucially (as I will further demonstrate in the next chapter), the sexual labor of COYOTE participants reconfigures earlier assumptions about the gendered double standard of sexuality, as it begins to shift the site of presumed sexual alienation from the body of the female prostitute to the body of the male client.

Thus far, I have explored the various ways that postindustrial cultural and economic patterns have served to reshape the practices and experiences of contemporary sex workers who inhabit different social spaces and professional tiers; in what follows, I move to the reformulated social meanings associated with purchasing sex—that is, to the client's point of view.

5 | Desire, Demand, and the Commerce of Sex

Suddenly, the car takes off. We're moving again, but I'm not quite sure whom we're following. Apparently, a woman has gotten into the car ahead of us with a date. We proceed at full speed about a block or two, over train tracks, to a deserted stretch of territory with few cars or people. The area is in fact completely barren except for a few abandoned warehouses. Despite the gleaming California sunshine, the atmosphere is tense.

Everything happens in a flash. In mere minutes, it's all over, we slam the brakes on, and two of the officers hop out. They motion for me to join them.

The other members of the Street Crimes unit have already arrived on the scene. They have stopped a blue Chevrolet truck and handcuffed the driver, a large but trembling man who is trying to be obsequious in spite of being terrified. Two of the officers have their guns pointed toward him. In addition to the arresting officer, the sergeant and another policeman also surround the suspect. Meanwhile, the female officers beckon the passenger, Carla, from her seat and begin to talk to her. They are trying to get her side of the story so that they can use it as evidence. Carla is high on drugs and rather weary but still lucid. She is apparently one of the numerous street prostitutes whom the officers know by name, since she has been arrested repeatedly during the ten or so years that she has been working. But today she is not the main focus of their attention.

I hover in the background, absorbing the drama of the surrounded man, the drawn guns, the momentary displays of power and fear. My heart pounding, I try to listen, feeling vaguely guilty about being a part of this. The arresting officer delivers a rapid-clip, tough-guy, made-for-TV monologue:

I want you to tell me what happened. . . . Remember, we've spoken to her so we know. . . . What were you thinking? . . . Did you use a condom? . . . No? So you came in her mouth? . . . Did you even look at her? Did you see that disgusting shit she has on her hands? Now it's all over your wee-wee. . . . Do you have a wife or girlfriend? Now you're going to go home and give whatever you just got to her. Every man's thought of it, but you don't need to take chances. Next time you're feeling horny, why don't you just buy some porn and jack off?

Before releasing their detainee, the officers issue him a written citation and a court date.

Much later that same evening, I arrive at a famed "erotic theater" with a friend, tired but intrigued. The theater has a reputation for being one of the most upscale of the seventeen legal sex clubs in the area, where strip-tease, lap dances, and, in recent years, hand jobs and blow jobs are widely if unofficially available for purchase. We wade through the small crowd of Asian businessmen standing outside and make our way to the entrance. A middle-aged man with glasses politely takes our money ($45 each) with no perceptible surprise that we should choose to come here—even though we are clearly the evening's only female customers. A basket of condoms sits prominently by the door.

Again in straightforward fashion, an employee proceeds to give us a tour and to describe the various shows. The rooms have names like the "VIP Club" and the "Luxury Lounge." The premises are dimly lit but clean, orderly, and rather spare. The floors are bare yet spotless. We head over to the main stage in the back room, where a young tanned and toned woman in a sparkly thong bikini is doing a dance to the accompaniment of strobe lights and disco. She twists and turns, gyrates and thrusts, opens and closes her legs. Her featured partner is a long, silver pole that protrudes upright from the floor. As the male customers watch the show, I watch *them*. They crane their necks to get a better view of the dancer. All of the seats are filled, and it's standing room only. "Imagine coming home to *that*," gushes a forty-something, white man in a dark business suit and red tie to one of his colleagues. The performance concludes with the dancer making her way into the audience and sidling up to individual men, who caress the surface of her body and push $20 bills under her garter.

Many of the customers are extremely young: under twenty-five, perhaps under twenty, white, baseball-capped and sporting casual attire. These contingents have clearly come in groups. The thirty- and forty-something, suited white businessmen seem to comprise another category, and also cluster together in groups of three or four. Then there are the loners—again, typically under fifty years of age, predominantly white, with a sprinkling of blacks and Latinos. All are able-bodied, of average looks and builds. By mere appearances, they certainly belie the stereotype that the sex industry is geared toward older men who can't find partners.

In a room called "Copenhagen Live," a central stage is encircled by a sunken ring of little cubicles, each partitioned off from the performance area by fine, black mesh curtains. This design allows the heads and bodies of the customers to protrude through to the stage, and for the women to protrude back through to the booths in the other direction. A surrounding wall of mirrors above the cubicles means that each customer can see every other customer, as well as the performers. Two young, beautiful women come out, both with gleaming, waist-length hair and very high heels, naked but for black-and-white midriff corsets which leave their breasts and genitals exposed. They perform a highly choreographed and stylized sex act together, kissing and licking. Then, despite an earlier staff person's admonishment that body parts must remain within the booths, the women come over individually to each booth to ask if anyone would like a "show." Both of them soon descend into the dark cubicles where they are grasped by eager hands, momentarily disappearing from our line of vision.

FIELD NOTES, SAN FRANCISCO BAY AREA, MAY 1999

Feminists and other scholars have debated theoretically what is "really" purchased in the prostitution transaction. Is it a relationship of domination? Is it love, an addiction, pleasure? Can sex be a service like any other? Only recently have they begun to tackle this question empirically.[1] This chapter draws on field observations of and interviews with male clients of commercial sex workers as well as the state agents who are entrusted with regulating them in order to probe the meanings ascribed by different types of consumers to commercial sexual exchange, and to situate such exchanges within the broader context of postindustrial transformations of sexuality and culture.[2]

I begin with the two paradoxical ethnographic images above. The first describes the new and growing phenomenon of the arrest of clients of female street prostitutes, an unprecedented strategy of direct state intervention in public expressions of heterosexual male desire. In the late 1990s, for the first time ever, U.S. cities such as San Francisco and New York began to boast arrest rates of male clients which approached those of female prostitutes, reversing a historical pattern that feminists had long criticized.[3] The second takes us to a local strip club, where (technically illegal) commercial sex acts are consumed as relatively un-problematic instances of sexual entitlement and male bonding.

In Western Europe and the United States, recent state efforts to problematize men's demand for sexual services—rising client arrests and reeducation via diversion programs such as "John School"; ve-hicle impoundment; stricter domestic and international laws on the patronage of illegal migrant or underage prostitutes and the possession of child pornography—have occurred in the face of an increasingly unbridled ethic of sexual consumption.[4] During the last thirty years, demand for commercially available sexual services has not only soared but become ever more specialized, diversifying along technological, spatial, and social lines. These contradictory social developments re-veal a tension between sex-as-recreation and the normative push for a return to sex-as-romance, a cultural counterpart of which can be found in the simultaneous emergence of Viagra and twelve-step languages of masculine sexual addiction. "Sex" as cultural imperative and technical quest, now freed from the bounds of domesticity and romance, and the rendering of nonrelationally bound erotic behavior as a pathological "addiction" are products of the same place and time.[5] The goal of this chapter is to unravel this paradox.

Some have attributed recent attempts to reform male sexuality to the gains of second-wave feminism, and even described a shift in social stigma from the seller to the buyer of sexual services.[6] Yet the influence of larger, structural factors has been neglected in most discussions. In fact, state interventions in (a typically lower-class tier of) male het-erosexual practices, and the regendering of sexual stigma in certain masculine middle-class fractions can both be linked to some of the broader transformations that have produced the burgeoning demand for sexual services in the first place. In the industrializing nineteenth and early twentieth centuries, the "wrong" in prostitution was seen to reside in the prostitute herself, and, in the classical writings of social science, prostitution as a social institution was portrayed as the su-preme metaphor for the exploitation of wage labor. With the transition from a production-based to a consumption-based economy, the focus of moral critique and political reform is gradually being displaced: the prostitute is increasingly normalized as either a "victim" or "sex worker," while attention and social sanction—at municipal, national, and transnational levels—are directed away from labor practices and toward consumer behavior.[7]

In what follows, I first sketch a brief genealogy of the academic and political discourses surrounding male sexual desire and consumer demand that have developed over the past century. I next take the reader to a variety of settings in which commercial sexual consumption takes place, in order to explore the meanings and motivations that contemporary clients ascribe to their own activities. In the final section, I contrast these framings with recent attempts by state agencies to reshape demand in the wake of a booming and diversifying sexual marketplace. My discussion throughout is based on fifteen in-depth interviews with male sexual consumers, a review of local newspapers and other print and electronic media, and ethnographic fieldwork in commercial sexual markets collected in five northern California and Western European cities.[8]

EXPLAINING COMMERCIAL SEXUAL DEMAND

Like that of social policy, the scholarly literature on prostitution has typically viewed the varied phenomena of sexual commerce through a narrow focus on the etiology, treatment, and social symbolism of the female prostitute. Although the moral reformers in the late nineteenth-century United States sought to problematize male sexuality, their campaign to replace the prevailing double standard of sexual behavior with a single female standard that would be officially encoded into state policy met with little success.[9] After the Progressive Era, far less social or scholarly attention was paid to prostitution, as sociology and psychology both reinscribed the double standard and rendered prostitution not only unproblematic for the male clientele but structurally integral to the institution of marriage.[10] In the 1970s and the 1980s, both the sociology of deviance and feminist theory saw the prostitute (but not the client) as a symbolically laden precipitate of larger social currents. Although some second-wave feminists critiqued the lack of attention to male clients, as well as the sexual double standard that underpinned it (as Gail Pheterson noted, "the characteristic of separating desire from love, which is considered neurotic in women, is recognized as 'typical' in men"), empirical literature with a sustained focus on male sexual clients has been slow to emerge.[11]

Over the course of the last two decades, a small but growing number of ethnographic and interview-based studies of client behavior have been undertaken by a new generation of social researchers.[12] Meanwhile, building on Kinsey's earlier—if methodologically flawed—work, as well as heeding feminist calls to render male sexual clients visible, quantitative researchers have begun to correlate proclivity for client behavior with other sociodemographic patterns.[13] Analyzing data from the 1993 University of Chicago National Health and Social Life Survey, researchers Elliot Sullivan and William Simon found factors such as age cohort, military experience, education, and racial/ethnic background to be statistically significant predictors of commercial sexual purchase.[14] In terms of racial patterns, for example, Sullivan and Simon found that, among men with no military experience, African American and Hispanic men were twice as likely as white men to have visited a prostitute.[15]

Commercial sexual proclivity has furthermore been shown by recent sociological researchers to vary systematically with a variety of attitudinal dispositions, including "socio-emotional problems," as measured by reported feelings of emotional and physical dissatisfaction, feeling unwanted and sexually unsatisfied, and, most interestingly, by "not hav[ing] sex as an expression of love."[16] It has also been correlated with a "commodified" view of sexuality, as measured by number of sexual partners, use of pornography, and the belief that one needs to have sex immediately when aroused.[17]

Finally, client behavior has increasingly been featured as a key component of broader qualitative studies on commercial sexual exchange.[18] A primary agenda of this work has, again, been to subject the heretofore invisible male sex buyer to a sociological and political gaze. Drawing on field data and interviews, qualitative researchers have generated typologies of clients and consumer motivations. Whereas sociological research on female prostitutes has typically been driven by questions of etiology (How did she get that way? Why would a woman do that?), this research highlights differences between men, but typically takes men's status as purchasers for granted. The primary motivations identified by these authors include clients' desire for sexual variation, sexual access to partners with preferred ages, racialized bodies, and specific physiques, the appeal of an "emotion-free" and clandestine sexual encounter, loneliness, marital problems, the quest for power and control, the desire to be dominated or for other "exotic" sex acts, and the thrill of violating taboos. While provocative and insightful, one deficit that characterizes the majority of this work is the failure to explain client motives with historical specificity, or to link clients' motives to social and economic institutions that might themselves structure the relations of gender dominance that are implied by the explanatory categories listed above. In general, typologies are presented as if they were distinct attributes of a transhistorical and unwavering masculinity.

Two notable exceptions to this tendency are the diversely situated anthropological and sociological accounts of client behavior by Anne Allison and Monica Prasad.[19] In Allison's *Nightwork,* an ethnography of a Tokyo "hostess club" where beautiful young women serve businessmen drinks and light their cigarettes, keep the banter flirtatious, and make their bodies available for groping, all at corporate expense, Allison draws on Frankfurt school theory in order to argue that "the convergence of play and work and player and worker, supposed and presupposed by the institution of company-paid entertainment, is a feature of any society progressing through the late stages of capitalism."[20] According to Allison, Japanese businessmen's nightly participation in the *mizu shobai,* or erotic nightlife, as well as their emotional distance from their wives and families, epitomizes this historical trend.

Meanwhile, in "The Morality of Market Exchange," an article that draws on telephone interviews with male sexual customers and which engages economic sociologists' classic distinction between market and premarket societies, Prasad argues that the prostitution exchange contains within it a form of morality that is specific to mass-market societies. Her interviews reveal that

> customers conduct the prostitution exchange in ways that are not very different from how most market exchanges are conducted today: information about prostitution is not restricted to an elite but is widely available; social settings frame the interpretation of this information; the criminalization of prostitution does not particularly hinder the exchange; and whether the exchange continues is often dictated by how well the business was conducted. In short, according to these respondents, in late-capitalist America sex is exchanged almost like any other commodity.[21]

Noting that her interviewees "praise 'market exchange' of sex for lacking the ambiguity, status-dependence, and potential hypocrisy that they see in the 'gift exchange' of sex characteristic of romantic relationships," Prasad goes on to remark that in the "fervently free-market 1980s and 1990s, romantic love might sometimes be subordinated to, and judged unfavorably with, the more neutral, more cleanly exchangeable pleasures of eroticism."[22]

Unlike many treatments of sexual clients, the contributions of Allison and Prasad situate sexual consumption within the context of an expanded and normalized field of commercial sexual transactions. Their analyses begin to reveal a shift from a relational to a *recreational* model of sexual behavior, a reconfiguration of erotic life in which the pursuit of sexual intimacy is not hindered but facilitated by its location in the marketplace.[23]

THE SUBJECTIVE CONTOURS OF MARKET INTIMACY

I'm by myself a lot, used to it, but sometimes I crave physical contact. I'd rather get it from someone I don't know because someone I do will want more. You get lonely. There's this girl right now I'm seeing. I like the attention. But that's it, in a nutshell. I find [prostitution] exciting, kind of fun. It's amazing that it's there. More people would participate if it weren't illegal. A lot of frustration in both sexes could be eliminated.

DON, 47, house painter

I feel guilty every time I cheat on my wife. I'm not a psychopath. I try to hide it as much as possible. I had a nonprofessional affair once. It was nice, and intimate, and I didn't have to pay! But I felt more guilty about that, messing with someone else's life, even though she knew I was married. You don't ever have to worry about that when you pay for it. I'm conservative by nature, but I believe in freedom of choice. If a woman wants to do it, more power to her! She's providing a service. I'm not exploiting her. Exploitation would be finding some hot 25-year-old who doesn't know any better and taking her to lunches, then to bed.

STEVE, 35, insurance manager

My wife has never understood my desire to do this. I have no problem with my wife. We have a good sexual relationship. There's a Vietnamese restaurant on Sixth and Market that I love, but I don't want to eat there every day...

RICK, 61, data processor

I started seeing escorts during a time when I didn't have many venues to meet women. I felt isolated. My friends had moved away, and I was lacking motivation. It's more real and human than jacking off alone. My first preference was to pick up women for casual sex. Since that wasn't happening, I got into the habit. It was so easy.

DAN, 36, research analyst

Among the disparate themes that animate clients' accounts of their motivations for purchasing sexual services runs one counterintuitive thread. As Monica Prasad and Anne Allison found, for increasing numbers of men erotic expression and the ethos of the commercial marketplace are by no means antithetical. Indeed, contemporary client narratives of sexual consumption challenge the key cultural opposition between public and private that has anchored modern capitalism.

Theorists of gender have sometimes regarded the recent growth of the commercial sex industry as a reactionary reassertion of male dominance in response to the gains of second-wave feminism, or as compensation for men's economic disempowerment in the postindustrial public sphere.[24] In such scenarios, the role of commercial sex is to provide the male client with a fantasy world of sexual subservience and consumer abundance that corrects for the real power deficits that he experiences in his daily life. While not disputing such accounts, I would like to suggest that men's quest for market-mediated sexual intimacy is guided by an additional set of historical transformations.

"Compensatory" arguments regarding men's persistent desire for commercial sexual encounters rest on the implicit premise that prostitution as an institution caters to needs that would preferably and more fulfillingly be satisfied within an intimate relationship in the private sphere of the home.[25] Yet for many sexual clients, the market is experienced as enhancing and facilitating desired forms of nondomestic sexual activity. This is true whether what the client desires is a genuine but emotionally bounded intimate encounter, the experience of being pampered and "serviced," participation in a wide variety of brief sexual liaisons, or an erotic interlude that is "more real and human" than would be satisfying oneself alone. The by now platitudinous insight that sexuality has been "commodified"—and by implication, diminished—like everything else in late capitalism does not do justice to the myriad ways in which the spheres of public and private, intimacy and commerce, have interpenetrated one another and been mutually transformed, making the postindustrial consumer marketplace a prime arena for securing varieties of interpersonal connection that circumvent this duality.

For many clients, one of the chief virtues of commercial sexual exchange is the clear and bounded nature of the encounter. In prior historical epochs, this "bounded" quality may have provided men with an unproblematic and readily available sexual outlet to supplement the existence of a pure and asexual wife in the domestic sphere. What is unique to contemporary client narratives is certain men's explicitly stated *preference* for this type of bounded intimate engagement over other relational forms. For at least some clients, paid sex is neither a sad substitute for something that one would ideally choose to obtain in a noncommodified romantic relationship, nor the inevitable outcome of a traditionalist Madonna/Whore double standard. Don, a forty-seven-year-old, never-married man from Santa Rosa, California, described the virtues of the paid sexual encounter this way:

> I really like women a lot, but they're always trying to force a relationship on me. I'm a nice guy, and I feel this crushing thing happen. Right now, I know a woman, she's pretty, nice, but if I make

love to her, she'll want a relationship. But I'm really used to living by myself. I go and come when I want, clean when I want. I love women, enjoy them, they feel comfortable around me. I've always had a lot of women friends. I flirt and talk to them, but I don't usually take the next step, because it leads to trouble!

Much is lost if we try to subsume Don's statements under pop-psychologizing diagnoses such as "fear of intimacy," or even a more covertly moralistic social-psychological descriptor like "techniques of neutralization."[26] In Don's preference for a life constructed around living alone, intimacy through close friendships, and paid for, safely contained sexual encounters, we also see evidence of a disembedding of the (male) individual from the sex-romance nexus of the privatized nuclear family. This is a concrete example of the profound reorganization of personal life that diverse social analysts have noticed occurring during the last thirty or so years.[27]

An additional advantage of market-mediated sexual encounters was articulated by Steve, a married, thirty-five-year-old insurance manager from a middle-class California suburb. Frustrated that sexual relations with his wife had been relatively infrequent since the birth of their child, Steve had decided to look for sex elsewhere. Although elements of Steve's story invoke the sexual double standard of eras past, the reasoning that he displayed during our interview also revealed a decidedly new twist. For Steve, the market-mediated sexual encounter is morally and emotionally preferable to the "nonprofessional affair" because of the clarifying effect of payment. Though he characterized himself as "conservative by nature," Steve had incorporated a fair amount of sex-worker rights rhetoric into his own discourse, describing the sexual agency of his paid "service providers" with tangible awe. Having grappled with feminist critiques of male sexual indulgence as "exploitative," he concluded that true exploitation resided in the emotional dishonesty of the premarket paradigm of seduction, rather than in the clean cash-for-sex market transactions that he participated in.

In my interviews with clients, many men were insistent that their patronage of the commercial sexual economy did not in any way result from problems or deficits in their primary sexual relationships.[28] Rick, a sixty-one-year-old data processor from San Francisco, emphasized that his sexual relationship with his wife was just fine, and likened his desire to pay different women for sex to other, less socially problematic consumer experiences ("There's a Vietnamese restaurant . . . that I love, but I don't want to eat there every day"). Rick's statement may be seen as a variant of the classic argument that prostitution is an expression of the male "natural appetite"—a perspective which, like Steve's above, is of course premised on a notion of the sexual double standard. As Carole Pateman has pointed out, in such arguments, "The comparison is invariably made between prostitution and the provision of food." [29] Significantly, however, Rick's explicit justification for patronizing prostitutes is less one of essential, biological drives than it is one of simple and entitled consumer choice. Rick's stated preference for variety presumes an underlying model of sexuality in which sexual expression bears no necessary connection to a domestic-sphere relationship, and in which a diversity of sexual partners and experiences is not merely substitutive but desirable in its own right.

In the same vein, Stephen, a fifty-five-year-old writer from San Francisco, described an exciting and sexually adventurous life at home with his female partner of eight years. He chose to supplement this with once-a-month paid sexual encounters involving female exotic dancers and transgender prostitutes that were "fun" and "intriguing." "Sometimes it's a really nice contact, how they touch me, how they move, but it's not for something I can't get at home," he explained. Stephen went on to elaborate on some of his motivations for patronizing prostitutes:

> When I grew up, I was younger and shorter than everyone else, convinced I wasn't sexually desirable to anyone. I was two years ahead in school, a total nerd. The notion that these glamorous women want to persuade me to have sex with them is incredible. I understand that it's not because of my looks. I could never get this many women who are this gorgeous to be sexual with me if I didn't pay.

Interviewees like Stephen and Rick challenge a common second-wave feminist presupposition that prostitution exists simply to satisfy sexual demands which nonprofessional women find distasteful or are too inhibited to perform. Though sexual dissatisfaction within marriage may have at least partly characterized the motivations of a prior era of male sexual clients, in the contemporary sexual marketplace paid sex is often not seen as compensation for something lacking in men's primary domestic relationships. [30] Rather, commercial sex provides access to multiple attractive partners that—in the wake of the historical shift from the family-based "good provider role" to the unfettered, consumeristic "playboy philosophy"—many male sexual clients feel that they are *entitled* to. [31] This philosophy is also made ap-

20 Elegantly dressed bouncers awaiting clients outside a "gentleman's club" in San Francisco (photo by author).

parent in the upscaling of commercial sex venues that has occurred in U.S. cities since the 1980s, what the anthropologist Katherine Frank has described as the "intensified focus on the creation of 'atmosphere' and luxury." [32] Over the last two decades, "gentleman's clubs" and commercial sexual services with names like "Platinum Crown Escorts," "Prestige Escorts," "The Gold Club," and "VIP Massage" have proliferated to cater to clients' fantasies of consumptive class mobility. [33] Within the terms of this new cultural logic of male dominance, clients conjure the sexual marketplace as the great social equalizer, where consumer capitalism democratizes access to a caliber of goods and services that in earlier eras would have been the exclusive province of a restricted elite. [34]

The dominant aesthetic of Amsterdam's brothels is characterized by densely juxtaposed symbols of exoticism and luxury. This evening, a colleague and I found ourselves in the "Jungle Room" of one mid-range locale, where zebra-skin bedding was accompanied by leopard-print pillows, brightly colored

21 Some advertisements for escort agencies, as featured in the 2001 San Francisco Yellow Pages. While the promise of erotic connection is merely implied, the appeal to clients' fantasies of class mobility is made explicit.

lava lamps were perched atop the tabletops and dressers, and ruby-red walls forged dramatic contrasts with thick, white shag carpeting.

Like the other large brothels in the city, this one advertised free limousine service, which we politely declined. On announcing our destination to the driver of the taxi that we opted for instead, the young man pivoted in his seat to offer us a knowing wink. As soon as we entered the club, we were greeted by Erica, a buxom, chatty woman in her mid-thirties, who wore a shimmery black evening gown and had elaborate, upswept hair. She took our coats and guided us to a bar with sleek, chrome banisters, highly polished countertops, and light fixtures that were brilliantly agleam. The few clients who were already there appeared to be lower middle-class white men, with rounded bellies filling out their checkered shirts and jeans. Even more strikingly, all of the men spoke Dutch and gave the appearance of being locals—in stark contrast to the jet-setting international business executives that regularly appear in the club's ads.

Eight white, Dutch-speaking women somewhere between the ages of twenty and thirty-five sat at the bar, talking to the customers who were present. A pair of hunched, smoking men dressed casually in denim jackets glowered at us from time to time, while the third man who was present ignored us. Fiftyish, balding, and squat, he sat chatting up a twenty-something woman with dark wavy hair. The women here were not dressed in provocative red-light district clothes but instead donned vaguely sexy yet still respectable attire, as if they had come to the bar for recreational purposes—casual flirtation or drinks. Indeed the entire arrangement seemed designed to simulate a naturalized bar scene, with the notable exceptions of the skewed gender ratio and the implicit social contract that had been entered into by all participants, which stipulated that here, tonight, the men could go into the "Jungle Room" with whomever they pleased.

FIELD NOTES, AMSTERDAM, 2001

BOUNDED AUTHENTICITY AND THE "GFE"

Here is another man's account of his commercial sexual activity, this time from an Internet chat room for patrons of strip clubs:

> I finally got to spend some quality time in the city by the Bay, compliments of my employer, who decided that I needed to attend a conference there last week. So, armed with a vast array of knowledge regarding the local spots, I embarked on a week of fun and frolicking. Unfortunately, I ended up spending too much time with conference goers so I only made three trips to clubs. I had an absolutely incredible time at both places. . . . At the first club, I adjourned to the Patpong room with Jenny, who asked me what I was interested in. I said that a couple of nude lap dances were on the agenda and I inquired as to her price: $60 each. Okay, no problem. I forked over the cash. After the two long dances she offered me a blow job for another $120. I said that would be heavenly and handed her the money. . . . It was an absolutely fabulous experience. I spent $30 on cover charges, $10 on tips, $240 with Jenny, and $300 with another girl named Tanya for a total of $580. Not bad for just over two hours of illicit fun. I'm used to paying that for decent outcall so this was a nice change of pace.

Like many of the interviewees described above, this man is unselfconscious about constructing his experience as a form of light and unproblematic commercial consumption ("two hours of illicit fun," "a nice change of pace"). For clients such as this (who may describe themselves as "hobbyists" or "enthusiasts" in Internet chat rooms), prostitution is primarily a pampering diversion financed by and casually sandwiched in between a week's worth of requisite, and presumably less pleasurable, professional activities.

Yet the paid sexual encounter may also represent to clients something more than just an ephemeral consumer indulgence. In their 1982 article, "The Phenomenology of Being a John," Harold Holzman and Sharon Pines argued that it was the fantasy of a mutually desired, special, or even romantic sexual encounter that clients were purchasing in the prostitution transaction—something notably distinct both from a purely mechanical sex act *and* from an unbounded, private-sphere romantic entanglement. They observed that the clients in their study emphasized the warmth and friendliness of the sex worker as characteristics that were at least as important to them as the particulars of physical appearance. Katherine Frank has also noted the ways in which patrons of strip clubs frequently pursue signs of a female dancer's "sincerity" before choosing to interact with her (many comment that they specifically avoid dancers "who [are] doing this just to make money").[35] The clients that I interviewed were similarly likely to express variants of the statement that "If her treatment is cold or perfunctory, I'm not interested." And in Web-based client guides to commercial sexual services such as "The World Sex Guide," reviewers are consistently critical of sex workers who are "clockwatchers," "too rushed and pushy," who "don't want to hug and kiss," or who "ask for a tip mid–sex act."

One of the most sought after features in the prostitution encounter has thus become the "girlfriend experience," or GFE. Ads for escorts in print media and online now routinely feature this in their advertisements, and there are entire Web pages where people who specialize in this service can advertise.

Here is a description of what a GFE session might consist of, an account that was posted to an Internet chat forum by one sexual client:

> A typical non-GFE session with an escort includes one or more of the basic acts required for the customer to reach a climax at least one time, and little else. A GFE type session, on the other hand, might proceed much more like a non-paid encounter between two lovers. This may include a lengthy period of foreplay in which the customer and the escort touch, rub, fondle, massage, and perhaps even kiss passionately. A GFE session might also include activities where the customer works as hard to stimulate the escort as she works to stimulate him. Finally, a GFE session usually has a period of cuddling and closeness at the end of the session, rather than each partner jumping up and hurrying out as soon as the customer is finished.

Earlier, we saw how San Francisco's white middle-class sex workers often strived to obtain a sense of emotional authenticity in their work, tailoring this experience into a purchasable (and desirable) commodity for their clients. The first tier of paid "intimacy providers" to offer their clients the GFE were indeed white, native-born sex workers in possession of sufficient cultural and bodily capital to fulfill their clients' fantasies of sex with a social equal. More recently, however, in client chat rooms and on Internet bulletin boards, men have begun to note that "foreign" women are also highly skilled practitioners of the service. One client observed that "Asian, Latin, and Eastern European women . . . are in my experiences the most intimate and open to this type of physical intimacy." As the GFE expands from a local, elite specialty service to a broadly advertised, mass-market sexual commodity (even constituting a standard feature of the "menus" of sexual services available in brothels worldwide), the initially broad and ill-defined spectrum of activities offered under this banner has metamorphosed into simple shorthand for modern prostitution's conventionally denied mouth-to-mouth kiss. The most "natural" of intimate gestures, now offered back to the client in denaturalized and explicitly commodified form, the kiss has become a highly prized emblem of intimacy and authenticity.

As with other forms of service work, successful commercial sexual transactions are ones in which the market basis of the exchange serves a crucial delimiting function that can also be temporarily subordinated to the client's fantasy of authentic interpersonal connection, as the following chat room description of an encounter in a commercial sex club illustrates:

> At the club, I had a memorable experience with a light-skinned black girl named Luscious. . . . We adjoined to the backstage area for one full-service session during the course of my visit. This time I brought my condoms. We began with the usual touchy feely. . . . I could feel she was just soaking, an indication her moans were not faked. Several minutes later I shot my load and used the conveniently located Kleenex dispenser to wash up. The most unusual aspect of this encounter is that Luscious didn't ask for money up front which is a first for a place of this type. I tipped her $60.

Even when the encounter lasts only minutes, from the client's perspective it may represent a meaningful and authentic form of interpersonal exchange. Clients such as the one quoted above are indeed seeking a real and reciprocal erotic connection, but a precisely delimited one. For these men, what is (at least ideally) being purchased is a sexual connection that is premised on bounded authenticity. As with the above client's invocation of the physical tangibility of Luscious's desire, other clients boasted of their ability to give sex workers authentic sexual pleasure, insisted that the sex workers they patronized liked them enough to offer them freebies or to invite them home for dinner, and proudly proclaimed that they had at times even dated or befriended the sex workers they were seeing.

the original
GFE Escorts Dot Com

Girlfriend Experience

GFE escorts is a worldwide GFE escort directory with listings in Atlanta, Miami, Columbus, Cleveland and more! No memberships and no monthly fees! Soon we will offer a GFE review board! join us in the new year 2002 and see what we have to offer you! **What is GFE?** GFE means girlfriend experience. GFE is Full service with a new meaning! This means that you are in a relaxed atmosphere, un-rushed, almost like you're with your 'real girlfriend'. It is less of a business transaction and more like a date with the woman of your dreams! You must be over the age of 18 (21 in some areas) so please, leave if you're not 18 or unsure of the age laws in your city. Otherwise, please click enter below.

HOME
ABOUT
CONTACT ME
SERVICES
AVAILABILITY
STATISTICS
GALLERY

About Me

About You

Let me introduce myself. . . I have always been fascinated and intrigued by the play between a man and a woman; not just the physical aspects, but the emotional, the psychological, the ritual. . . all delight and continue to amaze me.

Don't get me wrong, I love the sheer physicality of sexuality, but I think what best describes what I am about and what I offer is a Social Companion Service, a girlfriend experience without the attachment. However, I find myself trying to avoid brief encounters as I seek to establish meaningful communication and friendship, seeing only a few clientele, remaining somewhat exclusive.

That being said, I am very well educated and a great conversationalist, skilled entertainer and a confidant of refined men. I have always had a taste for excellence. . . I could

About You

My ideal gentleman is a mature, educated professional 35 and over. You are sophisticated, worldly, caring, sensual, health conscious and with a good sense of humor.

Honest-open communication regarding desires and expectations will be most rewarding for both of us and lead to a lasting friendship.

22 Buying and selling the "Girlfriend Experience": a sampling of advertisements from contemporary commercial sex Web sites. These advertisements democratize

Ava
A True Girlfriend Experience

5'6"
130lbs
36DD-24-35
Sexy gray eyes, long brown curly hair, smooth chocolate skin, full luscious lips. Pretty face, curvy body with a dynamite personality to match.

It couldn't get any better.

I offer a true girlfriend experience without the headache. My measurements are real and so am I. I offer full service without additional fees(greek is additional though).

Incall is available in Manhattan only on Mondays. Please reserve ahead. NY/NJ outcall available. Same day appointments available also. Please call an hour ahead of time.

Check out my reviews on TheEroticReview!

---

access to socially and sexually accommodating women while catering to the bounded authenticity that clients seek.

Clients' repeated claims of authentic interpersonal connection are particularly striking to consider in light of the fact the vast majority of sex workers (even those who were themselves pursuing a meaningful experience in their work) imposed very clear emotional boundaries between their customers and their nonprofessional lovers. Amanda, one of the few San Francisco sex workers that I spoke with who admitted to occasionally looking for lovers among her client pool, said that she had given up the practice of offering her preferred clients "bargain rates" or unpaid sexual arrangements because it inevitably met with dire results:

> They pretend to be flattered, but they never come back! If you offer them anything but sex for money they flee. There was one client I had who was so sexy, a professional dancer and tai chi practitioner, and really fun to fuck. Since good sex is a rare thing, I told him I'd see him for $20 (my normal rate is $250). Another guy, he was so sexy, I told him "come for free." Both of them freaked out and never returned. The men want an emotional connection, but they don't want any obligations. They don't believe they can have no-strings-attached sex, which is why they pay. They'd rather pay than get it for free.

Christopher, a male sex-worker who had also once tried to redefine his relationship with a client, recounted something similar: "I called a trick once because I wanted to have sex with him again. . . . We agreed in advance that it was just going to be sex for sex's sake, not for pay, and that was the last time I ever heard from him!" Critics of commercialized sex may misconstrue clients' desire for bounded authenticity if their implicit point of reference is the modernist paradigm of romantic love, premised on monogamous domesticity and intertwined life trajectories. Thus, Carole Pateman asks why (if not for the sake of pure domination) would "15 to 25 per cent of the customers of the Birmingham prostitutes demand what is known in the trade as 'hand relief,'" something which could presumably be self-administered.[36] Yet, as one client insisted, after explaining to me that he studied and worked all the time and consequently didn't have much opportunity to even meet women, let alone to pursue a romantic relationship, "It's more real and human than jacking off alone." This client reveals an underlying sexual paradigm which blends the "relational" with the "recreational"—a mode of eroticism that is compatible with the rhythms of his individually oriented daily life and, increasingly, with those of other men with similar white, middle-class sociodemographic profiles.

CONSUMPTION, COMPULSIVITY, AND SHAME

Compulsive sexuality has to be understood against the backdrop of circumstances in which sexual experience has become more freely available than before, and where sexual identity forms a core part of the narrative of self.

ANTHONY GIDDENS, *The Transformation of Intimacy* [37]

This is not to suggest that all of the clients that I spoke with regarded their patterns of sexual consumption with nonchalance and ease. Gary, an unpartnered forty-seven-year-old contractor from a small Bay Area city, was one of several clients I encountered who were too ashamed of their behaviors to even meet me for a face-to-face interview. Currently in therapy to deal with his compulsive behaviors around sexuality in general (and commercial sex in particular), throughout our telephone conversation Gary's emotional state oscillated between shameful frenzy and depressive desperation. In fact, he told me that he had answered my ad in the first place because he was feeling compulsive and out of control, and thought that by calling me (instead of a sex worker) he would be doing something to help himself: "reaching out," not "acting out."

Here is an excerpt from Gary's account of shopping for commercial sex:

> If I thought about it logically, I wouldn't do it. There are triggers. I work hard, long hours, live alone, and am comfortable enough. A lot of times I'll be home on a Friday night, I'll pick up the newspaper, look at the ads, get enticed, and then I'm gone. It's so easy. . . .
>
> But, you know, it's a tremendous financial drain. I've spent enough money in the massage parlors over the last twenty-seven years to buy myself a house. Some people snort houses, I do this. . . . You start to feel you can't get this unless you pay for it. That's the personal blow from this that you take that you keep to yourself. Plus there's the loss of money. It's like guilt, too, and shame. But you block that out when you're doing it, even if you feel it soon after. You feel like you're letting yourself down by not pursuing a relationship in more conventional ways. You're cheating yourself. As time goes on, you feel more and more distant from being able to have a normal relationship. Plus having such a secret aspect to your life, you feel dishonest with your world. People don't really know you. Although it's strange, I also know people who brag about it and are very open. . . .

Likening his subjective experience of buying sex to snorting drugs, Gary is clearly describing an "addictive," or at least compulsive, experience of his commercial sexual activity. This framing is in stark contrast to the deliberate, carefully considered redemptions of market intimacy and bounded authenticity described above, as well as to the open and bragging behavior that Gary has witnessed in some of his associates. Gary's guilt and shame around the purchase of sex congeal around the vast sums of money he has spent and the orienting of the self away from "normal relationships" and toward this easy yet esteem-damaging alternative. In various of my interviews with sexual clients—even ones in which the interviewees had first praised the benefits of market-mediated sexual exchange—similar themes of compulsivity, guilt, and shame emerged.

Several men described feeling "out of control" and "powerless" before making the purchase, driven and desperate while in active pursuit, and ashamed, secretive, fearful, or disappointed following the event. The three extracts below convey some of these men's subjective experiences of the prostitution encounter. All are quotes from men who had spent the earlier part of their interviews extolling the virtues of commercial sex:

> Nobody knows I do this. Nobody knows. Something comes over me. I could be driving along, and if I get a sexual thought, I need to take care of it. It could be going to a sexual arcade, or hiring someone. It's completely compulsive! I don't think about it in the morning. If I have a few hundred dollars, I want to see someone in twenty minutes.
>
> STEVE, 35

> One thing I feel shame about is the damn money. You know you could get it for free if you just put up with the damn other stuff. I'm not rich, I should be saving. But I just get these urges. Like today, coming to the city to meet you for this interview. I knew not to bring more than $20 with me, or I'd forget about everything I had to do and wind up at a strip club!
>
> DON, 47

> Sometimes, I'll be prowling the streets at night until 3:00 or 4:00 a.m., and come in to work after only four hours of sleep. I know that it's *compulsive*. One time, I was in Cape Cod on vacation, and I thought, "I have to get back to San Francisco, because there are no hookers here." The most uncomfortable part is defi-

nitely the compulsivity, the feeling like you don't have any power. And unfortunately, I'm one of those guys who feel let down afterwards. Afterwards, I worry: Did I get a disease? Are there pimps? How do I get home? Was my car broken in to? What will she use the money for? And I always want to spend more time. I think of all the negatives, that it was too rushed and disconnected. What I really want is some *connection*. . . .

   RICK, 61

How might we explain why some of the very same men who in one moment celebrate the safe parameters of market intimacy in the next breath describe their engagement with that intimacy as so very compulsive and psychically problematic? With Foucault-inspired critics such as Janice Irvine and Helen Keane, we could problematize the post-1970s efflorescence of discourses of addiction, whereby individuals' unfulfilled desires and consumptive excesses are interpreted as symptoms of underlying pathology. Through their internalization of these discourses, individuals themselves come to participate in the regulatory regimes of the psychotherapy industry and the state.[38] Alternatively, we might interpret these men's accounts of subjective suffering as both symbolic and material in origin—as an effect not only of Foucauldian biopower but of tangible, embodied conflicts with the mores of late-capitalist consumer culture.[39] Thus Anthony Giddens suggests that the normalization of nonrelationally bound sexuality, on the one hand, and the emergence of so much psychic stress around sexuality (in the form of compulsions and addictions), on the other hand, necessarily emerge in tandem. In this view, the more that sexual and other cultural practices are disembedded from their traditional ritual supports, the more the solitary self must subsume these behaviors under the banner of individual "lifestyle choices," and, for many, the subjective burdens prove to be overwhelming.

   Further insight into these men's accounts of the occasionally "addictive" quality of sexual purchase can also be gleaned from the works of diverse theorists of postmodern life, who argue that it is precisely the flexibility, transience, and flux of postmodernity that create simultaneous subjective longings for stability and permanence. These longings are evident in the postmodern surge of disparate forms of nostalgias and fundamentalisms—from the moral critique of consumerism to the ideology of family values to the quest for true love.[40] In the case of commercial sex, this reactivity can serve to explain clients' accounts of their desires for both bounded and unbounded authenticity, for commodified erotic exchange and the proverbial "free love." Clients' self-conflicting desires bespeak the very moment of social flux which has produced both normalized and "compulsive" engagements with commercial sexual activity. The act of sexual purchase thus serves as a temporary salve to clients' contradictory desires for both transience and stability, for fungible intimacy as well as durable connection. Meanwhile, culturally prominent discourses of "sex addiction" not only recast these conflicts in individualized terms but seek quite literally to capitalize on them, to rechannel clients' disparate needs and longings into more socially desirable directions.

THE STATE AND THE REDIRECTION OF DESIRE

It's 9 a.m. on a Saturday morning. In one of the only occupied rooms of the San Francisco Hall of Justice, I am seated in the back row of "John School," the city's pretrial diversion program for men who have been arrested for soliciting prostitutes. The city is proud of its program, which boasts a recidivism rate of less than 1 percent of first-time arrestees, who, for a mere $500, can have their records cleared. Approximately fifty or sixty men are in the room this morning, of diverse class and ethnic backgrounds (three of the men around me are accompanied by translators: one Spanish, one Arabic, one Cantonese).

More striking still is that there is nearly an equal number of media representatives in the room. By the end of the first hour, I have been introduced to journalists from TV20, the *London Times,* and *Self Magazine.* "There are representatives from different media organizations here each month," announces Evelyn, the program's feisty director, to the men. "I never do this class without media coverage." In stark contrast to the johns, the media people are predominantly thirty-something, stylish, educated women, acutely and tangibly fascinated by the spectacle of so many sheepish and docile men before them, and by the feminist fantasy of having the gender tables turned (now these men are quiet and still, and—at least until 5 p.m. this evening—they will be forced to remain that way and to listen). Although I am perhaps more conscious than they that it is as much class advantage as feminist victory that permits this witnessing, I notice too the at least superficial similarity between these women and me.

Yet according to the johns I chat with during the coffee breaks, very few are passively absorbing the information that is presented to them, and they are far from being persuaded of the error of their ways. The men say that John School is even worse than Traffic School—an all-day ordeal in a stuffy room with a whole procession of equally stuffy speakers. "This is bullshit." "I was trapped." "It's so hypocritical." "It should be legalized." "They act like it's something special, but all men do it. . . . Men and women just think differently. Men will fuck sheep, boys, anything. They are dogs."

The first presentation is led by an assistant district attorney and is entitled "Prostitution Law and Street Facts." Although John School is officially available to all men arrested for soliciting a prostitute, the structure of the program demonstrates that those who do get arrested comprise only a small and special subgroup of clients. This program is clearly geared for heterosexual men who shop the streets. During his presentation, the DA, trying to get the group to engage, asks: "How many of you were picked up in the Tenderloin? How many of you were picked up in the Mission?" He does not ask how many were picked up at the local erotic theater, or with an escort, or while cruising for a sex worker online, or even on Polk Street (where male and transgender street prostitutes work).[41]

The DA's objective is to scare the men out of their established patterns of behavior by gruesomely cataloging the potential legal repercussions of what they are doing—what it's like to get booked, to be herded into the paddy wagon, to spend the night in jail, or to be forced to take an HIV test—all likely consequences of a second arrest. He shows the class a brief video reviewing the laws. I am at first confused by the last image in the sequence: the captionless depiction of a man hunched over a computer screen. The DA's final words to the men are even more remarkable: "Next time you're thinking of going out on the street, do like this guy. Go on the Internet if you have to—but stay away from minors!"

The final presentation before the lunch break features a former street prostitute and ex–heroin addict who now runs a program to help prostitute women transform their lives and get off the streets. Seated beside her is a panel of three other formerly homeless and drug-addicted streetwalkers. Now clean and sober, well-scrubbed, well-fed, and conservatively attired, their appearances are not much different from other thirty- to forty-year-old professional women. Only their scathing and effusively expressed anger betrays a difference.

For the men, this is no doubt the most riveting panel of the day—at last, their attention seems focused; they sit tense and upright in their chairs. From their facial expressions and inclining postures, some even seem to be vaguely aroused. The rhetorical tactic employed by the women is a combination of shock therapy and a firm reassertion of the primacy of marital domesticity. "Most of the women I have worked with started turning tricks as children or teens," says one woman in a harsh, accusatory voice. "I learned a long time ago that it's not pedophiles involved in that, but the men that sit here in this room." Through teary eyes and clenched teeth, another panelist tells the men her own story of early sexual abuse, addiction, and rape. Her narrative, gripping and theatrical, ends with the following admonition:

> Once, I remember being crusty and dope sick, wearing yellow shorts, and walking around with blood caked on my thighs for two days. No one asked me what was wrong. I felt like a fallen woman that God, society, and my family would never forgive. . . . We're not out there because we like to suck dick, and you're not out there because you like us. You're the cause of our suffering, and you can become statistics yourselves. Try and realize, if you have to go back out—these women were hurt! A lot of you men are husbands, fathers, and grandfathers. What did you tell your significant others today? Hopefully, someday soon you'll learn how to have healthy relationships—with your *wives*.

In the afternoon, there are three additional presentations: one featuring representatives from organized neighborhood and merchant groups, another with a sergeant from the vice squad on the dynamics of pimping, and the final presentation by a therapist on "Sexual Compulsivity and Intimacy Issues." The neighborhood groups are represented by two men and a woman, white residents and small shopkeepers from the Tenderloin district. Together with the vice cop, they paint the johns as aggressors against family, community, and—rather ironically—business.[42] The harms that the johns are held responsible for are both symbolic and material. "Do you have sex in front of your children?" they ask. "Little boys in my neighborhood blow up condoms like balloons! You hear about victimless crimes, but our whole neighborhood is a victim! Fifteen-year-old girls turn tricks and twenty minutes later deliver babies. Millions of dollars pass through these girls, but at the end of the day they have nothing. All the way through this business, there are victims."

The final session, led by a licensed marriage and family counselor, relies on a twelve-step sexual addiction model of client behavior. The counselor is a white, middle-class, casually dressed man in his late thirties, an exemplar of northern California therapeutic culture and soft-spoken masculinity. He begins his presentation with a definition: "Sex addicts have trouble thinking of sex and love together, in the same relationship. They say, 'I love my wife, but I have sex with a prostitute.' The challenge is to do them together, to learn how to nurture relationship. This is not just a woman's job."

After distributing a "Sexual Addiction Screening Test" to the members of the class (with questions such as "Do you often find yourself preoccupied with sexual thoughts?" and "Has your sexual activity interfered with your family life?"), the therapist tries to enlist the class in a discussion about why

The Sexual Addiction Screening Test (SAST)

The Sexual Addiction Screening Test (SAST) is designed to assist in the assessment of sexually compulsive or "addictive" behavior. Developed in cooperation with hospitals, treatment programs, private therapists, and community groups, the SAST provides a profile of responses which help to discriminate between addictive and nonaddictive behavior. To complete the test, answer each question by placing a check in the appropriate yes/no column.

☐ yes ☐ no   1. Were you sexually abused as a child or adolescent?

☐ yes ☐ no   2. Have you subscribed or regularly purchased sexually explicit magazines like *Playboy* or *Penthouse*?

☐ yes ☐ no   3. Did you parents: have trouble with sexual behavior?

☐ yes ☐ no   4. Do you often find yourself preoccupied with sexual thoughts?

☐ yes ☐ no   5. Do you feel that your sexual behavior is not normal?

☐ yes ☐ no   6. Does your spouse [or significant other(s)] ever worry or complain about your sexual behavior?

☐ yes ☐ no   7. Do you have trouble stopping your sexual behavior when you know it is inappropriate?

☐ yes ☐ no   8. Do you ever feel bad about your sexual behavior?

☐ yes ☐ no   9. Has your sexual behavior ever created problems for you family?

☐ yes ☐ no   10. Have you ever sought help for sexual behavior you did not like?

☐ yes ☐ no   11. Have you ever worried about people finding out about your sexual activities?

☐ yes ☐ no   12. Has anyone been hurt emotionally because of your sexual behavior?

☐ yes ☐ no   13. Are any of your sexual activities against the law?

☐ yes ☐ no   14. Have you made promises to yourself to quit some aspect of your sexual behavior?

☐ yes ☐ no   15. Have you made efforts to quit a type of sexual activity and failed?

☐ yes ☐ no   16. Do you have to hide some of your sexual behavior from others?

☐ yes ☐ no   17. Have you attempted to stop some parts of your sexual activity?

☐ yes ☐ no   18. Have you ever felt degraded by your sexual behavior?

☐ yes ☐ no   19. Has sex been a way for you to escape your problems?

☐ yes ☐ no   20. When you have sex, do you feel depressed afterwards?

☐ yes ☐ no   21. Have you felt the need to discontinue a certain form of sexual activity?

☐ yes ☐ no   22. Has your sexual activity interfered with your family life?

☐ yes ☐ no   23. Have you been sexual with minors?

☐ yes ☐ no   24. Do you feel controlled by your sexual desire?

☐ yes ☐ no   25. Do you ever think your sexual desire is stronger than you?

23 The Sexual Addiction Screening Test, distributed at the San Francisco First Offender Program. Originally printed in Carnes (1989: 218–19).

men visit prostitutes. "Stress," volunteers one man. "Curiosity," says another. "Anger? Loneliness?" offers the therapist, and some of the men
agree. Finally, one john rouses himself out of boredom to protest. "Come on
already! It should just be legalized! Guys need a place to get relief." A police
officer from the Street Crimes unit who is seated to my left leans over to me
and whispers in my ear: "I agree. Anyway, I bet most of these men will now
just go indoors, where they don't have to worry about any of this."
        FIELD NOTES, SAN FRANCISCO, MAY 1999

Feminists have bemoaned—but also taken for granted—the sexual
double standard in the treatment of prostitution by the criminal justice
system. In 1993, the scholar and prostitutes' rights activist Gail Pheterson persuasively argued that

> Of course, the customer is also party to prostitution transactions
> and in countries where sex commerce is illegal, he is equally guilty
> of a crime. But such laws are not equally applied to customer and
> prostitute. . . . Nowhere is equal punishment enforced, however,
> partly because law officials are either customers themselves or
> they identify with customers. Prostitutes have numerous stories
> of the sexual demands of police, lawyers, judges, and other male
> authorities.[43]

Pheterson and other critics would never have predicted that, by
the mid-1990s, municipal and national governments might actually
intervene to challenge and reconfigure patterns of male heterosexual
consumption, and even mobilize feminist arguments in the service of
such interventions. Nor did they foresee that, despite a shared gender
and sexual identification with customers, male authorities might be
beholden to other social forces and political agendas that could lead
them to curtail the prerogatives of heterosexual interest. And they did
not anticipate how programs such as "John School" and the expanding and diversifying market in commercial sexual services might represent what only seem to be paradoxical facets of interconnected social
trends.
    Since the mid-1990s, "John Schools," "First Offender Programs,"
and "Client Reeducation Projects" have sprung up in American cities
as diverse as San Francisco and Fresno, California; Brooklyn and Buffalo, New York; Portland, Oregon; Las Vegas, Nevada; Kansas City,
Kansas; Norfolk, Virginia; and Nashville, Tennessee, as well as in Toronto and Edmonton in Canada and Leeds in the United Kingdom. Numerous other cities throughout the United States and Western Europe

have also considered implementing similar programs.[44] After decriminalizing prostitution in the late 1960s, in 1998 Sweden became the first national government to unilaterally criminalize the purchase of sexual services by male customers (a shift which I will explore in greater detail in the next chapter). In the United States, although the first sporadic and fleeting gestures toward the arrest of male clients date back to the 1970s, contemporary client reeducation programs must be seen as part of a new strategy of state intervention in male sexual behavior.

In both Oklahoma City and Kansas City, for example, city officials have begun to broadcast on cable television the photos and names of male clients arrested by police for prostitution-related offences.[45] In Huntington Woods, Michigan, the police released the names of 16,000 alleged prostitution customers on CD-ROM.[46] Police in various municipalities have also arranged for the names and faces of arrested clients to appear on city billboards and Web sites and in local newspapers.[47] Perhaps the most provocative recent example of john "outing" is "Webjohn," an online database organized by "concerned community members," featuring johns caught on video picking up or communicating with a known prostitute. The site's Mission Statement notably posits johns, not prostitutes, as vectors of disease, and declares two official aims: "to deny johns their anonymity" and "to offer any residential or business community in North America a cost-free and lawsuit-free mechanism to suppress street-level prostitution in the area." Taken together with a revision of legal codes to facilitate client arrests and to stiffen criminal penalties, "public outings" in the mass media, vehicle impoundment, revocation of driver's licenses, as well as fiercer prohibitions against the patronage of child prostitutes and the possession of child pornography, the new spate of social policies and cultural interventions constitutes an unprecedented attempt to regulate male heterosexual behavior.[48]

Anne Allison, Monica Prasad, and sociologists such as Mañuel Castells and Kamala Kempadoo have rightly pointed to the burgeoning demand for commercial sexual services as paradigmatic of various key features of late capitalism: the merging of public and private; the extension in depth and breadth of the service sector; the "individualization" of sex; and subjective preference for the neatly bounded commodity over the messy diffuseness of nonmarket exchange.[49] But missing from these accounts is a recognition of the fact that commercial sexual consumption is simultaneously being *normalized* and *problematized,* and that these two projects are linked. Underlying the lack of attention to the recent criminalization of consumer behavior is the neglect of two other key features of late capitalist society: the relationship between postindustrial poverty and gentrification, and the normative push on the part of some social activists to retain a modernist model of relationally bound sexual intimacy.[50]

"John Schools" are the outcome of an alliance between feminist antiprostitution activists, organized groups of predominantly lower middle-class community residents and shopkeepers (in Bourdieu's terms, the "old" petite bourgeoisie), and politicians and big businesses with interests in gentrifying neighborhoods such as San Francisco's Tenderloin and Mission districts. As described in chapter 2, these are neighborhoods which are home to the city's principal streetwalking strolls and the most socially marginal sectors of the commercial sex trade, yet which also stand close to the business district and to highly valuable real estate. Although the three groups indicated have disparate ideological and material agendas, as part of their agenda to eliminate street prostitution as a whole, they have joined forces to target the male patrons of prostitution's most public domain. In contrast to the moral wars of a century ago, contemporary campaigns against prostitution are chiefly concerned with cleaning up the gritty underbelly of an industry that is in practice left alone so long as it remains behind closed doors.[51] Attempts to eradicate the most "problematic" segments of the industry implicitly serve to legitimize the *unproblematic* parts which remain.

In this way, the district attorney's advice to the attendees of "John School" to turn on their computers can be rendered decipherable as an important step toward cleaner streets and gentrified neighborhoods. Thus, in 1994, when the San Francisco Board of Supervisors assembled a task force to investigate revisions to the city's prostitution policy, the primary and explicitly stated impetus was community and merchants' objections to disruptions on their streets.[52] Although police representatives and municipal politicians continue to frame their street-focused enforcement strategy as being in accordance with the preponderance of citizens' complaints, the effect of their policies is clearly to divert sex workers and customers into indoor and online commercial sex markets.

The new social policies targeting male sexual conduct and commercial consumption are not, however, absent of moral focus or content. The various strands of the ideological agenda behind programs such as "John School," like the interest groups behind it, are multiple but interweaving. Many contemporary feminist activists, like their feminist forerunners, are keen on challenging the male half of the sexual double standard. Given the emergence of the sexually consumeristic "playboy" ideal in the 1960s, the deregulation and normalization of pornography in the 1970s, and other predominantly male benefits of the sexual revolution, the reassertion of sexual domesticity and marital fidelity may be experienced as particularly crucial.[53] Responding to a similar constellation of concerns, the Tenderloin's middle-class residents and small-scale merchants can be seen as participating in both a material and a symbolic crusade against the incursion of market forces into a longed-for, protected sphere of family, neighborhood, and community.

CONCLUSION

The two historically unique and contradictory tendencies that I have documented here, namely burgeoning consumption and increased state intervention, should be understood within a broad array of economic and cultural transformations that have unfolded over the last thirty-five years and crystallized even more dramatically during the last decade. The pursuit of bounded authenticity that is encapsulated in men's demand for sexual commerce has been fostered by the shift from a relational to a recreational model of sexual intimacy, by the symbiotic relationship between the information economy and commercial sexual consumption, by the ways in which tourism and business travel facilitate the insertion of men into the commercial sexual marketplace, and, more generally, by the myriad mergings and inversions of public and private life that are characteristic of our era.

At the same time, the corresponding phenomena of postindustrial poverty and the gentrification of the inner city have led to an overlapping of ambitions between municipal politicians, developers, and feminist antiprostitution activists, who are jointly interested in "cleaning up" the male desires that contribute to the sullying of urban streets. "John Schools," as well as other measures that penalize a subgroup of the male clients of commercial sex workers, have emerged out of the confluence of these disparate political agendas. The recent crackdowns on johns and the normalization of other forms of commercial sex thus go hand in hand because, in addition to struggles over sex and gender, both the state policing of the street-level sex trade and the normalization of the sex business reveal a shared set of underlying economic and cultural interests: the excision of class and racial Others from gentrifying inner cities, the facilitation of the postindustrial service sector, and the creation of clean and shiny urban spaces in which middle-class men can safely indulge in recreational commercial sexual consumption.

6 | The State, Sexuality, and the Market

I am in the red-light district in Amsterdam, the prime tourist destination of the city. This morning, I was informed by a municipal tour guide that the neighborhood officially draws more visitors than the Anne Frank House and the Rijksmuseum combined. In addition to the thousands of daily visitors who travel here in the flesh, there are now millions more who choose to enter the city's sexual attractions "virtually." Many of the city's brothels and sex theaters sport live webcams, so that interested spectators can witness sexual activity in the Dutch capital from any location in the world—all by means of a few simple key strokes and a credit card.[1]

The district is safe and well policed, but the roaming packs of libidinous male tourists, rowdy and drunken crowds, wafting aromas of cannabis, ubiquitous fluorescent lights, and dense, multidirectional foot traffic are overwhelming to the senses, to say the least. From the fragments of dialogue that my ear casually perceives, it is clear that the buyers—like the sellers—hail from many different countries across Europe, North America, Africa, and Asia. Amsterdam's red-light district is a dense microcosm of the global sexual marketplace, where race and nation, as much as sex and gender, are culled and proffered as commodities for sale. The streets are divided into vague ethnic corridors, with Latin American women, Asian women, and African women clustered in separate sections from the white, often blonde, Eastern European women, who (judging from the sheer numbers of onlookers) seem to be the biggest draw.

An African woman leans her head out of a window at one point, and calls out in lilting English to an older heterosexual couple (one of several in the district): "You two come together?" Meanwhile, a drunken British tourist is leaning into the window of another woman with whom he has begun to negotiate. He explains that he would like to know the price. She motions him into her cubicle, indicating that this is something they can discuss inside. Instead, he extends his body over the window frame and leans in toward her, a gesture that seems to convey his refusal to enter her realm on anything other than his own terms. "I'm not going to be given orders by no fucking African woman!" he bellows.

Most of the women in the windows sit bored with half smiles, talking on cell phones, reading, or staring blankly into space. On the busier streets, lithe women dressed in bikinis or lingerie shake their bodies provocatively to the accompaniment of softly playing boom boxes, drawing the attention of dozens of gawking youth. I overhear one young man as he parts the red velvet curtains of an illuminated window before stepping back onto the pavement to rejoin his friends. "Holy shit! Where the fuck is *she* from?" The group proceeds to wind their way down to another ethnic corridor of the district. It is the sheer breadth and diversity of selection, the fungibility of consumer choices, that is the red-light district's biggest draw.

Last night, I visited a live show at one of the numerous sex theaters in the neighborhood. I chose the only one that specifically markets itself to a coed audience—even though I am told that all of the theaters in the neighborhood are owned by the same five individuals. I stood in a massive line behind a group of some forty or fifty sari-clad women and their husbands, who had just piled out of the tour bus that was parked in front. There were also several coed groups of well-scrubbed North American, Australian, and British college students on package holidays, already excited and in giggles. Meanwhile, the doorperson explained to a trio of concerned married couples why the show was good for women, too. "It'll get them excited for later," he said, winking at the men.

The theater itself was squeaky clean, brightly lit, and enormous, with phenomenal acoustics. The show, like the district itself, was geared specifically toward foreign tourists. The emcee, who described the various acts and from time to time solicited the participation of eager audience members, spoke entirely in English. I squeezed my way through the crowd into one of the plush seats arranged in graduated rows, just like any other theater. The members of the audience sat sipping beer, rather than munching popcorn, but otherwise it was quite like going to the movies. All watched politely as a young blonde woman dressed as a nun fellated a slightly older and darker Surinamese man dressed as a priest, while Gregorian chants played softly in the background. Then they went out into the audience, the robes came off and they proceeded to have full intercourse, splayed across the laps of giggling audience members. Beyond this limited form of audience participation, the only apparent difference between this and mainstream pornography was the lack of a money shot.[2] But, however risqué, the composition of the

24 Tourists lining up for entry into an erotic theater in the Amsterdam red-light district (photo by author).

crowd (including many heterosexual couples as well as groups of single women) made it clear that this form of sexual spectacle was thoroughly mainstream—if not quite "family friendly"—entertainment.[3]

FIELD NOTES, JUNE 1999

Thus far, my predominant focus has been on the city of San Francisco, where the de facto decriminalization of indoor sex work and the introduction of "John School" in the 1990s helped (in coordination with broad sweeping economic transformations) to reshape both the external contours and the subjective meanings of commercial sexual transactions for sex workers and clients alike. We have seen that while street-based sex workers and their clients were driven off the streets of the Tenderloin and Mission districts, new kinds of commodified intimate relations were being fostered behind closed doors. On the one hand, the privatization of commercial sex represented an exacerbation of modern-industrial trends, as commercial venues that had previously featured striptease and exotic dancing were converted into brothels offering the efficient provision of hand jobs, blow jobs, and sexual intercourse. At the same time, the privatization of sex commerce offered unprecedented opportunities for cultural normalization and for the market-mediated exchange of bounded authenticity, particularly for the city's digitally inclined new middle classes.

In this chapter, I turn my attention to Stockholm and Amsterdam, two cities comparable in size and economic structure to San Francisco, where I conducted fieldwork during the summers of 1995, 1999, 2002, and 2003.[4] As I noted in chapter 1, Sweden and the Netherlands represent two apparently antagonistic approaches to the state regulation of commercial sex and have served as exemplars for opposing factions of feminist theorists, social activists, and policy makers around the globe. As Barbara Hobson wrote, after researching and reviewing Swedish prostitution policy in the 1980s, "differences in approach go to the heart not only of a society's organization of class and gender but also of the state's role in regulating morals and markets. The study of prostitution becomes a two-way ideological mirror."[5] Sweden has often been upheld by feminist and other social researchers as both the exemplar of the interventionist welfare state and as "the nation in which equality has proceeded further than in any other Western country."[6] Since the 1970s, many commentators have assumed that brute manifestations of sexual, gender, and class inequality such as prostitution would wither away under a Swedish-style policy regime, featuring a well-tempered market and an interventionist social welfare state.[7] In similar fashion, social libertarian strands of feminism and cultural analysis have often looked to the Netherlands for a vision of the ways in which states might endorse both sexual freedom and social welfare. For this second group of commentators, the Netherlands has stood for the utopian melding of a strong welfare state, laissez-faire moral philosophy, and harm-reduction policy agendas around "victimless crimes" involving consenting adults, such as prostitution and drugs.[8]

Some of the distinctions that social critics have sought to emphasize in the course of transnational comparisons were apparently well evidenced in 1998, when Sweden became the first country in the world to officially encode prostitution as a form of gendered violence against women by criminalizing the purchase of sex (but not its sale) in commercial sexual transactions. A mere two years later, the Netherlands took several bold steps in the opposite direction when it became one of the first Western nations to acknowledge the burgeoning sex industry as a legitimate commercial sector like any other, removing adult, consensual prostitution activity from the criminal code and instead applying occupational health, hygiene, and safety guidelines.[9]

Although feminists, sex-worker advocates, and others have often taken "criminalization," "decriminalization," and "legalization" to represent radically divergent approaches to the regulation of commercial sex, this chapter highlights the ways that policy approaches which appear distinct on the surface can actually serve to facilitate similar shifts on the ground. In San Francisco, Stockholm, and Amsterdam, three quite disparate versions of policy reform in the late 1990s resulted in a common series of alterations to the social geography of sexual commerce: the removal of economically disenfranchised and racially marginalized streetwalkers and their customers from gentrifying city centers; the de facto tolerance of a small tier of predominantly white and relatively privileged indoor clients and workers; and the driving of illegal migrant sex workers further underground. While the broad constellation of attitudes toward gender and sexuality as well as other components of national and local cultures, histories, and regulatory strategies are by no means irrelevant to the configuration of sexual commerce in these cities, the shared realities ushered in by larger patterns of political economy have been more definitive in shaping its predominant forms.

In the pages that follow, I examine the genesis and consequences of the criminalization of prostitution in Sweden and the legalization of prostitution in the Netherlands, noting the salience of gentrification, globalization, and the exclusion of illegal migrants in both instances. After briefly summarizing the array of strategies that the two nations have historically employed to regulate sexual commerce, I draw on my own ethnographic research and analysis of government-sponsored reports to discuss the lived impact of the two divergent regulatory strategies. In the final section of this chapter, I return to the question that has undergirded much of the scholarly and political interest in transnational comparisons of U.S. and northern European approaches to the regulation of prostitution: whether and how contemporary state policies might be crafted toward better ends.

OVERVIEW: HISTORY AND POLICY

Activists and scholars have noted that there are three basic strategies that states have employed in the regulation of prostitution.[10] These strategies range from formal government recognition of prostitution as a legitimate sphere of market activity (legalization), to tacit condonement (decriminalization), to official prohibition of prostitution for both buyer and seller as well as prohibition of all prostitution-related activities (criminalization). A fourth strategy might be said to combine elements from the above three approaches. In the contemporary West, the regulatory systems of Nevada, the Netherlands, and Germany are frequently cited as exemplars of the first approach, while the remaining forty-nine U.S. states have typified the third strategy since the closing of the red-light districts during the Progressive Era.[11] As we have seen, in the late 1990s the city of San Francisco shifted from a criminalized to a de facto decriminalized system within the off-street market, while applying a more intensively policed form of criminalization to outdoor, street-level transactions.

In the 1970s, both the Netherlands and Sweden shifted from a strategy of prohibition by way of public decency laws passed at the turn of the century (laws which themselves succeeded a system of regulated brothel prostitution) to a "combined strategy" involving decriminalization of the prostitute-client transaction along with harsh penalties for prostitution-related activities such as pimping and pandering.[12] The previous public decency laws, like most prohibitive policies, were designed to remove prostitutes (but not their patrons) from public streets. At the same time, both states sought to supplement their legal approaches with an array of government-funded social service programs—programs that were targeted, almost exclusively, toward female prostitutes.[13]

Through the 1980s and 1990s, the contours of the legal frameworks in the two countries and the foci of their social services began to noticeably diverge in consequential ways. As with the 1996 attempt to decriminalize prostitution in San Francisco, and the subsequent implementation of "John Schools" in diverse cities, European municipalities, nation-states, and transnational bodies such as the European Union have found themselves scrambling to revise their prostitution policies.[14] Swedish and Dutch officials who are charged with regulating prostitution agree that the reasons for the states' revived interest in the regulation of sexual commerce are fairly straightforward: sexual commerce, regarded by some feminists as an archaic manifestation of traditional sex and gender arrangements, has not "withered away," even in what remain relatively strong welfare states such as Sweden and the Netherlands. Rather, it has taken on a wide array of new and diversified forms, which are remarkably consistent across national contexts: massage parlors, escort services, sex tourism, and cell phone and computer network contacts.[15] In addition to the extension of sexual commerce into new cultural terrains, concerns have also been stimulated by the expansion—or feared expansion—of migrant prostitution and human trafficking. The fear of trafficking has increasingly guided European prostitution policy since the early 1990s (nearly a decade before it became a pivotal domestic and foreign policy issue for the United States).[16] Significantly, neither Swedish nor Dutch feminist efforts to reform prostitution policy in the 1990s met with much success prior to the emergence of the trafficking debates. In both cases, feminist rearticulations of prostitution policy in accordance with the new framework of "trafficking" proved highly successful in gathering momentum, even if the legislation that eventually passed had some surprising consequences once put into practice. As I shall describe in the following sections, whereas in Sweden the criminalization of demand has been used to justify both the maintenance of public order and the protection of trafficked women, in the Netherlands the specter of sex trafficking has led to an explicit differentiation in social policy between "forced" and "voluntary" prostitution.[17]

THE FEMINIST STATE AND THE GLOBAL SEXUAL MARKETPLACE: CRIMINALIZING DEMAND

Sexuality is not something that can be bought or sold. Women are selling a totally empty body; men think they are buying something more. . . . Being a customer is like being a prostitute in that you must switch your mind off. It's like Dr. Jekyll and Mr. Hyde. That's why not all men can buy. A real, whole man who is socially functioning . . . will not be able to.

ELISABETH PETTERSSON, director of the Göteborg Prostitution Project and member of the 1993 Swedish Prostitution Commission[18]

The system's commodity and market-like character . . . set limitations. It involves a bond with more or less well-masked coldness and in a certain way, a double exploitation . . .

SVEN AXEL MÅNSSON, Professor of Social Welfare at the University of Göteborg and member of the 1993 Swedish Prostitution Commission[19]

In 1998, Sweden became the first country in the world to unilaterally criminalize the purchase of sex for male customers. Although clients are increasingly arrested in U.S., British, Canadian, and French cities, Sweden is the first and only country to penalize the customer—but not the prostitute—in written law. The new law was not part of the penal code but rather part of a package of laws called the Violence against Women Act, which also widened the definition of rape to include other acts in addition to sexual intercourse, increased social services for victims of domestic abuse, and stiffened penalties against genital cutting and sexual harassment.[20] Although framed in gender-neutral terms, the law understands prostitution to be a manifestation of gendered power relations, with female prostitutes serving male clients' sexual needs.[21] It thereby declares prostitution to be incompatible with the Swedish goal of gender equality.

As we have seen in our discussion of San Francisco's "John School," second-wave feminists have frequently bemoaned the sexual double standard in the treatment of prostitution by the criminal justice system (in which female sex workers are arrested, while the sexual behavior of their male clients is tacitly allowed). Apparently in response to concerns such as these, the Swedish Parliament reversed a historical trend in voting to criminalize the (presumptively male) buyer of sexual services, while leaving the (presumptively female) seller's decriminalized status intact. The text of the government bill stated plainly the Swedish Parliament's position, declaring "it is not reasonable to punish the person who sells a sexual service. In the majority of cases at least, this person is a weaker partner who is exploited by those who want only to satisfy their drives."[22] In 2002, a few years after the law's passage, the government instituted a vibrant public relations campaign that offered dramatic visual imagery promoting this view, blanketing 2,215 different public locations with color posters that informed potential customers and other citizens of sexual clients' newly criminalized (and pathologized) status.[23] One poster featuring a cluster of ordinary-looking middle-class men ominously announced that "one man in eight has bought sex." Another depicting a faceless male figure in a suit and tie declared it "time to flush the johns out of the Baltic." A third poster highlighted the gendered dimensions of the new cultural fears which were circulating around the emergence of the Internet and other new technologies: "More and more Swedish men do their shopping over the Internet. . . . It's a Crime to Buy Sex."

Though the posters and the official discourse which surrounded the law's passage both suggest that its primary objective was the extension of Sweden's celebrated "gender equality" policy to sexual as well as economic and political terrains, a closer examination of the diverse interests behind the passage of the new law reveals that gender rectitude was not the only guiding concern.[24] In origin as well as in consequence, Sweden's landmark legislation—pushed through Parliament with great fanfare by feminist Social Democratic politicians—has had as much to do with the symbolic politics surrounding questions of Swedish national identity as with questions of sex or gender per se. In fact, the Swedish Prostitution Committee's decision to implement the new law criminalizing clients emerged in tandem with heated

25 Swedish publicity posters following the passage of 1998 law criminalizing the purchase of sex (English language version for international distribution). Näringsdepartementet, Regeringskansliet http://www.regeringen.se/content/1/c6/02/36/39/531010d0.pdf.

social debates about whether or not Sweden should join the European Union. As the anthropologist Don Kulick has observed, "In the early 1990s . . . talk about prostitution had a subtext—in addition to being about the referent 'prostitution,' it was also about the EU and Sweden's relationship to it." [25] In addition to confronting the blurred boundaries between public and private and licit and illicit sex that the emergence of the Internet seemed to represent, Sweden was confronting the immediate and literal blurring of national boundaries through the specters of Europeanization and globalization. The 1998 law criminalizing the purchase of sex aimed to stabilize cultural and geopolitical boundaries simultaneously.

Though the law officially prohibits the client's behavior (a client who is uniformly depicted as white, middle-class, and computer-literate in the public relations posters), in many ways it is still the sex worker whose presence in Sweden is at issue—particularly the migrant sex worker. The national prostitution commission which ultimately recommended the new law was first established in 1993 to address a wide variety of concerns stemming from the "internationalization" of the new global order. Government officials were concerned both with an anticipated flood of migrants from the east in the wake of the recent Soviet collapse, as well as Sweden's impending and controversial entry into the European Union. [26] From its inception, one of the explicit goals of the commission was to seek a means to combat what they saw as the "free market" in sexual commerce advocated by the European "pro-prostitution lobby" and endorsed by the European Community Court. As Sven Axel Månsson, an outspoken member of the Swedish Prostitution Commission, cautioned: "A European Community member state cannot deny a foreign prostitute (from another member state) the right to work within its premises as long as prostitution is not illegal or subject to other repressive measures in that particular state. As most member states have decriminalized prostitution, [this] . . . opens the way for a free movement of 'sex workers' within Europe." [27] In language which highlighted the fear of an incursion of foreign sex workers, the Swedish Prostitution Commission declared arguments for the decriminalization of the European sex trade to be "alien to Swedish principles." [28]

Although the new Swedish policy marks an important shift from a social-service to a criminal justice system approach (the equivalent of 1.5 million U.S. dollars were given to the police, while no additional monies were given to social service agencies to enforce the new law), it has been taken by many Western feminists to represent an instance of aggressive state intervention against the incursion of global forces of inequality. [29] Government spokespersons routinely boast that the law has been an effective means of eliminating not only street prostitution but also trafficking in women. [30] Yet my own interviews with Swedish sex workers, law enforcement officials, government representatives, and activists uniformly suggest, first, that the presence of street-based and migrant sex workers in Sweden prior to the legislation was miniscule to begin with, and, second, that, if anything, the new legislation has actually served to augment, rather than delimit, the Swedish market in commercial sexual services. [31]

During our interviews, Swedish police officials routinely complained about the difficulties they faced in attempting to arrest clients, given that entrapment of any sort is illegal. [32] This is one reason, they say, that they have chosen to focus their attention on eliminating the most visible contours of commercial sex work from city streets. A second reason for the police's continued focus on street-level transactions likely has to do with what Swedish criminologists Toby Pettersson and Eva Tiby have referred to as the "problem of definition," whereby those individuals who do not conform to the stereotype of the street-based, strung-out "drug whore" (e.g., women who arrange commercial sexual contacts with their clients through Internet Web pages; male prostitutes who make contact with their clients in bars or chat rooms) may be difficult to recognize as prostitutes at all. Can "prostitution" be said to exist where there are no prostitutes? As one of Pettersson and Tiby's interviewees from the social service sector explained:

> Before [the new forms of contact came along] it was easy, black or white. Now it's become more confused somehow . . . the women who've been involved [before], it's been so obvious that they were prostitutes. ["]I'm a prostitute, kind of thing, I walk the streets.["] There's no mistaking it. But the closer you come to the other end, the more complicated it must become for the women too. It might be very good-natured and cosy, this man maybe buys dinner and yeah, then some regard it as a date. And then you get paid for it—it's a bit weird.[33]

Based on their interviews with Swedish police officials and social service workers, Pettersson and Tiby conclude that although the Swedish law explicitly sought to shift the stigma away from female prostitutes and toward male clients, "the traditional position of the bad woman as vendor and the invisible man as purchaser is preserved . . . [while] all other constellations, that may as well be considered to be prostitution, remain unproblematized."[34]

As my own police ride-alongs and various government reports reveal, urban streetwalking strolls constitute the sole focus of police attention, despite the fact that street prostitution represented a dwindling minority of the Swedish sex industry to begin with, and one in which proportionately few migrant prostitutes are employed.[35] Among the police officers, social workers, and street-based sex workers that I interviewed, there was broad consensus that the overwhelming majority of street prostitutes were Swedish citizens. While police officers admit that patrolling the streets has not accomplished much in terms of stemming the high-growth sectors of the industry—tourist-oriented strip clubs, massage parlors, and the new online services—as the following field note extract reveals, they often regard it as the most tangible way to make a difference.

Last night I spent several hours on prostitution patrol duty with Johannes, a member of the Stockholm police squad, observing the sparse handful of female prostitutes who were still on the streets of the central business district. Johannes was intimately acquainted with each woman's face, name, and personal history ("That one, she only comes out here when she's short of money, when she's going on vacation, or when she needs money to pay the rent"). Having left the neighborhood and on our way back to my flat in the Södermalm district, Johannes gestured to what he identified as one of fourteen illegal massage parlors in the city where sexual services were readily available for purchase. As we drove past, he chuckled quietly at the hypocrisy of Swedish prostitution policy: "These it is 'too difficult' to do anything about. It takes too much time, and it requires too much evidence." Johannes's comments echoed the observations of Sonja, an exotic dancer at the "company club" that I visited yesterday.[36] To my astonishment, she remarked casually that "the police don't care what goes on at the clubs. They're on our side [against the new law] and will wink when they ask us, "You have a g-string on, right?"

FIELD NOTES, JULY 2002

The Swedish sex workers that I spoke with insisted that since the law's passage, prostitution has not disappeared but rather moved underground. In cities such as Stockholm and Göteberg, with high-priced, glutted housing markets and thriving tourist industries, such enforcement strategies have conveniently served to displace streetwalkers from the very downtown areas that government and real estate officials are interested in developing.[37] As a consequence, the majority of streetwalkers have switched to different forms of client networking, resorting primarily to cell phones or the Internet. As in other Western European and U.S. cities, the vast majority of prostitution activity had in any event already moved indoors, free from the supervision of social workers and the scrutiny of the police.[38] In this sense, the law has hastened a shift in the social geography of commercial sex work—one common not only to Stockholm, but also to other postindustrial cities—that was already underway.

At 8 p.m. Sven Pettersson arrives, the police officer who has been assigned to show me around the city of Göteborg's prostitution strolls. He is a small, friendly man, dressed in a tan jacket and jeans. Although his unmarked navy blue vehicle is parked in front of my hotel, we decide to go exploring on foot.

Our first destination is the city's former red-light district, which, at least at this hour, seems to consist of nothing more than an isolated, empty street and its adjacent parking lot. It is utterly unpopulated, save for a pair of rumpled women in their mid-thirties with skinny, bruised arms and bloodshot eyes. They turn to glance at us briefly before stumbling away. About fifteen minutes later, a lone, matronly Polish woman appears. Sven knows her and explains that she is now married, no longer working, and legally residing in Sweden. Like many of the police officers I have met in Sweden, Sven stresses his comfortable, quasi-familial relationship with the women, at one point even pulling out the red rose–embossed business card of a friend who has recently left the streets.

We head over to the city's main cruising area, hoping to see a few of the city's male prostitutes, but this area, too, is completely empty. We do the next segment of the tour in his car, driving over to Göteborg's three other prostitution strolls, which are pristine, orderly, and again, devoid of any discernible prostitution activity. Sven indicates the few venues in the area with checkered pasts—the mall, the video store, the parking lot where prostitutes would take their johns. At the train station (the chief locus of street prostitution in many European cities) there has not been any activity for some time. Compared to 1995 (when a female research colleague and I walked through Göteborg's red-light district and were trailed by at least twenty or thirty cars, driven by men anxiously looking for dates), the city's street prostitution scene seems to have been radically transformed.

Before we part, I ask Sven what he thinks of Sweden's new law criminalizing the clients of prostitutes, and the 10 million crowns that was given to the police department to enforce it. I am somewhat taken aback when he issues an embarrassed laugh: "Do you want the official or the unofficial answer?" I (of course) request the latter. "The truth is that I am the whole prostitution patrol force!"

FIELD NOTES, JUNE 1999

THE CONSEQUENCES OF CRIMINALIZATION: TANYA'S STORY

Prior to the new law, selling sex without an intermediary was not a crime, although "living off the earnings of a prostitute" was.[39] With the shift from the streets to the Internet, many formerly independent sex workers who were engaged in legal activity have been impelled to rely on criminal intermediaries in order to contact clients. Several women that I spoke with noted the emergence and prevalence of "Internet pimps" over the last several years, whose job it is to help women run their businesses covertly. And, at least according to some, this growth in the illegal sector of the industry has actually paved the way for the arrival of more migrant prostitutes, as well as more traffickers.

Tanya was one individual I encountered who articulated the linkages between the new Swedish prostitution law and the broader transformations occurring in the Swedish sex industry clearly and unambiguously. A former street prostitute, Tanya was currently working as a "trafficker" (her term), facilitating the passage of Estonian women into Sweden to sell sex. Although it is impossible to say that Tanya's story is in any sense typical, her professional transition encapsulated some of the broader changes in the Swedish sex market that were identified by a number of the sex workers I spoke with.

During our interview, Tanya described the way in which street clients' newly born fear of arrest eventually led her to place an ad on the Internet. Because of her transsexual background, this was a potentially dangerous arrangement for her—unlike face-to-face contacts on the street, the clients that she met online did not necessarily know what they were "getting." Often clients would show up and be disappointed that she didn't have a conventionally legible female body. "They wanted the service," she explained, "just not from me." So Tanya decided to use her Internet skills and the client contacts that she had established to help other women make the shift indoors. While her initial employees were all Scandinavian women that she knew from the streets, she eventually came to employ less expensive Estonian women instead.

In her current business, she offers what she calls "a complete service" to the women, providing everything except for visas. Once they arrive at their contact point in Sweden, Tanya secures their apartments, arranges for clients, and takes care of security. She employs only one or two women at a time and arranges for them to stay in Sweden from anywhere between one week and three months. Although she is glad that she can pay the Estonian women approximately a third less than the Swedish ones for the same work, and acknowledges that she retains custody of the women's passports while they are in her employment, she insists that the arrangement she has with them is not exploitative:[40]

> Many of the girls are still in school, so they come [to Sweden] for only a short holiday. The average number of clients per day is three or four. I know one girl who earned 120,000 kronor [~ 16,000 U.S. dollars] after seven weeks. She had that much money in her pocket when she went home!
>
> The girls work in private apartments, normal houses. Some I can trust and some I can't. Once, a girl disappeared with my phone and my key, and then called to tell me that I would need to buy them back from her! So now I'm more careful. . . . There has been plenty of talk about "slave trading" in the business. In my case, not only do the girls want to come here to work, but they actually pay their Estonian contact person to get in touch with me. Most of them have done this work before. . . . It's in everybody's interest that the girls be happy and do good work.

It's a big market, and there are many countries who are asking for them. Sometimes, I can't even get enough girls, so I need to maintain my reputation as a good employer. Business only goes well when everyone is happy.

Some would argue (along with Tanya herself) that the new Swedish law has backfired in failing to curb either the demand for commercial sex or the incursion of migrant sex workers, thereby enabling businesses like Tanya's to thrive. Together with Kulick (2003), I would argue instead that it has served to assuage anxieties about national identity through a series of symbolic substitutions. Anxieties about slippery national borders are deflected onto anxieties about slippery moral borders, which affix themselves onto the bodies of female street prostitutes. The removal of these women from public streets can thereby pave the way for real estate developers, while bolstering Swedish national identity in the process.

THE AMBIVALENT EFFECTS
OF LEGALIZATION IN AMSTERDAM

Amsterdam's *tippelzone* is the architecturally elaborated street prostitution area that the Dutch government has provided for sex workers and their clients since 1997. The zone was created in order to transform furtive and dangerous sex-for-money or sex-for-drugs exchanges (which typically took place in the city's downtown area, behind the train station) into the safe, rational, and state-managed provision of sexual services. Given the *tippelzone*'s location in an industrial district some distance from the center of town, it is difficult to resist thinking of it as just another exceptionally well-maintained factory. The drop-in center is staffed by a full professional team of doctors, social workers, and Russian and Spanish language translators. The facilities and gates to the center are freshly painted in brightly colored hues. A neatly manicured lawn surrounds a smoothly paved ring road with protective shelters and comfortable benches for sex workers to rest their high-heeled, weary feet. There are phone booths in perfect working order at each ten-foot interval, and cleverly partitioned stalls so that clients and workers may park with privacy (complete with waste baskets for the disposal of condoms).

Each *tippelzone* boasts a *huiskamer,* or drop-in center for the workers. *Huiskamer* means "living room," which seems to bespeak the government's attempt to normalize and domesticate commercial sexual exchange. Open nightly from 9:00 p.m. to 5:00 a.m., the *huiskamer* provides all variety of medical and social services to street workers, including free coffee and tea, affordably priced condoms and sandwiches, and a "tippelteam" for regular police protection. The *huiskamer* is decorated with crepe-paper ornaments and boasts a big screen TV, an array of board games and posters, and large bowls of fresh fruit. On the bulletin board, there is a list of "dirty tricks" in three languages: Dutch, Russian, and Spanish, and an announcement posted for a workshop on immigration law. A video monitor patrols the entrance-way to the facility. The resident social workers advise the girls about every-thing—even prices. "We tell the girls not to go outside the zone. It's safe here. And we suggest that they not work under fifty guilders [~ 25 U.S. dollars]," explains Miryam, the young college student who has been employed part-time at the center for the last two years. "It's bad for self-esteem."

According to Miryam, some seven hundred cars drive through the area each night. In contrast to the city's official red-light district, geared primarily toward tourists, this is where the resident population (Dutch and foreign-born) comes to buy sex. Says Miryam, "A quiet night is when the cars, which range from pickup trucks to Porsches, are only twenty deep." From sixty to ninety different sex workers pass through the *huiskamer* each evening, and approximately one thousand different women use the center each month.

Half of the workers are *travestis* from Ecuador and Colombia, who have been migrating to Amsterdam since 1996;[41] the other half are Eastern European. At most four or five of the fifty or so sex workers present tonight are Dutch. "The Eastern European group is generally quiet and reserved, as they tend to work with pimps," explains Miryam. "The Polish and Rumanian groups are getting bigger and bigger; we have had increasing problems with criminality." Hardly any of the prostitutes who work here are addicted, be-cause the area is difficult for drug-dependent women to reach on foot (and far away from their supply of drugs). In theory, none of the women are under-age. The social workers admit that most of the women who work here do not have a visa. Some women work every night for two years; others leave after two weeks for Rotterdam or other European cities.

The atmosphere here is a surreal blend of legality and illegality, of work and fiesta. While I was talking with Miryam this evening, a tall, stunningly beautiful, Spanish-speaking *travesti* named Lola appeared before us to complain about a client from the prior evening—"Que me esta haciendo la vida imposible." She gave us the license plate number, to be promptly filed with the police. While forty or fifty other sex workers outside were selling safe and sanitary hand jobs and blow jobs, and the number of cars circling continued to multiply, Lola went in to join a group of another ten *travestis* who were clustered around the "living room" table, smoking, laughing, and sharing food while Latin rhythms played.

FIELD NOTES, JUNE 1999

26 Prostitution stroll and car park for customers in the Amsterdam *tippelzone* (photo: Jacqueline).

In the Netherlands, the legal reasoning in dealing with prostitution proceeded—at least on the surface—somewhat differently from the sequence in Sweden. On October 1, 2000, nearly two years after the passage of Sweden's Violence against Women Act, the Dutch Parliament revised the nation's legal code to legalize indoor prostitution and brothel keeping, officially transforming a black market economy into a business sector to be regulated like any other, subject to the usual labor codes and guidelines—including taxes and hygiene and safety regulations.[42]

To a diverse array of commentators, the new law became an instant symbol of political pragmatism and social tolerance. Within the Netherlands, the legislation passed with relatively little fanfare or controversy—most of the major interest groups were in agreement that prostitution had become a "fact of life" and should be dealt with accordingly.[43] As Jan Visser, then director of the Mr. A. de Graaf Stichting (the government-sponsored foundation specializing in prostitution-related issues) explained, "The management and control of dense city life have become too complex to allow a subculture to stay outside of the system."[44]

Yet there was one key provision of the new law legalizing the Dutch sex trade which received far less attention from the international press: the law stipulated that only adult, legal residents could be employed in indoor venues such as brothels, massage parlors, and sex clubs, and it mandated prison sentences of up to six years for individuals found guilty of forcing others to engage in prostitution, employing the services of a minor, or bringing others across national borders to engage in prostitution.[45] Brothels discovered to be employing or renting space to sex workers who were not legal residents of the European Union and/or lacking the proper documents would be shut down (and to facilitate enforcement of this provision, all prostitutes would now be required to carry proper identification papers with them). In a country where 50 to 60 percent of the sex trade was comprised of migrant women who had been working without official documents, this stipulation was, not surprisingly, enormous in its consequences. As one former member of the Dutch sex workers' rights organization, the Red Thread, observed during our interview, "At least 12,000 women were made illegal overnight."[46]

Immediately following the law's passage, nearly a quarter of the brothel windows in the red-light district were empty; many have been conspicuously papered with "for rent" signs ever since. While a sizable portion of illegal sex workers left the country for neighboring Germany or Belgium, those who remained were often relocated to the

27 Brothel windows for rent in the Amsterdam red-light district (photo by author).

*tippelzone*s or resorted to working in underground escort agencies and through the Internet. As the *tippelzone*s were initially constructed as a means to displace local drug-injecting streetwalkers, by the beginning of this decade the use of such zones by illegal migrants had begun to inspire sharp critiques. City officials complained that women who were engaged in sex-for-drugs preferred to remain in the downtown areas where they could be in greater proximity to their drugs. As the population of sex workers in the *tippelzone*s expanded and anti-immigrant sentiment gathered steam, the city's leaders were accused of running open-air brothels for illegal migrants, and pressure mounted on municipal governments to close the zones. In response to public outcry, the Amsterdam *tippelzone* (the city's last "zone of tolerance" for illegal migrant prostitutes) was shut down by municipal politicians in December 2003; the *tippelzones* in Rotterdam and The Hague have also since been eliminated.[47]

Meanwhile, reeling from the combined effects of a labor shortage and the additional costs entailed by complying with occupational health and safety codes, the majority of smaller sex businesses were forced to close up shop because they could not afford to pay taxes or to abide by the new labor guidelines. Women like Marie, an escort and former madam in her late thirties with a practical demeanor and a compelling, straightforward manner, recounted to me the daunting professional hurdles she faced on implementation of the new law. Over tea and biscuits in her sparsely decorated three-bedroom flat in the outskirts of Amsterdam, she noted that although she had previously rented out two of the bedrooms to other escorts, her options were currently limited to working alone:

> From the state's perspective, two women working together constitute a brothel that must be subject to controls. One day when I was working here the police came in, and one of the women who was working with me didn't have her identification papers with her. Although the woman was actually Dutch, with a thick Rotterdam accent, they threatened to take her to the police station to find out who she was. They came back two weeks later, and did the same thing with another girl who was actually from Brazil, who worked two days each week to send money back home, but whose husband didn't know that she was working. She freaked out, and said that she wouldn't work with me anymore. Eventually, it became hard to stay in business because under these circumstances, I could not get girls.
>
> The last straw was when I wanted to move upstairs to a bigger flat so that I could have more space. When I applied for the permit to run my business there, they asked if it was more than seven meters. I said that it was seven-ten. They told me, in that case, that I would need fire stairs, which would cost me 20,000 guilders [~ 10,000 U.S. dollars].
>
> At this point, I am in a totally different profession—I work twenty hours a week in a restaurant. So now, I don't need to pay for insurance or permits, and lower income at least means lower taxes. Occasionally I still see my regular clients, here, by myself, alone. I have the right to advertise, but I cannot work here

with a friend (which would be safer and more fun for me) because
then I would be considered a "business" and I would need fire stairs.

According to accounts by sex industry workers, local activists, and
the Dutch government, the size of the Dutch sex industry shrank by at
least 35 percent, leaving only the largest corporate enterprises behind.
Several of the self-employed sex workers that I spoke with during the
summers of 2002 and 2003 said that working conditions had become
so difficult, and the prices for sex work had fallen so low, that they
had even contemplated migrating to the United States to work—where
sex work is criminalized, and thus unregulated and higher paid. Only
the largest and most established sex clubs and escort agencies could
boast that, in the wake of the new law, they continued to glean high
profits.[48] A centralization of power has thus been achieved, pushing do
wn prices for sex and narrowing the range of potential employers. In
this way as well, the most profound effect of legalization has been a
reconfiguration of the scope and character of the Dutch sex industry,
away from the informally organized prostitution of the desperate (illegal migrants, underage prostitutes, and substance-dependent women)
and toward the centrally managed, rationalized sex work of white, na-
tive women and a handful of highly organized migrants.

In a discussion of prostitution regulatory strategy in the Netherlands, the legal scholar Chrisje Brants has described the subtle (and
distinctively Dutch) mode of social control known as *gedogen,* or "regulated tolerance." Brants emphasizes that the notion of tolerance that
is implied by the word should by no means be taken to imply down-
right approval. Rather, "it involves self-regulation, enforced if necessary through administrative rules, but always with the criminal law
as a threat in the background."[49] Consistent with Brants's analysis,
some local activists maintain that underpinning the official Dutch
policy legalizing prostitution is a more covert policy which rids the
country of many of its migrant workers.[50] This policy followed on the
heels of successive waves of legal restrictions to immigrants' rights (restricting the right to rent an apartment, to purchase insurance, etc.).[51]
The "trafficking debate" has been a crucial force in reshaping Dutch
prostitution policy in the service of a broader anti-immigrant agenda.
As Marieke Van Doorninck of the de Graaf Stichting has noted, "in
the 'forced vs. voluntary' distinction that the Dutch law has been premised upon, it is only the Dutch sex workers who have been deemed
capable of choice." Jo Doezema, a sex-workers' rights activist who has
worked in Amsterdam's red-light district, has similarly observed,

TABLE 1 Numbers of prostitutes and migrant prostitutes in some Western European countries in the late 1990s

	Inhabitants	Prostitutes	Migrant Prostitutes
Sweden	8.5 million	2,500	600–700
Norway	4.5 million	3,000	500–600
Denmark	5 million	6,000	2,000
Finland	6 million	4,000	1,750
The Netherlands	15 million	30,000	15,000
Germany	80 million	300,000	150,000

Sources: Randers-Pehrson and Jessen (2000, I); TAMPEP (2002, 242)

The "voluntary" prostitute is a Western sex worker, seen as capable of making independent decisions about whether or not to sell sexual services, while the sex worker from a developing country is deemed unable to make this same choice: she is passive, naive, and ready prey for traffickers. Potentially the most frightening division, however, created by the voluntary/forced dichotomy is that of sex workers into guilty/"voluntary" and innocent/"forced" prostitutes, which reinforces the belief that women who transgress sexual norms deserve to be punished. This division is thus a threat to the entire concept of women's human rights.[52]

Over the last few years, the population of migrant sex workers in the Netherlands has gradually begun to rise again. For many, the economic incentives to migrate are in and of themselves sufficient—whatever the legal consequences. But some sex-worker advocates now argue that those who might have been in a position to migrate and work autonomously in the Netherlands under the previous decriminalized system are now far more likely to become reliant on criminal networks for fake passports and identification papers. The process of securing false documents is not only costly and difficult for sex workers but constitutes a criminal offense. As Van Doorninck has stated, "It is easy to imagine that someone who was not a victim before—who was just here working independently—could become one under the new law."[53]

CONCLUSION: PARALLEL TRENDS

In recent decades, states and municipalities throughout North America, Australia, and Western Europe have sought to contain a burgeoning and diversifying sex trade through a variety of innovative measures—from stepped up enforcement against the perpetrators of "quality of life" crimes to the legalization of brothel keeping to increased client arrests. These efforts have arguably constituted a "third wave" of reform surrounding the state regulation of prostitution during the last century. If the first wave occurred with the closing of the red-light districts and the elimination of licensed brothel prostitution in the first decades of the twentieth century, and a second wave occurred with the liberalization of laws surrounding commercial sex in the 1970s, a new series of transformations has occurred in tandem with the postindustrial expansion and transnationalization of sexual commerce.

"Prosex" as well as "antiprostitution" feminists have produced diverse accounts of the gendered meanings that comprise the commercial sex-work transaction, arguing for an array of competing legal remedies—including decriminalization, legalization, and criminalization—and for the broader implementation of "Dutch" or "Swedish" policy models, as we have seen. Few commentators, however, have situated their analyses within the context of postindustrial transformations of sexuality and culture. My research demonstrates that the failure to situate sexual commerce within a broader political-economic framework can lead advocates to argue for opposing tactics which, once implemented, might have surprisingly similar effects on the ground. Whether sex work is decriminalized, legalized, or criminalized, the interests of real estate developers, municipal and national politicians, and business owners may overshadow the concerns of feminists and sex workers.

What is arguably most remarkable about the disparate array of legal strategies that Europeans and North Americans have implemented in recent years is how singular they have been in effect: The overarching trend has been toward the elimination of prostitution from city streets, coupled with the state-facilitated (or de facto tolerated) flourishing of the indoor and online sectors of the sex trade. Despite their seeming differences, the common focus of state interventions has been on eliminating the visible manifestations of poverty and deviance (both racial and national) from urban spaces, rather than the exchange of sex for money per se.

Different policy regimes and national cultures clearly can have an impact on the scope and character of the commercial sex trade. Sweden's prohibitive attitude toward prostitution (both before and after the new law) has been manifest in a comparatively small commercial sex sector of about 2,500 prostitutes, compared with a figure of about 30,000 in the Netherlands—a country with only twice Sweden's population.[54] Conversely, the Netherlands' pragmatic recognition of the sex trade as a legitimate sphere of commerce and employment has resulted in greater social legitimacy and working conditions for at least some parties, who have the opportunity to work free from police harassment, to openly declare their occupation on their bank accounts and tax forms, and to present themselves, in the words of Yvonne (one of the brothel owners that I interviewed) as "honest, hardworking businessmen" [*sic*].

Given these differences, the impulse among feminists and sex-workers' rights advocates to call on the example of either country in order to advance a particular normative agenda is understandable, but it is also fraught with difficulties. One of the key problems that can emerge is a simplification of political dynamics, including a failure to consider the multiple motives of political actors, notably those which surround questions of migration, national identity, and the gentrification of cities. In the wake of European unification and other global transformations, Sweden, the Netherlands, and other countries find themselves confronting similar material and symbolic dilemmas, ones which undergird and overshadow concerns about the regulation of commercial sex.

The global restructuring of capitalist production and investment that has taken place since the 1970s has meant that legal and illegal migrants in search of many different forms of work have continued to press against Western European and U.S. borders; meanwhile, for Swedish, Dutch, and other postindustrial city dwellers, deindustrialization, unemployment, and a lack of affordable housing have become the local face of the same global processes. For Swedish and Dutch citizens, the economic hardships entailed by unification have further contributed to a fragile and wavering sense of national identity. In the face of difficult-to-remedy structural transformations such as these, both Sweden and the Netherlands have created policies which reinforce a coherent sense of national identity by more closely regulating the prostitute body. In both cases, a semblance of cleanliness and order has been created by eliminating streetwalking and—in the case of the Netherlands—concentrating sex workers in corporate-run brothels.

Both countries, furthermore, make a show of policing illegal migrants, attempting to eliminate the most visible presence of migrant sex workers from public view. The national project is thereby reinforced and made to appear as "more moral" in each case—despite the fact that the policies of both countries have apparently served to strengthen the hands of the criminal networks that facilitate illegal migration. And, last, the policies of both Sweden and the Netherlands serve to better align each country with the local forces of globalization, facilitating gentrification and tourism. Despite some important surface-level contrasts, the cases of Stockholm, Amsterdam, and San Francisco demonstrate that regimes which legalize the sex trade as well as those which claim to seek its elimination share several common threads which link them to larger changes within the global economy.

Taken together, the cases also speak to a broader set of theoretical and political concerns about the state's role in achieving social reform—concerns which have long plagued feminist scholars interested in questions of prostitution, pornography, and other issues. As with the development of San Francisco's "John School," both the legalization of prostitution in the Netherlands and the criminalization of clients in Sweden were sought after and fought for by avowedly feminist constituencies. Yet as my own discussion in this chapter and the abundant literature on women's engagement with the state both reveal, feminist movements have good reason to be wary of forging alliances with nonfeminist state actors who claim to represent their best interests.[55] The question necessarily arises as to whether or not it is possible to forge a prostitution policy that simultaneously empowers sex workers and protects other women from the gendered sexualization of public space that certain feminists fear.[56] In this era of global flows of capital and culture, what are the potentials and limits of state policies that claim to speak on behalf of women? This is a critical question which my discussion in this chapter has anticipated, and which I shall address further in chapter 7, the conclusion to this book.

7 | Sexuality Debates and Pleasure Wars

At a 1999 academic conference entitled "Economic Justice for Sex Workers," the panelists and audience members drew the battle lines quickly, coalescing along the expected lines of ethical and political division into two opposing camps.[1] While the conference organizers and other sex-worker advocates argued passionately not only for "economic justice" but also for the decriminalization and social legitimation of sex work, a coalition of former prostitutes and antitrafficking activists rallied against the violence and exploitation that they perceived to be inherent in the sex trade and for the need to abolish the sex industry. With the tension building, Norma Jean Almodovar, cofounder of COYOTE, Los Angeles, and a former prostitute herself, stepped up to the podium to explain not only the potential economic benefits but also the erotic and emotional pleasures of prostitution. In response, a visibly agitated audience member jumped to her feet. "How could you enjoy sleeping with hundreds of men?" she demanded, "Sex is supposed to be intimate and private, with one person you love."

The rendition of the feminist sexuality debates that was enacted by the conference participants was both well rehearsed and illuminating, in that it brought to the fore the distinct normative visions of sexuality that have underpinned ideological conflict around commercialized sex over the last quarter-century.[2] During the same period that the feminist "sex wars" have continued to gather steam, within the broader political field contestations over issues such as gay marriage, abortion, and sex education have served as prominent signposts of widespread cultural conflict over shifting sexual relations and norms.[3] In this chapter, my aim is to decode recent "moral panics" around sexuality—in particular, mobilizations around prostitution and trafficking—by redescribing them as political and ethical disputes over what sexuality should *mean*.[4] It is my claim that many contemporary ideological struggles around sexuality have emerged in response to the rapid and large-scale economic and cultural transformations that have occurred with the rise of the postindustrial era.

My primary aim up until now has been to describe and interpret how contemporary modes of eroticism have been informed by new cultural and economic tendencies—a necessary precondition to the equally important work of evaluating these transformations ethically and politically.[5] In the following sections of this chapter, my goal is to revisit contemporary normative discussions around sexual commerce in light of the broad historical and cultural changes that the foregoing pages have described. After summarizing the theoretical model that has guided my analysis thus far, I turn my attention to feminist and other normative discussions of prostitution, drawing from published texts as well as from scholarly and activist contributions at conferences and policy meetings. In the final section of this chapter and by way of a conclusion, I return to the question posed in chapter 6 about the state's potential to advance an agenda of sexual and social justice.

EARLY MODERN, MODERN-INDUSTRIAL, AND POSTINDUSTRIAL PARADIGMS OF SEXUAL COMMERCE

The preceding chapters have described a dwindling sphere of publicly located cash-for-sex transactions among economically and racially marginalized inner-city dwellers, coupled with a burgeoning of private-sphere intimate exchanges among the white, native-born middle classes. We have seen that in postindustrial San Francisco, Amsterdam, and Stockholm, the boundaries of vice have been remapped in such a way so as to curtail the deviant underworld of modern prostitution, while the commercialization of erotic services overall has expanded. The array of spatial, social, and subjective transformations that have occurred in commercial sexual transactions suggests a transitional moment in paradigms of sexual commerce, one which may be comparable in scope and in magnitude to the consolidation of modern-industrial prostitution that took place a century prior. As Ruth Rosen, a historian of transformations in Progressive Era prostitution has noted, "Prostitution . . . tends to *mirror changes in family, women's lives, and sex roles*."[6] In this book, it has similarly been my claim that recent changes in the paradigmatic forms and venues of commercial sex are but the surface manifestations of broader shifts in the constitution of gender and sexuality, public and private, margin and center.

In table 2, I offer a typology of what I term "paradigms of sexual commerce," based on my own research and the existing historical record. It is intended to capture, in bold strokes and synoptic form, the shifting dynamics of sexual commerce described in the foregoing pages. This typology is not meant as a precise demarcation of discrete and non-overlapping historical epochs but is rather intended to be suggestive of broad cultural currents. My designation of three historical paradigms—"early modern," "modern-industrial," and "postindustrial"—is a heuristic device, facilitating the comprehension of social realities which are in fact much messier than this simple categorization permits. For example, the early-modern prototype of sexual barter never disappeared entirely but exists to this day as the dominant mode of commercial sexual exchange in many impoverished communities throughout the world, and, as we have seen in the preceding pages, in the sex-for-drugs barter economy of the inner city. Similarly, for migrant sex workers from developing nations (who find themselves confronting a set of economic and familial conditions which have made wage labor vital for their survival, including declining real wages, lower wage structures than for men, and longer working hours), participation in commercial sexual transactions may in some cases be more akin to modern-industrial prostitution than they are to the model of bounded authenticity that I have articulated in the preceding pages.[7] It is my contention that the paradigms that I have sketched nevertheless capture something important in terms of large-scale social change. They highlight the ways in which new forms and meanings of sexual exchange emerge at particular historical junctures, coexisting with, and at times eclipsing, the forms that preceded them.

WHAT'S *NOT* NEW

This typology is also not intended to suggest that the defining features of what I have termed the postindustrial paradigm of sexual commerce have emerged without important historical precedents. The rapidly expanding scope of sexual commerce at the turn of the last century has been well documented, along with the more general and widespread commodification of sexuality that some commentators suggest were the true targets of social reformers' campaigns against urban red-light districts and "white slavery."[8] As the historian Timothy Gilfoyle has noted, by the mid-nineteenth century, "for the first time in American life . . . sex became an objective consumer commodity."[9] During

TABLE 2 Paradigmatic distinctions between early-modern sexual barter, modern-industrial prostitution, and postindustrial sexual commerce. The three vertical columns suggest broad and historically overlapping cultural currents

	Early-Modern Sexual Barter	Modern-Industrial Prostitution	Post-Industrial Sexual Commerce
What is Sold	Companionship and sexual intercourse with unmarried men (vagrants, sailors, and other transients)	Heterosexual intercourse or receptive oral sex	Diversified and specialized array of sexual products and services (images, performances, acts)
Where the Exchange Takes Place	Tenements, taverns, bawdy houses, or small, remote streets	Red-light districts or urban tenderloins; sequestration serves to maintain social divide between "public" and "private"	Dispersed throughout the city and surrounding suburbs (in private homes, hotels and commercial venues; over the telephone and online); no clear division between the sexual ideologies of "public" and "private" space
State Inverventions	Prostitutes rarely prosecuted and clients exempt; vagrancy laws applied to "disorderly" women	Criminalized or regulated by state agents; where criminalized, gendered specification of "prostitution" as a crime	New legal focus upon "demand" and "trafficked women"; interventions concentrate on street-based exchanges and migrants
How the Exchange is Organized	Informally	Third party managers (pimps, madams, and other middlemen)	"Virtual" middlemen; corporate stripclubs, private ads
What is Bought	Satisfaction of social and carnal urges	Quick sexual release (the emotionally void counterpart of private sphere romance and love)	Bounded authenticity (relational meaning resides in the market transaction)

this period, a wide array of sexual services were made available for purchase in major urban centers (particularly to bourgeois men), including diverse forms of prostitution as well as erotic masked balls, private modeling shows, and pornography. A new urban culture of "sporting men," premised on consumer indulgence and the cultivation of fraternal bonds, inclined single as well as married men to partake in a "promiscuous paradigm" of sensual pleasure. Men's propensity to engage in such activities while outwardly espousing an amative/companionate sexual ethic constituted another important dimension of the gendered double standard which prevailed during this period.[10] At the same time, new, informal modes of sexual commerce—such as "treating" and "walking out"—abounded.[11] For young women, participation in casual prostitution provided access to a burgeoning commercial youth culture, to clothes and recreation, and to a potential means of escape from the stifling traditionalism of the family.[12]

There are also important precursors to the exchange of emotional intimacy in commercial sexual relations that I have described, examples of which span a wide range of periods and places. The tradition of the European courtesan (prized as much for conversation and culture as for her erotic capacities) and the "patronage prostitution" of Japanese geishas and Indian devadasis are well-known instances of emotionally expansive yet explicitly transactional erotic arrangements.[13] Historians have also noted that commodities other than sex were on offer in the luxury bordellos of eighteenth-century Paris, where clients would come to dine, to socialize, or to share confidences with the madam.[14] Sally Stanford, the San Francisco madam of an elite brothel in the 1920s, remarked in her autobiography that "men came to a place such as mine not for sex but for a whole batch of other reasons," including flattery and companionship.[15] Even Paul Cressey's 1933 study of the Chicago taxi dance hall revealed that many patrons were seeking affection, sociability, and romance from their paid partners.[16] The widespread range of such cases suggests that the "Taylorized sex" featured within the paradigm of modern-industrial prostitution may constitute an exception rather than the rule.[17] Although it is my contention that contemporary commercial sexual transactions are characterized by some decidedly new features—in terms of their formal organization, in terms of their mainstreaming within certain segments of the middle classes, and in terms of the explicitly bounded and commoditized (as opposed to naturalized) quality of the intimacy that is transacted—it is nonetheless possible to generate examples which demonstrate that sex workers have traded in capacities other than sex throughout much of history.

SEXUAL COMMERCE IN SOCIAL AND HISTORICAL CONTEXT

When I want sex, I go to work. When I want intimacy, I stay home with my two cats.

> CHRISTINA, 23, pornographic actress, speaking at the International Conference on Prostitutes' Rights, Van Nuys California, 1997

The postindustrial paradigm of sexual commerce is also unique in terms of the social structures which surround and contextualize it—its connection to a set of related transformations that have occurred within the broader spheres of economy, culture, and sexuality. As was noted in chapter 1, flexible accumulation, part-time and temporary work, dual wage-earner households, and a disappearing boundary between "production" and "consumption" have been the economic hallmarks of our era, replacing the production-centered economy of modern-industrial capitalism in which a male breadwinner could count on the relative geographic, temporal, and social stability of full-time employment. A structurally analogous set of changes has taken place within the organization of private life and in paradigms of kinship. Social demographers have pointed to the series of profound changes in family form and household composition that have occurred during this same period—including a decline in marriage rates, a doubling in the divorce rate, and a 60 percent increase in the number of single-person households. By 1988, nearly a third of American households consisted of a single individual. In Western European counties, single-person households have been the most rapidly growing household type since the 1960s, with 25 percent (in the United Kingdom) to 36 percent (in Sweden) of the population living alone. In the United States, the percentage of unmarried adults rose from 28 to 37 percent between 1970 and 1988. And according to the most recent census data in the United States, in 2000, fewer than a quarter of Americans were living in nuclear families.[18]

These structural transformations have had profound implications for the ways in which numerous individuals choose to conduct both their public and their private lives. As Arlie Hochschild has observed, the insecurity, tentativeness, and transience of intimate life have led many people to divest emotional meaning from their private-sphere relationships, reinvesting it instead in market relations, both as eager employees and as consumers. Through reliance on commercially available psychotherapy, child care, domestic labor, and take-out cuisine, they seek to provide their lives with the necessary "services"—and emotional meaning—that individuals of an earlier era could expect to secure in noncommodified, private-sphere relationships.[19] Meanwhile, Anthony Giddens has introduced the term "plastic sexuality" to refer to what he deems to be a new paradigm of sexuality, one which is non-reproductive, in principle reciprocal and egalitarian, and subjectively experienced as a property of the self. For Giddens, plastic sexuality is the erotic counterpart of the "pure relationship," a relationship entered into for no other reason but for the sake of the pleasure and intimacy it affords both partners.[20] Giddens's plastic sexuality, like the growing orientation toward bounded authenticity that I have described, bears an obvious resemblance to Laumann and colleagues' understanding of "recreational" sexuality, as well as to Bourdieu's notion of the "fun ethic" that has arisen in tandem with the ascent of the new middle classes.[21]

Drawing on my own research as well as on the theoretical contributions provided by other theorists of late capitalist intimacy, table 3 summarizes the model that I have developed to understand these interrelated economic and cultural transitions.[22]

I must caution again that my intention is not to suggest an absolutist, teleological model of history. What is crucial to recognize about the aspects of social life that are summarized under the heading of "late capitalism" in the final column is that rather than supplant the features of the prior historical epochs, they instead take their place (however

TABLE 3 Paradigms of work, kinship, and sexual ethics as they have emerged in three historical periods. In postindustrial culture, these paradigms exist simultaneously, within society as a whole and within particular individuals

	Early Modern Capitalism	Modern-Industrial Capitalism	Late Capitalism
Work	Domestic Production	Wage Labor	Service Work; "Creative" and "Flexible" Jobs
Kinship	Extended Kin Networks	Nuclear	Recombinant Families/ Isolable Individuals
Sexual Ethic	Procreative	Companionate/ Promiscuous (Gendered Double Standard)	Bounded Authenticity

comfortably or uncomfortably) right alongside. To some extent, all of us inevitably embody both "pre-" and "postmodern" cultural sensibilities. Yet—as with the series of economic, familial, and sexual transformations ushered in by modernity—the shift to a "postmodern" sexual ethic has been gradual and socially uneven. Nearly a quarter of Americans still live in nuclear families; more than half of the Americans, Japanese, and Finns, 40 percent of the British, and nearly 50 percent of Spanish and Italians continue to work in "nonflexible" jobs.[23] Despite the evident frailty of marriage and long-term relationships in contemporary Western society, romantic love remains a crucial repository of emotional meaning for significant numbers of individuals.[24] At the same time, millions of women and men across the globe who live in nonindustrialized areas rely on their own agricultural production, extended kin networks, and plentiful offspring for social and material sustenance. In brief, venturing into modernity, and postmodernity, has often been the privilege of individuals from specific classes, racial-ethnic backgrounds, regions and nations.

It should thus come as no surprise to find that more men than women, more middle-class professionals than working-class people, more of the young than the old, and more whites than blacks have been among the first social groups to fully participate in the new postindustrial paradigm of sexuality—as my research with sexual clients revealed.[25] Those who are geographically situated at the nodal points of the new information economy, and those who live alone or in "recombinant" families, are also those most likely to partake in market intimacy and in a recreational sexual ethic that is premised on bounded authenticity.[26] Men—not because of something inherent in male sexuality, but by virtue of the material conditions which have enabled a self-definition premised on autonomy and freedom—have been more inclined than women to adopt the new cultural model of sexuality.

Yet women, too, are increasingly participating in the postindustrial sexual economy, albeit in different forms than their male counterparts. Although the bounded authenticity that most women seek in their erotic lives is not necessarily provided by the direct sale or purchase of sexual services, there is nonetheless a growing market in sexually evocative romance novels, sex toys, "women-friendly" pornographic texts and performances, sex parties, sex classes, and sexual advice manuals for female consumers.[27] Certain thriving market segments that do not immediately appear to pertain to the "sex industry"—such as erotic lingerie and beauty products—also reflect the heightened importance of commercially situated sexual behavior to middle-class women.[28]

The emergence and success of these markets provide additional evidence that for growing numbers of both women and men, sexuality is currently being reconstructed as a series of isolable techniques that provide personal meaning and pleasure, as opposed to an expression of ongoing relationship with a particular individual.

The model of sexuality that I have outlined here is one that moves from political economy to eroticism and back again. While transformations in economy and kinship have produced a new paradigm of sexual ethics, this latter has itself been vital to transitions in extra-sexual domains. The prevalence of commercially available sexual exchange is merely one feature of the growing service economy which serves to redirect an ever-expanding set of human needs from noncommodified, domestic space to the (newly privatized and domesticated) market sphere. These services thus contribute to a fundamental reconstitution of the meaning and structure of the family, from an economic unit to the chief social repository of sex and intimacy, to an institution that is entered into ever more tentatively, conditionally, and contractually, premised on bonds that may in fact be severed if they come to no longer satisfy an individual's emotional needs.[29]

A sexual ethic that is premised on bounded authenticity—as opposed to an amative/companionate one—also makes possible the agile, isolable individual that contemporary economic life requires. As the sociologist of culture Ann Swidler has noted, "The need to be continually ready for new demands creates a wary avoidance of the entanglement in love and work, an eagerness to keep the self free and unconstrained."[30] Bounded authenticity lends itself less to engrossing time commitments or unwieldy rafts of dependents and more to intimate relations that are cost-efficient and well-suited to the structure of the modern corporation: temporary, detachable, and flexible. Whether in the public sphere of work, in the private sphere of the family, or in the embodied sphere of desire, the postmodern individual tends toward ever-increasing autonomy and mobility, unfettered by any form of binding or permanent social ties.

EVALUATING CONTEMPORARY SEXUAL MARKETS
The "privilege" of participation in a postindustrial paradigm of sexual commerce can perhaps best be described as an ambivalent one. As I found with the middle-class sex workers that I interviewed for this study—whose sexual labor required much more significant quantities of emotion work than did the sexual labor that was characteristic of modern-industrial prostitution—those who participate most fully in

the emotionally contained economy of recreational sex and bounded authenticity are also those whose psychic lives are most fully penetrated by the cultural logic of late capitalism. A thorough assessment of the costs and benefits of the incursion of the market into intimate life can therefore be a complex and difficult task—particularly for women. What Arlie Hochschild has termed "women's uneasy love affair with capitalism" is made all the more acute when we consider that many of the flourishing sectors of the late-capitalist service economy—such as child care, domestic labor, and sex work—are commercialized refinements of services that women have historically provided for free.[31] As service industry workers, women now conduct this labor within the context of market-generated (as opposed to status-based) social hierarchies.[32] As consumers, women as well as men increasingly have access to the particular conveniences, pleasures—and emotional confinement—of commercially mediated interpersonal relations. For women, as for men, passion, meaning, and connection do not disappear but are packed ever more tightly into market commodities.

Ethical and political disputes around sexual commerce, as well as other ideological struggles around sexuality, must be reevaluated in the light of these economic and cultural transformations. Conflicts over the social desirability of commercial sexual arrangements have often masked the broader cultural anxieties which percolate just below the surface: around relations of gender and power, as second-wave feminists have rigorously argued; but also in regards to the rapidly extending scope and reign of the market as well as the wide-ranging reorganization of kinship and intimacy. Those who have argued in favor of a return to the sexual mores of eras past (whether advocating for a procreative model, as in the Religious Right's condemnations of homosexuality, contraception, and abortion; or for an amative/companionate one, as in mainstream feminist and liberal-sociological critiques of commercialized intimacy) have typically failed to consider both the significance, and the trenchancy, of the material underpinnings of the new sexual ethos and its embodied forms.

Julia O'Connell Davidson is one critic who has sought to connect her own ethical evaluation of contemporary sex commerce to an analysis of the classed, raced, and gendered inequalities that have flourished under late capitalism.[33] As such, she aptly criticizes both "anti-" and "proprostitution" feminists for basing their positions on transhistorical understandings of sexuality which posit an inherent link between sexuality and self. In the case of antiprostitution feminists, this link is revealed via suggestions that once a woman sells sexual access to her body, she is damaged profoundly and irrevocably; in the case of pro-prostitution feminists, it is manifest through invocations of clients' "sexual needs" as a means to assert the social value of sexual labor. Although O'Connell Davidson convincingly disputes the notion that sexual commerce has any intrinsic value beyond that of other forms of service work (e.g., domestic work, shoe shining, or airline hostessing, all of which are premised on the prior existence of social inequalities), she herself neglects to specify why selling sex nonetheless remains more troubling to her than any of these other commercial forms. If there is no essential link between sexuality and self (as she maintains), why *not* sell sex? What is it, precisely, that makes it worse to sell sex than to sew garments, to clean houses, or to care for other people's children?

One response to this question is provided by feminist activists who have dedicated themselves to contemporary struggles around the "traffic in women." Feminists affiliated with groups like the Coalition Against Trafficking in Women (CATW) have argued that what is wrong with prostitution as opposed to other forms of service work is the inherency of the connection between prostitution, violence, and degradation. They maintain that "prostitution is a main battleground where women *as a class* are reduced to sex, denied equal humanity, and delivered up to such practices."[34] Whether or not these claims are capable of standing up to empirical scrutiny (a possibility rendered doubtful by my own and others' analyses of the diversity of lived experiences within the sex trade), such arguments are also problematic in their tendency to bracket the factors other than gender oppression that have facilitated the growth of contemporary sex markets. For example, Donna Hughes, a prominent antitrafficking activist, rightly asserts that "trafficking and prostitution are highly gendered systems that result from structural inequality between women and men on a world scale." She argues, however, that "the most crucial factor in determining where trafficking will occur is the activity of the traffickers. Poverty, unemployment, inflation, war, and lack of a promising future are compelling factors . . . but they are not the cause of trafficking."[35] While I agree that culture and structure must be seen as working in tandem, for Hughes, the problem of the sex industry is primarily one of sexually exploitative "bad" men; only to a lesser extent does it have to anything to do with global inequalities (which, in this rendition, are naturalized).

Yet a final problem with the CATW analysis is revealed by the title of another article which appeared on the organization's Web site: "Sex: From Intimacy to Sexual Labor, or Is It a Human Right to Prostitute?"[36]

According to this essay, prostitution is wrong even if women consent to the transaction, and even when abduction, deception, and trafficking have not occurred. For even under these circumstances, prostitution represents a violation of "an experience of human intimacy," and should be viewed not as a form of service work but as a practice akin to "paid rape." Echoing Høigård and Finstad's interpretation of the "double self," the (unspecified) author regards prostitutes' "refusing access to some parts of their bodies or use of their own beds, creating fictional life stories or other such measures" as futile attempts to ward off the inevitable damage that ensues when one's sexuality is deployed for monetary gain.[37] As with the audience member's spontaneous intervention at the 1999 "Economic Justice for Sex Workers" conference in San Francisco, these statements represent a rare moment in the prostitution debates in which a commentator's underlying sexual ethic is stated explicitly. For CATW activists, market-mediated sex cannot be intimate sex, and sexual relations that take place outside a framework of romance and domestic companionship (the modern-industrial paradigm) must be morally condemned.

Remaining attentive to the intertwining—and at times, contradictory—operations of diverse forms of power and oppression, I would like to instead argue for an ethical assessment of sexual commerce that melds feminist concerns around gendered power with a more complex consideration of the commodity form. Such an assessment follows in the footsteps of feminist philosophers such as Laurie Shrage and Debra Satz as well as cultural sociologists such as Viviana Zelizer, all of whom have strived to articulate a contextual and pluralist ethics of commercial sexual transactions. Thus, in her book *Moral Dilemmas of Feminism,* Shrage is sharply critical of any single and unitary account of the social origins, evolution, and meaning of prostitution, whether condemnatory or romanticist. Instead of attempting to answer the question "What's wrong with prostitution?" Shrage first poses the question "What is it?" Drawing on diverse sociohistorical studies, she compares different varieties of contemporary sex commerce with colonial Kenyan prostitution and prostitution in ancient Bablyon so as to highlight their particularities. She concludes that different varieties of prostitution may have different social meanings and, thus, demand different social responses. Perhaps prostitution "predicated on fertility worship or prostitution that functions as informal polyandry" need not be deterred or controlled.[38] Shrage's analysis undercuts the CATW assumption that there is a unity to all women's experiences which stems from sexual domination. Instead, she persuasively argues that women's sexual experiences harbor a *range* of potentially empowering, oppressive, and morally neutral meanings, as do different historical and cultural varieties of prostitution.[39]

Debra Satz has also argued that only a historically and culturally situated discussion of prostitution in its diverse variants will allow us to determine "what, if anything, is problematic about a woman selling sexual as opposed to secretarial labor."[40] Satz proceeds by proposing a range of "prostitute scenarios"—the fourteen-year-old heroin addict; the college-educated, Park Avenue call girl; the male prostitute who sells sex to other men—in order to consider who becomes a prostitute and why, how choices are made and preferences shaped, and what constitutes the likely range of alternatives for each of the above cases. Satz then considers to what extent different prostitutes are engaged in a "desperate exchange"—that is, an exchange in which the individual would never partake given any reasonable alternative. While for Satz there is nothing morally wrong with prostitution per se, her thought experiments lead her to conclude, crucially, that important barriers to degradation are established by a prostitute's ability to refuse to perform sex and to exercise informed consent; by her freedom to work without male brokerage; and by the existence of other viable life options.

In *The Purchase of Intimacy,* an intriguing exploration of the diverse social meanings that can append to different kinds of commodified intimate relations (within sexual coupling and more generally within household life), Viviana Zelizer similarly rejects what she terms the "hostile worlds" and "nothing but" analytic approaches to commercially mediated intimate encounters. Whereas the former posits a necessary contradiction between intimate social relations and monetary transfers (such that any contact between the two inevitably leads to moral contamination), the latter argues that intimate commercial transactions are "nothing but" another expression of rational action, oppression, or prevailing cultural values. Like Shrage and Satz, Zelizer instead advocates for a pluralist approach to evaluating intimate commercial commerce, an approach that she terms "differentiated ties." As in her earlier work on the complex social meanings contained within monetized transactions, a central contention of Zelizer's argument is that the precise means by which payments are exchanged and named is crucial for establishing the meaning of any given social relationship.[41]

Rather than taking commodification to be a self-evident totality, with Shrage, Satz, and Zelizer, I stress the ethical necessity of distinguishing *between* markets in sexual labor, based on the social location and defining features of any given type of exchange. This is not to suggest that there exists any simple and easily enforceable division between "forced" and "voluntary" prostitution or (applying a different moral valence) between "innocent" and "guilty" sex workers.[42] Rather, I am advocating for the careful and attentive scrutiny of precisely what is wrong—and, potentially, right—with different commercial sexual modalities. Satz's criteria for "desperate exchanges," for example, can provide us with one helpful starting point in this assessment.

With streetwalking, as with some of the other forms of "modern-industrial" prostitution that we have considered (e.g., in strip clubs and in red-light districts), women's economic marginalization and frequent exposure to physical violence and sexual control are indeed morally troubling features of the commercial sexual transaction—by Satz's as well as by most other ethical criteria. Within the drug markets of the Tenderloin and Mission districts, sex workers' persistent and severe intoxication can hardly render the notion of "informed consent" meaningful. To the extent that dynamics of force, violence, and exploitation are operative in any given sexual encounter or in the life course of particular sex workers, we should be ethically troubled and seek means to intervene (just as we should seek to intervene when force, violence, and exploitation occur with other kinds of unregulated labor).[43]

Looking beyond Satz's concerns with violence and exploitation, there are aspects of modern-industrial prostitution that—on careful examination—may be more difficult to ethically and politically assess. One such feature is sex workers' creation of a "divided self" as a means of psychic survival—a phenomenon which, as we saw in chapter 3, is often characteristic of low-status, alienating labor more generally. Yet as Arlie Hochschild has argued, the "surface acting" that is required for the enforcement of such a division may in some ways be less intrusive than the "deep acting" that many middle-class jobs require.[44] An additional complexity of moral evaluation is entailed by the fact that streetwalkers often regard their own work as participating in as well as challenging broader structures of oppression, both in terms of class and in terms of gender (recall that for many women, the quid pro quo exchange of cash for sex made sex work *less* morally troubling than other economic options, and *more* personally empowering than other forms of heterosexual intimacy). Although prostitution is rarely anyone's ideal economic or sexual arrangement, street-based sex workers have often described it as their best choice out of a very limited series of options.

Commercial sexual transactions of the postindustrial variety demand a distinct ethical appraisal. Not only are most of Satz's barriers to degradation present in the majority of instances, but many sex workers (like their clients) embrace a recreational sexual ethic that enables them to participate in sexual labor while maintaining an undivided, authentic-feeling self. As with the streetwalkers, payment for sexual services can function as a means of denaturalizing status-based social arrangements and inequalities—albeit in different ways. As we saw in chapters 3 and 4, whereas the streetwalkers challenged the moral divides between prostitution and other working-class jobs, and between sexual labor and marriage, COYOTE members rescripted both the content of heterosexual relations and the cultural divide between "good" and "bad" women. Sex-worker activists also traversed the boundaries of heterosexual domesticity by furthering the cultural normalization and political legitimacy of sex work.

Skeptics may protest that the individuals that I have chosen to represent under the banner of the postindustrial paradigm constitute atypical cases that are therefore inconsequential to an ethical assessment of the contemporary sex trade.[45] As I have argued earlier, although the women from COYOTE clearly constitute one pole on a spectrum of prevailing cultural patterns, my years of ethnographic research with diverse constituencies of sex workers have convinced me that they do not constitute a singularly freakish exception. Even *if* we were to consider their example as primarily a "limiting case," an analysis of their work is critical for assessing the range of possible meanings that can append to late-capitalist commercial sexual transactions. As we have seen, one feature that is highlighted by the "best case scenario" that they provide is the extent of the market's incursion into intimate life and vice versa. Their example also reveals the extent to which (even in the white, middle-class, upper tiers of the sex industry) incentives for engaging in sex work remain intricately tied to unequal relations of class and gender. As with the Tenderloin streetwalkers, the sexual labor of COYOTE members both challenges and participates in gendered and economic structures of oppression.

SEXUAL COMMERCE AND SOCIAL JUSTICE

At the Eighth Annual Domestic Violence Conference at Fordham University in New York City, the morning panelists are in the midst of a "Dialogue about Prostitution, Trafficking, and Domestic Violence." Two of the feminist activists featured on this morning's panel have taken to the stage, where they enact a well-rehearsed skit that is equal parts pedantry and political theater. "Women's bodies are more profitable than guns or drugs, plus they can be sold multiple times," announces one woman in a tone both authoritative and somber. "And they are easier to bring across the borders." Dressed smartly in a tweed suit and high-heeled pumps, she has the polished, impermeable veneer of a practiced politician. With studied guilelessness, her performance partner inquires, "But aren't they well paid once they are here?" "That's exactly what the traffickers would like you to believe!" the polished woman scoffs.

In the audience are some three hundred women—the majority, white middle-class feminist activists and lawyers. They are powerfully engaged with the speakers, inclining forward in their chairs in rapt attention. The speakers' graphic accounts of the sexual violence that prostituted women are forced to endure seems to serve as a viscerally stimulating "mirror of pornography" for all present—inspiring a wave of audible sighs and impromptu exclamations of disgust.[46]

Even more unusual than the speakers' performance is what is on the wall behind them: the full-color likeness of Margareta Winberg, Sweden's former Minister of Gender Equality, who beholds the audience members in eerie stillness from the enormous movie screen where her image is projected. A smiling facade with gray-blonde bangs and pearls looms large, setting the tone for the entire, weekend-long event: the celebration and dissemination of Swedish prostitution policy. Throughout the conference, the "Swedish plan" will emerge as feminist panacea and utopian state solution to the local problem of prostitution and to the global problem of international sex trafficking. The conference participants are in clear agreement: in order to end the commercial sexual exploitation of women, we must criminalize demand.

The day's events culminate with a screening of the 2002 Swedish film by Lucas Moodyson, *Lilja 4-Ever*. Although the film is a semi-fictional account, it has become a primary instructional tool for legislators, activists, and police officials seeking to understand the phenomenon of sex trafficking—both within Sweden and abroad.[47] As with other recent representations of trafficking, the tropes of peeling paint and bleak cityscapes stand in for the broader and more diffuse horrors of global economic injustice.[48] The film's final sequence relies on especially heavy symbolism: an angel attempts to guide Lilja, but he cannot prevent her from throwing herself into oncoming traffic, to her death.

FIELD NOTES, MARCH 2004

In light of my analysis of the experiential diversity and moral complexity of contemporary sex markets, the question that many readers may be eager to hear addressed is what "we" (feminists, sociologists, sexworkers' rights advocates, and other individuals concerned with social

justice) should seek to do about them. In chapter 6, I argued that feminists' single-minded focus on the legal remedies of decriminalization,
legalization, and criminalization has thus far failed to achieve either
empowerment or protection for women in the most vulnerable tiers of
the industry—much less the elimination or normalization of the global
sex trade. Here I will argue that those who have expressed ethical concerns about the expansion of sexual commerce should pay greater attention to the relationship between sexual and economic relations, not
only in crafting ethical evaluations of prostitution but also in forging
effective political remedies.

At the time of this writing, the mode of political intervention which
is garnering the most momentum nationwide is the criminalization of
sexual demand—that is, the "Swedish plan." [49] In accordance with
feminist ambitions to shift the stigma of prostitution from buyer to
seller, activist groups ranging from CATW to NOW have campaigned
for federal legislation to penalize prostitutes' customers. They have even
been joined in their efforts by right-wing and religious activists from
Concerned Women for America, the National Association of Evangeli-
cals, and the Southern Baptist Convention. [50] Male demand for sexual
services has been identified by a broad-based coalition of social actors
as the principal engine behind the "traffic in women," culminating in
the criminalization of "prostitute use" by the U.S. military, the foregrounding of demand at the Beijing + 10 meetings of the United Nations Commission on the Status of Women, and the incorporation of a
program to reduce demand for commercial sex acts as a core element
of the Trafficking Victims' Protection Reauthorization Act passed by
the U.S. Congress. [51]

Given my prior analysis of the class- and race-based enforcement
patterns of client-focused approaches to prostitution in San Francisco
and Stockholm, I am obviously skeptical about the efficacy of implementing such measures on a broader scale. In neither case is there compelling evidence that the criminalization of clients has been effective in
decreasing demand for off-street sexual services, or, more important,
for improving the lives of women in prostitution (the presumed impetus
for seeking to eliminate the sex trade). Nor do such policies do much
to address what are, I suspect, the more compelling issues for CATW
and other activists within the current campaign, who regard prostitution as "a violation of human intimacy." Those who seek to restore
the hegemony of procreative or amative models of sexuality would do
better to interrogate (and to challenge) the structural preconditions
of the new recreational sexual paradigm rather than to place the

livelihood of socially and economically marginalized women in further jeopardy.

As we have seen in chapters 5 and 6, in practice the criminalization of clients primarily serves as a street-sweeping device, facilitating the redevelopment of gentrifying urban centers. Meanwhile, there is gathering evidence that grouping all commercial sex acts together under the legal rubric of "trafficking" has the net effect of arresting and deporting the very migrant women that such laws purport to save. As Wendy Chapkis has demonstrated in her recent analysis of the effects of antitrafficking policies in the United States, those individuals who do not meet the legal and cultural criteria of the "innocent victim" (e.g., they are insufficiently young or naive, or are unwilling to testify against their alleged exploiters) will quickly get reclassified as "criminals" instead.[52] It was thus that in the summer of 2005 hundreds of state and federal law officers descended upon eleven massage parlors in San Francisco and other California cities in a highly sensationalized "rescue" of Korean migrants purportedly living under conditions of sexual slavery.[53] Of the nearly 150 women who were taken into police custody during the raid, more than half were immediately deported (and threatened with arrest by the Korean government on prostitution charges) when they were deemed by federal officials to have not been coerced. Of the remainder, forty-six women were forcibly retained by the federal government as material witnesses against the massage parlor operators, only a quarter of whom were eventually declared to be legitimate victims entitled to social services.[54] Ethnographic investigations that focus on the experiences of migrant sex workers have also demonstrated that although many migrants must endure violence, coercion, and privation in the course of their work (both within the sex trade and within other labor sectors), only a small minority conform to the images of "sexual slavery" that have been endlessly recycled by abolitionist feminist groups and the press.[55] For the overwhelming majority of female migrants, it is not brute force, pure deceit, or random abduction that propels them to engage in sexual labor, but rather the desire for economic, social, and geographic mobility; the potentially pleasurable aspects of being an object of affection and desire; and the allure of flexible schedules and instant cash.[56]

What measures *would* adequately address the physical and psychic harms that many women in the sex industry must face? The appeal of the organizers of the 1999 San Francisco conference to the principle of "economic justice" for sex workers (which focused on issues such as decriminalization, unionization, employee benefits, and the enforcement of occupational health and safety guidelines) is a fine starting point, but it does not go far enough. As COYOTE founder Margo St. James remarked at the symposium, the organizers' chosen topic was ironic, "given that no woman in America is even guaranteed the right to abortion, let alone economic autonomy." [57] Furthermore, as we have seen in the cases of both San Francisco and Amsterdam, decriminalization and labor rights for some sex workers are in practice quite compatible with the harassment, violation, and deportation of others—often carried out under the guise of "broken windows" policing or through well-intentioned but ultimately harmful efforts to combat sex trafficking via the en masse "rescue" of illegal migrants.

To seriously address the burgeoning economy in commercial sexual services in all of its diverse manifestations (including the circumstances of profound exploitation that some women find themselves in) would require a much more ambitious political agenda. First, it would require a sober analysis of the global inequalities (of sex, of class, of race, and of nation) that drive women into sexual labor, and of the ways that these inequalities are themselves created through specific practices and policies (e.g., through linkages between international debt and lending guidelines, price fluctuations in global commodity markets, and economic development policies). [58] It is precisely these trademark policies of neoliberal globalization which encourage indebted nations to respond to economic crises through the development of local tourist industries (including sex tourist industries) and to enhance local cash flow through migrant workers' remittances (including those garnered through sexual labor). As such, policies pertaining to globalization may be far more consequential than either the decriminalization, criminalization, or legalization of prostitution in shaping the size and formal contours of the sex trade.

A serious effort to engage with the structural preconditions behind the expansion of contemporary sex markets would also require us to confront the local faces of these same global processes, including the promotion of deindustrialized economies built on real estate speculation, retail trade, and financial services; redevelopment policies which eliminate affordable housing and recreate city centers as white, upper middle-class enclaves for consumption and leisure; and the continued transformation of the welfare state into a predominantly carceral enterprise. [59] In sum, the argument that I am making here is that feminists and other social commentators who are concerned about the existence

and augmentation of contemporary sex markets would be wise to identify the fight against corporate globalization (in both its transnational
and local guises) as pivotal to their interests.[60]

Taking into account the continued rightward drift of recent political
and cultural trends, it may seem a daunting task to find effective means
to combat the broad array of conditions that I have outlined above.
Although I agree that our abilities to reverse the course of globalization
or to breathe new life into a crumbling welfare state are highly unlikely
in the present political moment, there are more humble, direct, and re-
alizable interventions which might nonetheless be possible to achieve.
The existence of gender equity policies within the workplace and of
more general social and economic remedies to assist low-wage and migrant workers (such as living wage policies, training programs, and the
extension of basic labor protections to informal-sector employment)
would certainly render women's decisions to engage in sexual labor, at
all class levels, much more meaningful.[61] In 2003, Juhu Thukral and
Melissa Ditmore of the Urban Justice Center in New York interviewed
a diverse sample of street-based sex workers in order to document the
women's own assessments of their most pressing political needs. They
found that the single most important intervention that street-based
sex workers desired was not directly related to prostitution at all, but
rather to an inadequate supply of housing. Thukral and Ditmore observed that:

> The lack of any stable housing situation is a major factor con-
> tributing to the precarious situations in which street-based sex
> workers live. Homelessness creates a cycle of deepening impov-
> erishment that may be almost impossible to escape. The lack of
> a fixed address or a telephone number hinders attempts to find
> other employment. The high cost of even substandard short-stay
> accommodation imposes a financial burden that may be hard to
> meet without resorting to the "fast money" offered by illegal ac-
> tivities such as prostitution. Temporary accommodation creates
> an environment that is often not conducive to resolving other
> contributory problems such as substance dependency. Physical or
> mental illness resulting from the stress, discomforts, and dangers
> of homelessness carry additional personal and financial costs that
> make it harder to break the cycle.[62]

Their primary policy recommendations thus consisted of long-term
and transitional shelters, a "housing first" model for those who receive government assistance, and the redirection of federal, state, and

local monies away from arrest and incarceration and toward affordable residences.[63]

An awareness of the necessity of connecting struggles pertaining to sex work to a broader political and economic agenda has also been evidenced in the recent campaign to prevent the implementation of "prostitution-free" zones in Washington DC. Like its predecessor policy of "drug free zones," the creation of "prostitution-free zones" would criminalize economically and racially marginalized people who occupy public streets.[64] In the face of the proposed legislation, a broad-based coalition of local organizations joined together to express their strong and united opposition, proclaiming it a strategy to facilitate gentrification as well as to curb the rights to public assembly of migrants, the homeless, and sex workers. Comprised of peer-based projects for sex workers as well as advocacy groups for the homeless, LGBT issues and immigrants' rights, the Alliance for a Safe and Diverse DC emerged out of a political vision based on the mutual constitution of sexual and social justice. Although the alliance was not ultimately able to prevent implementation of the zones, its success in staving them off for a year nonetheless represents a successful model of sex-worker activism through coalition building. Significantly, the alliance has remained intact and politically active even after the city's decision to implement the zones, taking to the streets in order to document their impact on various DC communities and to overturn the policy on civil rights grounds.[65]

CONCLUSION

Whether we regard the flourishing of sexual commerce as merely one domain among others in an expanding global service economy or as a uniquely troubling manifestation of gross inequalities of gender, class, race, and nation will depend on the presence or absence of a normative orientation which views sexuality (particularly women's sexuality) as inextricably tied to procreation or romance. Yet in most debates about the social and economic significance of prostitution, interlocutors' own assumptions regarding the proper relationship between the spheres of sexuality, intimacy, and commerce have been left unarticulated. While ethical and political evaluations of prostitution often apply an unstated norm by presuming it to consist of a timeless set of practices and meanings, I suggest instead that normative discussions of sexual labor should begin with an understanding of the socially and historically specific meanings that affix to commercial sexual transactions, and to intimacy and sexuality more generally.

I have also argued that the emergence of a postindustrial paradigm of sexual commerce and of a sexual ethic that is premised on bounded authenticity represent important shifts in both the cultural logic of male dominance and in the cultural logic of capitalism. As such, they encapsulate new sets of social dangers as well as (in some cases) new occupational and relational possibilities. The fact that these shifts may have disparate effects for social actors pertaining to different genders or class fractions may be precisely what has inspired some parties' staunch opposition to the burgeoning commercial sex trade (in both its feminist and Religious Right guises). Yet critique alone cannot undo the structural transformations that have reinvented ethically complex exchanges as sexually and socially desirable commodities for increasing numbers of individuals. My intention in this book has been to reveal the material conditions under which particular erotic choices have become desirable in the first place, and to explain why both the desire for commercialized sex and the conditions for its realization have heightened, not wavered, during the current historical period. Throughout this work, I have sought to demonstrate structurally analogous and interlinked processes occurring simultaneously in economic, cultural, and erotic domains. As with many of the most politically difficult and theoretically complex issues of our era, I have argued that practices of sexual commerce must be situated squarely within these economic and cultural currents, rather than regarded as exceptions to be judged apart.

This project began in the fall of 1994 as a study of the San Francisco Task Force on Prostitution, formed a year earlier by then-Supervisor Terence Hallinan to look into the possibility of reforming prostitution policy in the city. I was fortunate in that my decision to embark on an empirical study of prostitution coincided with the task force's solicitation of a PhD student to assist with research on some of the issues surrounding legal reform. I had been intrigued by the abundant media coverage of the task force, which suggested that the feminists, prostitutes' rights activists, and neighborhood representatives that formed its core were considering legalizing prostitution (a solution which each of the above groups had historically opposed) and even contemplating such controversial public policy solutions as city-run brothels or municipal licensing. I wondered if and under what guise prostitutes' concerns were being represented in these considerations, who was doing the representing, and which (if any) feminist position would predominate when it came down to the nitty-gritty of policy reform. Most important, I was concerned about what the likely impact would be—for sex workers and other city residents—if the proposed reforms should come to pass.

Most of the prostitutes' rights leaders who held seats on the task force told me that they were either currently working as prostitutes or had worked as prostitutes in the past. Yet I was soon to discover that only a few had any experience with street prostitution—the main focus of the task force's attention. As I got to know them and the organizations they represented, I came to have a more subtle understanding of the complexity and diversity of local prostitution markets and the different social realities they entailed. Although my initial object of study was the task force itself, I decided to expand my project to include participant observation with sex workers working in diverse ways and at diverse levels, so that I might test empirically my growing suspicion that the dynamics and meanings of prostitution varied systematically across social space. I became particularly interested in the contrast between the self-employed sex workers that I had met in activist groups like COYOTE and the lived realities of commercial sex work for those who walked the streets.

Carol Leigh—task force member, prostitutes' rights activist, multimedia artist, and sex worker—had been doing condom distribution and outreach among street prostitutes for over a year by the time I met her. She was enthusiastic and welcoming when I asked if I might join her to do outreach. We spent the next six months as research and outreach partners: our agendas and analyses overlapped to a sufficient extent to forge a productive collaboration, even if they did not always perfectly coincide. With her fifteen-year tenure as a prominent local activist, Carol was instrumental in introducing me to a vast network of sex workers, activists, lawyers, social workers, and city officials who were crucial informants for this project. After several months of doing outreach together, when I began to devise my plan for going out on the streets as a "decoy," Carol's input was again critical for its conceptualization and realization. She helped me to do the work in such a way as to make it meaningful to the streetwalkers themselves—that is, by focusing on the police treatment of prostitutes—and provided hours and hours of invaluable background assistance during its execution. Each time I took to the streets, Carol (alone or, occasionally, with another activist) would take her post at the opposing corner to monitor and videotape me. We considered this to be a very necessary safety measure, given the hours of operation (normally, between 10:00 p.m. and 4:00 a.m.), the locations, and the generally risky circumstances. Although I spent most of my time as a decoy on the Geary-Mason stroll in the Theater district, I also spent several nights on the Geary-Leavenworth stroll in the Tenderloin. Greater safety (in the form of a more populated street) and the extent of my ability to successfully "pass" among different populations were the primary concerns that motivated this decision.

The majority of the streetwalkers were not only enthusiastic when I announced my intention to investigate the police treatment of streetwalkers—several women even offered me various forms of assistance. When I further indicated that I was prepared to get caught in a police sweep and be taken to jail along with everyone else (and that I planned to write about the experience) they provided helpful—if at times contradictory—advice that was intended to facilitate my getting arrested

("You need to run when we run, so they know you're a 'ho.'" "Just stand there when they come by. Then they'll definitely get you." "You need to walk with another girl."). After a period of time, when newer women began to arrive on the strolls who had not been informed of my project or my intentions, they often assumed that I was simply another working girl. This was an impression that could be hard to shake even after I had the chance to try and explain my project face to face. (On one occasion while describing my research to a group of women that I had only recently come to know, their faces suddenly melted into smiles of recognition: "Oh yeah—you're the girl who's trying to sue the cops!")

Although the police demanded to see my identification and threatened to bring me to jail various times, in the end I was never actually arrested. The first few times that I was apprehended by the police, my identification card would be run and after no prior arrests were revealed on the small electronic monitor, I would usually be told to leave the area with a smirk or a stern warning ("If you're still out here when we circle back again, you're going to jail!"). But it didn't take long before I became somewhat of a known entity among the members of the Tenderloin vice squad—rather than believing me when I told them that I was a researcher, I think they too suspected I was an activist whose primary objective was to sue them for false arrest (some of my street-based fieldwork coincided chronologically with the two high-profile lawsuits that I discuss in chap. 3). Within a short period of time, whenever I would get hustled into the paddy wagon with the other women, I alone would be escorted back out of the car and onto the curb with relative courtesy.

My subsequent research was also the product of some important—and politically diverse—collaborations. Victoria Schneider, a dynamic sex workers' rights activist and then-active street prostitute, and Norma Hotaling, founder and current director of the SAGE Project (dedicated to abolishing the commercial sexual exploitation of women and children) were, in different ways, important guides to the SROs and prostitution strolls of San Francisco's Mission district. Jerry Skolnick, the author of pioneering ethnographic studies on the dynamics of policing, introduced me to the members of the vice squad in a neighboring municipality (given my known association with San Francisco's streetwalkers, I thought it wise to make my primary police contacts elsewhere).[1] This introduction enabled me to spend the summer accompanying them on their twice-weekly prostitution patrols, as well as to forge contacts with police departments in a number of other cities.[2]

In a series of ever-widening concentric circles, my project expanded outward for several years, as I reached for broader and broader contexts to make sense of what I saw. In 1995, I made my first trip to Scandinavia to research alternative state policies surrounding prostitution, following in the footsteps of earlier feminist sociologists who had turned to northern Europe to interrogate the construction of various social issues under conditions of relative gender and economic equality.[3] My first summer of research took me to Copenhagen, Denmark; Oslo, Norway; and Göteborg, Sweden, where I conducted my initial cross-national comparative study of the treatment of prostitution by different social welfare states. In each of the cities that I visited, my field research was enabled by collaborations with experienced researchers and activists who had ongoing contacts with various participants in the local sexual economy and who generously served as my guides to brothels, massage parlors, street prostitution strolls, the police, and government agencies.[4]

This research was also facilitated by the fact that nearly everyone I encountered in Scandinavia and subsequently in the Netherlands spoke English with great fluency—not simply university researchers, police officers, and state officials, but also a majority of the sex workers.[5] As I was soon to discover, English is the lingua franca of the European sex trade, particularly in highly touristed cities where both the workers and the clients hail from a multitude of regions.[6] Had I been conducting an in-depth psychological study of local clients, or investigating the subjective experiences of a particular population of migrant sex workers, it is unlikely that English would have been a sufficient linguistic medium for carrying out my research. But given that the objective of my investigations was to understand policy transformations and their consequences, communicating in English seemed adequate for my purposes.[7]

The focus of my research only began to narrow again in 1998, when I learned that Sweden and the Netherlands were revising their prostitution policies, and that both countries had assembled task forces similar to the one that I had served on in San Francisco. These two cases were of particular interest to me because Sweden and the Netherlands had both been hailed as "gender utopias" by various groups of feminist activists and the press, yet (as I describe in chap. 6) the two countries were changing their laws in opposite directions. I realized that by confining my analysis to the cases of San Francisco, Amsterdam, and Stockholm, I would be able to compare the lived dynamics of contemporary prostitution under three different legal regimes, in cities that shared a number of common features, including size, economic infrastructure, and reputations for social progressivism.

Despite the comparative dimensions of this project, I am aware that critics may question my choice of the San Francisco Bay Area as a primary field site, doubting the generalizability of claims that are culled from research conducted in such a historically unique coastal city. It is important to recall, however, that—as Rebecca Solnit and Susan Schwartzenberg point out in their recent book, *Hollow City*—in the late 1990s San Francisco relinquished its 150-year-old status as an urban "refuge and anomaly" to become the repository of over a third of the nation's venture capital and the global headquarters of the Internet economy. Even in the wake of more recent economic downturn, many of the features which still define the city, the "barrage of novelty item restaurants, websites, technologies, and trends . . . the numbness of incessant work hours and the anxiety of destabilized jobs, homes, and neighborhoods," also provide an increasingly apt description of life in other twenty-first century postindustrial cities.[8]

The reasoning that ultimately informed my conviction that I could base broader claims on a study conducted in San Francisco was thus similar to that articulated by Judith Stacey regarding her selection of California's Silicon Valley for research on postmodern families. As I note in chapter 1, although San Francisco is neither a typical nor a "representative" U.S. location, the fact that postindustrial cultural transformations are "more condensed, rapid, and exaggerated" here than elsewhere clearly may very well render them easier to perceive.[9] An underlying premise of my argument is that the frequently touted "particularity" of sexual culture in the San Francisco Bay Area (as a seat of both liberal tolerance and radical mobilizations around sexual diversity) is as much about the particular economic and social features of the region as it is about a geographically specific "culture" per se.[10]

Had I conducted my research in a different subset of well-touristed, postindustrial cities I would likely have gleaned findings that were similar to—though by no means identical with—those reached by virtue of the cases under consideration here. Indeed, in my less detailed examinations of patterns of sexual commerce in some other cities (I currently live in New York and lived in Barcelona for several years in the early 1990s), I have seen variations of some of the same trends which I witnessed in this study. These nodal points of transnational economic and cultural processes have become key sites of sexual transformation as well, giving rise to a rapid proliferation of sexual commerce. In newly industrializing or nonurban settings, my findings would presumably have been quite different. Recent studies of sexual commerce in developing nations have pointed to a set of dynamics motivating sex workers, clients, and state actors which are structurally distinct from the ones that I describe in this work, although (as I argue in chap. 7) they are intricately intertwined.[11]

SEXUAL POLITICS AND POSITIONALITY
IN ETHNOGRAPHIC FIELDWORK

I begin to exit my car and Carol comes over to greet me. "You look beautiful, wonderful," she says. "But about those stockings . . . " I really tried my best, spent several hours in front of the mirror in fact, but learning the code of an alien aesthetic is more difficult than I had imagined, even for someone like me with an observant, interested eye. This weekend, the women on the street told me to strive for the seeming contradiction (to my aesthetic sense) of "nice, normal, classy," with "big hair" and "lots of makeup." I weakly tried to explain this to Carol in my defense. She maintained that my error had been to fall too heavily on the "classy" side, then enlisted a woman off the street to help itemize the failings of my outfit: the stockings should be sheer, rather than opaque. The miniskirt was good, but the jacket was too concealing. My shoes were square-toed, when they should have been pointed. And the scarf would have to go, even though it was barely 40 degrees. Bracing myself against the wind, I wondered silently if the female police decoys were able to do any better.

Apparently, most of the men in the neighborhood are less discerning critics. I took my post on the corner of Geary and Mason, while Carol and her video camera took theirs a safe distance away. The short walk over from my car made me nervous—I'm not used to being stared at as this particular kind of exotic object. Despite the fact that I looked straight ahead and strode vigorously with swinging fists, in the eyes of male onlookers I had been magically transformed (reminding me of the lascivious reactions to Jack Lemmon's character in the movie *Some Like It Hot*, when he first dons a dress). Men yelled at me, cars pulled over close, the male cashier and the pimps stared at me as I walked into the candy store on O'Farrell Street to buy gum. But I also noticed that some of the women seemed like they were maybe more comfortable with me hanging around. Standing alongside Sherry as she flagged down cars, tonight was the first time that I had the courage to even try to arrange an interview.

FIELD NOTES, NOVEMBER 29, 1994, SAN FRANCISCO TENDERLOIN

I embarked on this study after spending several years as a graduate and undergraduate student delving into the legacy of the feminist "sexuality debates" that had emerged to destabilize scholarly and activist consensus a decade earlier. Were prostitution and pornography forms of gender violence, as some feminist activists and scholars claimed? Or should they be situated alongside the provision of other commercially available services simply as "work," as sex workers' rights activists across the globe were increasingly mobilizing to argue? In the early 1990s, most of these conversations still took place at an abstract level—very little empirical work existed on the lived conditions of contemporary prostitution.[12] I was further encouraged to begin an empirical study of prostitution by a 1993 essay by Lynn Chancer entitled "Prostitution, Feminist Theory, and Ambivalence: Notes from the Sociological Underground." In a bold move, Chancer called on feminist scholars to conduct detailed ethnographic and, ideally, participant-observational studies of prostitution in all its various guises. If male sociologists could study crack users, street gangs, and ghetto boxers up close, why was prostitution always considered from a distance?[13]

My very first night of doing "decoy" research confirmed for me the ethnographer's maxim that one's embodied proximity to an object of inquiry determines what one can see.[14] It was not until I myself spent the hours dressing, applying makeup, and self-scrutinizing that I fully understood the work entailed in the transformation of the body into an object of consumption for a specified market. Situating myself in this way also enabled me to understand what Gail Pheterson and other feminist theorists have described as the "whore stigma" in new and profound ways.[15] Despite the fact that I had explained to most of the people I encountered (sex workers, pimps, johns, and others) that I was doing research, at times it was difficult for them to grasp the fact that I wasn't really working as a prostitute. Identified and treated like a streetwalker by the outside world, I myself came to internalize this identity to some extent even after the fieldwork was completed (my heart continuing to skip a beat whenever I happen to be jaywalking and a police car comes into view).

In his book, *Distinction*, Pierre Bourdieu has cautioned that when intellectuals attempt to understand social others through a provisional and deliberate entry into their worlds, the result is likely to be an apprehension of these worlds through schemes of perception and appreciation which still pertain to intellectuals' own *habitus*.[16] Writing from a very different epistemological and methodological position, the feminist theorist Donna Haraway has also argued that, "one cannot relocate in any possible vantage point without being accountable for that movement."[17] As a white, middle-class feminist academic, my claims to speak with authority about the lives of individuals whose worlds I initially entered on a "provisional and deliberate" basis are both politically and methodologically fraught, despite the many lasting and important friendships that emerged for me as a result of this fieldwork. Nor can I fail to recognize the degrees of social distance that, in many cases, made this entry into others' worlds possible in the first place, and allowed me to return home to my own comparatively comfortable surroundings at night's end.

During my fieldwork, I chose to address some of the political dimensions of this dilemma through the collaborative research strategies described above and through my growing activist engagement in issues pertinent to sex workers' lives (participating in demonstrations, writing letters, testifying in court, advocating for sex workers' rights at municipal hearings, etc.). In terms of the methodological dilemmas entailed by "studying down," other sociologists have often sought to address this problem through a strategy of long-term corporal immersion in their subjects' phenomenal worlds, not only "stepping into the ring" but staying there for a period of time sufficient to develop an embodied (as well as conscious) mastery of others' experiences. In this way, it has been suggested that some of the difficulties of perception entailed by the researcher's social relocation might be overcome. As Loïc Wacquant, author of *Body and Soul* (a recent ethnographic study of ghetto boxers) has argued,

> it is imperative that the sociologist submit himself [*sic*] to the fire of action *in situ*; that to the greatest extent possible he put his own organism, sensibility, and incarnate intelligence at the epicenter of the array of material and symbolic forces that he intends to dissect, that he strive to acquire the appetites and the competencies that make the diligent agent in the universe under consideration.[18]

Likewise, in *Islands in the Street* (a study of American street gangs) Martin Sanchez Jankowski seeks to establish his ethnographic authority through a similar means, noting that he "participated in nearly all the things they did. I ate where they ate, I slept where they slept, I stayed with their families, I traveled where they went, and in certain situations where I could not remain neutral, I fought with them."[19]

Had my objective been to focus on the ongoing experiences of a single and relatively coherent group of individuals, it might have been desirable for me to make this the primary methodological strategy of my own research. I might, for example, have rented an apartment in the Tenderloin and lived in the neighborhood full time, or decided that it was necessary to turn tricks myself (a methodology which would have presented its own independent set of dilemmas, as I discuss below). When I provisionally shifted my focus away from the Tenderloin toward other field sites in 1996, my plan had been to return to the streets for another period of intensive fieldwork the following year. Yet I was soon to discover that the world of streetwalking that I had begun to research in the early 1990s was rapidly disappearing, and that my primary contacts on the streets had already moved on to other venues (as I describe in chaps. 2 and 3). Given the serendipity that is an inevitable feature of ethnographic fieldwork, I decided that my best course of action was to change locales along with my displaced informants, adapting my research strategy to the rapid social and spatial transformations that I was witnessing.[20] As Michael Burawoy has argued with respect to conducting field research under conditions of late capitalist flux and transience, what is often required is to "rethink the meaning of fieldwork, to release it from solitary confinement [and] from being bound to a single place and time."[21]

My fieldwork with COYOTE was to some extent much easier, not only because it usually took place in surroundings to which I was more accustomed, but because the sociodemographic profile of most of the members (in terms of criteria such as age, race, educational background, and residence) was strikingly similar to my own. Even more important, I already shared a good deal of the language, behaviors, practices, expectations, and perceptions that comprised their *habitus*. I did not anticipate that this would be the case before I began my study, but it did make the research process run surprisingly smoothly, both in formal fieldwork and through the provision of ample opportunities for more informal encounters that lead to an easy and natural deepening of social ties (I would often run into members unexpectedly at the gym, at a café, or through common acquaintances). When I began this research, I could not honestly say that "some of my best friends" were sex workers. By the time that I completed it, this was a very apt description of my social world. With COYOTE's sex-worker activists, the chief methodological danger that I faced was not the trenchant blindness of social difference but rather my own inadvertent transition from nonparticipating observer into nonobserving participant (i.e., as close friend and collegial activist), to employ William Foote Whyte's oft-quoted phrase.[22]

During my fieldwork and interviews with clients, the relational context was different once again. I had already spent a significant amount of time chatting informally with male patrons in the commercial sex venues that I'd visited when I decided to pursue a series of more systematic, in-depth interviews. I placed an ad in two sex newspapers where many of the local sex workers advertised (one targeted toward a straight audience, the second targeted toward gay men) which consisted of three simple sentences: "HAVE YOU PAID FOR SEX? IF SO, FEMALE RESEARCHER WANTS TO INTERVIEW YOU! PLEASE CALL [voice mail number]." Placing this ad proved to be a highly successful strategy for supplementing the sample of clients that I had generated through the "snowball" method of asking sex workers for client referrals. I received approximately fifty telephone messages in response to my ad in the first day alone. With the straight clients, in particular, I was fully expecting to be treated like a sex-worker surrogate and to consider the men's transference with me as an additional form of data. Indeed, when I asked men why they had chosen to respond to my ad, several emphasized its novelty among the spate of other sexual possibilities being advertised. They said things like "It seemed like it would be something interesting and different to try" or "It was different from the other [sex worker] ads, so I thought I'd call yours first." What was most illuminating for me—both in terms of the interview process and in terms of what it revealed about some of the emotional expectations they brought with them to commercial sexual encounters—was the way in which the men simultaneously regarded our interview sessions as an erotic verbal adventure and a form of meaningful emotional support. Many of the men were ready to talk for hours about their experiences and expressed a clear sense of relief at being able to tell their stories to a young(ish) and pleasant woman who was also a friendly and eager listener. "Nobody knows I do this, nobody knows," confessed one man, looking desperately into my eyes. Another man bubbled over with emotion when he noted at the end of our interview how much he appreciated talking to me, especially given how much cheaper it was than a visit to his psychotherapist.[23]

As various commentators have noted, one of the potential dangers of a "follow the bodies" approach to multisited research is the risk that it poses of being spread too thin, of forcing the researcher to respond, move, reflect, and write at a less leisurely pace than the one to which some ethnographers have often been accustomed.[24] Certainly, in my own work, I at times felt this to be the case, as I watched myself move through a confusing series of social transitions, subjective identifications, and political and psychic allegiances in response to shifting fieldwork imperatives. To what extent this motion may have compromised the thoroughness of my own "moral and sensual conversion" to the lifeworlds of the individuals under consideration, I cannot say.[25] But I am certain that there are also crucial advantages to conducting field-work in this way, to spending my evenings trolling for prostitutes with the police and my nights with sex-worker activists at the peep show, to moving back and forth between "John Schools" and streetwalking strolls, and to circuiting through various cities. Principal among these advantages is the ability to weave together a narrative which explores the complex interconnections between different social groups and be-tween various times and places, to replace the "fiction of the social whole" with an ethnographic rendering of a highly complex social system.[26]

There is a final methodological dilemma that I faced in this proj-ect which merits special mention. To return to the challenge posed by Chancer in the article which partially inspired this work: why not con-duct a *fully* participant-observational study of prostitution? Chancer herself provides a compelling answer to this question, noting the likely array of professional consequences that a female ethnographer would face were she herself to engage in prostitution—from repeated jokes to humiliation to both overt and covert discrimination to perceptions of her as a martyr or a freak. Whereas male urban ethnographers often reap both personal and professional benefits from their entry into dan-gerous fieldwork settings—reinforcing their own and others' percep-tions of them as enviably "hip" or macho—a female ethnographer of prostitution who engaged in fully participational research would most likely inspire a host of uncomfortable reactions, ranging from titilla-tion to repulsion to deliberate distancing—none of which are particu-larly advantageous to an academic career.[27]

In a 1998 afterword to her original essay, Chancer notes two sets of responses from her colleagues that were inspired by her article's ini-tial publication: on the one hand, a series of whispered inquiries about whether she herself had ever worked as a prostitute (otherwise, how else to explain her interest in such a sordid and unseemly topic?); on the other hand, a spate of communications from a new generation of feminist ethnographers such as Wendy Chapkis (who herself sold sex to female clients in an Amsterdam brothel for one day as part of her field-work) which seemed to signal new possibilities for breaking the par-ticipant-observational taboo.[28] The contradictory developments that Chancer reports suggest to me a number of additional questions that contemporary ethnographers of prostitution ought to consider, ones which I feel I am particularly well suited to address as a result of having conducted this research. First: What are the potential methodological gains to be had by a fully participant-observational study of prostitution? And second: How do whatever gains might ensue from full participation balance against the lingering political and professional difficulties of conducting this sort of investigation?

Although there has been a flurry of recent writings about the potential analytic insights to be gleaned through "sex in the field" as an explicit research strategy—mostly, though not exclusively, authored by men[29]—in my case, I do not think that engaging in sex-for-pay would have revealed a tremendous amount more about the sets of social relations that I was seeking to understand. The qualities which still contribute to sexuality's stigmatized status as an object of empirical inquiry (the blend of conscious and unconscious aspects, the visceral reactions it generates, its potential to entail a loss of boundaries) might have transformed any such firsthand experiment into a solipsistic foray of self-discovery rather than the careful and attentive inquiry into others' experiences that I intended. If I had myself engaged in sex work prior to initiating this study, or if for other reasons I was already skilled in the provision of bounded authenticity (e.g., if I had previously worked as a massage therapist or as a social worker) it is possible that my experience of providing paid sexual services as part of the research experience would have been less dramatic and personally transformative and thus more sociologically illuminating.

I did, however, occasionally accompany sex workers when they went on dates to meet clients, and was once even introduced to a client as a potential "double" for a session, which admittedly facilitated greater ethnographic familiarity with the practices and mores that I was exploring.[30] No doubt, had I chosen to engage in sex work myself, I would have had many more occasions to be in intimate proximity to clients in their "natural" settings and might have learned things that I was unable to detect through interviews or through my observations in the more public regions of brothels, massage parlors, and strip clubs. Nonetheless, the potential methodological advantages that such an opportunity would have provided need to be considered alongside the lingering political and professional difficulties that Chancer points to.

Writing this book some seven years after Chancer's afterword was published, I fear that the cautious optimism that she expressed about the potential for contemporary researchers to delve into a fully ethnographic study of prostitution with a sense of professional candor and permission may not yet be fully warranted. Although my own project was intentionally and explicitly multisited in design, it is revealing to me that none of my colleagues or acquaintances were ever particularly curious about whether or not I had *purchased* sex, or how intimately I was engaged in the task force proceedings. Instead, the salient question on most people's minds (often hinted at or insinuated, rather than spoken directly) was the same question that plagued Chancer on publication of her essay: whether or not I had myself worked as a prostitute.[31] Although Chancer applauds the fact that Wendy Chapkis can both hold an academic job and admit to having sold sex (even for one day), her own analysis of the tight relationship between sex, sexism, and the gendered distribution of stigma within prostitution suggests that the fact that Chapkis received only female clients is not an insignificant detail. Despite the recent efflorescence of ethnographic work on sexual commerce, the only two female ethnographers that I am aware of who have admitted to engaging in sexual labor with male clients for the purpose of their research both chose to leave the academy on publication of their books.[32]

In her afterword, Chancer notes that she intended for her article to illuminate not simply something about the phenomenon of prostitution but also, and perhaps more important, something about the nature of current ethnographic and social science research in general.[33] I obviously agree with Chancer's observation that there are good, practical reasons that female sociologists have typically chosen to study prostitution "at a distance." Although some (most frequently, male) ethnographers have put themselves at physical risk in the name of social science, the bravery and heroism that are associated with such efforts continue to enhance their sense of identity as men as well as their status as academics. By contrast the female ethnographer of prostitution must make herself vulnerable in profound and potentially intimate ways, both within any performance of sex work and within its later reportage. The "whore stigma" is capable of producing very real social and professional dangers, ones which cannot be found in the mirror image of masculinist social science. The success of recent efforts to craft a fully embodied "carnal sociology," to seek redress for the disappearance of the body from a century of sociological inquiry, remains limited.[34] Despite the important transformations in the social meaning and individual experience of sexuality that have transpired in recent decades, within sociological circles only particular kinds of bodies and sexualities have been afforded the freedom and safety to appear in their entirety.

CHAPTER ONE

1. Throughout this book, names and identifying details of individuals and commercial venues have been changed so as to protect their anonymity. Names of public figures and of geographical locations have been left unmodified in order to preserve the social specificity of this account. When requested, I have employed some sex workers' actual or "working" names in order to facilitate self-recognition.

2. In her 1913 work, *A New Conscience, and an Ancient Evil,* the social reformer Jane Addams provided a classic statement of this position when she surmised that "In that vast and checkered undertaking of its own moralization to which the human race is committed, it must constantly free itself from the survivals and savage infections of the primitive life from which it started. Now one and then another of the ancient wrongs and uncouth customs which have been so long familiar as to seem inevitable, rise to the moral consciousness of a passing generation; first for uneasy contemplation and then for gallant correction" (quoted in Hobson 1987, p. 154). For a more recent account of the changing "double standard" and the consequent decline of the sex trade, see Bullough and Bullough (1987: 291ff.).

3. For a few prominent examples from the plethora of recent accounts, see Landesman (2004), Malarek (2003), and the numerous op-ed pieces by Nicholas Kristof that have appeared in the *New York Times* in recent years (e.g., Kristof 2004).

4. On structural violence, see Farmer (1997, 2005), Parker (2001), and Padilla (forthcoming).

5. See, e.g., Ehrenreich (1989), Ross (1989), Wright (1985), Bourdieu (1984), and Florida (2002).

6. Of the multitude of recent works on postindustrial global economic transformations, two massive edited collections—Held and McGrew (1999) and Lechner and Boli (2000)—are indicative of this omission. While they include sections on the implications for politics, culture, and identity, only one essay, notably titled "The Gender Dimension" (Steans 2000) makes any mention of

the body or sexuality. David Harvey's well-known treatment of the transition from Fordism to flexible accumulation (1990) and Saskia Sassen's analysis of the emergence and significance of global cities (1998) also lack sustained discussions of the sexual domain.

7. By the "international sex trade," I am not referring to a coordinated social or economic network, but to a highly diversified set of spatially dispersed transactions and social actors.

8. See, e.g., Bell (1978), Harvey (1990), Esping-Andersen (1990), Leidner (1993), Hondagneu-Sotelo (2001), Turkle (1995), and Castells (1996).

9. Hochschild (1994a, 1997), Stacey (1991, 1996), Coontz (1997).

10. Hochschild (1994b, 1997), Swidler (1980), Giddens (1992), Illouz (1997).

11. Luker (1984), D'Emilio (1993).

12. Castells (1996: 25), Seidman (1991: 121), Giddens (1992), Bauman (1998: 26).

13. Altman (2001: 1).

14. Foucault (1978).

15. Laumann (1994).

16. Bauman (1998: 27).

17. Simmel ([1907] 1971: 122).

18. Marx ([1844] 1978); Engels ([1884] 1978). According to legal theorist Margaret Radin, "[I]nalienability has had a central place in our legal and moral culture. Yet there is no one sharp meaning for the term 'inalienable.' Sometimes inalienable means nontransferable; sometimes only nonsalable. Sometimes inalienable means nonrelinquishable by a rightholder; sometimes it refers to rights that cannot be lost at all. . . . Something that is market-inalienable is not to be sold, which in our economic system means it is not to be traded in the market" (Radin 1987: 1849–50).

19. Marx ([1844] 1978: 96).

20. Engels maintained that under capitalism monogamy applied to women only; under communism, it would become a reality for men as well ([1884] 1978).

21. Despite the fact that male prostitution was also prevalent in urban centers during this period, male prostitutes were typically subsumed under the new and more socially salient banner of "homosexuals" in sociological, medico-psychological, and political discourses (Weeks [1981] 1997, Kaye 2003).

22. Viviana Zelizer has referred to the normative vision in the social sciences that places rigid moral boundaries between market and intimate domains as "the hostile worlds view" (Zelizer 2005, 2002).

23. Sanger p. 29, quoted in Stansell (1982: 173).

24. Rosen (1982).

25. Langum (1994: 18, 27), Donovan (2006: 29–31).

26. In Britain, attention to the phenomenon of white slavery was sparked somewhat earlier and was also given fuel by journalistic exposés, most notably "The Maiden Tribute of Modern Babylon" by the reformer William Stead. In 1885, Stead published a series of articles which detailed his purchase of a thirteen-year-old girl from her parents for one pound (Hobson 1987: 142).

27. Langum (1994: 15).
28. Although Durkheim's classic work *Suicide* cast in social terms what had previously been seen as the most "individual" of human actions, he was quite explicit about what he regarded as the presocial nature of the human body. Durkheim's sole intervention into questions of sexuality was a discussion of sex education (1911: 29–52). A partial English version of this text is provided in Durkheim ([1911] 1979: 140–48).
29. Freud ([1912] 1963: 64).
30. Ellis ([1906] 1936: 254).
31. Davis ([1937] 1985).
32. At the forefront of American sociology during the interwar years, the University of Chicago sociologists known as the Chicago school produced detailed, empirical accounts of the surrounding urban milieu (see Sumner 1994: 42).
33. Cressey (1932), Thomas (1923), Hobson (1987: 189), Thornton (1997: 13).
34. Heap (2003: 461); see also Irvine (2003: 433) and Rubin (2002: 23).
35. Sumner (1994: 203).
36. Cavan (1970), Young (1970), Davis (1971), Winick and Kinsie (1971), Bryan (1972), Hirschi (1972), Cohen (1980), Schur (1984).
37. In a frequently cited critique of the myopic focus on "nuts, sluts, and 'preverts'" in sociological deviance theory, Alexander Liazos highlighted the neglect of "other, more serious and harmful forms of 'deviance' . . . such things as poverty and exploitation, the war in Vietnam, unjust tax laws, racism and sexism, and so on, which cause psychic and material suffering for many Americans, black and white, men and women" (Liazos 1985: 374).
38. Davis (1971: 299). Symbolic interactionism was the reigning paradigm in qualitative sociology in the 1950s and 1960s. In contrast to positivist statistical analysis and behaviorist psychology, it advocated the study of social action as a reflexive, purposive, and creative response to objective social conditions (Sumner 1994: 42).
39. See Snitow et al. (1983), Vance (1989), and Duggan and Hunter (1995).
40. Leigh (1997: 225), Pheterson (1993: 39), Kempadoo and Doezema (1998: 3).
41. MacKinnon (1989: 3).
42. Barry (1979; 1995), MacKinnon (1987), Jeffreys (1997).
43. On the troubling emergence of the term "prosex feminism" to capture the views of feminists who sought to emphasize the potential for pleasure *as well as* danger in patriarchal heterosexual relations, see Vance (1989). In accordance with Vance's critique, I employ the term within quotation marks to highlight some of the difficulties that are entailed by this designation.
44. McClintock (1993: 1).
45. St. James (1987: 84).
46. For an analysis of similar developments within the field of social history, see Gilfoyle (1999). For a sampling of recent sociological and anthropological research on contemporary sex workers, see McClintock (1993), McKeganey and Barnard (1996), Pheterson (1996), Scambler and Scambler (1997), Chapkis (1997), O'Connell Davidson (1998), Flowers (1998), Kulick (1998), Prieur (1998), Brock (1998), Dank (1999), and Weitzer (2000c).

47. On male sex workers, see West (1993), McNamara (1994), Pettiway (1996), Aggleton (1999), Weeks (1985), and Kaye (2003). On pimps and profiteers, see Månsson (1987), Faugier and Sargeant (1997), and Hodgson (1997). On clients, see Allison (1994), Frank (2002a, 1998), Sullivan and Simon (1998), and Campbell (1998). Recent works on sex tourism, migrant sex work, and transnational correspondence marriages include Brennan (2004), Constable (2003), Cheng (forthcoming), Padilla (forthcoming), Kempadoo and Doezema (1998), Kempadoo (1999a), Agustín (2005, 2003, 2000), Thorbek and Pattanaik (2002), and Ehrenreich and Hochschild (2002).

48. See, e.g., Bell (1987), French (1988), Leigh (2004), Stubbs (1994), Mattson (1995), Plachy and Ridgeway (1996), Macy (1996), Nagle (1997a), Delacoste and Alexander (1998), Hughes and Roche (1999), Bernstein Sycamore (2000), Jameson (2004), and Farley (2003). Early precursors of the sex-worker memoir include *Gypsy,* the 1957 best-selling autobiography of stripper Gypsy Rose Lee, and Xaviera Hollander's 1972 publication of *The Happy Hooker,* both of which became major motion pictures.

49. The phrase refers to the reinscription and rhetorical reinforcement of a "culturally normative heterosexual organization of desire" in certain feminist texts that purport to be engaged in its critique (Brown 1995: 86). See also Doezema (2001).

50. The film concerns a Russian teenage girl who is trafficked into Sweden in the wake of post–Soviet economic collapse. The film has been a huge commercial as well as political success. It has been widely screened at national and international conferences on prostitution, and the Swedish Film Institute received 1.5 million kronor from the Swedish government to encourage high school students and members of the military to see the film (Kulick 2005).

51. As the journalist Timothy Egan has documented, "The General Motors Corporation, the world's largest company, now sells more graphic sex films every year than Larry Flynt, owner of the Hustler empire. The 8.7 million Americans who subscribe to DirecTV, a General Motors subsidiary, buy nearly $200 million a year in pay-per-view sex films from satellite providers." Meanwhile, Rupert Murduch's satellite subsidiary EchoStar "makes more money selling graphic adult films . . . than Playboy, the oldest and best-known company in the sex business, does with its magazine, cable, and Internet business combined" (Egan 2004; see also "GOP = Grumpy Old Pornographers" 2005, Rich 2004a, and Rich 2004b).

52. In turn-of-the-century London, surveys estimated that some 16,000 women were working as prostitutes; by 1912, the high-water mark of organized prostitution in U.S. cities, New York had over 1800 "vice resorts" and an estimated 15,000 prostitutes (Walkowitz 1980, D'Emilio and Freedman 1988: 210). By comparison, recent estimates indicate that there may be approximately 50,000 illicit sex workers currently working in New York City (Weidner 2001: 189). Such figures suggest that the number of illegal sex workers has increased threefold while the size of the general population has approximately doubled; they do not take into account sex workers who are employed in the rapidly expanding noncriminalized commercial sex sectors, such as stripping and phone sex.

53. In his book *Reefer Madness,* Eric Schlosser reports that in the United States, the number of major strip clubs roughly doubled between 1987 and 1992. Today there are about 2,300 of these clubs nationwide, with annual revenues ranging from $250,000 to $5 million each. The salaries of featured dancers in these venues have also exploded, with the nation's top porn actresses earning $15,000–$20,000 a week to dance at strip clubs (2003: 181). Meanwhile, Linda Williams has identified "the most eye-opening statistic" as the following: "Hollywood makes approximately 400 films a year, while the porn industry now makes 10,000 to 11,000. Seven hundred million porn videos are rented each year" (Williams 2004: 2).

54. Williams (2004: 3).

55. Schlosser (1997: 44).

56. Schenker (2004).

57. Over 3,000 pages of material were consulted from print and online media between 1994 and 2001. Online research involved a review of Web sites and chat rooms where sex workers advertise and consult with one another, and sites and list-serves where patrons exchange experiences and other information.

58. For synthetic discussions of challenges to the objectivist fieldwork tradition, see Emerson (2001: 20–24); Clifford and Marcus (1986), and Wolf (1996). For a recent critique of "linear, univocal, monological, and monochromatic texts" in sociological ethnography, see Wacquant (2005:444).

59. An extract from Harold Cohen's field notes as they appear in his book, *Deviant Street Networks,* is indicative of the objectifying and "othering" gaze that has often prevailed in sociological treatments of prostitution: "On August 2, 1977 at 10.30 p.m. I observed two women on 32nd Street and Fifth Avenue. Although at this time several prostitutes were present at this location I concluded that these women were not part of the permanent street scene. . . . Both were dressed in what appeared to be conservative and expensive clothes. They were not dressed in a promiscuous manner, nor did they have on excess makeup. . . . In fact they kept very much to themselves staring downward toward the sidewalk or looking at each other but avoiding eye contact with other street actors. After a few minutes they disappeared from view and were never again seen by this researcher" (Cohen 1980: 22).

60. For example, I provide few graphic close-ups of specific sexual transactions, except where I consider such inclusions to be pivotal to the ensuing theoretical discussion. Nor do I linger over my own libidinal experiences in the field, as a handful of ethnographers of sexual commerce have elected to do (e.g., Odzer 1994; for an example of an erotically tinged attempt at clinical realism, see Massey and Hope 2005). A fuller discussion of the unique challenges posed by embracing prostitution as an object of ethnographic inquiry is included in the methodological appendix to this book.

61. See, e.g., Burawoy et al. (1991, 2000), Willis and Trondman (2000), Scheper-Hughes (1992), Kligman (1998), Salzinger (2003), Marcus (1998), and Stacey (1991).

62. Stacey (1991).

63. For an analysis of the three "worlds" of welfare capitalism—liberal, corporatist, and social-democratic—see Esping-Anderson (1999 and 1990).

64. Following a similar logic, I employ other elements of the dominant lexicon in my field notes as well—referring, e.g., to women on the street as "girls," to the customers as "tricks," "dates," or "johns," and to the police as "cops."

65. The state of California is similar to most U.S. states in defining the crime of prostitution as "any lewd act between persons for money or other consideration" (West's Annotated California Codes 1999).

66. See, e.g., Harvey (1990 and 2003), Block (1990), Burawoy (2000), Comaroff and Comaroff (2000), and Duggan (2003).

67. The evidence suggests that the numbers are on the rise. When I did a rough count of print and Web-based advertisements in 2001, there were approximately 3,000 ads. By 2005, there were 5,000 advertisements on one popular local Web site alone. Unlike the more general expansion of sexual commerce described above, this multiplication most likely represents a shift in sex workers' means of working and advertising (rather than a sudden and dramatic increase in the number of sex workers per se).

CHAPTER TWO

1. The San Francisco Municipal Police Code §215 states that "It shall be unlawful for any person to engage in or be a party to or to solicit or invite any other person to engage in or be a party to any lewd, indecent, or obscene act or conduct" (San Francisco Task Force on Prostitution 1996, app. D).

2. Institutionalized prostitution, in the sense of regulated brothels, also existed during earlier periods of Western history, albeit on a much smaller scale. On the rise and decline of municipal brothels in medieval Europe, see Otis (1985). On the legal regulation of prostitution in ancient Rome, see McGinn (1998).

3. Gilfoyle (1992), Walkowitz (1980), Rosen (1982), Hobson (1987), Trumbach (1995), Agustín (2005), Svanström (2000), D'Emilio and Freedman (1988), Baldwin (1999).

4. For men of this period, "copulatory orgasm at regular intervals was regarded not merely as pleasure . . . but as a biological necessity for both mental and physical health" (Baldwin 1999: 359).

5. Male prostitutes during this period were typically subsumed under the new and more socially salient banner of "homosexuals" in sociological, medico-psychological, and political discourses (Weeks 1981, Kaye 2003).

6. Between the years of 1910 and 1915, more than thirty-five U.S. states and municipalities conducted major investigations of prostitution (D'Emilio and Freedman 1988: 210).

7. The hallmarks of modern-industrial prostitution—growth, formal organization, and legal regulation—emerged at different times in different places (e.g., Parisian prostitution was widespread and regulated on an unofficial scale already by the late 1700s; by the 1860s, most Western European metropolitan cities also had some sort of regulatory system). In the still-rural United States and in Scandinavia, however, the formal features of modern-industrial prostitution only developed in the final decades of the nineteenth century (see, e.g.,

Svanström 2000; Hobson 1987). On the emergence of regulated prostitution in colonial contexts, see Levine (2003) and White (1990). On male prostitutes' different relationship to stigma in the late nineteenth century, see Weeks (1981) and Kaye (2003).

8. Gilfoyle (1992: 309). The Progressive Era marks the time of national transformation from a kin-based, rural society to a modern-industrial nation, spanning roughly the period from 1880 to 1920 (see Luker 1998).

9. The 1910 Mann Act (Ch. 395, Stat. 825–27) prohibited the interstate traffic in women for "immoral purposes."

10. Writing in 1933, William C. Reckless described post–Progressive Era vice in a way that epitomized the Chicago school's focus on economic, political, and moral "disorganization" as the social underpinnings of crime (Reckless 1933).

11. Rosen (1982).

12. Hobson (1987: 156–57).

13. Reckless (1933: 15), Shumsky and Springer (1981: 73), Baldwin (1999).

14. Hobson (1987: 140, 157), Boutellier (1991: 204), Walkowitz (1980). Despite the prominent role played by international voluntary associations among European abolitionists (see, e.g., Limoncelli 2006), there were nonetheless discernible national differences among local social movements to eliminate regulated prostitution. As opposed to the more libertarian British, e.g., "the Swedes were . . . strongly suppressionist, refusing to allow the state to ignore prostitution and insisting that, if commercial sex were not to be outlawed altogether, at least the law on public order should be enforced to end solicitation" (Baldwin 1999: 390).

15. The so-called "French regulation system" became the model for much of Europe during the early decades of the nineteenth century. One of its chief theorists was the physician Alexandre Jean Baptiste Parent-Duchâlet. His landmark book, *De la prostitution dans la ville de Paris,* advocated not only the sequestration of prostitutes within special districts but their restriction to enclosed houses with barred windows and frosted windowpanes. Such houses could therefore be discreet from the outside yet subject to complete surveillance (Parent-Duchâlet 1836; see also Svanström 2000: 92).

16. Sterk-Elifson and Campbell (1993), Marshall and Marshall (1993), Boutellier (1991), Van der Poel (1995), Brants (1998).

17. "Abolitionism" is a term which was used to describe the late nineteenth-century feminist movement to eliminate prostitution. It is premised on the notion that prostitution constitutes a social harm that states should work to extinguish (Outshoorn 2004c: 7–8, Limoncelli 2006). In the Netherlands, prostitution policy unofficially reverted back to regulationism over the course of the twentieth century, with local authorities limiting prostitution to well-defined areas. In Sweden, application of the 1885 Vagrancy Act became the dominant legislation for controlling prostitutes, enabling state authorities to intercept and confine women who were not "honorably" employed (Outshoorn 2004b: 185, Söderblom 1992: 219).

18. The contributions of the midcentury Chicago school of sociology constitute an important exception. See, e.g., Reckless (1933), as well as Robert Park's

well-known discussion of distinct "moral regions" within the city (Park, Burgess, and MacKenzie [1925] 1967).

19. Shumsky and Springer (1981: 72). Shumsky and Springer point to an article by the anthropologist Jennifer James, "Mobility as an Adaptive Strategy" (1975) as a paradigmatic instance of this argument. James argues that "local and national mobility [is] crucial to survival as a streetwalker," stressing the importance to prostitutes of mobility "as both a survival and social strategy."

20. Reckless (1933: 271); see also Lynd and Lynd ([1929] 1957: 113) and Lynd and Lynd (1937: 163).

21. Accounts of the prevalence of Chinese prostitutes in the early American West are overwhelmingly beholden to a "scarcity" model of naturalized heterosexual desire. Benjamin Tong, e.g., refers to Chinese men's "critical shortage of women for companionship," and Judy Yung has explained the arrival of large numbers of immigrant prostitutes to San Francisco as a result of "the scarcity of women" (Tong 1994, Yung 1995, both quoted in Luibhéid 2002: 183; see also Light 1974 and Hirata 1979). Such explanations beg a prior critical question: namely, men's desire for women at all. Given the likelihood of intragender sexual intimacies during a period when "heterosexuality" was not yet fully consolidated as a regulatory system, it is difficult to account for the specific demand for *female* prostitutes among otherwise unattached working-class males (see Stryker and Van Buskirk 1999, Chauncey 1994).

22. Tong (1994: 111).

23. Chan (1991: 97), quoted in Tong (1994: 118). These measures anticipated the Chinese Exclusion Act of 1882, as well as the Page Law of 1875—the explicit aim of which was to prevent the flow of Chinese prostitutes and other "undesirables" into the nation (Luibhéid 2002: 31).

24. Shumsky and Springer (1981: 74). The term "transitional zone" derives from Chicago sociologist Ernest Burgess's spatial model of five concentric zones within the city. See Burgess (1925).

25. Bowden (1967), quoted in Shumsky and Springer (1981: 78).

26. San Francisco Grand Jury (1910), quoted in Kerr (1994) and Shumsky and Springer (1981).

27. San Francisco Department of Public Health (1911), quoted in Kerr (1994: 32) and Shumsky and Springer (1981:81).

28. Leigh (1996: 5); on the shifting boundaries of the Barbary Coast, see also Barnhart (1986) and Asbury (1933).

29. Mullen (1993).

30. In an article published in the *San Francisco Chronicle,* Mrs. Genevieve Allen, the executive director of the San Francisco Center of the California Civic League, reported that of the five hundred women on the Barbary Coast that her organization had approached, only ten accepted offers of help. She indicated, furthermore, that "Although every big business house in the city stood ready to give employment to women who were competent to fill positions . . . she kn[ew] of but one woman who went to work. She took a place as a demonstrator." Another investigator visited forty women, of whom "3 said they were willing to get married; 23 announced they would stay in the old line

of business; 8 were going to join relatives, 3 were willing to work at honest employment; and 3 were undecided" (*San Francisco Chronicle,* January 31, 1917, www.sfmuseum.org/hist/vice.html).

31. Kerr (1994).

32. Corbin (1990: 338). In France, the regulated brothel system was dismantled in 1946 (Svanström 2000: 5).

33. Månsson (1981: 311).

34. Mr. A. de Graaf Stichting (2004).

35. Rosen (1982: 172). See also Winick and Kinsie (1971: 132), and Gail Sheehy's pronouncement in her well-regarded 1971 exposé that "the street hooker . . . far outnumbers anybody in the business" (35).

36. In the late 1990s, the image of the streetwalker was only beginning to be displaced by the ascendance of a new figure in the popular press: that of the young, vulnerable "trafficking victim" (Kempadoo 1999b).

37. See, e.g., Weitzer (2000c), Brock (1998), and Elias et al. (1998).

38. Alexander (1987: 189). For a critical discussion of the genesis of such estimates, see Chapkis (1997: 234 n. 16).

39. See the rough numerical breakdown of sexual commerce in San Francisco that I provide in chap. 1. Because of the skewed focus of police departments toward street prostitution, arrest statistics are notoriously unreliable for estimating indoor/outdoor distributions.

40. The Bay Area's subway system is called BART (Bay Area Rapid Transit).

41. Zamora (1998), Gordon (1998), Peterson (1998).

42. Beginning in the summer of 1997, the national chain Déjà Vu Inc., which operates over eighty strip clubs in fourteen states, bought four San Francisco clubs within a two-block area (Kaye 1999b). Déjà Vu has continued to purchase adult-oriented businesses in the city and currently owns ten of the seventeen properties.

43. Among the massage parlors that appear in the city's official registry (previously maintained by the Police Department and currently maintained by the Department of Public Health) are some facilities which do not provide erotic services to their clients (such as the San Francisco Hilton and Nordstrom's Spa). Nevertheless, the general trend in which sexually oriented massage parlors became both more numerous and more widely dispersed throughout the city has been well documented. See, e.g., Kuczynski (2001), Kaye (1999b), and Huang (1998a, 1998b).

44. On the gentrification of San Francisco in the 1990s, see generally Solnit and Schwartzenberg (2000), Hartman (2002), and Brook, Carlsson, and Peters (1998).

45. Smith (1996). Urban ethnographers have provided ample discussion of the consequences of such policies for the homeless (Kozol 1995), the mentally ill (Barr 2001), racial minorities (Anderson 1993), and the working classes (Smith 1996), but they have had little to say about their impact on sexual commerce—or, for that matter, questions of sex and gender more generally.

46. MacDonald (1994).

47. For an overview of the causes and consequences of gentrification in the San Francisco Mission district, see Alejandrino (2000).
48. Smith (1996: 6).
49. See also Zukin (1982: 19), Sassen (1994), and Wilson (1996).
50. Waters and Hudson (1998: 304).
51. On the postindustrial burgeoning of the global tourist trade and the transformation of U.S. and Western European cities from sites of production to spaces of consumption, see Fainstein and Judd (1999).
52. Waters and Hudson (1998).
53. San Francisco Task Force on Prostitution (1994).
54. In addition to myself, these included representatives from Offices of the City and from pertinent community organizations (a full list of participants is provided in San Francisco Task Force [1996]). I discuss my own means of gaining entrée to the Task Force in the methodological appendix.
55. The inclusion of sex-worker activists on the San Francisco Task Force can of course be viewed within the context of the city's "specialness" vis-à-vis the overt incorporation of sexual minorities into the uppermost tiers of the political process (see, e.g., Castells [1983]; DeLeon [1992]). Whether this inclusion in fact moved the city closer to the vision of complete decriminalization that many activists advocated for is another matter, one that this and subsequent chapters critically interrogate.
56. Field notes, August 31, 1994. On the changing character of neighborhood antiprostitution campaigns since the 1970s (in San Francisco and elsewhere), see Weitzer (2000b). On the prevalence of residents' objections to adult-oriented businesses in Kansas City neighborhoods as similarly rooted in considerations of land use and business practices rather than questions of traditional morality, see Kelly and Cooper (2000: 49).
57. San Francisco Task Force on Prostitution (1996: 27–29).
58. These numbers vary somewhat from those which appear in the San Francisco Task Force on Prostitution's *Final Report* (see fig. 5); statisticians who were consulted at both the California Bureau of Justice and the San Francisco Police Department over a period of several months were unable to explain the discrepancies between the two sets of figures. Despite the differences in absolute numbers, the overall trend that is documented by both sets of data—the shift from arrests for prostitution to arrests for disorderly conduct—is consistent.

    The California penal code defines "disorderly conduct" to include "lewd or dissolute conduct" in public space, loitering "without apparent reason," and public intoxication (Table 4B, Adult Misdemeanor Arrests by Gender, Offense, and Arrest Rate in San Francisco County, http://stats.doj.ca.gov/cjsc _stats/prof03/38/4B.htm ; §647, http://leginfo.ca.gov).
59. A fuller discussion of this program and its impact is provided in chap. 5.
60. Sanchez (2003). For accounts of similar transformations in New York, Toronto, and Milan, see Weidner (2001), McNamara (1994), Brock (1998), and Danna (2002). In New York, the Disney Corporation made elimination of the public face of sex commerce an explicit condition of its "revitalization" of Times Square.

CHAPTER THREE

1. For a fuller description of some of the epistemological, methodological, and political issues entailed by this fieldwork, see the methodological appendix.

2. For an elaboration of this concept, see Bourdieu (1984), Bourdieu and Wacquant (1992), and Wacquant (1995).

3. It is likely that some of the women that I encountered on the street were under eighteen (though none directly acknowledged this to me); most of my closest confidantes were women nearer my own age at the time, in their mid-twenties. Early in my research, Eve (who was twenty-six) explained to me with a wink that "On the streets, all the girls are over eighteen, if you know what I mean." She also told me that she would occasionally report exceptionally young women to the police, reasoning that "There are some kids who just really shouldn't be out here . . . they're not old enough to choose."

4. See, e.g., Walkowitz (1980), Rosen (1982), Høigård and Finstad (1992). In a 1994 pilot study of predominantly street-based sex workers conducted by the San Francisco SAGE project, women identified housing (78 percent), job training (73 percent), drug treatment (67 percent), health care (58 percent), and child care (34 percent) as critical interventions that would make it possible for them to leave the streets (Hotaling et al. 2003: 261). In a 1990 survey of forty-five female street-based sex workers in the Tenderloin, Weinberg, Shaver, and Williams reported that 39 percent had not completed high school, and 37 percent had only a high school degree (1999: 507). An oft-quoted 1982 survey of two hundred San Francisco street prostitutes by Silbert and Pines documented the prevalence of early sexual abuse among streetwalkers. Silbert and Pines found that over 60 percent of their sample were victims of incest and sexual abuse between the ages of three and sixteen (Silbert and Pines 1982: 471, 479), approximately four times the estimated figure for women generally (Russell 1986: 60). I am aware of no comparable studies on the prevalence of sexual abuse among indoor sex workers. For a critique of the idea that sexual abuse *automatically* predisposes women to prostitution, see Kaye (2004).

5. Women typically charged their clients by the act, with prices starting at $100 for fellatio and $400 for vaginal intercourse (the two most common requests) plus hotel fees.

6. Notably, when I first asked the women on the "upper-" and "middle-class" strolls to tell me about the places where street prostitution took place in the city, the commercial sex markets of Hyde and Capp streets did not even figure into their mental templates.

7. Lisa Maher has similarly noted the market correspondence between the minimum price for sexual exchanges and the retail price for drugs. In Bushwick, Brooklyn, where she conducted her fieldwork, crack cocaine had a low unit price of $5 in the 1990s, which was also the minimum rate for oral sex. Women on these streets widely referred to $5 blow jobs as "crackfares" (Maher 1997: 134). The interdependence of street sex and drug economies in cities throughout the world has also been noted by Cecilie Høigård and Liv Finstad, and is revealed by the formula "price of a fix = [minimum] price of a trick."

They found this formula to be applicable in each of the nine cities that they investigated (Høigård and Finstad 1992: 42–43).

8. For an elaboration of this point, see Bernstein (1999) and Pheterson (1996: 30).

9. For a notable exception, see Maher (1997).

10. Høigård and Finstad (1992).

11. Hughes and Roche (1999), Farley (2003), Pateman (1988), MacKinnon (1989).

12. Ironically, prefeminist empirical scholarship on prostitution may have been *more* likely to emphasize axes of difference than later research. Typically, however, much of this work employed a "client's eye" view in presenting different commercial sex markets in one-dimensional hierarchical tiers, based on the likely class of the patrons and the "objective" desirability of the sex workers. For some historically diverse instances of sex-worker typologies by rank, see Sanger (1859), Winick and Kinsie (1971), Sheehy (1971), and Diana (1985).

13. Female prostitutes at all levels earn considerably more than their male counterparts. At the time this research was conducted, prices for San Francisco male street prostitutes ranged from $20 to $50. The top price for the off-street male escorts I interviewed was $150 an hour, approximately half as much as the majority of female escorts in this study. As some feminists have noted, modeling and prostitution comprise the only two occupations for which women as a group are paid more than men (see, e.g., MacKinnon 1987: 25).

14. Interestingly, commentators on both sides of the feminist "sexuality debates" have pointed to women's frequent justification of sex work in economic terms as the basis for quite disparate political agendas (the normalization and destigmatization of "sex work" on the one hand; the foregrounding of the socially coercive basis of women's choice to engage in "prostitution" on the other). Much of the literature which seeks to recast "prostitution" as "sex work" explicitly tries to foreground questions of labor and economic incentive (see, e.g., McLeod 1982, Delacoste and Alexander 1987, Leigh 1994c, Chapkis 1997, and especially Jenness 1993). For abolitionist feminist arguments that are premised on these same framings, see Høigård and Finstad (1992) and O'Connell Davidson (2002).

   On the emergence of a labor frame among prostitutes in the late nineteenth century, see Rosen (1982), Walkowitz (1980), and Hobson (1987). On contemporary male and transgender prostitutes' greater propensity to foreground the role of *pleasure* (as opposed to work) in sexual labor, see Perkins and Bennet (1985) and Weinberg, Shaver, and Williams (1999).

15. Weinberg, Shaver, and Williams (1999: 511).

16. As Lisa Maher notes, boundary setting is also important for drug-using prostitutes, even if the boundaries do not necessarily serve to demarcate actual practices but simply ideals. The women in Maher's study described the exchange of sex for crack (rather than cash) as something they might do under certain circumstances, but which nonetheless entailed a compromise of principle (Maher 1997: 143).

17. Edwards (1993: 98). See also Perkins and Bennett (1985) and McLeod (1982).

18. On the use of condoms as symbolic vehicles for "taking control" with clients, see Faugier and Sargeant (1997).
19. Høigård and Finstad (1992).
20. The convention of adopting working names has been insufficiently analyzed in the sex-work literature, though Høigård and Finstad (1992: 69) view the practice as a means of hiding one's "true self" and Katherine Frank (2002a: 303) suggests that it can be a pragmatic device for securing some safety and distance when dealing with overly persistent clients. In accordance with Høigård and Finstad's analysis, my fieldwork also points to a doubling of self for many women but in less melodramatic ways than they have sketched. As Richard Sennett and Jonathan Cobb's classic text, *The Hidden Injuries of Class,* makes clear, working-class laborers of many stripes commonly experience a "divided self" (Sennett and Cobb 1972: 191–219). See also Hochschild (2003: 102).
21. The phrase "emotional labor" derives from the work of Arlie Hochschild (1983: 7), who argues that "this kind of labor calls for a coordination of mind and feeling," drawing on a source of self "that we honor as deep and integral to our individuality." For additional discussion of "emotional labor" in sex work, see Chapkis (1997).
22. On the average duration of sex-work careers, see Alexander (1996). Note, however, that among their sample of thirty-seven female street prostitutes in the San Francisco Tenderloin, Weinberg, Shaver, and Williams reported the "mean number of years worked" as 9.73 (1999: 510).
23. Pendleton (1997: 77).
24. The other facilitators were members of the National Lawyer's Guild and the sex-workers' activist group, the Coalition on Prostitution.
25. According to some estimates, nearly seven out of ten street prostitutes are regularly raped on the job (see, e.g., Neland [1995], Silbert [1980], Farley et al. [2003]).
26. Walkowitz (1980), Rosen (1982), Hobson (1987).
27. Contemporary sociological treatments of brothel owners and madams are few, but see Hausbeck and Brents (2000), Wiltz (2000) and Heyl (1979).
28. See §266h, San Francisco Task Force on Prostitution (1994, Legal Committee Exhibits).
29. In Norway and Sweden, newspapers that run advertisements for commercial sexual services have been subject to pimping charges as a result of feminist antiprostitution activism. Since the mid-1990s, the Exotic Dancers Alliance, a San Francisco–based union for exotic dancers, has charged that many of the local strip clubs effectively act as pimps by forcing dancers to engage in prostitution so that they will be able to pay the mandatory (and exorbitantly high) stage fees that the clubs demand in exchange for providing the women with a place to work. Thus far, the EDA has not succeeded in bringing criminal charges against the owners or management. For a detailed discussion of these practices and dancers' complaints, see Brook (1998) and Steinberg (2004).
30. Ethnographic accounts of the relationship between prostitutes and pimps include Milner and Milner (1972), Wacquant (1994), Hodgson (1997), Maher (1997), and Epele (2002).

31. Slim ([1969] 1987), Milner and Milner (1972), Wacquant (1994).
32. Hodgson (1997).
33. Pimp-controlled women were typically issued "cash quotas" (among the women I studied, approximately $500) and were expected to turn over their entire night's earnings to their men. Their male partners assumed the responsibility of allocating these monies for expenses.
34. Epele (2002: 168).
35. Høigård and Finstad (1992: 134). See also Miller (1995).
36. According to the San Francisco District Attorney's Office, an average of a dozen people are prosecuted on pimping charges in the city every year (Brannon 1998). Between 2000 and 2003, there were 3,345 arrests made for the misdemeanor offense of prostitution and 54 arrests for pimping (Sergeant David Makofsky, San Francisco Police Department Statistics Unit, personal communication, January 20, 2005). Recent conversations with law enforcement officials suggest, however, that new federal legislation designed to combat human trafficking (see chap. 7) will increasingly be used to target pimps as "domestic traffickers," making them eligible for criminal sentences of up to thirty years. See also Wilgoren (2006).
37. See generally the San Francisco Task Force on Prostitution (1996, app. D), detailing the San Francisco Municipal Police Code sections 215, 225, and 240, which prohibit lewd and indecent acts, soliciting prostitution and making an offer or agreement to commit prostitution. The California State Penal Code defines "public nuisance" as "[a]nything which is injurious to health, or is indecent, or offensive to the senses, or an obstruction to the free use of property" (*West's Annotated California Codes* 1999, §370).
38. San Francisco Task Force on Prostitution (1994, Legal Committee Exhibits).
39. Although such practices are evidently illegal, the police officers I spoke with generally admitted that it sometimes became necessary to blur legal boundaries in the process of making an arrest.
40. In 1994, the San Francisco District Attorney's Office came under fire for its practice of using condoms as evidence in prostitution cases. In August of that year, after heated political pressure from sex-workers' rights activists, the San Francisco Board of Supervisors requested that the office stop using the practice on public health grounds (see Strupp 1994; Levy 1994).
41. Pheterson (1996: 31).
42. Wilson and Kelling (1982).
43. Pheterson (1996: 89).
44. Goffman (1963).
45. The "broken windows" thesis posits that "serious street crime flourishes in areas in which disorderly behavior goes unchecked" (Wilson and Kelling 1982: 34). By the early 1990s, Wilson and Kelling's ideas had become leading criminal justice theories, serving to shape the proliferation of order-maintenance policing strategies (Harcourt 2001: 3).
46. On the relationship between "quality of life" campaigns and what Andrea McArdle and Tanya Erzen have termed "the new police brutality," see McArdle and Erzen (2001).

47. Davis (1995).
48. Davis (1995).
49. See Goldberg (1995).
50. I discuss Margo St. James's bid for office in greater detail in chap. 4.
51. Maher (1997: 182). I am aware of no systematic studies of the disparate police treatment of prostitutes by race, but accounts of these disparities can be found in Lockett (1995), Pheterson (1996), and Leigh (1994d). On the overrepresentation of African American women in San Francisco jails, see San Francisco Task Force on Prostitution, app. D: Arrest and Incarceration Statistics. For discussions of the intersecting dynamics of gender, race, and urban policing more generally, see, e.g., Gore, Jones, and Kang (2001), Sudbury (2002), and Silliman and Bhattacharjee (2002).
52. For fuller descriptions of this case, see Kligman (1999) and Laird (1999). At a set of hearings sponsored by the San Francisco Task Force on Prostitution in November of 1994, Kiki Whitlock, a transgender sex worker, reported an experience of being illegally strip-searched during incarceration that was nearly identical to Victoria Schneider's (San Francisco Task Force on Prostitution 1996, app. D: Testimony, History, and Index).
53. On one occasion, Eve casually volunteered to me that she thought cops and prostitutes were ideally suited to one another romantically, leading me to wonder if she had at some point had more intimate dealings with the San Francisco Police Department that might have facilitated her better treatment.
54. Chevigny (2001).
55. Maher and Curtis (1998: 113, 123), quoted in Nolan (2001).
56. California's "Three Strikes and You're Out Law" (§667) was passed in 1994.
57. By the late 1990s, the smallest rooms in San Francisco's residential hotels typically cost between $400 and $500 a month and availability was scarce. Between 1993 and 1998 (the years during which San Francisco would officially become the toughest housing market in the nation) the city lost approximately 1,000 rooms to demolition and renovation (Thompson 1998).
58. Feldman et al. (1993: 149), emphasis mine.
59. In the words of one turn-of-the-century prostitute quoted by Ruth Rosen in her book, *The Lost Sisterhood:* "I lay on de bed, and he do what he want. Ees nawthing, you know—maybe wan, two minutes. Si! I can make heem do eet queeker, but mo' all de time eet ees not necessary. He ees queeck by himself" (Rosen 1982: 92).
60. On the rise of prostitution within San Francisco's strip clubs, see Brook (1998) and Steinberg (2004). According to Steinberg, the transformation of strip clubs into de facto houses of prostitution actually occurred in two phases. The first was in 1980, when the Mitchell Brothers'–O' Farrell Theater introduced the idea (borrowed from a strip club in New York) that their clients "could sit with, roll around with (and to some ill-defined extent) touch the nude bodies of their revered fantasy objects" for tips. The practice quickly spread to other clubs in the city, and by the end of the decade, "lap dancing had established itself from coast to coast as a new, often predominant, form

of sexual entertainment" (Steinberg 2004: 4). The second phase was initiated in the mid-1990s with the introduction of private booths and more explicit cash-for-sex transactions.

61. Warner (1999).

62. Some recent critics of the heightened legal prohibitions surrounding sex work have tended to speak as if the control of class- and race-neutral "public sex" were all that were at issue. The volume *Policing Public Sex* (Dangerous Bedfellows 1996) is solidly anchored in an analysis of the role played by gentrification and neoliberalism in shaping the contours of contemporary urban sexuality and as such constitutes an important corrective to this trend. Even here, however, chapters refer to the "twilight of commercial sex" in New York and "the new outlaw sexualities," as if the policing associated with such phenomena were spread evenly across classed and raced social space (45, 185). Yet as Christian Parenti has noted, at precisely the moment that New York street prostitutes were being arrested en masse, "the number of New York city yellow pages devoted to escort services jumped from seventeen before the crackdown to forty-eight after" (Parenti 1999: 79).

An observation from my fieldwork provides a further illustration of how the policing of "public sex" has dramatically different consequences for different populations. One of the most striking things I perceived when I left the Tenderloin each night was how differently my sexualized attire would be read and reacted to once I returned home to my own neighborhood (a white, middle-class "hipster" enclave of bars, cafés, and small boutiques at the westernmost edge of the Mission district). Walking around in my short skirt, upswept hair, and high heels, in the Tenderloin I bore the stamp and stigma of a "public woman" and was treated accordingly. Yet in my own neighborhood I seemed like any other dressed-up young woman returning home from an evening on the town: I could walk wherever I chose without risk of police interception, enter commercial establishments and be greeted respectfully, and jaywalk and "loiter" with abandon.

CHAPTER FOUR

1. St. James received the endorsements of Mayor Willie Brown, District Attorney Terrence Hallinan, and State Assemblyman John Burton, among other prominent figures.

2. Irvine (1996), Carroll (1996).

3. Bowman and King (1996), Lewis and Opatrny (1996), Opatrny (1996).

4. See Steinberg (2004), Kaye (1999b), and Kooy (2001).

5. Kooy (2001: 121).

6. The majority of the Lusty Lady theater operates as a "peep show," where customers stand in small booths and deposit coins to reveal naked dancers behind plate glass windows. Prior to unionization, three of the thirteen windows in the club had one-way windows, which, according to dancers, facilitated clients' clandestine videotaping of the women. Spurred by concerns about one-way windows in the peep show booths, as well as questions of racial discrimination, inconsistent disciplinary procedures, and the lack of

a sick leave policy, the dancers voted 57 to 15 to unionize. See Kooy (2001), Brooks (1997), and the broadly circulated documentary film made by former Lusty Lady dancer Julia Query, *Live Nude Girls Unite* (2000). In 2003, the Lusty Lady theater was again in the news, this time for becoming the nation's first cooperatively owned erotic theater. When management threatened to close the club due to dwindling profits, the dancers decided to purchase it for themselves. See Koopman (2003) and Friend (2004).

7. Lane (2000).

8. "The Sex Business" (1998: 22). See also Droganes (2000), Schlosser (1997), Greenfeld (1999), Prial (1999), Egan (2000), Jackson (2000), and "Sex, News, and Statistics" (2000).

9. Koerner (2000: 34).

10. Boulware (1999); see also Learmonth (1999), Mieszkowski (2000), and Kahn (2000). Danni Ashe, a former porn star and stripper from Seattle, emblematized entrepreneurial success in this mold. By 1997, her hugely successful erotic Web site was grossing $2.5 million annually and garnering favorable attention from mainstream media outlets, including the *Wall Street Journal,* the *New York Times,* the *Boston Globe,* and the *LA Times* (Lane 2000: 221).

11. There were, however, increasing attempts to convey the potential dangers of "cybersex addiction." See, e.g., Steven B. (1999), Drudis (1999), and Brody (2000).

12. I conducted and transcribed face-to-face interviews of two to four hours in length with four men and eleven women (several of whom were interviewed on multiple occasions) and engaged in more informal conversations with some fifty to sixty individuals. A fuller discussion of the methodology that guided my research is provided in the methodological appendix.

13. See, e.g., Kristof (2004), Landesman (2004), Brinkley (2000), Seib (2000), and Shepard (2000).

14. St. James (1989: xvii). For an analysis of the emergence of COYOTE in the early 1970s, see Jenness (1993). During the course of my research, COYOTE splintered into a number of more specialized political and professional organizations for sex workers, including the Exotic Dancer's Alliance, the Cyprian Guild, the Sex Workers' Outreach Project, Sex Workers Organized for Labor, Human and Civil Rights and numerous online communities, with many members participating in multiple groups simultaneously. For the sake of simplicity, I refer to participants (both frequent and occasional) in these distinct yet allied organizations as if they all pertained to the same group. See www.bayswan.org for an up-to-date listing of sex-worker self-advocacy groups nationwide. For a listing of international organizations, see www.nswp.org.

15. See, e.g., Wynter (1987), West (1987), Farley (2003), and Hughes and Roche (1999). See also the volume *Prostitution, Power, and Freedom,* written by the sociologist Julia O'Connell Davidson (1998), who poses the challenge this way: "Those who wish to defend the institution of prostitution often state that there are individuals who enjoy working as prostitutes. . . . I think that we can allow for the possibility that these individuals are providing a faithful account of their own subjective experience without this in any sense

undermining the more general argument that prostitution is an institution which founders upon the existence of economic and political conditions that compel people to act in ways in which they would not otherwise choose to act." She goes on to state that the "tiny minority of individuals who are attracted to prostitution by the intrinsic qualities of 'sex work'" shall thus fall outside the scope of her analysis (5). Not only does this assessment ignore a growing middle-class constituency within the sex industry; it also psychologizes their concerns. O'Connell Davidson thereby fails to grapple at a sociological level with the conditions that have enabled this new group of sex workers to thrive.

16. During an interview, Michael (a sex worker and documentary filmmaker) joked that "Everyone who pays me to have sex with them is like a patron of the arts." Annie Sprinkle, a well-known pornographic actress turned performance artist, has similarly quipped that "the sex industry is a much bigger funder of the arts than the NEA [National Endowment for the Arts]—I'm sure of it!" (Juno and Vale 1991: 39). Indeed, the majority of COYOTE participants that I came to know identified not only as sex workers but also as writers, students, and performance and visual artists.

17. Delacoste and Alexander (1987: 342), Leigh (2004: 66).

18. Queer political activism, in contrast to the gay liberation movement which historically preceded it, is avowedly antiassimilationist. As Steve Epstein has written, "Queerness . . . stands in opposition to the inclusionary project of mainstream lesbian and gay politics, with its reliance on the discourses of civil liberties and civil rights. In this sense, queerness is often a marker of one's distance from conventional norms in all facets of life, not only the sexual" (Epstein 1993: 153). It is somewhat ironic that prostitutes' rights movements have sought legitimacy under the banner of "sex work," given that for Marx and other early socialist critics, what was wrong with wage labor or "work" was precisely that it resembled prostitution (Marx [1844] 1978: 103).

19. See, e.g., Bell (1987), Nagle (1997a), Leigh (1994a, 1994c, 2004), and Sprinkle (1998).

20. As Patricia Hill Collins writes, "[A]ll Black women are affected by the widespread controlling image that African American women are sexually promiscuous, potential prostitutes. . . . [Historically] the prostitution of Black women allowed white women to be the opposite; Black "whore" makes white "virgins" possible. This race/gender nexus fostered a situation whereby white men could then differentiate between the sexualized woman-as-body who is dominated and "screwed" and the asexual woman-as-pure-spirit who is idealized and brought home to mother" (Collins 1990: 174–76). For a similar argument, see Smith (1994).

21. ACT UP (Aids Coalition to Unleash Power) is an AIDS activist organization with chapters in San Francisco and other urban centers. The San Francisco–based Harvey Milk Club serves gay, lesbian, bisexual, and transgender interests in the Democratic party. The organization is named after the late San Francisco Supervisor (the first openly gay elected official in California). *Whorezine* was a locally produced magazine (no longer in publication) that

      included sex-work oriented news, commentary, artwork, and a "dirty tricks" list alerting escorts to potentially dangerous clients.

22. Florida (2002). Florida's notion of the "creative class"—a social formation specific to late twentieth-century technologically advanced urban economies—shares certain common features with earlier sociological notions of postindustrial society's "new class," as well as with Pierre Bourdieu's notion of the "new petite bourgeoisie." I discuss the latter in greater detail below.

23. Milkman and Dwyer (2002), McCall (2001), Sassen (2002).

24. Scholten and Blaze (2000).

25. These ads appeared in the April 6, 1999, "Help Wanted" section of the *Daily Californian*.

26. Girl-X (1997: 20).

27. Bourdieu (1984: 357).

28. Bourdieu (1984: 367).

29. Sprinkle (1998: 118–19).

30. Urban Justice Center (2005: 32).

31. Bourdieu (1984: 365).

32. In discussing entrapment, Diana is referring to the police practice of arresting sex workers at the point that they agree to engage in a sex act for money. The officers that I observed during my fieldwork would typically make arrests only after a transaction was verbally agreed on and an "act of furtherance" had occurred. Legally speaking, an act of furtherance is a gesture that indicates that the sex worker is prepared to carry through with her end of the bargain.

33. See also Urban Justice Center (2003).

34. See, e.g., Huang (1998a and 1998b).

35. Boulware (1999), Schwartz (2001), Goodell (2001), Jacobs (2004).

36. The erotic review sites that clients frequent are also subdivided by market niche. One high-end site (which reviews only female escorts who advertise on the Internet) asks clients to rate women on a 1 to 10 scale in terms of both appearance and performance (e.g., 9 = "I forgot it was a service"). There are also sites geared specifically toward budget shoppers, the most well-known of which advertises itself as a place where "Cheap Bastards Find Quality Ladies."

37. Bourdieu (1984: 368).

38. See also Meretrix (2001) and www.escortsupport.com (2004). The blogspot www.sacredwhore.com (last accessed 6/1/05) contains a listing of online publications and links to sixteen distinct online communities, including separate chat rooms for sacred whores, queer sex workers, and sex workers' partners. There are also a growing number of "how to" books and Web sites for clients, which advise men on the particulars of locating sex workers, tipping, and session etiquette. See, e.g., Christina (2004), Itiel (1998), and Fuffle and Spanks (2003).

39. See, e.g., Queen (1997) and Stubbs (1994).

40. See, e.g., Monet (1994: 58).

41. For related accounts, see the documentary film, "Big Girls: Big, Beautiful Women in the Adult Entertainment Industry" (dir. Sara McCool, 2000), and Frank (2002a), Funari (1997), and Chapkis (1997).

42. Hamlin (2002); Landes (2005). As part of her activist agenda, MacAllister regularly conducts "big burlesque" exotic dancing workshops in the Bay Area, providing instruction in "everything from tassel-twirling, to stage presence, to costume and makeup tips." See www.bigburlesque.com. (last accessed 5/30/2005).

43. See also Lever and Dolnick (2000).

44. As the San Francisco–based sex worker and writer Carol Queen has argued, "We create sexual situations with very clear boundaries, for ourselves and for our clients. In fact, one of the things that people are paying us for is clear boundaries. . . . Same thing with seeing a psychotherapist; there you are paying someone to tell your secrets to, someone you can trust will not judge you and who at least won't interrupt you in the middle and start telling you their secrets. Instead, you are getting focused attention" (quoted in Chapkis 1997: 77).

45. Mullings (2000: 229). See also MacCannell (1976), Mowforth and Munt (1998), and West and Carrier (2004). On the quest for authenticity in sex tourism, see Padilla (forthcoming).

46. Frank (2002a). The burgeoning genres of "amateur," "reality," and "alternative" porn also exemplify many men's preference for commercially mediated access to "real" women (rather than seasoned professionals). See, e.g., Patterson (2004) and Mayer (2004).

47. On strippers' own strategic signaling of authenticity to their clients, see Wood (2000) and Massey and Hope (2005).

48. The notion of "counterfeit intimacy" is developed in Foote (1954), Boles and Garbin (1974), and Ronai and Ellis (1989). The writings of Arlie Hochschild distinguish between the practices of "surface acting" and "deep acting" in emotional life (2003: 92–93). While the former conveys something akin to Erving Goffman's notion of impression management, the latter term is used synonymously with "emotional labor" (see chap. 3, n. 21 above). Hochschild notes that middle-class jobs typically call for "deep acting" ("an appreciation of display rules, feeling rules"), while working-class jobs "more often call for the individual's external behavior and the products of it" (102). This contrast also captures the distinction I am seeking to make between postindustrial and modern-industrial forms of sexual labor.

49. The terms "front stage" and "back stage" derive from Erving Goffman's dramaturgical analysis of social roles and the management of identity. See Goffman (1959) and MacCannell (1976).

50. For one woman's story of her oscillations between sex worker and client, see Monet (1997).

51. Pateman (1988: 184). Carole Pateman presents a radical feminist critique of renditions of the shift from status to contract which regard this transition as a move toward freedom and equality (see, e.g., Maine [1861] 1917). She argues that procontract defenders of prostitution typically envision a world in which prostitution is universalizable, where "Anyone who needs a sexual service should have access to the market, whether male or female, young or old, black or white, ugly or beautiful, deformed or handicapped. . . . The female hunchback as well as the male hunchback will be able to find a seller of services"

(192). Pateman insists, however, that such a vision is naive from a feminist point of view, given that the very existence of prostitution is predicated on the prior existence of gendered domination.

52. See Milkman and Dwyer (2002), McCall (2001), Esping-Andersen (1999, 1990), and Sassen (1998).

53. See U.S. Bureau of Census (2001). Drawing on the latest census data, the *New York Times* has reported that San Francisco has the lowest percentage of children under eighteen of any large city in the nation (14.5 percent, as compared with 25.7 percent nationwide). Seattle, Boston, Honolulu, Portland, Miami, Denver, Minneapolis, Austin, and Atlanta ("all considered, healthy, vibrant urban areas") follow closely behind (Egan 2005). The best-known statement of the relationship between postindustrial economies and the rise of gay culture (though he mistakes the direction of the causal relationship) is Richard Florida's *The Rise of the Creative Class* (2002). See also Castells (1997: 202–21) and Knopp (1992).

54. See Williams (2004) and Juffer (1998). In September of 2001, Tracy Quan's semi-autobiographical *Diary of a Manhattan Call Girl* was designated a *Cosmopolitan* magazine "chick pick" (other titles included the fictional *Asking for Trouble,* about a single woman who falls in love with a male escort) ("Fab Fall Reads" 2001: 342). More recently, adult film actress Jenna Jameson's *How to Make Love Like a Porn Star* spent several months on the *New York Times* bestseller list (Wyatt 2004).

55. Dudley (2004).

56. St. John (2004).

57. Bellafante (2001).

58. In an article which documents the surge in San Francisco women willing to work as exotic dancers in the mid-1990s, Kerwin Kaye quotes one dancer's observations regarding the sudden influx: "It became very trendy to be a stripper, and you could actually say 'I'm an exotic dancer' on your housing and employment applications. When I first started working, people put down that they were therapists, or management was willing to say that you worked in the office there. But by the time I left, you could say that you worked . . . and no one blinked an eye . . . it became socially acceptable to be a stripper in San Francisco. And everyone and her sister was taking off her clothes" (Kaye 1999b: 50).

CHAPTER FIVE

1. See n. 10 below.

2. My focus in this chapter is on heterosexual male desire and consumption patterns—the primary commercial sex market in which the state intervenes, and the almost exclusive focus of state discourse. In touristic urban centers, heterosexual prostitution is estimated to comprise approximately two-thirds of the overall market (Leigh 1994b). Although there is some literature on the emergence of women as consumers of pornographic spectacles and images (Juffer 1998; Ehrenreich, Hess, and Jacobs 1986), and on the recent phenomenon of female sex tourism to the Caribbean (de Albuquerque 1998, O'Connell

Davidson 1998), there is still scant evidence that any significant number of female clients of prostitutes—either lesbian or heterosexual—exists domestically. The lack of such a market reveals a great deal about the persistently gendered nature of commercial sexual consumption.

3. See, e.g., Pheterson (1993) and Lefler (1999). The first arrests of clients in the United States (which were intermittent and few in number) followed a 1975 case brought by the American Civil Liberties Union before a California state court, which noted "the plain unvarnished fact . . . that men and women engaged in proscribed sexual behavior are not treated equally" (MacDonald 1978, C5). On the increase in client arrest rates in mid-1990s San Francisco, see Marinucci (1995a), describing a 25 percent increase in client arrest rates, and (1995b), quoting San Francisco Police Department statistics indicating a dramatic rise in prostitution-related arrests of male clients, to 1,000 of 4,900 total. By 2002, men accounted for 75 percent of all prostitution-related arrests in San Francisco, and by 2004, the city was arresting twice as many men as women for prostitution-related offenses (Hargrove 2005, Conroy 2006). On the emergence of a similar phenomenon in New York City carried out as part of Mayor Rudolph Giuliani's "Quality of Life" campaigns, see Pierre-Pierre (1994) and Nieves (1999). In 2005, aggregate national data suggested that men accounted for slightly more than one-third of all people arrested on prostitution-related charges (Hargrove 2005).

4. Recent federal legislation in the United States has included the Trafficking Victims Protection Reauthorization Act (2005), which stipulates stepped up interventions against clients of prostitution (see chap. 7), and the Protect Act (2003), which strengthens penalties against the production, distribution, and possession of child pornography and the patronage of underage prostitutes abroad (U.S. Dept. of Justice 2003).

5. Janice Irvine (1993) notes that the literature of twelve-step groups specializing in sexual addiction defines the disorder thus: "Any form of sex with one's self or with partners other than the spouse is progressively addictive and destructive. Thus, for the married sexaholic, sexual sobriety means having sex only with the spouse, including no form of sex with one's self. For the unmarried . . . freedom from sex of any kind. For all . . . progressive victory over lust" (213).

6. See, e.g., Kulick (2005), Kaye (1999a).

7. Since the year 2000, "demand" has become the new buzzword among policy makers and activists, largely as a response to the 1998 Swedish law unilaterally criminalizing the purchase (but not the sale) of sexual services. A fuller analysis of the Swedish law and its repercussions is provided in chap. 6.

8. Twelve of the client interviews were conducted face-to-face and lasted from one to four hours each. The remaining interviews were conducted over the telephone. Interviewees were residents of four different San Francisco Bay Area municipalities and were recruited through referrals from sex-worker informants and through ads placed in local heterosexual and gay male sex newspapers. They were patrons in a range of different commercial sex markets, including massage parlors, independent sex workers, street prostitutes, escort

agencies, telephone sex, and strip clubs. Fourteen of the fifteen interviewees were white; the other interviewee identified as Mexican. While to some extent this reflects the racially skewed and stratified composition of sex-industry consumers, another salient issue here may have been my means of contacting participants. Snowball samples were generated through white, educated, indoor sex workers, who tend to have an upper-income and predominantly white clientele. Furthermore, interviewees who responded to my ad may have done so in part as a kind of therapy-seeking behavior. Although the response to my ads was overwhelming—I had approximately fifty responses to the two ads in the first day alone—the kinds of people who responded may have mirrored the kinds of people who seek out psychotherapy, who are again, disproportionately white and middle-class.

Although the majority of my data in this chapter derive from fieldwork and in-depth interviews, data were also gleaned through Internet chat rooms that clients frequent. To the extent that my analysis relies on chat room data, the question of reliability may emerge for some readers because of the potential difficulty in ascertaining the extent to which the accounts presented are fantasy-driven and thus (partially or entirely) fictional. In my research, I addressed this potential concern in two ways: by making sure that my online observations were consistent with my observations in other venues, and by viewing this material as less reflective of clients' actual practices than of their subjective desires and meanings.

9. Luker (1998). Scattered efforts to intervene in patterns of male sexual consumption have even earlier precedents. For example, Jennine Hurl-Eamon (2004) has described the arrest of a handful of male patrons of Westminster prostitutes between 1690 and 1720.

10. See, e.g., Davis ([1937] 1985), Schwarz (1954), Greenwald (1958), and Parsons (1960). In some midcentury texts, normalized and pathologized constructions of commercial sexual consumption exist side by side. Schwarz (1954) and Greenwald (1958), e.g., present similar "john typologies," in which the "compulsive" consumer is pathologized while the "occasional" consumer is normalized.

11. Pheterson (1993: 55). For some second-wave feminist critiques of the gendered double standard in the enforcement of prostitution laws, see McIntosh (1978), Milman (1980), Hobson (1987) and Høigård and Finstad (1992).

12. Relevant studies include Månsson (1987), Prieur and Taksdahl (1993), Allison (1994), Atchison, Fraser, and Lowman (1998), Campbell (1998), Prasad (1999), Frank (1998, 2002a), and Anderson and O'Connell Davidson (2003).

13. Despite the radicalism that has been attributed to Kinsey (and often used to discredit him), in ironic conformity with the functionalism and normative marital model of his time, Kinsey distinguished between a category of "occasional buyers" (69 percent of the adult male population) and those for whom prostitutes were a frequent form of "sexual outlet." He found that 21 percent of white men with a college education, 26 percent of white men without a college education, and 33 percent of African American men with a college education pertained to the latter group. No data were included on African

American men with less than a college education because of problems with sampling (Sullivan and Simon 1998: 153).

14. As is typical in the literature, Sullivan and Simon narrowly equate "paid sex" with the patronage of prostitutes, ignoring other types of commercial sexual transactions (lap dancing, phone sex, etc.). According to their findings, the rate of men who have visited prostitutes is just 1 in 20 for men age eighteen to twenty-four, but is 1 in 3 for men age fifty-three to sixty. They report that military service increases the chances that a man will have paid for sex by 23 percent, and that "more education initially tends to cause decreases in the likelihood of prostitution visitation, bottoming out at trade school degrees, and then results in increases in prostitution patronage continuing through advanced degrees" (1998: 150).

15. Sullivan and Simon (1998: 139–40). I consider this particular finding to be quite questionable, given contravening ethnographic evidence from my own and others' research. In San Francisco, sex workers of all racial and ethnic backgrounds and working at a variety of levels described a preference for white and Asian customers. African American female street prostitutes working with pimps told me that their men often discouraged them from seeing black customers because they were seen as competition. One African American "independent" street prostitute remarked that "Brothers always think they can get freebies. I don't date black men." The sole African American man on one municipal vice squad explained to me that black men rarely got rotated to vice because it was difficult for them to go undercover as johns when they were doing prostitution arrests.

    This tendency was particularly pronounced in indoor and upscale commercial sex markets, both heterosexual and gay. Three different women who had worked in Nevada's legalized brothels explained that when a white customer presented himself at the door, the women who were working that evening were required by the house to "line up" for selection, but when an African American man presented himself, line-up was not obligatory. Among the indoor independent sex workers that I came to know in San Francisco, there was a particular preference for Asian and then white "dot-commers" and other businessmen, who were seen as the most polite, reliable, and lucrative source of income. One white sex worker I spoke with pulled her advertisement from the print media and decided to only advertise online so as to better target her preferred market niche. Approximately half of her exclusively middle-class-and-up clientele was white; the other half was Asian. For other accounts of the paradigmatic whiteness of sex-industry consumers, see Flowers (1998), Nagle (1997b), Ophelian (1999), Gant (2000), and Leigh (2004: 26).

16. Sullivan and Simon (1998: 152).

17. Monto (2000).

18. See, e.g., Høigård and Finstad (1992), McKeganey and Barnard (1996), Flowers (1998), O'Connell Davidson (1998), and Kulick (1998).

19. Allison (1994), Prasad (1999).

20. Allison (1994: 23).

21. Prasad (1999: 188).

22. Prasad (1999: 181, 206). Katharine Frank (2002a) has similarly sought to situate her study of contemporary strip club patrons within the context of postmodern cultural transformations. However, in contrast to the accounts above, Frank argues that clients' persistent desire for authentic intimate encounters with strippers occurs *despite* (rather than because of) its location within a postmodern cultural milieu.

23. In *The Social Organization of Sexuality,* Edward Laumann and his colleagues use the terms *relational* and *recreational* to designate distinct normative orientations toward sexual behavior (1994). Here, I use the terms both to distinguish between different normative models and to indicate the successive emergence of historically specific configurations of sexual and emotional life. In contrasting *recreational* sexuality with *relational* sexuality, I seek to distinguish the former from the romantic residues and intertwined life trajectories that typically accompany the notion of a "relationship," but I do not mean to suggest that it must lack a meaningful intersubjective component.

24. See, e.g., Giddens (1992), O'Connell Davidson (1998), Kimmel (2000), and Månsson (2001).

25. See also Stein (1974), who argues that men's primary reason for seeking out call girls is to receive oral sex, which their wives are reluctant to perform.

26. See Sykes and Matza (1957).

27. See, e.g., Swidler (1980), Ehrenreich (1983), Giddens (1992), Hochschild (1994a), and Rountree (2000). Giddens's *Transformation of Intimacy* (1992) employs a "compensatory" model of men's participation in commercial sex, while also describing more general reconfigurations in late capitalist paradigms of intimacy.

28. Although I did not speak with the clients' primary sexual partners directly, I did ask my interviewees if their partners were inclined to see their commercial sexual activity in the same way as themselves. Notably, most men reported that they chose not to tell their partners about their activities. The reactions of the partners who were told ranged from grudging acceptance to hurt and disapproval, providing evidence of the extent to which heterosexual men (figured mostly as desiring subjects) and their female partners (figured mostly as exchangeable objects) may have divergent interests with respect to the proliferation and normalization of sexual commerce.

29. Pateman (1988: 198).

30. On clients' motivations during the Progressive Era, see Rosen (1982: 97).

31. Ehrenreich (1983).

32. Frank (2002a: 25).

33. In cities which cater to new middle-class consumers, the democratization of sexual access to women is typically coded in a language of luxury; in postmodern cities which cater to working-class tourists a different language may prevail. A recent visit to Las Vegas, Nevada, for example, revealed that a frequent motif among the 100+ escort ads in the Yellow Pages is "discount rates." Advertisers boast that they provide the "lowest prices" for their services and may even offer "money back guarantees." One 2006 ad for an erotic massage parlor featured "discounts for first-time callers," "discounts for

extended time," "discounts for repeat customers," and "discounts for senior citizens."

34. Marx was the first to note the ironic leveling capacity of market transactions, though in lament rather than in celebration: "That which is for me through the medium of *money*—that for which I can pay (i.e., which money can buy) that am *I*, the possessor of the money. The extent of the power of money is my power. Money's properties are my properties and essential powers—the properties and powers of its possessor. Thus what I *am* and *am capable* of is by no means determined by my individuality. I am ugly, but I can buy for myself the most *beautiful* of women" (Marx [1844] 1978: 103).

35. Frank (2002a: 205).

36. Pateman (1988: 199).

37. Giddens (1992: 77).

38. Irvine (1993), Keane (2002). See also Kaye (2002), who notes that "Beginning in the early 1980s . . . a proliferation of recovery groups rose to address almost every imaginable sort of compulsion: sex, love, gambling, overeating, "undereating" (i.e., anorexia), impotence, shoplifting, self-mutilation, overspending." Kaye observes that "although the diversity is remarkable, it is not infinite. A behavior must simultaneously be subjectively desired and socially problematized in order to be seen as an 'addiction' (e.g., while there may be 'women who love too much,' thanks to the relational changes wrought by feminism, there are as yet no 'women who love *their children* too much')."

39. In Foucault's lexicon, "biopower" refers to Western power in its modern incarnation, "characterized by increasing organization of population and welfare for the sake of increased force and productivity" (see Dreyfus and Rabinow 1982: 7–8).

40. See, e.g., Harvey (1990), Castells (1997), Illouz (1997), and Jakobsen (2002). The political theorist Wendy Brown has devised the term "reactionary foundationalism" to refer to the postmodern longing for fixity and durable attachments (Brown 1995). For a modern-industrial precursor to this argument, see Simmel ([1907] 1971).

41. In a 2002 study of the "John School" program in Toronto, Wortley, Fischer, and Webster also found that relatively few of the program participants came from affluent or professional/managerial backgrounds. They similarly postulated that "the types of men who ultimately attend the John School program may reflect the demographics of the neighborhoods and individuals that are most often targeted by police 'sting' operations and other antiprostitution initiatives" (378). In a 2005 analysis of clients arrested for prostitution in Chicago during a four-month period, John Conroy evaluated arrest photos to conclude that of 524 images, more than 80 percent appeared to be African American or Hispanic. "Suburbanites and tourists accounted for less than one mug shot in five, and even in this group nearly three johns in five were black or Hispanic. The wealthy suburbs north of Evanston had not a single representative" (Conroy 2006).

42. Ruth Rosen observed a split between the interests of large- and small-scale business owners earlier in the century, when large-scale business interests

(real estate agents, landlords, and owners of saloons and breweries) supported organized brothel prostitution, whereas small shopkeepers opposed it (Rosen 1982: 77). This split seems to parallel contemporary trends.

43. Pheterson (1993: 44).

44. Marinucci (1995a and b), Kilman and Watson-Smyth (1998), Symbaluk and Jones (1998), Lefler (1999), Monto (2000), Nieves (1999), Weitzer (2000b), "Norfalk's 'John School'" (2005).

45. Hamilton (1999), Weitzer (2000b).

46. "Names" (1999), "Suburban Detroit" (1999).

47. Lewis (1999), Fowler (2003), McCord (2004), "Durham Police" (2004), "Convicted Johns" (2005), Conroy (2006).

48. Lefler (1999), "NSW" (1999), Weitzer (2000b), "Urban Warrior" (2004), Botonis (2004).

49. Castells (1996), Kempadoo (1998).

50. In cities other than San Francisco, the moral project of retaining a relational paradigm of sexual intimacy is one that is often shared by prominent fractions of both feminist and evangelical Christian movements, and which has arguably contributed to the "strange bedfellows" phenomenon of their joint activism around prostitution. This overlap is apparent in the recent development of faith-based client intervention programs such as Operation Destiny in Danville, California. The program helps men to cease their engagement in "inappropriate" sexual behaviors, such as patronizing prostitutes, and to redirect their energies toward their families and God (Hughes 2004).

51. Weitzer (2000b).

52. San Francisco Task Force on Prostitution (1994).

53. See, e.g., Ehrenreich (1983), Juffer (1998).

CHAPTER SIX

1. For a discussion of the scope and profitability of the online sex industry in Amsterdam (the epicenter for Europe), see Davies and Wonke (2000).

2. As described by Linda Williams (1989), by the late 1970s, the "money shot" (i.e., the depiction of the external ejaculation of the penis for the sake of narrative climax) became a staple feature of hard-core pornographic film. Presumably, it is eliminated from live pornographic performances such as the one described in order to enable men to complete their four to six daily performances.

3. In November of 2005, the travel company Thomas Cook came under fire by feminist groups in the United States and Britain for launching guided family tours of the Amsterdam red-light district. The slogan "under threes go free" was purportedly featured in the company's advertisements (Gallagher 2005, Hunt 2005, Bowes 2005).

4. All three cities have approximately 750,000 residents and economies weighted heavily toward tourism, business and personal services, and high technology (Smith 1996, Milkman and Dwyer 2002, Swedish Institute 2001, Terhorst et al. 2003). My fieldwork consisted of sixty formal interviews with key figures involved in national prostitution debates (government officials, public

prosecutors, social workers, police officers, academic specialists, feminist organizers, and sex-workers' rights activists) as well as on-site observations on streetwalking strolls, in brothels, bars, and massage parlors, drop-in centers, and other social service facilities. While the bulk of my research was conducted in Amsterdam and Stockholm, I also conducted some fieldwork in several smaller Dutch and Scandinavian cities (e.g., in Utrecht, Leiden, and the Hague in the Netherlands, and in Göteborg in Sweden), as well as in Oslo, Norway, and Copenhagen, Denmark. I have provided a fuller description of my research process in the methodological appendix.

5. Hobson (1987: 30).
6. Gelb (1989: 138), Wolfe (1989), Lenneer-Axelson (1991a). As such, it is interesting to note that it is also a country in which there has been a marked absence of any strong or tangible second-wave women's movement. The relative gender equality that Sweden is noted for has been achieved not through the civil sphere but through the early incorporation of "women's interests" into formal government institutions. According to Hobson (1999), the downsizing of the Swedish public sector in the 1990s has, however, led to a recent spate of more vocal feminist activism.
7. Hobson (1987), Jeffreys (1997), Boëthius (1999), Farley and Kelly (2000).
8. Hobson (1987), Chapkis (1997), Weitzer (2000b), Kuo (2002). "Harm reduction" refers to social-service approaches to prostitution and drug dependency that seek to reduce the associated harms without requiring the abolition of the sex industry or total abstinence by the drug user (Sorge 1991; Kilvington, Day, and Ward 2001).
9. Legalized prostitution can also be found in Austria, Germany, Australia, and New Zealand, as well as in the state of Nevada. See Outshoorn (2004), Hausbeck and Brents (2000), Perkins et al. (1994), and Jordan (2005).
10. See, e.g., Van Wesenbeeck (1995), Barry (1995), Alexander (1987), Leigh (1998), and Weitzer (2000b). Leigh (1998) articulates the differences between these models from a perspective that is akin to my own view, arguing that they merely represent "ideal types" within a field of highly complex configurations of policy.
11. The fact that the United States is often held to be a nation that relegates most of its moral issues to regulation by the market (Wolfe 1989, Esping-Andersen 1990), yet officially prohibits the exchange of sexual services for payment, might at first blush appear to present a contradiction. Although theorists writing in the utilitarian tradition have often embraced market logics to argue against state intervention in prostitution, economic logics have also been used to justify its prohibition (Satz 1995). Barbara Hobson has described a tension in the United States between a commitment to free market principles and a tradition of intervention in moral concerns, thus explaining its history of "radical swings in policy between all-out campaigns against prostitution and sufferance of its existence" (1990: 4). On the exceptionalism of Nevada (historically rooted in a migrant mining economy and a culture of "cowboy," antifederalist libertarianism), see Hausbeck and Brents (2000).
12. Hobson (1987), Høigård and Finstad (1992), Davis (1993).

13. Less frequently, social work and reeducation programs have also attempted to target clients, as with the Swedish KAST project which began in 1997, featuring social workers doing outreach to male sexual clients and offering them counseling (Torgny Sjögren, KAST, interview, June 18, 1999). By the beginning of this decade, severe budget cuts in the Netherlands began to severely inhibit service provision of all sorts. The red-light district's Prostitution Information Center lost its government funding and the Mr. A. de Graaf Stichting, the Dutch research institute for prostitution issues, founded in 1961, closed its doors.

14. Hobson (2005), Outshoorn (2004a, 2005), Kligman (2005), Kilvington, Day, and Ward (2001).

15. Månsson (1981: 311), Jan Visser, Mr. A. de Graaf Stichting, interview, June 9, 1999.

16. Definitional struggles over what constitutes the crime and human rights violations of "trafficking" continue to abound. The most recent United Nations Protocol against Trafficking in Persons defines trafficking broadly, to encompass multiple forms of forced migration and forced labor beyond prostitution (including, most commonly, domestic work, sweatshop labor, and agricultural work). Nevertheless, many antitrafficking activists and state agents deem trafficking to be synonymous with all forms of prostitution, whether forced or voluntary (see, e.g., Saunders 2004; Saunders and Soderlund 2004).

17. On the conflation of feminism, nationalism, and antitrafficking sentiment in the passage of the 1998 Swedish law prohibiting the purchase of sex, see Kulick (2003) and Gould (2002). Joyce Outshoorn (2004b) and Marieke Van Doorninck of the Mr. A. de Graaf Stichting (interview, July 2002) have both noted the gap between Dutch feminist demands and state policies regarding the rights of illegal migrant sex workers. See also Doezema (1998) and Norwegian Ministry of Justice (2004).

18. Interview, June 18, 1999.

19. Månsson (1992: 10).

20. *Violence against Women Fact Sheet* (1999).

21. Within Sweden, variants of commercial sexual exchange that depart from the classical heterosexual exchange model of women offering services to men have been insufficiently acknowledged or understood. The crafters of a recent survey of online sexual services in Sweden were thus baffled to discover that of 2,668 entries, the majority of the sellers were men (National Board of Health and Welfare 1999).

22. *Violence against Women Fact Sheet* (1999).

23. Nordic Baltic Campaign (2002). On the relationship between the new Swedish law and the invention of a new category of "pervert" in Swedish society, see Kulick (2005).

24. Since the 1960s and 1970s, the hallmarks of Swedish gender equality policy have included state-run child care programs and generous parental leave and pension systems which have allowed Swedish women to enter the labor force in record numbers. See Florin and Nilsson (1998), Earles (2004), Hobson (1999), and Rabo (1997). Beginning in the late 1970s, feminist-identified

parliamentarians sought to intervene in the sexual arena as well. Through the 1980s, antipornography legislation was made stricter through successive bans on child pornography (1980), on sexual violence in films and videos (1986), and on sexual violence in pictures and print (1989) (Bygdeman and Lindahl 1994: 72). Feminist interventions in prostitution policy date back to 1977, when the government created its first "prostitution project," sending a team of researchers and social workers to Malmö to investigate and to attempt to curb the prostitution explosion in one Swedish port city. The project gave rise to similar efforts in Göteborg, Stockholm, and Noorkjøping, and led to the government's creation of the first national prostitution commission (Månsson 1981: 311). The report that was eventually issued by the commission resulted in a new national prostitution policy which aimed to address the problem both through legal measures and through expanded social services. In 1982, the law against vagrancy was removed from the penal code and was supplanted by several key policy revisions: profiteering (including newspaper advertising and the renting out of flats) was prohibited; pornographic "live shows" in places open to the public were banned; prostitution was criminalized for sellers under twenty years of age; and the Swedish government was required by law to fund research on methods of preventing prostitution (Swedish Prostitution Commission 1993; *Women and Men* 1995). For additional discussion of feminist interventions in Swedish sex law, see Kulick (2003, 2005).

25. Kulick (2003: 207).

26. The results of the referendum vote by which Swedish voters elected to enter the European Union were closely divided: 52.2 percent of voters were in favor, and 46.9 percent of voters were against (Kulick 2003: 214 ftnt. 15).

27. Månsson (1992: 8).

28. Swedish Prostitution Commission (1993: 3–4). The 1993 committee initially recommended the criminalization of both the buyer and the seller, arguing that bilateral criminalization would have the greatest general deterrent effect. This proposal was rejected by virtually all government parties consulted, largely on the grounds that women who were already victimized by prostitution should not be made to suffer further penalties (Norwegian Ministry of Justice 2004; interview with Anne Rygh Pedersen, Swedish Social Democratic Party, July 22, 1999).

29. See, e.g., Boëthius (1999), Farley and Kelly (2000), and Raymond (2003).

30. Winberg (2002), Ekberg (2002), Swedish Ministry of Foreign Affairs (2003), Orback (2005).

31. Before the passage of the new law, there were never more than 1,000 street prostitutes in all of Sweden, even according to the most liberal estimates (Kulick 2003: 200), with street prostitution constituting no more than a third of the overall market (Norwegian Ministry of Justice 2004). Data collected through the 1990s reveal that approximately one quarter of Swedish prostitutes were migrants, compared to upward of 50 percent and as much as 80 percent in countries such as the Netherlands and Germany (Randers-Pehrson and Jessen 2000: 1; TAMPEP 2002: 243ff).

32. Unlike in the United States, even the use of police decoys is considered entrapment. As of 2001, the police had made eighty-six arrests and twenty convictions (Anders Gripelov, head of the Prostitution Patrol Force, interview, July 8, 2002).

33. Pettersson and Tiby (2003: 163). Another definitional difficulty is entailed by the Swedish law's equation of the crime of prostitution with the purchase of a "temporary sexual relationship." ("Anyone who for remuneration procures a temporary sexual relationship will be guilty—if their action is not punishable by some other offense according to the penal code—of purchasing sexual services, and will be sentenced to fines or prison for not more than six months.") As Kulick rightfully inquires: "What does 'temporary' mean exactly? Should it cover regular clients, who maintain long term relationships with individual sex workers, or are they exempt from prosecution? And . . . what exactly constitutes 'a sexual relationship'? . . . what exactly has to be done to whom for a given interaction to be considered 'sexual'?" (2003: 202).

34. Pettersson and Tiby (2003: 154).

35. The Swedish police have been involved in only one case which involved sex purchased indoors. In a 2003 case associated with trafficking, a list of clients was found by the police while going through the computer records of a Stockholm brothel. Due to strict laws against entrapment, the police conduct no undercover operations in brothels—whether or not trafficking is suspected (Norwegian Ministry of Justice 2004: 10).

36. Swedish "company clubs" are the approximate equivalent of "gentleman's clubs" in the United States.

37. On the law's exclusion of Swedish sex workers from city streets, see also Östergren (2004); on the spatialization of social hierarchy in Sweden, see Pred (2000).

38. Roane (1998), Israely (2000), Davies and Wonke (2000).

39. The penal code provides that a person "promoting or improperly deriving economic advantage from another person having casual sexual relations in return for payment can be convicted of procuring and imprisoned for up to four years. . . . Procuring can include, not only the more traditional activities of the pimp or the panderer, but also other forms of promotion such as sex advertisements in newspapers, travel arrangements and so on. Special penal liablility—the same as for procuring—is incurred . . . by a property owner when a tenanted apartment is used for prostitution" (Swedish Prostitution Commission 1993: 3).

40. As Tanya explained to me,"For a Swedish girl working by herself, it's usually 1,500 [kronor] for an hour of services. Sometimes, on the street, the client would be able to bargain her down to 1,000 kr. Now that it's only drug addicts left on the street, the price has gone way down. A blow job was usually 500 kr. So when I started to employ Swedish girls, I would charge 1,500 to 3,000 (for a half hour or one hour), and take half. Now if I want to make the same profit with the Estonian girls, I pay 500 kronor per girl, which leaves 750 for me for a half hour date. The meeting costs the client 1,250. So it's slightly cheaper for him, and he gets a higher quality girl. For a one-hour

date, the price is 1,600 to 2,500. The girl gets 500 for half an hour, and 800 for one hour. But actually, I have found that the girls are happy with even less, anywhere from 300 to 500, so I have started paying that." At the time the interview was conducted, the exchange rate was approximately 9 kronor to the dollar. Thus, each woman would earn approximately $30 to $50 for a half-hour date, while Tanya would earn $80. For an hour date, the women whom Tanya employed would earn approximately $90, and Tanya would earn $180.

41. For an ethnographic account of some of the conditions that propel Latin American transvestite prostitutes to seek employment in the European sex industry, see Kulick (1998).

42. In anticipation of the law's passage, the city of Amsterdam began to officially regulate prostitution through a system of licenses in 1996 (Mr. A. de Graaf Stichting 2004).

43. Van Oostveen (1997).

44. Visser (1997: 4).

45. TAMPEP (2002), Outshoorn (2004b).

46. Although the women had technically been working illegally even before the passage of the new law, their places of employment had not been regularly policed.

47. Interview with Kersten Van Dalen, night manager of the Amsterdam *huiskamer,* October 9, 2003; "Rotterdam Shuts Door" (2004); van Soomeren (2004).

48. Hugo, Dutch Association of Sex Club Owners, interview, July 1999; Yvonne, spokesperson for the Excellent Group (Dutch Brothel Owner's Association), interview, July 18, 2002.

49. Brants (1998: 624).

50. Marieke Van Doorninck, Mr. A. de Graaf Stichting, interview, July 18, 2002; Licia Brussa, TAMPEP (Transnational AIDS/STD Prevention among Migrant Prostitutes in Europe), interview, July 8, 2003.

51. Van Doorninck, interview, July 18, 2002.

52. Doezema (1998: 42). A cogent critique of the "forced vs. voluntary" distinction in prostitution policy has also been provided by Chapkis (2005).

53. Van Doorninck, interview, July 18, 2002.

54. Randers-Pehrson and Jessen (2000: 1), TAMPEP (2002: 242). Providing precise statistical counts of sex-industry workers is notoriously difficult, as numbers are generally gleaned from police or social workers; using official counts of identifiable prostitutes as measures of the size of the sex industry in general presents even greater difficulties. Nonetheless, the numbers can serve as a rough portrait of differences in the scope and character of sexual commerce in diverse contexts.

55. See, e.g., Walkowitz (1980), Beisel (1997), Luker (1998), and Brown (1995).

56. The sexualization of public culture has also inspired antiprostitution activism on the part of women's organizations that do not consider themselves feminist. Evangelical Christian women have historically played an active role in

shaping prostitution policy not only in the United States but also in countries such as Norway, Britain, and the Netherlands (Hobson 1987).

CHAPTER SEVEN

1. The "Economic Justice for Sex Workers" Symposium took place at the University of California, Hastings College of the Law in San Francisco, California, on March 28, 1999. For a summary of the proceedings, see Shah (1999).
2. In similar fashion, contemporary struggles within queer politics and theory over questions of assimilationism—e.g., the pursuit of marriage or other forms of state-recognized, rights-endowed partnerships, versus the celebration of a "public" sexuality that is unmoored by durable romantic attachments—are conflicts that have emanated from the dramatic and multifaceted cultural changes that have taken place in postindustrial societies since the late 1960s. Pertinent discussions of the queer "pleasure wars" include Pendleton (1996), Warner (1999), and Crain (1997).
3. On the meaning of recent cultural struggles around gay marriage and gay rights, see Seidman (2005), Chauncey (2004), and Stein (2001). On abortion wars, see Luker (1984), Ginsburg (1989), Petchesky (1990), and Saletan (2004). On the sociological significance of contemporary debates around sex education in schools, see Irvine (2002) and Luker (2006).
4. The term "moral panic" was first deployed by British sociologist Stanley Cohen (1972) and has been used by recent theorists to describe the anxieties that crystallize in the political and cultural field over particular constellations of sexual behaviors, often resulting in severely punitive responses from the state. See, e.g., Rubin (1989), Duggan and Hunter (1995), Warner (1999), and Stein (2001).
5. Durkheim ([1901] 1982), Bourdieu and Wacquant (1992).
6. Rosen (1982: 173). Italics in original.
7. Kempadoo (1998), Agustín (2000: 2), Brennan (2004: 27), O'Connell Davidson and Sánchez Taylor (2005).
8. Acker (2002), Gilfoyle (1992), Ullman (1997).
9. Gilfoyle (1992: 18).
10. Gilfoyle (1992: 102), Chudacoff (1999: 38).
11. Stansell (1982), Peiss (1989).
12. Stansell (1982: 185).
13. See Griffin (2001), Dalby (1983), Downer (2001), and Ramberg (2006). Indeed, many contemporary sex workers have themselves sought to elicit the comparison between the GFE and these earlier modes of commercial sexual engagement, creatively blending pre- and postmodern elements in their self-descriptions as "tantric sex practitioners" or "modern day courtesans." The Web site of one sex-worker activist of Indian descent notes that she offers "an in-call and out-call service for professional clients who are seeking a girl friend experience with a genuinely affectionate Devadasi escort."
14. Norberg (1998).
15. Stanford (1966: 72), quoted in Rosen (1982: 94).

16. Cressey (1932: 129).
17. The term "Taylorized sex" derives from the work of Alain Corbin (1990).
18. U.S. Bureau of the Census (1989, 1992, 2001), Sorrentino (1990), Kellogg and Mintz (1993).
19. Hochschild (1997).
20. Because Giddens's (1992) "plastic sexuality" still bears a connection to a notion of private-sphere, durable romantic relationships, he uses the term "episodic sexuality" to refer to what for him is a more troubling cultural offshoot. Episodic sexuality is gendered masculine, compulsive in nature, and aims to neutralize the anxieties that are stimulated by the threat of intimacy contained in the pure relationship and the relative emancipation of women. As such, episodic sexuality often finds expression in practices of commodified sex such as the consumption of pornography.
21. Laumann et al. (1994), Bourdieu (1984).
22. For a fuller discussion of these theorists, see chap. 1.
23. Manuel Castells defines "nonflexible" employment as full-time, year-round, salaried work with over three or more years in the same company (Castells 2001).
24. Illouz (1997), Beck and Beck-Gernsheim (1995), Ingraham (1999). Laurie Schaffner and I have noted that it is precisely during this period in which increasing numbers of heterosexuals have structured their lives outside the confines of marriage that an organized gay and lesbian movement has mobilized to gain access to marital rights (Bernstein and Schaffner 2005: xviii).
25. See Laumann et al. (1994: 518–29) for similar findings pertaining to recreational sex as well as a detailed statistical breakdown of the correlation between normative sexual orientation and membership in master status groups in the United States.
26. Judith Stacey uses the term "recombinant families" to describe the "diverse, fluid, and unresolved" mélange of contemporary American familial arrangements: "[W]omen and men have been creatively remaking American family life during the past three decades of postindustrial upheaval. Out of the ashes and residue of the modern family, they have drawn on a diverse, often incongruous array of cultural, political, economic, and ideological resources, fashioning these resources into new gender and kinship strategies to cope with postindustrial challenges, burdens, and opportunities" (1991: 16–17).
27. See Snitow (1983), Loe (1998), and Juffer (1998). The burgeoning sexual self-help industry, geared largely toward female consumers, emphasizes sexual skills, variety, and adventure. In addition to a steady proliferation of sexual advice columns, books, and Web sites (far too numerous to count), there are currently over a dozen venues in San Francisco (as well as similar offerings in other urban centers) that feature hands-on instruction in assorted sexual techniques (Hardy 2001).
28. Wolf (1991), Brumberg (1997), Schaffner (2006).
29. See also Foucault (1978), Rubin (1975), Giddens (1992), and Rountree (2000).
30. Swidler (1980: 240).

31. Hochschild (1997: 229). The English Collective of Prostitutes (ECP) and its U.S. affiliate, US PROStitutes Collective (USPROS), are for this reason both affiliates of the International Wages for Housework Campaign. The two organizations have campaigned vigorously for "the abolition of the prostitution laws which punish women for refusing to be poor and/or financially dependent on men" (English Collective of Prostitutes, 1992).

32. On child care, see Hochschild (2000, 1997, 1994b), and Hondagneu-Sotelo (2001). On domestic labor, see Salzinger (1991), Romero (1992), and Parreñas (2000). For an intriguing analysis of women's "unpaid sex work" in private-sphere, long-term heterosexual relationships, see Duncombe and Marsden (1996).

33. O'Connell Davidson (2002).

34. CATW (1998). Italics in original.

35. Hughes (2000: 10).

36. CATW (1998).

37. Høigard and Finstad (1992). A fuller discussion of their analysis of prostitutes' "divided self" is provided in chap. 3.

38. Shrage (1994: 119).

39. Shrage (1994).

40. Satz (1995: 63).

41. Zelizer (1994, 2005). Following Zelizer's model, a careful study of the distinct payment practices in different types of commercial sexual encounters (tipping, payment before or after services, etc.) would be worthy of pursuit.

42. Doezema (1998), Chapkis (2005).

43. On the abuse of domestic laborers, see Anderson and O'Connell Davidson (2003). On the exploitation of workers in the garment trades, see Ross (1997). On illegal migrant workers' general vulnerability to violence and abuse, see Kyle and Koslowski (2001) and Bales (1999).

44. Hochschild (2003: 102). According to Hochschild, whereas many middle-class jobs place a premium on an individual's capacity to manage feelings via a strategy that she terms "deep acting" or "emotion work," working-class jobs more often require "surface acting" only. "The creation and sustaining of meanings go on . . . but it is not what the boss pays for." Further discussion of this distinction is provided in chaps. 3 and 4.

45. In an impassioned letter to the editors of *Marie Claire* magazine regarding a July 2005 article entitled "Prostitution Gives Me Power" (featuring interviews with middle-class Dutch prostitutes engaged in what I would term the "postindustrial" paradigm of sex work), John Miller, Director of the U.S. Department of State Office to Monitor and Combat Trafficking in Persons, expressed outrage at the magazine for "choosing to glamorize this issue with a few highly atypical examples." Though it did not appear in the magazine, Miller's letter was widely circulated on antiprostitution Web sites and list-serves (see, e.g., Wigdon 2005).

46. As noted above (see chap. 1, n. 49), Wendy Brown's apt phrase refers to the feminist reinscription of a culturally normative heterosexual organization of desire.

47. The film is purported to be (very loosely) based on an actual series of events. For further discussion of the film and its international dissemination, see Kulick (2005).

48. For an elaborated analysis of the prevalence of these motifs in recent antitrafficking films, see Vance (forthcoming).

49. Unlike in Sweden, however, where prostitution does not constitute a crime for the women who sell sex, in the United States (where prostitution is defined as a crime for both parties) most municipalities are simply shifting their enforcement patterns to achieve greater parity between prostitute and client arrests.

50. Even the Vatican has come on board to endorse the criminalization of demand. On July 12, 2005, the Vatican issued a statement calling for prostitutes' clients to face legal penalties and to receive counseling as a means to combat "modern day slavery" (Associated Press 2005).

51. The Trafficking Victims Protection Reauthorization Act of 2005 (H.R. 972) amends the military manual for court martial such that any service member convicted of patronizing a prostitute can receive dishonorable discharge, forfeiture of all pay and allowances, and up to one year of confinement (Wood 2006; Schogol 2006). It also authorizes federal funds for the arrest and prosecution of sex purchasers as well as client reeducation programs and the publication of arrestees' names and addresses. Its specific objective is the elimination of international sex trafficking and domestic prostitution, both broadly defined to included consensual adult sex work.

52. Chapkis (2005); see also Kempadoo (2005a) and Miller (2004). The Trafficking Victims Protection Act (TVPA) of 2000 stipulated that migrants in the United States who were deemed to be victims of trafficking would be eligible for T-visas (granting them temporary residency, work permits, and the possibility of welfare support). Although the U.S. government currently estimates that 14,500–17,000 people are trafficked into the country each year for commercial sex and forced labor (a figure that was downgraded in 2004 from its prior estimate of 50,000 per year), by April of 2006 fewer than a thousand T-visas had been issued (U.S. Department of Justice 2006).

53. "I thought they were going after Osama bin Laden," said one neighborhood resident who witnessed the raid. "There were many people running at full speed. I thought there was a terrorist attack" (Van Derbeken and Kim 2005; see also Squatriglia 2005; Marshall 2005; and Rosenzweig and Kang 2005).

54. Van Derbeken and Kim (2005); Law Enforcement Instructors Alliance, Human Trafficking and Vice National Training Seminar, Las Vegas, Nevada, March 20–22, 2006.

55. As Kamala Kempadoo has noted, debt bondage, indentured labor, and exploitative contractual arrangements are the most common forms of forced labor, with slaves making up the smallest proportion of all cases. Whereas slavery is premised on property relations ("the permanent and legal ownership of one human being by another and the power invested in the owner to command that property at will") the more typical forms of migrant exploitation are in fact *contractual,* derived from the principle of the exchange value of labor in the free market (Kempadoo 2005a: xx).

56. Agustín (2005: 69). See also Kempadoo and Doezema (1998), Kempadoo (2005a, 2005b), Thorbek and Pattanaik (2002), and Cheng (2004a, 2004b, forthcoming).
57. St. James (1999: 6).
58. O'Connell Davidson and Sánchez Taylor (2005: 84). See also Kempadoo (1998).
59. Hartman (2002), Zukin (1995), Wacquant (2001).
60. This argument is indebted to Julia Sudbury's analysis of the "political and economic chain reaction" that has given rise to the twenty-first century prison-industrial complex, involving "a symbiotic and profitable relationship between politicians, corporations, the media and state correctional institutions that generates the racialized use of incarceration as a response to social problems rooted in the globalization of capital" (Sudbury 2002: 61).
61. Newman (2000); Wijers and van Doorninck (2002).
62. Urban Justice Center (2003: 80).
63. Other useful interventions that Thukral and Ditmore identify include substance abuse remedies, counseling, job training, health care, money management services, funding for peer support networks, and police training to better intervene in situations of violence against prostitutes (those which are initiated by members of their own forces, as well as by other parties). For those sex workers who are found to be trafficked, appropriate policy would consist of referring women to appropriate social service agencies, rather than arresting, detaining, or deporting them (Urban Justice Center 2003, 2005).
64. For a sociological analysis of the raced and classed effects of implementing "prostitution-free" zones in Portland, Oregon, see Sanchez (2003).
65. Lynsen (2006); interviews with Penelope Saunders, Executive Director of Different Avenues, Washington DC, July 22, 2005 and September 7, 2006.

APPENDIX
1. See Skolnick (1966, 1988, 1993).
2. Within a few years time, my prior street-based research was sufficiently in that past that I was able to complete some ride-alongs with the San Francisco police department as well.
3. A discussion of this literature is provided in chap. 6.
4. These individuals are listed individually and thanked profusely in the acknowledgments to this book.
5. Furthermore, nearly all of the relevant academic literature and government reports contained comprehensive summaries in English (if they were not simultaneously published in English originally). In the few cases in which relevant documents appeared only in Dutch or Swedish, I relied on research assistants for translations.
6. English also occupies a privileged role—one that to the best of my knowledge, has not been theorized—in European sexual subcultures more generally. Not only brothels, but also many other commercial sexual venues (from porn stores to lesbian S/M clubs) have English names and feature English-language descriptions in their advertising.

7. On a few occasions when I encountered migrant sex workers from Latin America who did not possess facility in English, I was able to speak with them in Spanish, in which I am fluent.

8. Solnit and Schwartzenberg (2000: 14). See also Zukin (1995), Smith (1996), Florida (2002).

9. Stacey (1991, 26).

10. Indeed, various of my COYOTE interviewees identified the "openness" of San Francisco's sexual culture and the political and cultural power of the local LGBQT (lesbian, gay, bisexual, queer, transgender) community as factors which made their entry into sex work possible, providing a model of legitimacy for queer citizenship that sex workers could then emulate. One woman actually identified the most unique feature of the Bay Area as its receptivity to New Age spiritual practices, indicating that she might not have become an erotic masseuse had she lived within a context in which it was unacceptable to bring tantra into her work. When I pressed this group of interviewees as to whether of not they thought they would still have entered into sex work had they lived elsewhere, most said that the only other U.S. cities in which they could imagine doing sex work were Portland, Seattle, and New York—cities whose socioeconomic profiles are, in many respects, similar to San Francisco (McCall 2001; Smith 1996; Egan 2005).

11. See, e.g., Brennan (2004), Wilson (2004), Kempadoo (2005b), Padilla (forthcoming), Cheng (forthcoming).

12. My own attempt to provide a provisional resolution to these debates is conveyed in the article, "What's Wrong with Prostitution? What's Right with Sex Work? Comparing Markets in Sexual Labor." See Bernstein (1999).

13. Chancer (1993).

14. See, e.g., Wacquant (2004), Emerson (2001), Sanchez Jankowski (1991), Goffman (1974).

15. Pheterson (1993), Chancer (1993).

16. Bourdieu (1984: 372–73). In Bourdieu's work, the term "habitus" refers to socially specific capacities to think, feel, and act in particular ways. As such, the term mediates between individual and social levels of experience. For a concise discussion of the genealogy of the term and its usage in Bourdieu's work, see Wacquant (2004b).

17. Haraway (1991: 192).

18. Wacquant (2004: viii).

19. Sanchez Jankowski (1991: 13).

20. On serendipity in fieldwork, see Pieke (2000) and Cheng (forthcoming: app. 1).

21. Burawoy (2000: 4).

22. Whyte (1943: 321). For a thoughtful discussion of social distance as an impediment to clear vision in ethnographic fieldwork, see Duneier (2001).

23. For discussions of transference and countertransference in fieldwork, see Hollway and Jefferson (2001), Gordon (1998), and Williams (2002).

24. Scheper-Hughes (2002: 35); see also Marcus (1998).

25. Wacquant (2004: vii).

26. Marcus (1998: 31–56).
27. Note, e.g., Wacquant's framing of his first fieldwork challenge with boxers as a heroic masculine quest: "Would I be capable of *learning this roughest and most demanding of sports,* of mastering its rudiments so as to carve out for myself a small place in the simultaneously fraternal and competitive world of the Sweet science of bruising, to weave with the members of the gym relationships of mutual respect and trust and thereby, eventually, carry out my field investigation of the ghetto?" (italics in original) (Wacquant 2004: x). The gentlemanly bravura that Sanchez Jankowski displays through his declaration that he was ready to fight if called on provides a further instance of the pursuit of masculine gender affirmation through ethnographic research.
28. Chapkis (1997).
29. See Zussman (2002), Goode (2002), and Kulick and Willson (1995). The masculinist underpinnings of this fieldwork tradition date back to Erving Goffman's often quoted remark that "you don't really know people until you've slept with them" (Zussman 2002: 475). In a recent special issue of the journal *Qualitative Sociology* on "Sex in Research," Joseph Hermanowicz embraces Goffman's dictum with gusto, deploying "sex in the field" as a metaphor for his point-by-point plan for gaining access to field subjects—e.g., offering jocular encouragement to budding qualitative sociologists to "probe" and "persist" (Hermanowicz 2002). While sex-in-the-field remains a largely male strategy within sociological fieldwork, within anthropology women have begun to critically explore their own erotic subjectivity not as an empiricist strategy for "gaining access," but as a potential vehicle for achieving theoretical and substantive knowledge. See, e.g., Kulick and Willson (1995).
30. A "double" is the sex trade vernacular for an encounter in which two sex workers are paid to service one client. The occasion that I refer to occurred early in my fieldwork. Lydia, a Tenderloin streetwalker who I was beginning to forge a closer bond with, invited me to come along with her and one of her regular clients for a date. She offered to pay me $40 of the total sum collected "just to watch," and more money if I decided to participate. Considering this an extraordinary fieldwork opportunity, I indeed accompanied her back to the Tenderloin nightclub that was to be our rendezvous point with the client in question. After a short period of chatting with them, for what were at the time still vague and intangible reasons to me, I said goodbye to them both and respectfully departed.
31. The anthropologist Angie Hart has described a similar experience upon completion of her fieldwork on prostitution in Spain. See Hart (1998).
32. Katherine Frank worked as a stripper for her research in *G-Strings and Sympathy;* Amy Flowers worked as a phone-sex operator for her study, *The Fantasy Factory* (Frank 2002a; Flowers 1998).
33. As Chancer has written, "The sociological study of sex tends to evoke a sociological study of sociology . . . a 'meta' level of analysis is created that shifts attentions from sex to sexual reactions to its study" (1998: 199).
34. Wacquant (2004).

BIBLIOGRAPHY

Acker, Caroline Jean. 2002. *Creating the American Junkie: Addiction Research in the Classic Era of Narcotic Control.* Baltimore: Johns Hopkins University Press.

Aggleton, Peter, ed. 1999. *Men Who Sell Sex: International Perspectives on Male Prostitution and HIV/AIDS.* Philadelphia: Temple University Press.

Agustín, Laura. 2005. "At Home in the Street: Questioning the Desire to Help and Save," in *Regulating Sex: The Politics of Intimacy and Identity,* ed. Elizabeth Bernstein and Laurie Schaffner. New York: Routledge.

———. 2003. "Sex, Gender, and Migration: Facing Up to Ambiguous Realities." *Soundings* 23 (spring).

———. 2000. "Working in the European Sex Industry: Migrant Possibilities." *OFRIM/Suplementos,* June. English translation available at http://www.swimw.org (last accessed April 26, 2002).

Alejandrino, Simon Velasquez. 2000. *Gentrification in San Francisco's Mission District: Indicators and Policy Recommendations.* San Francisco: Mission Economic Development Association.

Alexander, Priscilla. 1998. "Prostitution: Still a Difficult Issue," in *Sex Work: Writings by Women in the Sex Industry,* ed. Fédérique Delacoste and Priscilla Alexander. 2nd ed. Pittsburgh: Cleiss Press, pp. 184–231.

———. 1996. "Making a Living: Women Who Go Out," in *AIDS and Women's Experiences,* ed. Maxine Ankrah et al. New York: Columbia University Press, pp. 75–90.

———. 1987. "Prostitution: A Difficult Issue for Feminists," in *Sex Work: Writings by Women in the Sex Industry,* ed. Fédérique Delacoste and Priscilla Alexander. Pittsburgh: Cleiss Press, pp. 184–215.

Allison, Anne. 1994. *Nightwork: Sexuality, Pleasure, and Corporate Masculinity in a Tokyo Hostess Club.* Chicago: University of Chicago Press.

Almaguer, Tomás. 1993. "Chicano Men: A Cartography of Homosexual Identity and Behavior," in *The Lesbian and Gay Studies Reader,* ed. Henry Abelove, Michele Aina Barale, and David M. Halperin. New York: Routledge, pp. 255–74.

Almas, Elsa. 1994. "Sexology in Norway: Conceptualization of Sexuality." *Nordisk Sexologi* 12: 78–95.

Altman, Dennis. 2001. *Global Sex*. Chicago: University of Chicago Press.

Anderson, Bridget, and Julia O'Connell Davidson. 2003. "Is Trafficking in Human Beings Demand Driven? A Multi-Country Pilot Study." Geneva, Switzerland: International Organization for Migration, http://www.iom.int.

Anderson, Elijah. 1993. *Streetwise*. Chicago: University of Chicago Press.

Asbury, Herbert. 1933. *The Barbary Coast: An Informal History of the San Francisco Underworld*. New York: Thunder's Mouth Press.

Associated Press. 2005. "Vatican: Punish Clients of Prostitution." *Miami Herald*, July 12. http://www.miami.com/mid/miamiherald/news/12109288.htm (last accessed July 22, 2005).

Atchison, Chris, Laura Fraser, and John Lowman. 1998. "Men Who Buy Sex: Preliminary Findings of an Exploratory Study," in *Prostitution: On Whores, Hustlers, and Johns,* ed. John Elias et al. New York: Prometheus Books, pp. 172–204.

Baldwin, Peter. 1999. *Contagion and the State in Europe, 1830–1930*. Cambridge: Cambridge University Press.

Bales, Kevin. 1999. *Disposable People: New Slavery in the Global Economy*. Berkeley: University of California Press.

Barnhart, Jacqueline. 1986. *The Fair But Frail: Prostitution in San Francisco, 1849–1900*. Reno: University of Nevada Press.

Barr, Heather. 2001. "Policing Madness: People with Mental Illness and the NYPD," in *Zero Tolerance: Quality of Life and the New Police Brutality in New York City,* ed. Andrea McArdle and Tanya Erzen. New York: New York University Press, pp. 50–85.

Barry, Kathleen. 1995. *The Prostitution of Sexuality: The Global Exploitation of Women*. New York: New York University Press.

———. 1979. *Female Sexual Slavery*. New York: New York University Press.

Bauman, Zygmunt. 1998. "On Postmodern Uses of Sex." *Theory, Culture, and Society* 15 (3–4): 19–35.

Beck, Simon. 1997. "Lusty Ladies Crack the Whip." *South China Morning Post,* April 27, p. 13.

Beck, Ulrich, and Elizabeth Beck-Gernsheim. 1995. *The Normal Chaos of Love,* trans. Mark Ritter and Jane Wiebel. Cambridge: Polity Press.

Bell, Daniel. 1978. *The Cultural Contradictions of Capitalism*. New York: Basic Books.

Bell, Laurie, ed. 1987. *Good Girls, Bad Girls: Feminists and Sex Trade Workers Face to Face*. Toronto: Seal Press.

Bell, Shannon. 1995. *Whore Carnival*. New York: Autonomedia.

———. 1994. *Reading, Writing, and Rewriting the Prostitute Body*. Bloomington: Indiana University Press.

Bellafante, Gina. 2001. "Front Row." *New York Times,* Aug. 14, p. B8.

Bernstein, Elizabeth. 1999. "What's Wrong with Prostitution? What's Right with Sex-Work? Comparing Markets in Female Sexual Labor." *Hastings Women's Law Journal* 10 (1): 91–119.

Bernstein, Elizabeth, and Laurie Schaffner. 2005. "Regulating Sex—An Introduction," in *Regulating Sex: The Politics of Intimacy and Identity,* ed. Elizabeth Bernstein and Laurie Schaffner. New York: Routledge, pp. xi–xxv.

Bernstein Sycamore, Matt, ed. 2000. *Tricks and Treats: Sex Workers Write about Their Clients.* New York: Harrington Park Press.

Bishop, Ryan, and Lilian S. Robinson. 1998. *Night Market: Sexual Cultures and the Thai Economic Miracle.* New York: Routledge.

Block, Fred. 1990. *Postindustrial Possibilities: A Critique of Economic Discourse.* Berkeley: University of California Press.

Boëthius, Maria-Pia. 1999. "Current Sweden: The End of Prostitution in Sweden?" Svenska Institutet, http://www.si.se.infoSweden/604.cs?hit1= Prostitution &hit2 (last accessed Feb. 26, 2001).

Boles, J., and A. P. Garbin. 1974. "The Strip Club and Customer-Stripper Patterns of Interaction." *Sociology and Social Research* 58: 136–44.

Botonis, Greg. 2004. "Cars Returned after Prostitution Sweep." *Los Angeles Daily News,* May 15.

Boulware, Jack. 1999. "Web Rouser." *San Francisco Weekly,* March 31–April 6, pp. 19–26.

Bourdieu, Pierre. 1984. *Distinction: A Social Critique of the Judgement of Taste,* trans. Richard Nice. Cambridge, MA: Harvard University Press.

Bourdieu, Pierre, and Loic J. D. Wacquant. 1992. *An Invitation to Reflexive Sociology.* Chicago: University of Chicago Press.

Bourgois, Philippe. 1995. *In Search of Respect: Selling Crack in El Barrio.* Cambridge: Cambridge University Press.

Boutellier, Johannes. 1991. "Prostitution, Criminal Law, and Morality in the Netherlands." *Crime, Law, and Social Change* 15: 201–11.

Bowden, Martyn John. 1967. *The Dynamics of City Growth: An Historical Geography of the San Francisco Central District, 1850–1931.* PhD diss., University of California, Berkeley.

Bowes, Gemma. 2005. "Red Light Tour Condemned as 'Sick.'" *Observer,* Nov. 13.

Bowman, Catherine, and John King. 1996. "S.F. Supervisor Incumbents Triumph." *San Francisco Chronicle,* Nov. 6, p. A1.

Brannon, Johnny. 1998. "Pimps: Targets of Sharpened Police Enforcement." *San Francisco Independent,* April 14.

Brants, Chrisje. 1998. "The Fine Art of Regulated Tolerance: Prostitution in Amsterdam." *Journal of Law and Society* 25 (4): 621–35.

Brennan, Denise. 2004. *What's Love Got to Do with It? Transnational Desires and Sex Tourism in the Dominican Republic.* Durham: Duke University Press.

Breyer, Johanna. 1998. "Gender Discrimination and Solicitation Crimes." Unpublished ms., on file with the author.

Brinkley, Joel. 2000. "CIA Reports Widespread Immigrant Sexual Slavery." *San Francisco Examiner,* April 2, p. A-3.

Brock, Deborah R. 1998. *Making Work, Making Trouble: Prostitution as a Social Problem.* Toronto: University of Toronto Press.

Brody, Jane. 2000. "Cybersex Gives Birth to a Psychological Disorder." *New York Times,* May 16, p. F7.

Brook, James, Chris Carlsson, and Nancy J. Peters, eds. 1998. *Reclaiming San Francisco: Theory, Politics, Culture.* San Francisco: City Lights Books.

Brook, Kerwin. 1998. "Peep Show Pimps: San Francisco Strip Clubs May Be Pushing Dancers into Prostitution." *San Francisco Bay Guardian,* Feb. 4, pp. 18–21.

Brooks, Siobhan. 2000. "Listening to Lust: A Conversation with Sonya Roberts about Aural Sex," in *Male Lust: Power, Pleasure, and Transformation,* ed. Kerwin Kaye et al. New York: Hayworth, pp. 199–205.

———. 1997. "Dancing towards Freedom," in *Whores and Other Feminists,* ed. Jill Nagle. New York: Routledge, pp. 252–56.

Brown, Wendy. 1995. *States of Injury: Power and Freedom in Late Modernity.* Princeton, NJ: Princeton University Press.

Brumberg, Joan Jacobs. 1997. *The Body Project: An Intimate History of American Girls.* New York: Vintage.

Bryan, James H. 1972. "Apprenticeships in Prostitution," in *The Social Dimension of Human Sexuality,* ed. Robert R. Bell and Michael Gordon. Boston: Little, Brown.

Bullough, Vern, and Bonnie Bullough. 1987. *Women and Prostitution: A Social History.* Buffalo, NY: Prometheus Books.

Burawoy, Michael. 2000. "Introduction: Reaching for the Global," in *Global Ethnography: Forces, Connections, and Imaginations in a Postmodern World,* Michael Burawoy et al. Berkeley: University of California Press, pp. 1–41.

———. 1991. "The Extended Case Method," in *Ethnography Unbound: Power and Resistance in the Modern Metropolis,* Michael Burawoy et al. Berkeley: University of California Press, pp. 271–91.

Burgess, Ernest. [1925] 1996. "The Growth of the City: An Introduction to a Research Project," reprinted in *The City Reader,* ed. Richard T. LeGates and Frederic Stout. London: Routledge.

Bygdeman, Marc, and Katarina Lindahl. 1994. *Sex Education and Reproductive Health in Sweden in the Twentieth Century.* Report for the International Conference on Population and Development in Cairo.

Campbell, Rosie. 1998. "Invisible Men: Making Visible Male Clients of Female Prostitutes in Merseyside," in *Prostitution: On Whores, Hustlers, and Johns,* ed. John Elias et al. New York: Prometheus, pp. 155–72.

Carnes, Patrick. 1989. *Contrary to Love: Helping the Sexual Addict.* Minneapolis, MN: Compcare Publishers.

Carroll, Jerry. 1996. "Halloween's Big, Scary Parties." *San Francisco Chronicle,* Oct. 22, p. E1.

Castells, Manuel. 2001. "The Network Society." Paper presented at the Center for Working Families, University of California, Berkeley.

———. 1997. *The Information Age: Economy, Society, and Culture,* vol. 2: *The Power of Identity.* Oxford: Blackwell.

———. 1996. "The Net and the Self: Working Notes for a Critical Theory of the Informational Society." *Critique of Anthropology* 16 (1): 9–38.

———. 1983. *The City and the Grassroots: A Cross-Cultural Theory of Urban Social Movements.* Berkeley: University of California Press.

Cavan, Sherri. 1970. "B-Girls and Prostitutes," in *Observations of Deviance*, ed. Jack Douglas. New York: Random House, pp. 55–64.

Chan, Sucheng. 1991. "The Exclusion of Chinese Women, 1870–1943," in *Entry Denied: Exclusion and the Chinese Community in America, 1882–1943*, ed. Sucheng Chan. Philadelphia: Temple University Press, pp. 94–146.

Chancer, Lynn Sharon. 1998. *Reconcilable Differences: Confronting Beauty, Pornography, and the Future of Feminism*. Berkeley: University of California Press.

———. 1993. "Prostitution, Feminist Theory, and Ambivalence: Notes from the Sociological Underground." *Social Text* 37: 143–73.

Chapkis, Wendy. 2005. "Soft Glove, Punishing Fist: The Trafficking Victims Protection Act of 2000," in *Regulating Sex: The Politics of Intimacy and Identity*, ed. Elizabeth Bernstein and Laurie Schaffner. New York: Routledge, pp. 51–67.

———. 1997. *Live Sex Acts: Women Performing Erotic Labor*. New York: Routledge.

Chauncey, George. 2004. *Why Marriage?: The History Shaping Today's Debate over Gay Equality*. New York: Basic Books.

———. 1994. *Gay New York: Gender, Urban Culture, and the Making of the Gay Male World, 1890–1940*. New York: Harper Collins.

Cheng, Sea-ling. Forthcoming. *Transnational Desires: Migrant Entertainers in US Military Camp Towns in South Korea*. Philadelphia: University of Pennsylvania Press.

———. 2004a. "Interrogating the Absence of HIV/AIDS Interventions for Migrant Sex Workers in South Korea." *Health and Human Rights: An International Journal* 7(2): 193–205.

———. 2004b. " 'R and R' on a 'Hardship Tour' ": GIs and Filipina Entertainers in South Korea." *American Sexuality Magazine* 1 (5).

Chevigny, Paul. 2001. Foreword to *Zero Tolerance: Quality of Life and the New Police Brutality in New York City*, ed. Andrea McArdle and Tanya Erzen. New York: New York University Press, pp. vii–xiii.

Christina, Greta, ed. 2004. *Paying for It: A Guide by Sex Workers for Their Clients*. Oakland, CA: Greenery Press.

Chudacoff, Howard P. 1999. *The Age of the Bachelor: Creating an American Subculture*. Princeton, NJ: Princeton University Press.

Clifford, James, and George E. Marcus, eds. 1986. *Writing Culture: The Poetics and Politics of Ethnography*. Berkeley: University of California Press.

Coalition Against Trafficking in Women (CATW). 1998. "Sex: From Intimacy to 'Sexual Labor' or Is it a Human Right to Prostitute?" http://www.uri.edu/artsci/wms/hughes/catw/sex.htm (last accessed Nov. 9, 1998).

Cohen, Bernard. 1980. *Deviant Street Networks: Prostitution in New York City*. Lexington: Lexington Books.

Cohen, Stanley. 1972. *Folk Devils and Moral Panics: The Creation of Mods and Rockers*. Cambridge: Blackwell.

Collins, Patricia Hill. 1990. *Black Feminist Thought: Knowledge, Consciousness, and the Politics of Empowerment*. New York: Routledge.

Coman, Julian. 2000. "Prostitutes in Bondage to Red Tape in Holland Legislation Bring Bureaucracy to the World's Oldest Profession." *Sunday Telegraph* (London), Nov. 5, p. 33.

Comaroff, Jean, and John L. Comaroff. 2000. "Millennial Capitalism: First Thoughts on a Second Coming." *Public Culture* 12 (2): 291–343.

Conroy, John. 2006. "The Electronic Pillory." *Chicago Reader,* April 7, sec. 1.

Constable, Nicole. 2003. *Romance on a Global Stage: Pen Pals, Virtual Ethnography, and "Mail Order" Marriages.* Berkeley: University of California Press.

"Convicted Johns to Be Displayed in Oakland." 2005. *World News,* March 14.

Coontz, Stephanie. 1997. *The Way We Really Are: Coming to Terms with America's Changing Families.* New York: Basic Books.

Corbin, Alain. 1990. *Women for Hire: Prostitution and Sexuality in France after 1860.* Cambridge, MA: Harvard University Press.

Crain, Caleb. 1997. "Pleasure Principles." *Lingua Franca* 7 (8): 26–38.

Cressey, Paul. 1932. *The Taxi-Dance Hall.* New York: Greenwood Press.

Dalby, Liza. 1983. *Geisha.* New York: Vintage Books.

Dangerous Bedfellows, eds. 1996. *Policing Public Sex: Queer Politics and the Future of AIDS Activism.* Boston: South End Press.

"Danish Parliament Approves Legalization of Prostitution." 1999. Associated Press Online, March 5, Lexis-Nexis.

Dank, Barry, ed. 1999. *Sex Work and Sex Workers: Thematic Issue of Sexuality and Culture,* vol. 2. New Brunswick, NY: Transaction Publishers.

Danna, Daniela. 2002. "Street Prostitution and Public Policies in Milan, Italy." Paper presented at the conference "Sex Work and Public Health," in Milton Keynes, UK, Jan. 18–20.

Davies, Guy, and Anthony Wonke. 2000. "Media: We Want Porn: Virtual Brothels in Amsterdam, Not Head-Scratching Mainstream Broadcasters, Have Sorted the Future of Television and the Web." *Guardian* (London), Nov. 13, p. 8.

Davis, Fania. 1995. Letter to James A. Quadra, San Francisco Deputy City Attorney, Re: *Dotson v. Yee, San Francisco Task Force on Prostitution Final Report,* app. D.

Davis, Kingsley. [1937] 1985. "The Sociology of Prostitution," in *Theories of Deviance,* ed. Stuart H. Traub and Craig B. Little. Itasca, IL: F. E. Peacock Publishers, pp. 8–21.

Davis, Nanette, ed. 1993. *Prostitution: An International Handbook of Trends, Problems, and Policies.* Westport, CT: Greenwood Press.

———. 1971. "The Prostitute: Developing a Deviant Identity," in *Studies in the Sociology of Sex,* ed. James M. Henslin. New York: Meredith Corporation, pp. 297–325.

De Albuquerque, Klaus. 1998. "Sex, Beach Boys, and Female Tourists in the Caribbean." *Sexuality and Culture* 2: 467–79.

Delacoste, Fédérique, and Priscilla Alexander, eds. 1998. *Sex Work: Writings by Women in the Sex Industry,* 2nd ed. Pittsburgh: Cleiss Press.

———. 1987. *Sex Work: Writings by Women in the Sex Industry.* Pittsburgh: Cleiss Press.

DeLeon, Richard Edward. 1992. *Left Coast City: Progressive Politics in San Francisco, 1975–1991.* Lawrence: University Press of Kansas.

D'Emilio, John. 1993. "Capitalism and Gay Identity," in *The Lesbian and Gay Studies Reader,* ed. Henry Abelove et al. New York: Routledge, pp. 467–479.

D'Emilio, John, and Estelle B. Freedman. 1988. *Intimate Matters: A History of Sexuality in America.* New York: Harper and Row.

Diana, Lewis. 1985. *The Prostitute and Her Clients: Your Pleasure Is Her Business.* Springfield, IL: Charles C. Thomas Publishers.

Doezema, Jo. 2001. "Ouch! Western Feminists' 'Wounded Attachment' to the 'Third World Prostitute.'" *Feminist Review* 67: 16–31.

———. 1998. "Forced to Choose: Beyond the Voluntary v. Forced Prostitution Dichotomy," in *Global Sex Workers: Rights, Resistance, and Redefinition,* ed. Kamala Kempadoo and Jo Doezema. New York: Routledge, 34–51.

Donovan, Brian. 2006. *White Slave Crusades: Race, Gender, and Anti-Vice Activism, 1887–1917.* Urbana and Chicago: University of Illinois Press.

Downer, Lesley. 2001. *Women of the Pleasure Quarters.* New York: Broadway Books.

Dreyfus, Hubert L., and Paul Rabinow. 1983. *Michel Foucault: Beyond Structuralism and Hermeneutics.* Chicago: University of Chicago Press.

Droganes, Constance. 2000. "Toronto the Naughty," *National Post,* Jan. 22, http://www.nationalpost.com.

Drudis, Eric. 1999. "Study Finds New Sexual Revolution On-line." *San Francisco Examiner,* April 1, p. A16.

Dudley, Melinda. 2004. "Sex Workers Fight Stigmas with Multimedia Art Show." *Daily Bruin,* Feb. 23, http://www.dailybruin.ucla.edu/news/articles.asp?id = 32156 (last accessed May 31, 2005).

Duggan, Lisa. 2003. *The Twilight of Equality? Neoliberalism, Cultural Politics, and the Attack on Democracy.* Boston: Beacon Press.

Duggan, Lisa, and Nan D. Hunter. 1995. *Sex Wars: Sexual Dissent and Political Culture.* New York: Routledge.

Duncombe, Jean, and Dennis Marsden. 1996. "Whose Orgasm Is This Anyway? 'Sex Work' in Long-term Heterosexual Couple Relationships," in *Sexual Cultures: Communities, Values, and Intimacy,* ed. in Jeffrey Weeks and Janet Holland. New York: St. Martin's Press.

Duneier, Mitchell. 2001. "On the Evolution of *Sidewalk,*" in *Contemporary Field Research: Perspectives and Formulations,* ed. Robert M. Emerson. Prospect Heights, IL: Waveland Press, 167–188.

"Durham Police Post 'Johns' on Web." 2004. *NBC 17,* Dec. 8.

Durkheim, Emile. [1915] 1951. *Suicide: A Study in Sociology,* trans. John Spaulding and George Simpson, ed. George Simpson. New York: Free Press.

———. [1914] 1973. "The Dualism of Human Nature and Its Social Conditions," in *On Morality and Society,* ed. Robert Bellah. Chicago: University of Chicago Press, pp. 149–63.

———. [1911] 1979. *Durkheim: Essays on Morals and Education,* ed. W. S. F. Pickering, trans. H. L. Sutcliffe. Boston: Routledge and Kegan Paul.

———. 1911. "L'education Sexuelle." *Bulletin de la Société Française de Philoso-phie* 11: 29–52.

———. [1901] 1982. *The Rules of Sociological Method: Selected Texts on Sociology and Its Method,* trans. W. D. Halls, ed. Steven Lukes. New York: Free Press.

Earles, Kimberly. 2004. "Women and the Assault on Welfare in Sweden." *Social-ism and Democracy* 18 (1): 107–35.

Edwards, Susan. 1993. "Selling the Body, Keeping the Soul: Sexuality, Power, and the Theories and Realities of Prostitution," in *Body Matters: Essays on the Sociology of the Body,* ed. Sue Scott and David Morgan. London: Falmer Press, pp. 89–104.

Egan, Timothy. 2005. "Vibrant Cities Find One Thing Missing: Children." *New York Times,* March 24, http://www.nytimes.com (last accessed June 3, 2005).

———. 2000. "Technology Sent Wall Street into Market for Pornography." *New York Times,* Oct. 23, pp. A1, A20.

Ehrenreich, Barbara. 1989. *Fear of Falling: The Inner Life of the Middle Class.* New York: Harper Collins.

———. 1983. *The Hearts of Men: American Dreams and the Flight from Commit-ment.* New York: Doubleday.

Ehrenreich, Barbara, Elizabeth Hess, and Gloria Jacobs. 1986. *Re-Making Love: The Feminization of Sex.* New York: Anchor Press.

Ehrenreich, Barbara, and Arlie Russell Hochschild. 2002. *Global Woman: Nan-nies, Maids, and Sex Workers in the New Economy.* New York: Metropolitan Books.

Ekberg, Gunilla. 2002. "The International Debate about Prostitution and Traffick-ing in Women: Refuting the Arguments." *Seminar on the Effects of Legalization of Prostitution Activities—A Critical Analysis.* Stockholm: Regeringskansliet.

Elias, James, Vern Bullough, Veronica Elias, and Gwen Brewer, eds. 1998. *Prosti-tution: On Whores, Hustlers, and Johns.* New York: Prometheus Books.

Ellis, Havelock. [1906] 1936. *Studies in the Psychology of Sex.* Vol. 2. New York: Random House.

Emerson, Robert M. 2001. *Contemporary Field Research: Perspectives and For-mulations.* Prospect Heights, IL: Waveland Press.

Engels, Friedrich. [1884] 1978. "The Origin of the Family, Private Property, and the State," in *The Marx-Engels Reader,* ed. Robert Tucker. New York: W. W. Norton, pp. 734–60.

English Collective of Prostitutes. 1992. *Prostitute Women and AIDS: Resisting the Virus of Repression.* London: Crossroads Books.

Epele, María. 2002. "Excess, Scarcity, and Desire amongst Drug-Using Sex-Workers," in *Commodifying Bodies,* ed. Nancy Scheper Hughes and Loic Wac-quant. London: Sage, pp. 161–81.

Epstein, Steven. 1993. "A Queer Encounter: Sociology and the Study of Sexuality," in *Queer Theory/Sociology,* ed. Steven Seidman. Cambridge, MA: Blackwell, pp. 145–68.

Erickson, David John, and Richard Tewksbury. 2000. "The 'Gentlemen' in the Club: A Typology of Strip Club Patrons." *Deviant Behavior: An Interdisciplin-ary Journal* 21: 271–93.

EscortSupport.com, 2004. *Escorting Tip Guide.* Sacramento, CA: OJO Publishing.

Esping-Anderson, Gøsta. 1999. *Social Foundations of Postindustrial Economies.* Oxford: Oxford University Press.

———. 1990. *The Three Worlds of Welfare Capitalism.* Princeton, NJ: Princeton University Press.

European Intervention Projects AIDS Prevention for Prostitutes (EUROPAP). 1998. *Hustling for Health: Developing Services for Sex Workers in Europe.* Amsterdam: TAMPEP International Foundation.

———. 1994. *Final Report.* Amsterdam: TAMPEP International Foundation.

"Fab Fall Reads." 2001. *Cosmopolitan* (Sept.): 342.

Fainstein, Susan S., and Dennis R. Judd. 1999. "Global Forces, Local Strategies, and Urban Tourism," in *The Tourist City,* ed. Dennis R. Judd and Susan F. Fainstein. New Haven, CT: Yale University Press, pp. 1–21.

Farley, Melissa, ed. 2003. *Prostitution, Trafficking, and Traumatic Stress.* Binghamton, NY: Haworth.

———. 1994. "Letter to the Editor." *Off Our Backs* (Aug.–Sept.).

Farley, Melissa, and Vanessa Kelly. 2000. "Prostitution: A Critical Review of the Medical and Social Sciences Literature." *Women and Criminal Justice* 11 (4).

Farley, Melissa, et al. 2003. "Prostitution and Trafficking in Nine Countries: An Update on Violence and Posttraumatic Stress Disorder," in *Prostitution, Trafficking, and Traumatic Stress,* ed. Melissa Farley. Binghamton, NY: Haworth, pp. 33–75.

Farmer, Paul. 2005. *Pathologies of Power: Health, Human Rights, and the New War on the Poor.* Berkeley: University of California Press.

———. 1997. "On Suffering and Structural Violence: A View from Below," in *Social Suffering,* ed. Arthur Kleinman, Veena Das, and Margaret Lock. Berkeley: University of California Press, 261–83.

Fass, Paula. 1977. *The Damned and the Beautiful: American Youth in the 1920's.* Oxford: Oxford University Press.

Faugier, Jean, and Mary Sargeant. 1997. "Boyfriends, Pimps and Clients," in *Rethinking Prostitution: Purchasing Sex in the 1990s,* ed. Graham Scambler and Annette Scambler. London: Routledge, pp. 121–39.

Feldman, Harvey W., Frank Espada, Sharon Penn, and Sharon Byrd. 1993. "Street Status and the Sex-for-Crack Scene in San Francisco," in *Crack Pipe as Pimp: An Ethnographic Investigation of Sex-for-Crack Exchanges,* ed. Michael S. Ratner. New York: Lexington Books, 133–59.

Florida, Richard. 2002. *The Rise of the Creative Class.* New York: Basic Books.

Florin, C., and Nilsson, B. 1998. "'Something in the Nature of a Bloodless Revolution': How New Gender Relations Became Gender Equality Policy in Sweden in the Nineteen-Sixties and Seventies," in *State Policy and Gender System in Two German States and Sweden, 1945–1989,* ed. R. Torstendahl. Lund: Bloms I Lund Tryckeri AB, pp. 11–78.

Flowers, Amy. 1998. *The Fantasy Factory: An Insider's View of the Phone Sex Industry.* Philadelphia: University of Pennsylvania Press.

Foote, N. N. 1954. "Sex as Play." *Social Problems:* 159–63.

Foucault, Michel. 1978. *The History of Sexuality,* vol. 1: *An Introduction,* trans. Robert Hurley. New York: Random House.

Fowler, Bree. 2003. "Prostitute Solicitors to Go on Detroit TV." Associated Press, March 4.

Frank, Katherine. 2002a. *G-Strings and Sympathy: Strip Club Regulars and Male Desire.* Durham: Duke University Press.

———. 2002b. "Stripping, Starving, and the Politics of Pleasure," in *Jane Sexes it Up: True Confessions of Feminist Desire,* ed. Merri Lisa Johnson. New York: Four Walls Eight Windows Press, 171–207.

———. 1998. "The Production of Identity and the Negotiation of Intimacy in a 'Gentleman's Club.'" *Sexualities* 1 (2): 175–203.

French, Dolores, with Linda Lee. 1988. *Working: My Life as a Prostitute.* New York: E. P. Dutton.

Freud, Sigmund. [1912] 1963. "The Most Prevalent Form of Degradation in Erotic Life," in *Sexuality and the Psychology of Love,* ed. Philip Rieff. New York: Collier Books, pp. 58–70.

Friend, Tad. 2004. "Naked Profits: The Employees Take Over a Strip Club." *New Yorker,* July 12 and 19, pp. 56–61.

Fuffle, Kerr, and Roscoe Spanks. 2003. *Paying for Sex: The Gentleman's Guide to Web Porn, Strip Clubs, Prostitutes, and Escorts.* Victoria, British Columbia: Trafford Press.

Funari, Vicki. 1997. "Naked, Naughty, Nasty: Peep Show Reflections," in *Whores and Other Feminists,* ed. Jill Nagle. New York: Routledge.

Gallagher, Paul. 2005. "Thomas Cook's Latest Holiday . . . Red Light Tours for the Kiddies." *The Daily Mirror,* Nov. 14, http://www.mirror.co.uk.news (last accessed Nov. 14, 2005).

Gamson, Joshua. 1991. "Silence, Death, and the Invisible Enemy: AIDS Activism and Social Movement 'Newness,'" in *Ethnography Unbound: Power and Resistance in the Modern Metropolis,* Michael Burawoy et al. Berkeley: University of California Press, pp. 35–58.

Gant, Larry. 2000. "Uncomfortable Questions: Black Men and Heterosexual Commercial Sex," in *Male Lust,* ed. Kerwin Kaye et al. New York: Haworth Press, pp. 287–95.

Gelb, Joyce. 1989. *Feminism and Politics: A Comparative Perspective.* Berkeley: University of California Press.

Gender Equality in Norway: National Report to the Fourth United Nations Conference on Women in Beijing. Oct. 1994. Oslo: Royal Ministry of Foreign Affairs.

Giddens, Anthony. 1992. *The Transformation of Intimacy: Sexuality, Love, and Eroticism in Modern Societies.* Stanford: Stanford University Press.

Gilfoyle, Timothy J. 1999. "Prostitutes in History: From Parables of Pornography to Metaphors of Modernity." *American Historical Review* 104 (1): 117–41.

———. 1992. *City of Eros: New York City, Prostitution, and the Commercialization of Sex, 1790–1920.* New York: W. W. Norton.

Ginsburg, Faye D. 1989. *Contested Lives: The Abortion Debate in an American Community.* Berkeley: University of California Press.

Girl-X. 1997. "Will Moan for Rent Money." *Hip Mama: The Parenting Zine*. Special issue, "Mamas on Call: Doing the Sex Industry," no. 13, pp. 20–24.

Goffman, Erving. [1974] 1989. "On Fieldwork," comp. Lyn H. Lofland. *Journal of Contemporary Ethnography* 18 (2): 123–32.

———. 1963. *Stigma: Notes on the Management of Spoiled Identity*. New York: Simon and Schuster.

———. 1959. *The Presentation of Self in Everyday Life*. Garden City, New York: Doubleday.

Goldberg, Leslie. 1995. "Nurse Settles False Arrest Suit." *San Francisco Examiner,* http://www.sfgate.com.

Goldsmith, Belinda. 1999. "Swedish Law Fails to Curb Prostitution." *Reuters Online,* July 5. Infonautics (last accessed March 3, 2000).

Goldsmith, Margie. 2003. "Crunch Fitness Gets Kinky with 'Whipped,'" *Metro Sports New York,* May, p. 11.

Goode, Erich. 2002. "Sexual Involvement and Social Research in a Fat Civil Rights Organization." *Qualitative Sociology* 25 (4): 501–34.

Goodell, Jeff. 2001. "How to Run a Successful Silicon Valley Business." *New York Times Magazine,* April 8, pp. 52–54.

Gooding-Williams, Robert, ed. 1993. *Reading Rodney King: Reading Urban Uprising*. New York: Routledge.

"GOP = Grumpy Old Pornographers." 2005. *Fairfield County Weekly News,* Jan. 13, www.fairfieldweekly.com (last accessed Jan. 24, 2005).

Gordon, Avery. 1998. *Ghostly Matters: Haunting and the Sociological Imagination*. Minneapolis: University of Minnesota Press.

Gordon, Linda. 1990. "Family Violence, Feminism, and Social Control," in *Women, the State, and Welfare,* ed. Linda Gordon. Madison: University of Wisconsin Press, pp. 178–98.

Gordon, Rachel. 1998. "Supes OK Crackdown on Massage Parlors." *San Francisco Examiner,* Sept. 23.

Gore, Dayo Folayan, Tamara Jones, and Joo-Hyun Kang. 2001. "Organizing at the Intersections: A Roundtable Discussion of Police Brutality through the Lens of Race, Class, and Sexual Identities," in *Zero Tolerance: Quality of Life and the New Police Brutality in New York City,* ed. Andrea McArdle and Tanya Erzen. New York: New York University Press, pp. 251–71.

Gould, Arthur. 2002. "Sweden's Law on Prostitution: Feminism, Drugs, and the Foreign Threat," in *Transnational Prostitution: Changing Global Patterns,* ed. Susanne Thorbek and Bandana Pattanik. London: Zed Books, 201–17.

"Government Computers Used to Solicit Prostitutes." 2000. Agence France Presse Online, Feb. 23, Lexis-Nexis (last accessed Feb. 2, 2001).

Greenfeld, Karl Toro. 1999. "Taking Stock in Smut." *Time,* April 19, p. 43.

Greenwald, Harold. 1958. *The Elegant Prostitute: A Social and Psychoanalytic Study*. New York: Walker Publishing.

Griffin, Susan. 2001. *The Book of the Courtesans: A Catalogue of Their Virtues*. New York: Broadway Books.

Hamilton, Arnold. 1999. "Lurid Tactics: Oklahoma City Threatens Prostitution Participants Glare of TV Publicity." *Dallas Morning News,* March 18, p. 33A.

Hamlin, Jesse. 2002. "A Burlesque Show that Fills the Stage: It's Not Over Until the Fat Lady Strips." *San Francisco Chronicle,* June 13, http://www.sfgate.com.

Haraway, Donna. 1991. *Simians, Cyborgs, and Women: The Reinvention of Nature.* New York: Routledge.

Harcourt, Bernard E. 2001. *Illusion of Order: The False Promise of Broken Windows Policing.* Cambridge, MA: Harvard University Press.

Hardy, Lisa Allyn. 2001. "Sex in the City: Where to Learn about the Birds, the Bees, and Sexual Bliss." *San Francisco Bay Guardian,* May 23, p. 31.

Hargrove, Thomas. 2005. "Men Make Up One-Third of Prostitution Arrests." Scripps Howard News Service, Feb. 17.

Hart, Angie. 1998. *Buying and Selling Power: Anthropological Reflections on Prostitution in Spain.* Boulder, CO: Westview Press.

——. 1994. "Missing Masculinity? Prostitutes' Clients in Alicante, Spain," in *Dislocating Masculinity: Comparative Ethnographies,* ed. Andrea Cornwall and Nancy Lindisfarne. New York: Routledge, pp. 48–66.

Hartman, Chester. 2002. *City for Sale: The Transformation of San Francisco.* Berkeley: University of California Press.

Harvey, David. 2003. *The New Imperialism.* Oxford: Oxford University Press.

——.1990. *The Condition of Postmodernity: An Enquiry into the Origins of Cultural Change.* Cambridge: Blackwell.

Hausbeck, Kathryn, and Barbara Brents. 2000. "Inside Nevada's Brothel Industry," in *Sex for Sale: Prostitution, Pornography, and the Sex Industry,* ed. Ronald Weitzer. New York: Routledge, pp. 217–43.

Heap, Chad. 2003. "The City as Sexual Laboratory: The Queer Heritage of the Chicago School." *Qualitative Sociology* 26 (4): 457–89.

Hekma, Gert. 2005. "How Libertine Is the Netherlands? Exploring Contemporary Dutch Sexual Cultures," in *Regulating Sex: The Politics of Intimacy and Identity,* ed. Elizabeth Bernstein and Laurie Schaffner. New York: Routledge, pp. 209–25.

Held, David, and Anthony McGrew, eds. 2000. *The Global Transformations Reader: An Introduction to the Globalization Debate.* Cambridge: Polity Press.

Hermanowicz, Joseph C. 2002. "The Great Interview: Twenty-five Strategies for Studying People in Bed." *Qualitative Sociology* 25 (4): 479–99.

Heyl, Barbara Sherman. 1979. *The Madam as Entrepreneur: Career Management in House Prostitution.* New Brunswick, NJ: Transaction Books.

Hirata, Lucie Cheng. 1979. "Free, Indentured, Enslaved: Chinese Prostitutes in Nineteenth-Century America." *Signs* 5 (1): 3–29.

Hirschi, Travis. 1972. "The Professional Prostitute," in *The Social Dimension of Human Sexuality,* ed. Robert Bell and Michael Gordon. Boston: Little, Brown, pp. 249–68.

Hobson, Barbara. 2005. "Introduction." *Social Politics* (spring): 1–2.

Hobson, Barbara Meil, ed. 2002. *Making Men into Fathers: Men, Masculinities, and the Social Politics of Fatherhood.* Cambridge: Cambridge University Press.

——. 1999. "Women's Collective Agency, Power Resources, and Citizenship Rights," in *Extending Citizenship, Reconfiguring States,* ed. Michael Hanagan and Charles Tilly. Lanham: Rowman and Littlefield, pp. 149–77.

————. 1987. *Uneasy Virtue: The Politics of Prostitution and the American Reform Tradition.* Chicago: University of Chicago Press.

Hochschild, Arlie Russell. 2003. *The Commericalization of Intimate Life: Notes from Home and Work.* Berkeley: University of California Press.

————. 2000. "The Nanny Chain." *American Prospect* 11 (4): 32–36.

————. 1997. *The Time Bind: When Work Becomes Home and Home Becomes Work.* New York: Metropolitan Books.

————. 1994a. "The Commercial Spirit of Intimate Life and the Abduction of Feminism: Signs from Women's Advice Books." *Theory, Culture, and Society* 2: 1–24.

————. 1994b. *The Second Shift.* New York: Avon Books.

————. 1983. *The Managed Heart: Commodification of Human Feeling.* Berkeley: University of California Press.

Hodgson, James F. 1997. *Games Pimps Play: Pimps, Players, and Wives-in-Law.* Toronto: Canadian Scholars' Press.

Høigård, Cecilie, and Liv Finstad, 1992. *Backstreets: Prostitution, Money, and Love,* trans. Katherine Hanson, Nancy Snipe, and Barbara Wilson. University Park: Pennsylvania State University Press.

Hollander, Xaviera. 1972. *The Happy Hooker: My Own Story.* New York: Dell Publishing.

Hollway, Wendy, and Tony Jefferson. 2000. *Doing Qualitative Research Differently.* London: Sage.

Holzman, Harold, and Sharon Pines. 1982. "Buying Sex: The Phenomenology of Being a John." *Deviant Behavior* 4: 89–116.

Hondagneu-Sotelo, Pierrette. 2001. *Doméstica: Immigrant Workers Cleaning and Caring in the Shadows of Affluence.* Berkeley: University of California Press.

Hotaling, Norma, et al. 2003. "Been There Done That: SAGE, a Peer Leadership Model among Prostitution Survivors," in *Prostitution, Trafficking, and Traumatic Stress,* ed. Melissa Farley. Binghamton, NY: Haworth.

Huang, Renata. 1999. "Bunco Squad: Police Brass Can't Account for a Rogue Vice Operation." *San Francisco Weekly,* March 3–9.

————. 1998a. "Policing the Vice Squad: Investigations Launched into Money Collected from Massage Parlor Workers." *San Francisco Weekly,* Dec. 16, http://www.sfweekly.com (last accessed May 28, 2005).

————. 1998b. "Wages of Vice: Police Find a Way to Make Money by Busting Massage Parlors." *San Francisco Weekly,* Dec. 2, http://www.sfweekly.com (last accessed May 28, 2005).

Hughes, Donna. 2004. *Best Practices to Address the Demand Side of Sex Trafficking.* Aug. S-INLEC-04-CA-0003. http://www.uri.edu/artsci/wms/hughes/ (last accessed June 15, 2005).

————. 2000. "The 'Natasha' Trade: The Transnational Shadow Market of Trafficking in Women." *Journal of International Affairs* 53 (2): 625–51.

Hughes, Donna, and Clare Roche, eds. 1999. *Making the Harm Visible: Global Sexual Exploitation of Women and Girls.* Kingston, RI: Coalition Against Trafficking in Women.

Hunt, Jacqueline. 2005. "Letter to the Editor." *Observer,* Nov. 20.

Hurl-Eamon, Jennine. 2004. "Policing Male Heterosexuality: The Reformation of Manners Societies' Campaign against the Brothels in Westminster, 1690–1720." *Journal of Social History,* http://www.findarticles.com/p/articles/mi_m2005?is_4_37?ai_n6137406/print (last accessed July 22, 2005).

Illouz, Eva. 1997. *Consuming the Romantic Utopia: Love and the Cultural Contradictions of Capitalism.* Berkeley: University of California Press.

Ingraham, Chrys. 1999. *White Weddings: Romancing Heterosexuality in Popular Culture.* New York: Routledge.

Irvine, Janice M. 2003. "'The Sociologist as Voyeur': Social Theory and Sexuality Research, 1910–1978." *Qualitative Sociology* 26 (4): 429–57.

———. 2002. *Talk about Sex: The Battles over Sex Education in the United States.* Berkeley: University of California Press.

———. 1993. "Regulated Passions: The Invention of Inhibited Sexual Desire and Sex Addiction." *Social Text* 37: 203–27.

Irvine, Martha. 1996. "Former Hooker Sets Sights on San Francisco City Hall." Associated Press, Sept. 30, http://web.lexis-nexis.com.

Israely, Jeff. 2000. "Old Trade, New Tack: Italy Considers Legalizing Prostitution in Order to Control It." *San Francisco Chronicle,* Sept. 25, p. A12.

Itiel, Joseph. 1998. *A Consumer's Guide to Male Hustlers.* New York: Harrington Park Press.

Jackson, Robert. 2000. "The Dirty Business of Internet Porn." AlterNet. Nov. 17, www.alternet.org (last accessed Nov. 21, 2000).

Jacobs, Andrew. 2004. "Call Girls, Updated." *New York Times,* Oct. 12.

Jakobsen, Janet. 2002. "Can Homosexuals End Western Civilization As We Know It? Family Values in a Global Economy," in *Queer Globalizations: Citizenship and the Afterlife of Colonialism,* ed. Arnaldo Cruz-Malavé and Martin Manalansan. New York: New York University Press, pp. 49–71.

James, Jennifer. 1975. "Mobility as an Adaptive Strategy," *Urban Anthropology* 4: 349–64.

Jameson, Fredric. 1984. "Postmodernism, or the Cultural Logic of Late Capitalism." *New Left Review* 146.

Jameson, Jenna. 2004. *How to Make Love Like a Porn Star.* New York: Regan Books.

Janus, Sam, Barbara Bess, and Carol Saltus. 1977. *A Sexual Profile of Men in Power.* Englewood Cliffs, NJ: Prentice Hall.

Jeffreys, Sheila. 1997. *The Idea of Prostitution.* North Melbourne: Spiniflex.

Jelinek, Pauline. 2004. "Troops May Be Tried for Using Prostitutes." Associated Press. Sept. 22, http://cnn.netscape.cnn.com (last accessed Sept. 22, 2004).

Jenness, Valerie. 1993. *Making It Work: The Prostitutes' Rights Movement in Perspective.* New York: Aldine de Gruyter.

Jensen, Torben. 1994. "Buffer in a Social-Political Minefield: Social Work with Male Prostitution." Paper presented June 9 at the University of Göteborg, Sweden.

Jensen, Torben, Ida Koch, Annalise Konstad, and Anders Dahl. 1990. *Prostitution i Danmark.* Copenhagen: Socialforskningsinstiuttet.

Jessen, Liv. 1995. "Why Prostitution in a Welfare State?" Paper presented at Innledning på seminar FN-toppmøtes Forum-konferanse, March, Copenhagen.

Johnson, Merri Lisa. 1999. "Pole Work: Autoethnography of a Strip Club," in *Sex Work and Sex Workers*. Special issue of *Sexuality and Culture*, 2: 149–57.

Jordan, Jan. 2005. *The Sex Industry in New Zealand: A Literature Review*. Wellington: New Zealand Ministry of Justice. http://www.courts.govt.nz/pubs/reports/2005/sex-industry-in-nz-literature-review/index.html (last accessed June 15, 2005).

Juffer, Jane. 1998. *At Home with Pornography: Women, Sex, and Everyday Life*. New York: New York University Press.

Juno, Andrea, and V. Vale, eds. 1991. *Angry Women*. Re/Search Publications.

Kahn, Michael. 2000. "Web 'Porn-trepreneurs' Get Internet Business Tips." Reuters, Jan. 25.

Kaplan, Bernard D. 1995. "Anti-Prostitution Mood Sweeps Sweden." *San Francisco Examiner*, March 30, p. A17.

Kaplan, Gisela. 1992. *Contemporary Western European Feminism*. New York: New York University Press.

Kaye, Kerwin. 2004. "Sexual Abuse and the Wholesome Family: Feminist, Psychological, and State Discourses," in *Regulating Sex: The Politics of Intimacy and Identity*, ed. Elizabeth Bernstein and Laurie Schaffner. New York: Routledge.

———. 2003. "Male Prostitution in the Twentieth Century: Pseudo Homosexuals, Hoodlum Homosexuals, and Exploited Teens. *Journal of Homosexuality* 46 (1–2): 1–77.

———. 2002. "Consuming Addiction: Obsession and the Control of Everyday Life." Unpublished ms. on file with the author.

———. 1999a. "Male Sexual Clients: Changing Images of Masculinity, Prostitution, and Deviance in the United States, 1900–1950." Unpublished ms., on file with the author.

———. 1999b. "Naked but Unseen: Sex and Labor Conflict in San Francisco's Adult Entertainment Theaters," in *The Politics of Sexuality*, ed. Barry M. Dank and Roberto Refinetti, vol. 3 of *Sexuality and Culture*. New Brunswick, NJ: Transaction Publishers, pp. 39–69.

Keane, Helen. 2002. *What's Wrong with Addiction?* New York: New York University Press.

Kellogg, Susan, and Steven Mintz. 1993. "Family Structures," in *Encyclopedia of American Social History*, vol. 3, ed. M. C. Cayton et al. New York: Scribner, pp. 1925–41.

Kelly, Eric Damian, and Connie Cooper. 2000. *"Everything You Always Wanted to Know about Regulating Sex Businesses. . . ."* Chicago: American Planning Association. Planning Advisory Service Report Number 495/496.

Kempadoo, Kamala. 2005a. "From Moral Panic to Global Justice: Changing Perspectives on Trafficking," in *Trafficking and Prostitution Reconsidered: New Perspectives on Migration, Sex Work, and Human Rights*, ed. Kamala Kempadoo. Boulder, CO: Paradigm Publishers, pp. vii–xxxiv.

———. 2005b. *Trafficking and Prostitution Reconsidered: New Perspectives on Migration, Sex Work, and Human Rights*. Boulder, CO: Paradigm Publishers, pp. vii–xxxiv.

———. 2004. *Sexing the Caribbean: Gender, Race, and Sexual Labor.* New York: Routledge.

———, ed. 1999a. *Sun, Sex, and Gold: Tourism and Sex Work in the Caribbean.* Lanham, MD: Rowman and Littlefield.

———. 1999b. "Slavery or Work? Reconceptualizing Third World Prostitution." *Positions* 7 (1): 225–37.

———. 1998. "Introduction—Globalizing Sex Workers' Rights," in *Global Sex Workers: Rights, Resistance, and Redefinition,* ed. Kamala Kempadoo and Jo Doezuma. New York: Routledge.

Kempadoo, Kamala, and Jo Doezuma, eds. 1998. *Global Sex Workers: Rights, Resistance, and Redefinition.* New York: Routledge.

Kerr, Courtney. 1994. "A Geographic History of Prostitution in San Francisco." *Urban Action: San Francisco State University's Journal of Urban Affairs,* pp. 30–35.

Kilman, Lisa, and Kate Watson-Smyth. 1998. "Kerb Crawlers Offered Aversion Therapy Course." *Independent,* Aug. 3, p. 5.

Kilvington, Judith, Sophie Day, and Helen Ward. 2001. "European Prostitution Policy: A Time of Change?" *Feminist Review* 67: 78–93.

Kimmel, Michael. 2000. "Fuel for Fantasy: The Ideological Construction of Male Lust," in *Male Lust: Power, Pleasure, and Transformation,* ed. Kerwin Kaye et al. New York: Haworth, pp. 267–73.

Kinsey, Alfred, Wardell Pomeroy, and Clyde E. Martin. 1948. *Sexual Behavior in the Human Male.* Philadelphia: W. B. Saunders Company.

Kligman, David. 1999. "Transexual Gets Damages After S.F. Cops' Strip Search." *San Francisco Examiner,* April 20, p. A-6.

Kligman, Gail. 1998. *The Politics of Duplicity: Controlling Reproduction in Ceaucescu's Romania.* Berkeley: University of California Press.

Kligman, Gail, and Stephanie Limoncelli. 2005. "Trafficking Women after Socialism: To, Through and From Eastern Europe." *Social Politics* (spring): 118–40.

Knopp, L. 1992. "Sexuality and the Spatial Dynamics of Capitalism." *Environment and Planning* 10 (6): 607–744.

Koerner, Brendan I. 2000. "A Lust for Profits." *U.S. News and World Report,* March 27.

Koopman, John. 2003. "Lusty Lady Becomes First Worker-Owned Strip Club: From Boas and High Heels To Boardrooms and High Finance." *San Francisco Chronicle,* June 26, p. A17.

Kooy, Heidi. 2001. "Trollops and Tribades: Queers Organizing in the Sex Business," in *Out at Work: Building a Gay-Labor Alliance,* ed. Kitty Krupat and Patrick McCreery. Minneapolis: University of Minnesota Press, pp. 112–33.

Kozol, Jonathan. 1995. *Amazing Grace: The Lives of Children and the Conscience of a Nation.* New York: Harper Collins.

Kristof, Nicholas. 2004. "Loss of Innocence." *New York Times,* Jan. 28, http://www.nytimes.com (last accessed Jan. 28, 2004).

Kuczynski, Alex. 2001. "Racy Magazine Ads Pose Inconsistency in Publishers' Stance." *New York Times,* March 12, pp. C1 and C11.

Kulick, Don. 2005. "Four Hundred Thousand Swedish Perverts." *GLQ* 11 (2): 205–35.

———. 2003. "Sex in the New Europe: The Criminalization of Clients and the Swedish Fear of Penetration." *Anthropological Theory* 3 (2): 199–218.

———. 1998. *Travesti*. Chicago: University of Chicago Press.

Kulick, Don, and Margaret Willson, eds. 1995. *Taboo: Sex, Identity and Erotic Subjectivity in Anthropological Fieldwork*. London: Routledge.

Kuo, Leonore. 2002. *Prostitution Policy: Revolutionizing Practice through a Gendered Perspective*. New York: New York University Press.

Kyle, David, and Rey Koslowski, eds. 2001. *Global Human Smuggling: Comparative Perspectives*. Baltimore: Johns Hopkins University Press.

Laird, Cynthia. 1999. "SF TG Wins $755K in Strip Search Suit." *Bay Area Reporter*, April 22.

Landes, Emily. 2005. "Burlesque Boom: Bay Area 'Burly Girls' Are Shaking Their Tassles Once Again." *Time*, April 4, p. 79.

Landesman, Peter. 2004. "Sex Slaves on Main Street," *New York Times Magazine*, Jan. 25.

Lane, Frederick S. 2000. *Obscene Profits: The Entrepreneurs of Pornography in the Cyber Age*. New York: Routledge.

Langum, David J. 1994. *Crossing over the Line: Legislating Morality and the Mann Act*. Chicago: University of Chicago Press.

Larsson, Stig. 1983. *Konshandeln: Om Prostitueratdes Villkor*. English summary. Stockholm: Skeab.

Lasch, Christopher. 1979. *Haven in a Heartless World: The Family Besieged*. New York: Basic Books.

Laumann, Edward O., John H. Gagnon, Robert T. Michael, and Stuart Michaels. 1994. *The Social Organization of Sexuality: Sexual Practices in the United States*. Chicago: University of Chicago Press.

Learmonth, Michael. 1999. "Siliporn Valley." *San Jose Metro*, Nov. 11–17, pp. 20–29.

Lechner, Frank J., and John Boli, eds. 2000. *The Globalization Reader*. Oxford: Blackwell.

Lefler, Julie. 1999. "Shining the Spotlight on Johns: Moving toward Equal Treatment of Male Customers and Female Prostitutes." *Hastings Women's Law Journal* 10 (1): 11–37.

Leidner, Robin. 1993. *Fast Food, Fast Talk: Service Work and the Routinization of Everyday Life*. Berkeley: University of California Press.

Leigh, Carol. 2004. *Unrepentant Whore: Collected Works of Scarlot Harlot*. San Francisco: Last Gasp.

———. 1998. "A Brief History of Prostitution in San Francisco." *San Francisco Task Force on Prostitution Final Report,* app. D: Testimony, History, Index.

———.1997. "Inventing Sex Work," in *Whores and Other Feminists,* ed. Jill Nagle. New York: Routledge, pp. 223–32.

———, ed. 1994a. "In Defense of Prostitution," in special issue of *Gauntlet: Exploring the Limits of Free Expression* 1.

————. 1994b. "Prostitution in the United States—The Statistics," in special issue of *Gauntlet: Exploring the Limits of Free Expression* 1: 17–19.

————. 1994c. "Thanks Ma," in *Uncontrollable Bodies: Testimonies of Identity and Culture*, ed. Rodney Sappington. Seattle: Bay Press, pp. 243–63.

————. 1994d. "Black Women and Prostitution," in special issue of *Gauntlet: Exploring the Limits of Free Expression* 1: 113–16.

Leiner, Marvin. 1994. *Sexual Politics in Cuba: Machismo, Homosexuality, and AIDS*. Boulder, CO: Westview Press.

Lenneer-Axelson, Barbro. 1991a. "Swedish Men and Equality." Paper presented at the Department of Social Work, University of Göteborg.

————. 1991b. "Sexology, Sexual Policy and Sex Education in Sweden, 1920–1990." Pamphlet. Stockholm: Swedish Association for Sex Education.

Lever, Janet, and Deanne Dolnick. 2000. "Clients and Call Girls: Seeking Sex and Intimacy," in *Sex for Sale: Prostitution, Pornography, and the Sex Industry*, ed. Ronald Weitzer. New York: Routledge, pp. 85–103.

Levine, Philippa. 2003. *Prostitution, Race, and Politics: Policing Venereal Disease in the British Empire*. New York: Routledge.

Levy, Dan. 1994. "Supervisors Summon D.A. to Talk about Condoms as Evidence." *San Francisco Chronicle*, Aug. 16, p. A16.

Lewis, Diane. 1999. "Naming 'Johns': Suicide Raises Ethical Questions about Policy." *FineLine: The Newsletter on Journalism Ethics* 2 (6): 3.

Lewis, Gregory, and Dennis J. Opatrny. 1996. "New S.F. Board of Supervisiors." *San Francisco Examiner*, Nov. 6, http://sfgate.com.

Liazos, Alexander. [1972] 1985. "The Poverty of the Sociology of Deviance: Nuts, Sluts, and Perverts," in *Theories of Deviance*, ed. Stuart H. Traub and Craig B. Little. Itasca, IL: F. E. Peacock, pp. 373–95.

Light, Evan. 1974. "From Vice District to Tourist Attraction: The Moral Career of American Chinatowns, 1880–1940." *Pacific Historical Review* 43: 367–94.

Limoncelli, Stephanie. 2006. "International Voluntary Associations, Local Social Movements and State Paths to the Abolition of Regulated Prostitution in Europe, 1875–1950." *International Sociology* 21 (1): 31–59.

Lockett, Gloria. 1995. "CAL-PEP: The Struggle to Survive," in *Women Resisting AIDS: Feminist Strategies of Empowerment*, ed. Beth Schneider and Nancy E. Stoller. Philadelphia: Temple University Press, pp. 208–19.

Loe, Meika. 1998. "Dildos in Our Toolboxes: The Production of Sexuality at a Pro-Feminist Sex Toy Store." *Berkeley Journal of Sociology* 43: 97–137.

Lopez, Steve. 2000. "Hold the Pickles, Please: This Drive-Through Has a New Menu Item." *Time*, Oct. 2, p. 6.

Luibhéid, Eithne. 2002. *Entry Denied: Controlling Sexuality at the Border*. Minneapolis: University of Minnesota Press.

Luker, Kristin. 2006. *When Sex Goes to School: Warring Views on Sex— and Sex Education— Since the Sixties*. W. W. Norton and Company.

————. 1998. "Sex, Social Hygiene, and the State: The Double-Edged Sword of Social Reform." *Theory and Society* 27: 601–34.

————. 1984. *Abortion and the Politics of Motherhood*. Berkeley: University of California Press.

Lynd, Robert S., and Hellen Merrell Lynd. 1937. *Middletown in Transition: A Study in Cultural Conflicts.* New York: Harcourt, Brace, Jovanovich.

———. [1929] 1957. *Middletown: A Study in Modern American Culture.* New York: Harcourt, Brace, Jovanovich.

Lynsen, Joshua. 2006. "Trans Activists Question D.C. Prostitution Bill." *Washington Blade.* March 31, www.washingtonblade.com (last accessed Sept. 2, 2006).

MacCannell, Dean. 1976. *The Tourist: A New Theory of the Leisure Class.* New York: Schocken Books.

MacDonald, Heather. 1994. "San Francisco Gets Tough with the Homeless." *City Journal,* (autumn), http://www.city-journal.org/article01.php?aid=1368 (last accessed Feb. 21, 2006).

MacDonald, William. 1978. *Victimless Crimes: A Description of Offenders and Their Prosecution in the District of Columbia.* Washington, DC: Institute for Law and Social Research.

MacKenzie, John. 1998. "Sex Trade Booming as Asia Busts," *Scotland on Sunday,* Oct. 18, p. 21.

MacKinnon, Catharine A. 1989. *Toward a Feminist Theory of the State.* Cambridge, MA: Harvard University Press.

———. 1987. *Feminism Unmodifed: Discourses on Life and Law.* Cambridge, MA: Harvard University Press.

———. 1982. "Feminism, Marxism, Method, and the State: An Agenda for Theory." *Signs: Journal of Women in Culture and Society* 7 (3): 515–44.

Macy, Marianne. 1996. *Working Sex: An Odyssey into Our Cultural Underworld.* New York: Carroll and Graf Publishers, Inc.

Maglin, Nan Bauer, and Donna Perry, eds., 1996. *"Bad Girls"/"Good Girls": Women, Sex, and Power in the Nineties.* New Brunswick, NJ: Rutgers University Press.

Maher, Lisa. 1997. *Sexed Work: Gender, Race, and Resistance in a Brooklyn Drug Market.* Oxford: Oxford University Press.

Maine, Sir Henry. [1861] 1917. *Ancient Law.* London: J. M. Dent and Sons.

Malarek, Victor. 2003. *The Natashas: Inside the New Global Sex Trade.* New York: Arcade Press.

Månsson, Sven-Axel. 2001. "Men's Practices in Prostitution: The Case of Sweden," in *A Man's World? Changing Men's Practices in a Globalized World,* ed. Bob Pease and Keith Pringle. London: Zed Books, 135–49.

———.1992. "Brothel Europe: International Prostitution and Traffic in Women." Unpublished ms.

———. 1987. *The Man in Sexual Commerce,* trans. Vernon Boggs and Birgitta Borafia. Lund: Lund University.

———. 1981. *Konshandelns Framjare Och Profitorer.* Lund: Doxa.

Marcus, George E. 1998. *Ethnography through Thick and Thin.* Princeton, NJ: Princeton University Press.

Marinucci, Carla. 1995a. "A School for Scandal." *San Francisco Examiner,* April 16, pp. A1 and A16.

———. 1995b. "S.F. Vice Squad Focuses on Pimps." *San Francisco Examiner,* July 26, http://www.sfgate.com (last accessed Jan. 13, 2005).

———. 1995c. "International Praise for S.F. 'School for Johns.'" *San Francisco Examiner,* Nov. 14, p. A2.

Marshall, Carolyn. 2005. "Agents Said to Dismantle a Korean Sex Ring." *New York Times,* July 2, http://www.nytimes.com/2005/07/02/national/02sex.html? (last accessed July 2, 2005).

Marshall, Ineke Haen, and Chris E. Marshall. 1993. "Prostitution in the Netherlands: It's Just Another Job!" in *Female Criminality: The State of the Art,* ed. Concetta C. Culliver. New York: Garland Publishing, pp. 225–47.

Martin, Emily. 1994. *Flexible Bodies: The Role of Immunity in American Culture from the Days of Polio to the Age of Aids.* Boston: Beacon Press.

Martin, Glen. 1996. "North Beach Strippers Unite: Dancers Could Be First in the Country to Unionize." *San Francisco Chronicle,* Aug. 14, p. A15.

Marx, Karl. [1844] 1978. "The Economic and Philosophic Manuscripts of 1844," in *The Marx-Engels Reader,* ed. Robert C. Tucker. New York: W. W. Norton, pp. 66–126.

Massey, Joseph E., and Trina L. Hope. 2005. "A Personal Dance: Emotional Labor, Fleeting Relationships, and Social Power in a Strip Bar," in *Together Alone: Personal Relationships in Public Places,* ed. Calvin Morrill, David A. Snow, and Cindy H. White. Berkeley: University of California Press, pp. 66–93.

Mattson, Heidi. 1995. *Ivy League Stripper: A True Story.* New York: St. Martin's Press.

Mayer, Vicki. 2004. "Soft-core in TV Time: The Political Economy of a 'Cultural Trend.'" Unpublished ms., on file with the author.

McArdle, Andrea, and Tanya Erzen. 2001. *Zero Tolerance: Quality of Life and the New Police Brutality in New York City.* New York and London: New York University Press.

McCall, Leslie. 2001. *Complex Inequality: Gender, Class, and Race in the New Economy.* New York: Routledge.

McClintock, Anne. 1993. "Sex Workers and Sex Work: Introduction." *Social Text* 37: 1–11.

McCord, Julia. 2004. "Neighbors Fight Back against Prostitution." *Omaha World Herald,* July 31.

McGinn, Thomas. 1998. *Prostitution, Sexuality, and the Law in Ancient Rome.* New York: Oxford University Press.

McIntosh, Mary. 1978. "Who Needs Prostitutes: The Ideology of Male Sexual Needs," in *Women, Sexuality, and Social Control,* ed. Carol Smart and Barry Smart. London: Routledge, pp. 53–65.

McKay, Jim. 1996. "Exotic Dancers Take Steps to Organize." *Pittsburgh Post-Gazette,* Aug. 18, p. F9.

McKeganey, Neil, and Marina Barnard. 1996. *Sex Work on the Streets: Prostitutes and Their Clients.* Buckingham, UK: Open University Press.

McLeod, Eileen. 1982. *Women Working: Prostitution Now.* London: Croom Helm.

McNamara, Robert P. 1994. *The Times Square Hustler: Male Prostitution in New York City.* Westport, CT: Praeger Press.

McNeil, Donald G., Jr. 2000. "The Joy of the Red Light District: A Police Guide." *New York Times,* July 21, http://www.nytimes.com (last accessed Feb. 26, 2001).

Meretrix, Magdalene. 2001. *Turning Pro: A Guide to Sex Work for the Ambitious and Intrigued.* Emeryville, CA: Greenery Press.

Merry, Sally Engle. 2001. "Spatial Governmentality and the New Urban Social Order: Controlling Gender Violence through Law." *American Anthropologist* 103 (1): 16–30.

Mieszkowski, Katharine. 2000. "Naked Ambition." *San Francisco Bay Guardian,* Feb. 9, p. 46.

Milkman, Ruth, and Rachel E. Dwyer. 2002. "Growing Apart: The 'New Economy' and Job Polarization in California, 1992–2000," in *The State of California Labor 2002.* University of California Institute for Labor and Employment, http://www.ucop.edu/ile/scl/2002 (last accessed Feb. 22, 2003).

Miller, Eleanor. 1986. *Street Woman.* Philadelphia: Temple University Press.

Miller, Eleanor M., Kim Romenesko, and Lisa Wondolkowski. 1993. "The United States," in *Prostitution; An International Handbook of Trends, Problems, and Policies,* ed. Nanette Davis. Westport, CT: Greenwood Press, pp. 300–327.

Miller, Jody. 1995. "Gender and Power on the Streets: Street Prostitution in the Era of Crack Cocaine." *Journal of Contemporary Ethnography* 23 (4): 427–52.

Milman, Barbara. 1980. "New Rules for the Oldest Profession: Should We Change Our Prostitution Laws?" *Harvard Women's Law Review* 3: 1–82.

Milner, Christina, and Richard Milner. 1972. *Black Players: The Secret World of Black Pimps.* Boston: Little, Brown.

Minton, Torri. 1996. "SF Sex Club Workers OK Union, 57–15." *San Francisco Chronicle,* Aug. 31, p. A17.

"Modern-Day Slavery." 2004. *Washington Times,* Aug. 1, http://www.washingtontimes.com (last accessed Aug. 1, 2004).

Monet, Veronica. 1997. "No Girls Allowed at the Mustang Ranch," in *Whores and Other Feminists,* ed. Jill Nagle. New York: Routledge, pp. 167–70.

———. 1994. "A Day in the Life of a Prostitute," in *In Defense of Prostitution,* ed. Carol Leigh. *Gauntlet: Exploring the Limits of Free Expression* 1: 58–66.

Montgomery, Heather. 2001. *Modern Babylon? Prostituting Children in Thailand.* New York: Berghahn Books.

Monto, Martin. 2000. "Why Men Seek Out Prostitutes," in *Sex for Sale: Prostitution, Pornography, and the Sex Industry,* ed. Ron Weitzer. New York: Routledge, pp. 67–85.

Morgan, Robin, ed. 1984. *Sisterhood Is Global: The International Women's Movement Anthology.* New York: Doubleday.

Mowforth, Martin, and Ian Munt. 1998. *Tourism and Sustainability.* New York: Routledge.

Mr. A. de Graaf Stichting. 2004. "History of Prostitution in Amsterdam." http://www.mrgraaf.nl/history.htm (last accessed Dec. 28, 2004).

Mullen, Kevin. 1993. "When Prostitution Was Semi-Legal in Frisco." *San Francisco Examiner,* Dec. 29.

Mullings, Beverly. 2000. "Fantasy Tours: Exploring the Global Consumption of Caribbean Sex Tourisms," in, *New Forms of Consumption: Consumers, Culture, and Commodification,* ed. Mark Gottdiener. Lanham, MD: Rowman and Littlefield, pp. 227–51.

Nagle, Jill, ed. 1997a. *Whores and Other Feminists.* New York: Routledge.

———. 1997b. "Showing Up Fully: Women of Color Discuss Sex-Work," in *Whores and Other Feminists,* ed. Jill Nagle. New York: Routledge, pp. 195–210.

Nair, Yasmin. 2004. "How Trafficking Became Sexy: Behind the Myths of a Slave Economy." *Clamor* 28 (Aug.): 49–51.

"Names of Alleged U.S. Prostitute Clients Released." 1999. Reuters Online, Jan. 13, http://www.infonautics.com (last accessed March 3, 2000).

National Board of Health and Welfare. 1999. *Kånnedom om Prostitution 1998–9.* March 7, 2001. http://www.sos.se/sos/publ/refereng/0003005e.htm (last accessed March 7, 2001).

Neland, Vicki. 1995. *Council for Prostitution Alternatives Handbook.* Portland, OR.

Nelson, Adie, and Barrie W. Robinson. 1994. *Gigolos and Madames Bountiful: Illusions of Gender, Power, and Intimacy.* Toronto: University of Toronto Press.

Newman, Katherine S. 2000. *No Shame in My Game: The Working Poor in the Inner City.* New York: Vintage Books.

Nieves, Evelyn. 1999. "For Patrons of Prostitutes, Remedial Instruction." *New York Times,* March 18, pp. A1 and A20.

Nolan, Thomas W. 2001. "Galateas in Blue: Women Police as Decoy Sex Workers." *Criminal Justice Ethics* (winter/spring): 62–67.

Norberg, Kathryn. 1998. "Prostitution in Eighteenth-Century Paris: Pages from a Madam's Notebook," in *Prostitution: On Whores, Hustlers, and Johns,* ed. James E. Elias et al. Amherst, MA: Prometheus Books, pp. 61–80.

Nordic Baltic Campaign Against Trafficking in Women. 2002. *Final Report.* Nordic Council of Ministers, http://www.nordicbalticcampaign.org.

"Norfalk's 'John School' Tries to Curb Prostitution by Targeting Customers." 2004. http://www.wavy.com.

Norwegian Ministry of Justice and Police Affairs. 2004. *Purchasing Sexual Services in Sweden and the Netherlands: Legal Regulation and Experiences,* ed. Ulf Stridbeck. (G-0637).

"Nude Dancers Don Union Label." 1996. *Washington Post,* Sept. 1, p. A10.

"NSW: New Laws to Nab Drivers Prowling for Prostitutes." 1999. AAP General News Online (Australia) 11–16. http://www.infonautics.com (last accessed March 3, 2000).

O'Connell Davidson, Julia. 2002. "The Rights and Wrongs of Prostitution." *Hypatia* 17 (2): 84–97.

———. 1998. *Prostitution, Power, and Freedom.* Ann Arbor: University of Michigan Press.

O'Connell Davidson, Julia, and Jacqueline Sánchez Taylor. 2005. "Travel and Taboo: Heterosexual Sex Tourism to the Caribbean," in *Regulating Sex: The*

Politics of Intimacy and Identity, ed. Elizabeth Bernstein and Laurie Schaffner. New York, Routledge, pp. 83–99.

Odzer, Cleo. 1994. *Patpong Sisters: An American Woman's View of the Bangkok Sex World.* New York: Arcade Publishing.

Olsen, Frances E. 1983. "The Family and the Market: A Study of Ideology and Legal Reform." *Harvard Law Review* 96 (7).

Opatrny, Dennis J. 1996. "Election '96." *San Francisco Examiner,* Nov. 7, http://sfgate.com.

Ophelian, Annalise. 1999. "Performing Power: Agency and Intersectionality in Professional Sadomasochism." Unpublished ms., on file with the author.

Orback, Jens. 2005. "Legal and Other Normative Measures to Combat Trafficking in Women and Girls with a Focus on the Demand." Speech by the Swedish Minister for Gender Equality at the Forty-ninth Session of the United Nations Commission on the Status of Women, March 1.

Orloff, Ann. 1993. "Gender and the Social Rights of Citizenship: The Comparative Analysis of Gender Relations and Welfare States." *American Sociological Review* 58: 303–28.

Östergren, Petra. 2004. "Sexworkers' Critique of Swedish Prostitution Policy." Article available at http://www.petraostergren.com.

Otis, Leah Lydia. 1985. *Prostitution in Medieval Society: The History of an Urban Institution in Languedoc.* Chicago: University of Chicago Press.

Outshoorn, Joyce. 2005. "The Political Debates on Prostitution and Trafficking of Women." *Social Politics* (spring): 141–55.

———, ed. 2004a. *The Politics of Prostitution: Women's Movements, Democratic States, and the Globalisation of Sex Commerce.* Cambridge: Cambridge University Press.

———. 2004b. "Voluntary and Forced Prostitution: The "Realistic Approach" of the Netherlands," in *The Politics of Prostitution: Women's Movements, Democratic States, and the Globalization of Sex Commerce,* ed. Joyce Outshoorn. Cambridge: Cambridge University Press, pp. 185–204.

———. 2004c. "Introduction: Prostitution, Women's Movements, and Democratic Politics," in *The Politics of Prostitution: Women's Movements, Democratic States, and the Globalisation of Sex Commerce,* ed. Joyce Outshoorn. Cambridge: Cambridge University Press, pp. 1–221.

Overall, Christine. 1992. "What's Wrong with Prostitution? Evaluating Sex Work." *Signs: Journal of Women in Culture and Society* 17 (4): 705–24.

Padilla, Mark. Forthcoming. *Looking for Life: Male Sex Work, HIV/AIDS, and the Political Economy of Tourism in the Dominican Republic.* Chicago: University of Chicago Press.

Parent-Duchâlet, Alexandre Jean Baptiste. 1836. *De la prostitution dans la ville de Paris.* Paris: J. B. Baillière.

Parenti, Christian. 1999. *Lockdown America: Police and Prisons in the Age of Crisis.* London: Verso.

Park, Robert, Ernest W. Burgess, and Roderick MacKenzie. [1925] 1967. *The City.* Chicago: University of Chicago Press.

Parker, Richard. 2001. "Sexuality, Culture, and Power in HIV/AIDS Research." *Annual Review of Anthropology* 30: 163–79. Annual Reviews, US.

Parker, Robert E. 1994. *Flesh Peddlers and Warm Bodies: The Temporary Help Industry and Its Workers.* New Brunswick, NJ: Rutgers University Press.

Parreñas, Rhacel Salazar. 2000. "Migrant Filipina Domestic Workers and the International Division of Reproductive Labor." *Gender and Society* 14: 560–80.

Parsons, Talcott. 1960. *Structure and Process in Modern Society.* New York: Free Press.

Pateman, Carole. 1988. *The Sexual Contract.* Stanford: Stanford University Press.

Patterson, Zabet. 2004. "Going On-line: Consuming Pornography in the Digital Era," in *Porn Studies,* ed. Linda Williams. Durham, NC: Duke University Press, 104–27.

Peiss, Kathy. 1989. " 'Charity Girls' and City Pleasures: Historical Notes on Working Class Sexuality, 1880–1920," in *Passion and Power: Sexuality in History,* ed. Kathy Peiss and Christina Simmons. Philadelphia: Temple University Press, pp. 57–69.

Pendleton, Eva. 1997. "Love for Sale: Queering Heterosexuality," in *Whores and Other Feminists,* ed. Jill Nagle. New York: Routledge, pp. 73–83.

———. 1996. "Domesticating Partnerships," in *Policing Public Sex: Queer Politics and the Future of Aids Activism,* ed. Dangerous Bedfellows. Boston: South End Press, pp. 373–95.

Perkins, Roberta, and Garry Bennet. 1985. *Being a Prostitute: Prostitute Women and Men Now.* Sydney: Allen and Unwin.

Perkins, Roberta, Garrett Prestage, Rachel Sharp, and Frances Lovejoy, eds. 1994. *Sex Work and Sex Workers in Australia.* Sydney: University of New South Wales Press.

Petchesky, Rosalind. 1990. *Abortion and Women's Choice: The State, Sexuality, and Reproductive Freedom.* Boston: Northeastern University Press.

Peterson, Laura. 1998. "Massage Parlors Getting Cold Shoulder from City, Tenderloin." *San Francisco Independent,* July 14.

Pettersson, Toby, and Eva Tiby. 2003. "The Production and Reproduction of Prostitution." *Journal of Scandinavian Studies in Criminology and Crime Prevention* 3: 154–72.

Pettiway, Leon E. 1996. *Honey, Honey, Miss Thang: Being Black, Gay, and on the Streets.* Philadelphia: Temple University Press.

Pheterson, Gail. 1996. *The Prostitution Prism.* Amsterdam: Amsterdam University Press.

———. 1993. "The Whore Stigma: Female Dishonor and Male Unworthiness." *Social Text* 37: 39–65.

———, ed. 1989. *A Vindication of the Rights of Whores.* Seattle: Seal Press.

Pieke, Frank. 2000. "Serendipity in Anthropology and Culture," in *Anthropologists in a Wider World: Essays on Field Research,* ed. P. Dresch, W. James, and D. Parkin. New York, Oxford: Berghahn.

Pierre-Pierre, Garry. 1994. "Police Focus on Arresting Prostitutes' Customers." *New York Times,* Nov. 20, http://www.nytimes.com.

Plachy, Sylvia, and James Ridgeway. 1996. *Red Light: Inside the Sex Industry.* New York: Powerhouse Books.

Plummer, Ken. 1995. *Telling Sexual Stories: Power, Change, and Social Worlds.* London: Routledge.

Polanyi, Karl. 1957. *The Great Transformation.* Boston: Beacon Press.

Prasad, Monica. 1999. "The Morality of Market Exchange: Love, Money, and Contractual Justice." *Sociological Perspectives* 42 (2): 181–215.

Pred, Allan. 2000. *Even in Sweden: Racisms, Racialized Spaces, and the Geographical Imagination.* Berkeley: University of California Press.

Prial, Dunstan. 1999. "IPO Outlook: 'Adult' Web Sites Profit, though Few are Likely to Offer Shares." *Wall Street Journal,* March 8, p. B10.

Prieur, Annick. 1998. *Mema's House, Mexico City: On Transvestites, Queens, and Machos.* Chicago: University of Chicago Press.

Prieur, Annick, and Arnhild Taksdal. 1993. "Clients of Prostitutes: Sick Deviants or Ordinary Men? A Discussion of the Male Role Concept and Cultural Changes in Masculinity." *NORA* 2: 105–14.

Pro-Sentret. 1992. "Prostitution: Social Problem or Just Another Woman's Job?" Unpublished ms.

Quan, Tracy. 2001. *Diary of a Manhattan Call Girl.* New York: Crown Publishers.

Queen, Carol. 1997. *Real Live Nude Girl: Chronicles of Sex-Positive Culture.* San Francisco: Cleis Press.

Rabo, Annika. 1997. "Gender Equality Policy in Post-Welfare Sweden," in *Anthropology of Policy: Critical Perspectives on Governance and Power,* ed. Cris Shore and Susan Wright. London: Routledge, pp. 107–36.

Radin, Margaret Jane. 1996. *Contested Commodities.* Cambridge, MA: Harvard University Press.

———. 1987. "Market Inalienablity." *Harvard Law Review* 100 (8): 1849–1937.

Ramberg, Lucinda. 2006. *Given to the Goddess: Devadasis, Kinship, Ethics.* PhD diss., Department of Anthropology, University of California at Berkeley.

Randers-Pehrson, Arne, and Liv Jessen. 2000. "Northern Regional Report Part II: Overview of the Situation in Each Country." European Network for HIV/STD Prevention in Prostitution. http://www.europap.net/regional/northen _regional_part_II.htm. (last accessed March 14, 2001).

Raymond, Janice G. 2003. "Ten Reasons for Not Legalizing Prostitution." *Journal of Trauma and Practice* 2: 315–32.

Reckless, Walter C. 1933. *Vice in Chicago.* Chicago: University of Chicago Press.

Reynolds, Helen. 1986. *The Economics of Prostitution.* Springfield: Charles C. Thomas.

Rich, Frank. 2004a. "On 'Moral Values,' It's Blue in a Landslide." *New York Times,* Nov. 14, www.nytimes.com (last accessed Sept. 4, 2006).

———. 2004b. "The Plot against Sex in America." *New York Times,* Dec. 12, www.nytimes.com (last accessed Sept. 4, 2006).

Roane, Kit R. 1998. "Prostitutes on Wane in New York Streets but Take to Internet." *New York Times,* Feb. 23, pp. A1 and B4.

Robinson, Paul. 1976. *The Modernization of Sex: Havelock Ellis, Alfred Kinsey, William Masters, and Virginia Johnson.* New York: Harper and Row.

Robinson, Tony. 1995. "Gentrification and Grassroots Resistance in San Francisco's Tenderloin." *Urban Affairs Review* (March): 483–513.

Romero, Mary. 1992. *Maid in the U.S.A.* New York: Routledge.

Ronai, Carol Rambo, and Carolyn Ellis. 1989. "Turn-ons for Money: Interactional Strategies of the Table Dancer." *Journal of Contemporary Ethnography* 18 (3): 271–98.

Rosen, Ruth. 1982. *The Lost Sisterhood: Prostitution in America, 1900–1918.* Baltimore: Johns Hopkins University Press.

Rosenzweig, David, and K. Connie Kang. 2005. "Raids on Brothel Rings Net 45 Arrests: L.A. and Bay Area Groups Are Suspected of Smuggling Hundreds of South Korean Women." *Los Angeles Times,* July 2, http://www.latimes.com/news/local/la-me-smuggling2jul02,1,1419111,full.story?coll=la-utilities-sport s&ctrack=1&cset=true (last accessed July 6, 2005).

Ross, Andrew, ed. 1997. *No Sweat: Fashion, Free Trade, and the Rights of Garment Workers.* New York: Verso.

———. 1989. *No Respect: Intellectuals and Popular Culture.* New York: Routledge.

"Rotterdam Shuts Door on Street Prostitutes." 2004. *Novum Nieuws,* March 17, www.expatica.com (last accessed Sept. 17, 2006).

Rountree, William. 2000. *Contracting Intimacy: Transforming Property, Parenting, and Meaning in Intimate Relationships.* PhD diss., Department of Sociology, University of California at Berkeley.

Rubin, Gayle. 2002. "Studying Sexual Subcultures: Excavating the Ethnography of Gay Communities in Urban North America," in *Out in Theory: The Emergence of Lesbian and Gay Anthropology,* ed. Ellen Lewin and William L. Leap. Urbana and Chicago: University of Illinois Press, pp. 17–69.

———. 1989. "Thinking Sex: Notes for a Radical Theory of the Politics of Sexuality," in *Pleasure and Danger: Exploring Female Sexuality,* ed. Carole Vance. London: Pandora, pp. 267–320.

———. 1975. "The Traffic in Women: Notes on the 'Political Economy' of Sex," in *Toward an Anthropology of Women,* ed. Rayna Reiter. New York: Monthly Review Press, pp. 157–211.

Russell, Diana E. H. 1986. *The Secret Trauma: Incest in the Lives of Girls and Women.* New York: Basic Books.

Sahlins, Marshall. 1972. *Stone Age Economics.* New York: Aldine.

Saletan, William. 2004. *Bearing Right: How Conservatives Won the Abortion War.* Berkeley: University of California Press.

Salzinger, Leslie. 2003. *Genders in Production: Making Workers in Mexico's Global Factories.* Berkeley: University of California Press.

———. 1991. "A Maid by Any Other Name: The Transformation of 'Dirty Work' by Central American Immigrants," in *Ethnography Unbound: Power and Resistance in the Modern Metropolis,* by Michael Burawoy et al. Berkeley: University of California Press, pp. 139–61.

Sanchez, Lisa. 2003. "Sex and Space in the Global City," in *Globalization under Construction,* ed. Richard Warren Perry and Bill Maurer. Minneapolis: University of Minnesota Press, pp. 239–73.

Sanchez Jankowski, Martin. 1991. *Islands in the Street: Gangs and American Urban Society.* Berkeley: University of California Press.

San Diego Police Department. 1994. "'Glitter Track': The Use of a Temporary Restraining Order to Solve the Prostitution Problem."

San Francisco Task Force on Prostitution. 1996. *Final Report.* Submitted to the Board of Supervisors of the City and County of San Francisco, California. Available online at http://www.bayswan.org/1TF.html (last accessed May 17, 2006).

———.1994. *Interim Report.* Submitted to the Board of Supervisors of the City and County of San Francisco, California.

Sanger, William. 1859. *History of Prostitution: Its Extent, Causes, and Effects throughout the World.* New York: Harper and Brothers.

Sassen, Saskia. 2002. "Global Cities and Survival Circuits," in *Global Woman: Nannies, Maids, and Sex Workers in the New Economy,* ed. Barbara Ehrenreich and Arlie Russell Hochschild. New York: Metropolitan Books, pp. 254–75.

———. 1998. *Globalization and Its Discontents: Essays on the New Mobility of People and Money.* New York: New Press.

———. 1994. *Cities in a World Economy.* Thousand Oaks, CA: Pine Forge Press.

Satz, Debra. 1995. "Markets in Women's Sexual Labor." *Ethics* 106: 63–85.

Saunders, Penelope. 2004. "Prohibiting Sex Work Projects, Restricting Women's Rights: The International Impact of the 2003 U.S. Global AIDS Act." *Health and Human Rights: An International Journal* 7 (2): 179–93.

Saunders, Penelope, and Gretchen Soderlund. 2004. "Threat or Opportunity? Sexuality, Gender, and the Ebb and Flow of Traffic as Discourse," *Canadian Journal of Women's Studies* 22 (3, 4): 16–24.

Scambler, Graham, and Annette Scambler. 1997. *Rethinking Prostitution: Purchasing Sex in the 1990s.* London: Routledge.

Schaffner, Laurie. 2006. *Girls in Trouble with the Law.* New Brunswick, NJ: Rutgers University Press.

Schenker, Jennifer L. 2004. "In Europe, Cellphone Profits Go Up as Clothes Come Off." *New York Times,* May 4.

Scheper-Hughes, Nancy. 2002. "Commodity Fetishism in Organs Trafficking," in *Commodifying Bodies,* ed. Nancy Scheper-Hughes and Loïc Wacquant. London: Sage Publications, pp. 31–63.

———. 1992. *Death without Weeping: The Violence of Everyday Life in Brazil.* Berkeley: University of California Press.

Schlosser, Eric. 2003. *Reefer Madness: Sex, Drugs, and Cheap Labor in the American Black Market.* Boston: Houghton Mifflin.

———. 1997. "The Business of Pornography." *U.S. News and World Report,* Feb. 10, pp. 43–52.

Schogol, Jeff. 2006. "Patronizing a Prostitute Is Now a Specific Crime for Servicemembers." *Stars and Stripes,* Jan. 7, http://www.estripes.com/article.asp?section=104&article=33300&archive=true (last accessed Jan. 14, 2006).

Scholten, Jenny, and Nicki Blaze. 2000. "Digital Cleavage: Women Are on the Wrong Side of the Gender Divide at Comdex." *San Francisco Bay Guardian,* Nov. 29, http://sfbg.com (last accessed May 22, 2005).

Schur, Edwin M. 1984. *Labeling Women Deviant: Gender, Stigma, and Social Control.* New York: McGraw Hill.

Schwartz, John. 2001. "New Economy: Even in Downturn, Sex Still Sells." *New York Times,* April 9, http://www.nytimes.com (last accessed April 12, 2001).

Schwarz, Oswald. 1954. "The Prostitute and Her Customers," in *Men: The Variety and Meaning of Their Sexual Experience,* ed. A. M. Krich. New York: Dell Publishing, pp. 233–43.

Seib, Gerald F. 2000. "Sex Trafficking: The Dark Side of the New World." *Wall Street Journal,* May 17, p. A28.

Seidman, Steven. 2005. "From Outsider to Citizen," in *Regulating Sex: The Politics of Intimacy and Identity,* ed. Elizabeth Bernstein and Laurie Schaffner. New York: Routledge, pp. 225–47.

———. 1992. *Embattled Eros: Sexual Politics and Ethics in Contemporary America.* New York: Routledge.

———. 1991. *Romantic Longings.* New York: Routledge.

Sennett, Richard, and Jonathan Cobb. 1972. *The Hidden Injuries of Class.* New York: Vintage Books.

"Sex, News, and Statistics: Where Entertainment on the Web Scores." 2000. *Economist Online,* Oct. 7, http://www.economist.com (last accessed Oct. 19, 2000).

Sex Work Consumer's Guide. 1994. Informational pamphlet. Hollywood, CA: COYOTE.

Seymour, Andrew. 2000. "Strip Club Scrutiny: Cops Eyeballing Parlours for Prostitution in Wake of Dancers' Complaints." *Ottawa Sun,* Feb. 29, p. 5.

Shah, A. Minal. 1999. Introduction to symposium issue: *Economic Justice for Sex Workers. Hastings Women's Law Journal* 10 (1): 1–5.

Sheehy, Gail. 1971. *Hustling: Prostitution in Our Wide Open Society.* New York: Dell Publishing.

Shepard, Paul. 2000. "Sex Trade Flourishing, U.S. Says," Associated Press, Feb. 23.

Shephard, Benjamin. 2001. "Analysis of the 1995 Amendments of the New York Zoning Law." Unpublished ms., on file with the author.

Shrage, Laurie. 1994. *Moral Dilemmas of Feminism: Prostitution, Adultery, and Abortion.* New York: Routledge.

Shumsky, Neil Larry, and Larry M. Springer. 1981. "San Francisco's Zone of Prostitution," *Journal of Historical Geography* 7 (1): 71–89.

Silbert, Mimi. 1980. *Sexual Assault on Prostitutes.* Research Report to the National Center for the Prevention and Control of Rape.

Silbert, Mimi, and Ayala M. Pines. 1982. "Entrance into Prostitution." *Youth and Society* 14 (4): 471–93.

Silliman, Jael, and Anannya Bhattacharjee, eds. 2002. *Policing the National Body: Race, Gender, and Criminalization.* Cambridge, MA: South End Press.

Simmel, Georg. [1907] 1971. "Prostitution," in *On Individuality and Social Forms,* ed. Donald N. Levine. Chicago: University of Chicago Press, pp. 121–26.

Simons, Marlise. 1998. "Dutch Say a Sex Ring Used Infants on the Internet." *New York Times,* July 19, p. 5.

Skolnick, Jerome H. 1993. *Above the Law: Police and the Excessive Use of Force.* New York: Free Press.

———. 1988. "The Social Transformation of Vice." *Law and Contemporary Problems* 51 (1): 9–31.

———. 1966. *Justice without Trial: Law Enforcement in Democratic Society.* New York: Wiley.

Slim, Iceberg. 1987. *Pimp: The Story of My Life.* Los Angeles: Holloway House.

Smith, Neil. 1996. *The New Urban Frontier: Gentrification and the Revanchist City.* London: Routledge.

Smith, Valerie. 1994. "Split Affinities: The Case of Interracial Rape," in *Theorizing Feminism: Parallel Trends in the Humanities and Social Sciences,* ed. Anne C. Hermann and Abigail J. Stewart. Boulder, CO: Westview Press, pp. 155–71.

Smith-Rosenberg, Carroll. 1985. *Disorderly Conduct: Visions of Gender in Victorian America.* New York: Oxford University Press.

Snitow, Ann, et al., eds. 1983. *Powers of Desire: The Politics of Sexuality.* New York: Monthly Review Press.

Söderblom, Tomas. 1992. *Horan och batongen: prostitiution och repression I folkhemmet.* Stockholm: Didlunds Bokförlag.

Solevåg, Asbjørn. 1993. "Male Prostitution and Sex-Work Related HIV Prevention." Unpublished ms.

Solnit, Rebecca, and Susan Schwartzenberg. 2000. *Hollow City: The Siege of San Francisco and the Crisis of American Urbanism.* London: Verso.

Sorge, Rod. 1991. "Harm Reduction: A New Approach to Drug Services." *Health/PAC Bulletin* (winter): 70–99.

Sorrentino, Constance. 1990. "The Changing Family in International Perspective." *Monthly Labor Review* (March): 41–58.

Sprinkle, Annie. 1998. *Post-Porn Modernist: My Twenty-five Years as a Multimedia Whore.* San Francisco: Cleis Press.

Squatriglia, Chuck. 2005. "SF Massage Parlors Raided as Part of Smuggling Probe." *San Francisco Chronicle,* July 1, http://www.sfgate.com/cgi-bin/article.cgi?file=/chronicle/archive/2005/07/01/BAmassage01.DTL (last accessed May 17, 2006).

Stacey, Judith. 1991. *Brave New Families: Stories of Domestic Upheaval in Late Twentieth Century America.* New York: Basic Books.

Stanford, Sally. 1966. *The Lady of the House.* New York: G. P. Putnam.

Stansell, Christine. 1982. *City of Women: Sex and Class in New York, 1789–1860.* Urbana: University of Illinois Press.

Steans, Jill. 2000. "The Gender Dimension," in *The Global Transformations Reader: An Introduction to the Globalization Debate,* ed. David Held and Anthony McGrew. Cambridge: Polity Press, pp. 366–74.

Stein, Arlene. 2001. *The Stranger Next Door: The Story of a Small Community's Battle over Sex, Faith, and Civil Rights.* Boston: Beacon Press.

Stein, Martha L. 1974. *Lovers, Friends, Slaves . . . The Nine Male Sexual Types: Their Psycho-Sexual Transactions with Call Girls.* New York: G. P. Putnam's Sons.

Steinberg, David. 2004. "Lap Victory." *San Francisco Weekly,* Sept. 8, http://www.sfweekly.com.

Sterk-Elifson, Claire, and Carole A. Campbell. 1993. "The Netherlands," in *Prostitution: An International Handbook on Trends, Problems, and Policies,* ed. Nanette J. Davis. Westport, CT: Greenwood Press, pp. 191–207.

Steven B. 1999. "A Cautionary Tale." *San Francisco Bay Times,* May 13, pp. 8–11.

St. James, Margo. 1999. "Economic Justice for Sex Workers." *Hastings Women's Law Journal* 10 (1): 5–11.

———. 1989. Preface to *A Vindication of the Rights of Whores,* ed. Gail Pheterson. Seattle: Seal Press, pp. xvii–xx.

———. 1987. "The Reclamation of Whores," in *Good Girls/Bad Girls: Feminists and Sex Trade Workers Face to Face,* ed. Laurie Bell. Seattle: Seal Press, pp. 81–88.

St. John, Warren. 2004. "Parties Where an ID Is the Least of What You Show." *New York Times,* Jan. 11, sec. 9.

Strupp, Joe. 1994. "Flap over Use of Condoms as Evidence." *San Francisco Independent,* Aug. 19.

Stryker, Susan, and Jim Van Buskirk. 1996. *Gay by the Bay: A History of Queer Culture in the San Francisco Bay Area.* San Francisco: Chronicle Books.

Stubbs, Kenneth Ray, ed. 1994. *Women of the Light: The New Sacred Prostitute.* Larkspur, CA: Secret Garden.

"Suburban Detroit Police Release Names of Prostitution Ring's Clients." 1999. Associated Press Online, Jan. 15, http://www.freedomforum.org (last accessed Jan. 12, 2000).

Sudbury, Julia. 2002. "Celling Black Bodies: Black Women in the Global Political Industrial Complex." *Feminist Review* 70: 57–75.

Sullivan, Barbara. 1997. *The Politics of Sex: Prostitution and Pornography in Australia since 1945.* Cambridge: Cambridge University Press.

Sullivan, Elroy, and William Simon. 1998. "The Client: A Social, Psychological, and Behavioral Look at the Unseen Patron of Prostitution," in *Prostitution: On Whores, Hustlers, and Johns,* ed. James Elias et al. Amherst, NY: Prometheus Books, pp. 134–55.

Sumner, Colin. 1994. *The Sociology of Deviance: An Obituary.* Cambridge: Cambridge University Press.

Svanström, Yvonne. 2000. *Policing Public Women: The Regulation of Prostitution in Stockholm, 1812–1880.* Stockholm: Atlas Akademi.

Sward, Susan. 2000. "Dancer Says Strip Club Patron Raped Her: Mitchell Brothers Encouraged Prostitution, Suit Maintains." *San Francisco Chronicle,* Feb. 20, p. A19.

Swedish Association for Sex Education (RSFU). 1990. *Vision, Reality, Activities: Programme of Principles Adopted at RFSU's Annual Meeting in May.*

Swedish Institute. 2001. "Fact Sheet on Swedish Industry." November.

Swedish Ministry of Foreign Affairs. 2003. *Poverty and Trafficking in Human Beings: A Strategy for Combating Trafficking in Human Beings through Swedish International Development Cooperation.* Stockholm: Regeringskansliet.

Swedish Ministry of Industry, Employment, and Communications. 2004. "Fact Sheet on Prostitution and Trafficking in Women." Jan., http://www.naring.regeringen.se/fragor/jamstalldhet/.

Swedish Prostitution Commission. 1995. *Betänkande av 1993 års Prostitutionsutredning.* SOU:15. English summary.

———. 1993. "Committee Terms of Reference." Minutes from Cabinet Meeting of March 11.

Swidler, Ann. 1980. "Love and Adulthood in American Culture," in *Themes of Work and Adulthood,* ed. N. J. Smelser and E. H. Erikson. Cambridge, MA: Harvard University Press.

Sykes, Gresham M., and David Matza. 1957. "Techniques of Neutralization: A Theory of Delinquency." *American Sociological Review* 22: 664–70.

Symbaluk, D. G., and K. M. Jones. 1998. "Prostitution Offender Programs: Canada Finds New Solutions to an Old Problem." *Corrections Compendium* 23 (11): 1–2 and 8.

TAMPEP (Transnational AIDS/STD Prevention Among Migrant Prostitutes in Europe Project). 2002. *Final Report,* vol. 1.

———. 1996/1997. *Final Report.*

Terhorst, Pieter, et al. 2003. "Amsterdam: It's All in the Mix," in *Cities and Visitors: Regulating People, Markets, and City Space,* ed. Lily Hoffman, Susan Fainstein, and Dennis Judd. Oxford: Blackwell, pp. 75–91.

"The Permissive Dutch, in Life and Death." 2000. *Economist Online,* Dec. 2, Lexis-Nexis (last accessed Feb. 2, 2001).

"The Sex Business." 1998. *Economist,* Feb. 14, pp. 17–26.

Thomas, William I. 1923. *The Unadjusted Girl.* Boston: Little, Brown.

Thompson, Clay. 1998. "Concrete Jungle: In the Nation's Toughest Housing Market, Staying Off the Street Is Tougher Than Ever." *San Francisco Bay Guardian,* Oct. 7–13.

Thorbek, Susanne, and Bandana Pattanaik, eds. 2002. *Transnational Prostitution: Changing Global Patterns.* London: Zed Books.

Thornton, Sarah. 1997. "Introduction to Part 1," *The Subcultures Reader,* ed. Ken Gelder and Sarah Thornton. London: Routledge.

Tong, Benjamin. 1994. *Unsubmissive Women: Chinese Prostitutes in Nineteenth-Century San Francisco.* Norman and London: University of Oklahoma Press.

Trumbach, Randolph. 1995. *Sex and the Gender Revolution: Heterosexuality and the Third Gender in Enlightenment London.* Chicago: University of Chicago Press.

Turkle, Sherry. 1995. *Life on the Screen: Identity in the Age of the Internet.* New York: Touchstone.

Ullman, Sharon. 1997. *Sex Seen: The Emergence of Modern Sexuality in America.* Berkeley: University of California Press.

United Nations Protocol to Prevent, Suppress, and Punish Trafficking in Persons, Especially Women and Children, Supplementing the Convention against Transnational Organized Crime. 2000. http://www.uncjin.org/Documents/Conventions/dcatoc/final_documents_2/convention_%20traff_eng.pdf (last accessed May 17, 2006).

Urban Justice Center. 2005. *Behind Closed Doors: An Analysis of Indoor Sex Work in New York City.* New York: Sex Workers' Project at the Urban Justice Center.
———. 2003. *Revolving Door: An Analysis of Street-Based Prostitution in New York City.* New York: Sex Workers' Project at the Urban Justice Center.
"Urban Warrior: Hook Up with Hooker, Cops Will Hook Up Your Car." 2004. *Philadelphia Daily News,* June 12.
U.S. Bureau of the Census. 2001. "Household and Family Characteristics: Summary Tables." June 13, http://www.census.gov/population/www/socdemo/hh-fam-sum98tab.html.
———. 1992. *Marriage, Divorce, and Remarriage in the 1990's.* Washington, DC: U.S. Government Printing Office Current Population Reports, pp. 23–180.
———. 1989. *Studies in Marriage and the Family.* Washington, DC: U.S. Government Printing Office Current Population Reports, pp. 23–162.
U.S. Department of Justice. 2006. Report on Activities to Combat Human Trafficking, Fiscal Years 2001–2005. http://www.usdoj.gov/whatwedo/whatwedo_ctip.html (last accessed May 1, 2006).
———. 2003. "Fact Sheet—Protect Act." http://www.usdoj.gov/opa/pr/2003/April/03_ag_266.htm (last accessed May 17, 2006).
Van Derbeken, Jaxon, and Ryan Kim. 2005. "Alleged Sex-trade Ring Broken up in Bay Area: Police Say Koreans in Massage Parlors Were Smuggled in." *San Francisco Chronicle,* July 2, http://www.sfgate.com/cgi-bin/article.cgi?file=/c/a/2005/07/02/MNGDLDIDVD1.DTL (last accessed July 2, 2005).
Van der Poel, Sari. 1995. "Solidarity as Boomerang: The Fiasco of the Prostitutes' Rights Movement in the Netherlands." *Crime, Law, and Social Change* 23 (1): 41–65.
Van Doorninck, Marieke. 2002. "A Business Like Any Other? Managing the Sex Industry in the Netherlands," in *Transnational Prostitution: Changing Global Patterns,* ed. Susanne Thorbek and Bandana Pattanik. London: Zed Books, pp. 193–201.
Van Oostveen, Noortje. 1997. "Prostitution—a Fact of Life." Informational pamphlet, Communications Department of the City of Amsterdam.
Van Soomeren, Paul. 2004. "Design against Kerb Crawling: Tippelzones." Paper presented at the International CPTED Conference, Sept. 13–17, Brisbane, Australia, www.e-doca.net (last accessed Sept. 17, 2006).
Van Wesenbeeck, Ine. 1995. *Prostitutes' Well-Being and Risk.* Amsterdam: VU University Press.
Vance, Carole. Forthcoming. "Hiss the Villain: Depicting Sex Trafficking," in *Ethnography and Policy: What Do We Know about "Trafficking"?* ed. Carole S. Vance. Santa Fe, NM: School for American Research Press.
———, ed. 1989. *Pleasure and Danger: Exploring Female Sexuality.* London: Pandora Press.
Violence against Women Fact Sheet. 1999. News and Information from the Swedish Government Offices on Issues Related to Violence against Women. July 6. http://www.kvinnifrid.gov.se/regeringen/faktaeng.htm.
Visano, Livy. 1987. *This Idle Trade.* Ontario, Canada: VitaSana Books.
Visser, Jan H. 1997. "The Dutch Law Proposal on Prostitution: Text and Explanation." http://www.mrgraaf.nl (last accessed May 1, 2001).

Wackermann, Paul-Claude. 2000. "Swedish Prostitutes Become a Virtual Problem." *Agence France Presse Online,* Jan. 26, Lexis-Nexis (last accessed Feb.12, 2001).

Wacquant, Loïc J. D. 2005. "Shadowboxing with Ethnographic Ghosts: A Rejoinder." *Symbolic Interaction* 28 (3): 441–47.

———. 2004a. *Body and Soul: Notebooks of an Apprentice Boxer.* Oxford: Oxford University Press.

———. 2004b. "Habitus," in *International Encyclopedia of Economic Sociology,* ed. Milan Zafirovski. London: Routledge.

———. 2001. "The Penalization of Poverty and the Rise of Neoliberalism." *European Journal on Criminal Policy and Research* 9: 401–12.

———. 1995. "Pugs at Work: Bodily Capital and Bodily Labour among Professional Boxers." *Body and Society* 1: 65–95.

———. 1994. "Inside the Zone: The Social Art of the Hustler in the Contemporary Ghetto." Russell Sage Working Paper no. 49. New York.

Walker, James, and Peter Jennings. 1998. "San Francisco's Class on Prostitution." ABC *World News Tonight with Peter Jennings,* Jan. 6. KGO, San Francisco.

Walkowitz, Judith R. 1980. *Prostitution and Victorian Society: Women, Class, and the State.* Cambridge: Cambridge University Press.

Warner, Michael. 1999. *The Trouble with Normal: Sex, Politics, and the Ethics of Queer Life.* New York: Free Press.

———, ed. 1993. *Fear of a Queer Planet: Queer Politics and Social Theory.* Minneapolis: University of Minnesota Press.

Waters, Rob, and Wade Hudson. 1998. "The Tenderloin: What Makes a Neighborhood?" in *Reclaiming San Francisco: Theory, Politics, Culture,* ed. James Brook, Chris Carlsson, and Nancy J. Peters. San Francisco: City Lights Books, pp. 301–16.

Weber, Max. [1915] 1946. "Religious Rejections of the World and Their Directions," in *From Max Weber,* ed. Hans Gerth and C. Wright Mills. New York: Oxford University Press, pp. 323–59.

Weeks, Jeffrey. 1985. *Sexuality and Its Discontents: Myths, Meanings, and Modern Sexualities.* London: Routledge and Kegan Paul.

———. [1981] 1997. "Inverts, Perverts, and Mary-Annes," in *The Subcultures Reader,* ed. Ken Gelder and Sarah Thornton. London: Routledge, pp. 268–81.

Weidner, Robert. 2001. *"I Won't Do Manhattan": Causes and Consequences of a Decline in Street Prostitution.* New York: LFB Publishing.

Weinberg, Martin, Frances Shaver, and Colin J. Williams. 1999. "Gendered Sex Work in the San Francisco Tenderloin." *Archives of Sexual Behavior* 28 (6): 503–21.

Weisberg, D. Kelly. 1985. *Children of the Night: A Study of Adolescent Prostitution.* Lexington, MA: Lexington Books.

Weitzer, Ron. 2000a. "Why We Need More Research on Sex Work," in *Sex for Sale: Prostitution, Pornography, and the Sex Industry,* ed. Ron Weitzer. New York: Routledge, pp. 1–17.

———. 2000b. "The Politics of Prostitution in America," in *Sex for Sale: Prostitution, Pornography, and the Sex Industry,* ed. Ron Weitzer. New York: Routledge, pp. 159–81.

———, ed. 2000c. *Sex for Sale: Prostitution, Pornography, and the Sex Industry.* New York: Routledge.

Wessenlingh, Isabelle. 2000. "Dutch Apply 'Avant-Garde' Legislation to Social Problems." Agence France Presse Online, Dec. 20, Lexis-Nexis (last accessed Feb. 12, 2001).

West, Donald J., in association with Buz de Villiers. 1993. *Male Prostitution.* New York: Harrington Park Press.

West, Paige, and James G. Carrier. 2004. "Ecotourism and Authenticity: Getting Away from It All?" *Current Anthropology* 45 (4): 483–91.

West, Rachel. 1987. "U.S. Prostitutes Collective," in *Sex Work: Writings by Women in the Sex Industry,* ed. Fédérique Delacoste and Priscilla Alexander. Pittsburgh: Cleis Press, pp. 266–71.

West's Annotated California Codes. 1999 (supp. 2001). § 370, § 647B, and § 647C.

Whisman, Vera. 1993. "Identity Crisis: Who Is a Lesbian Anyway?" in *Sisters, Sexperts, Queers: Beyond the Lesbian Nation,* ed. Arlene Stein. New York: Penguin, pp. 47–61.

White, Luise. 1990. *The Comforts of Home: Prostitution in Colonial Nairobi.* Chicago: University of Chicago Press.

Whyte, William Foote. 1943. *Street Corner Society.* Chicago: University of Chicago Press.

Wigdon, Amelia. 2005. "Marie Claire Puts a Positive Spin on Prostitution." July 20, http://www.cwfa.org/articles/8581/CWA/family/index.htm (last accessed May 1, 2006).

Wijers, Marjan, and Marieke van Doorninck. 2002. "Only Rights Can Stop Wrongs: A Critical Assessment of Anti-Trafficking Strategies." Paper presented at EU/IOM STOP European Conference on Preventing and Combating Trafficking in Human Beings—A Global Challenge for the Twenty-first Century. Sept. 18–20, European Parliament, Brussels, Belgium, available at http://www.walnet.org/csis/papers/wijers-rights.html (last accessed May 1, 2006).

Wilgoren, Debbi. 2006. "Area Juvenile Sex Rings Targeted Using Anti-Trafficking Laws." *Washington Post,* March 6, p. A-1.

Williams, Christine. 2002. "To Know Me is To Love Me? Response to Eric Goode," *Qualitative Sociology* 25 (4): 557–60.

Williams, Linda. 2004. "Porn Studies: Proliferating Pornographies On/Scene: An Introduction," in *Porn Studies,* ed. Linda Williams. Durham: Duke University Press, 1–27.

———. 1989. *Hardcore: Power, Pleasure, and the 'Frenzy of the Visible.'* Berkeley: University of California Press.

Williams, Terry. 1992. *Crackhouse: Notes from the End of the Line.* New York: Penguin.

Wilson, Ara. 2004. *The Intimate Economies of Bangkok.* Berkeley: University of California Press.

Wilson, James Q., and George L. Kelling. 1982. "Broken Windows." *Atlantic Monthly* (March): 29–37.

Wilson, William Julius. 1996. *When Work Disappears: The World of the New Urban Poor.* New York: Knopf.

Wiltz, Christine. 2000. *The Last Madam: A Life in the New Orleans Underworld*. Cambridge, MA: Da Capo Press.

Winberg, Margareta. 2002. "Speech by the Deputy Prime Minister." *Seminar on the Effects of Legalization of Prostitution Activities—A Critical Analysis*. Stockholm: Regeringskansliet.

Winick, Charles, and Paul M. Kinsie. 1971. *The Lively Commerce: Prostitution in the United States*. Chicago: Quadrangle Books.

Wolf, Diane L., ed. 1996. *Feminist Dilemmas in Fieldwork*. Boulder, CO: Westview Press.

Wolf, Naomi. 1991. *The Beauty Myth: How Images of Beauty Are Used against Women*. New York: Doubleday.

Wolfe, Alan. 1989. *Whose Keeper? Social Science and Moral Obligation*. Berkeley: University of California Press.

Women and Men in Sweden: Facts and Figures. 1995. Stockholm: SCB.

Women's Front of Norway. 1994. Informational Pamphlet.

Wood, Elizabeth Anne. 2000. "Working in the Fantasy Factory: The Attention Hypothesis and the Enacting of Masculine Power in Strip Clubs." *Journal of Contemporary Ethnography* 29 (1): 5–31.

Wood, Sara. 2006. "DOD Personnel Face Stricter Human Trafficking Laws." *Black Hills Bandit*. April 21, http://www.blackhillsbandit.com/articles/2006/04/21/news/news02.txt (last accessed April 22, 2006).

Wortley, Scot, Benedikt Fischer, and Cheryl Webster. 2002. "Vice Lessons: A Survey of Prostitution Offenders Enrolled in the Toronto John School Diversion Program." *Canadian Journal of Criminology* 44 (4): 369–402.

Wright, Erik Olin. 1985. *Classes*. London: Verso.

Wyatt, Edward. 2004. "Sex, Sex, Sex: Up Front in Bookstores Near You." *New York Times*, Aug. 24, p. E1.

Wynter, Sarah. 1987. "Whisper: Women Hurt in Systems of Prostitution Engaged in Revolt," in *Sex Work: Writings by Women in the Sex Industry*, ed. Fédérique Delacoste and Priscilla Alexander. Pittsburgh: Cleis Press, pp. 266–71.

Young, Wayland. 1970. "Prostitution," in *Observations of Deviance*, ed. Jack Douglas. New York: Random House, pp. 64–89.

Yung, Judy. 1995. *Unbound Feet: A Social History of Chinese Women in San Francisco*. Berkeley: University of California Press.

Zamora, Jim Herron. 1998. "Front-line Soldiers in War on Sex." *San Francisco Examiner*, Nov. 8.

Zelizer, Viviana. 2005. *The Purchase of Intimacy*. Princeton, N.J.: Princeton University Press.

———. 2002. "The Purchase of Intimacy." *Law and Social Inquiry* 25: 817–44.

———. 1994. *The Social Meaning of Money*. New York: Basic Books.

Zukin, Sharon. 1995. *The Cultures of Cities*. Cambridge, MA: Blackwell.

———. 1982. *Loft Living: Culture and Capital in Urban Change*. Baltimore: Johns Hopkins University Press.

Zussman, Robert. 2002. "Editor's Introduction: Sex in Research." *Qualitative Sociology* 25 (4): 473–76.

Wanted" ads for, 81; mainstreaming of, 14, 108, 141; mirror of, 13; "money shot," 229*n*2; nineteenth century, 171; for women, 174
Portland, Oregon, 38, 240*n*10
postindustrialism: antiprostitution campaigns in, 2; bounded authenticity and, 102–6; cultural transformations, 5, 7, 15–16, 21, 114, 165, 193; gay culture and, 223*n*53; and gender, 81, 199, 174; market intimacy in, 119–25; paradigms of sexual commerce, 168–75, 180–81; public/private divide and, 4, 140 (*see also* public/private divide); service sector and, 5, 141; terminology, 18. *See also* capitalism: late; postmodernism; service economy
postmodernism: cultural transformations, 227*n*22; family and, 6, 175, 193; reactionary foundationalism and, 228*n*40; addiction and, 133; sexual ethic, 174; tourism and, 103 (*see also* tourism). *See also* capitalism: late; postindustrialism
poverty: gentrification and, 33–36, 140; sex trafficking and, 3, 177; sex work and, 42–43, 44, 61, 66–67, 169, 177, 184–87. *See also* homelessness
Prasad, Monica, 117, 119, 139
Pretty Woman (film), 12
privatization: and gender, 5, 175, 176; and public sex, 68–69; of "public women," 73, 102, 109; and race, 68–69, 109; and sexual commerce, 68–69, 140
procuring, 233*n*39. *See also* pimps
PROMISE (Prevention, Referral, Outreach, Mentoring and Intervention to End Sexual Exploitation), 77
prostitutes. *See* sex workers
prostitution: arrest statistics, 34, 37, 38; and consent, 52, 145, 162–63, 178–80, 186; criminalization of, 24–25, 56, 139, 148–56; decline of

modern-industrial, 30–34, 37–39, 69; early modern, 24, 67, 169–70; early social critics, 7–11, 24; and empowerment, 11–12, 51, 178; historical regulation of, 24–25, 26–29, 146–47, 208*n*7–209*n*7; as metaphor, 7–8; modern-industrial, 23–24, 29, 42, 47–49, 67, 75, 110–11, 169–71, 180, 208*n*7; and normative heterosexuality, 50–52, 96–98, 108; postindustrial, 69, 74–75, 110–11, 141, 169–70, 172, 175, 180–81; terminology, 11, 17–18; typology, 169–72, 173–74; underage, 42–43, 48, 66, 115, 135–36, 139. *See also* specific issues; specific settings
Prostitution Information Center (Amsterdam, the Netherlands), 231*n*13
psychotherapy, 96–97, 102, 133, 173, 225*n*8
public decency laws. *See* legislation
public/private divide, 24, 47–48, 52, 119, 141, 168–69, 170; new boundaries of, 102, 140; commercial sex as blurring, 14, 74, 150; and emotional life, 5, 7, 38, 119, 125–26, 172–73; and family life, 5, 23–24, 48, 121; and the Internet, 14, 74, 150; and "public women," 7, 24, 42, 60, 170 (see also gendered double standard, "good girl/bad girl" divide, Madonna/Whore divide); and the self, 49, 67, 101–2, 107–8, 180. *See also* privatization
public sex, policing of, 68, 218*n*62

"quality of life" campaigns, 2, 37, 62–64, 164, 216*n*46, 224*n*3. *See also* "broken windows" policing; gentrification
Quan, Tracy, 223*n*54
Queen, Carol, 222*n*44
queer politics, 50–51, 220*n*18, 235*n*2, 235*n*3. *See also* gay liberation
Query, Julia, 219*n*6